# ENGLAND!

*An Uncommon Guide*

*Also by Lawrence & Sylvia Martin:*

THE STANDARD GUIDE TO MEXICO

THE STANDARD GUIDE TO THE CARIBBEAN

*by Sylvia Martin:*

I, MADAME TUSSAUD (*novel*)

YOU MEET THEM IN MEXICO

*Lawrence &*
*Sylvia Martin*

# ENGLAND!

*An*

*Uncommon*

*Guide*

*McGraw-Hill Book Company, Inc.*

NEW YORK    TORONTO    LONDON

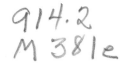

To four dauntless travelers:
    Stephanie and Valeria over here
    Beryl and Reggie over there
And to two who stayed at home:
    Claw de Pussy and the Striped Pants Kid

# CONTENTS

PART III   TEN SALLIES INTO ENGLAND

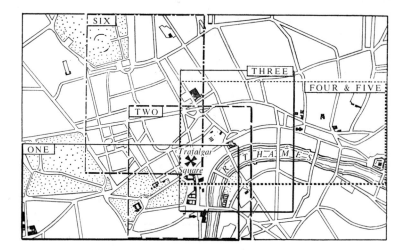

# MAPS

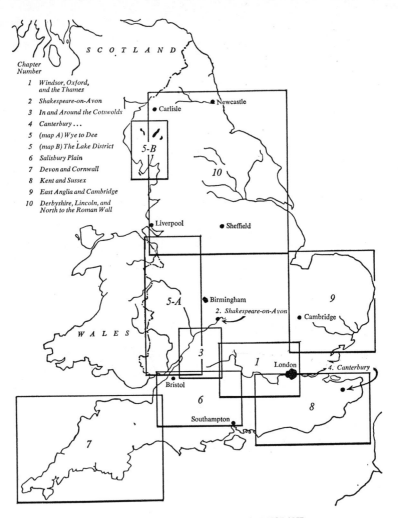

SCOTLAND

WALES

5-B

10

5-A

3

9

1

6

8

7

Carlisle

Newcastle

Liverpool

Sheffield

Birmingham

2. Shakespeare-on-Avon

Cambridge

London

4. Canterbury

Bristol

Southampton

MAP KEY FOR TEN SALLIES INTO ENGLAND

# PREFACE

Our affair with England began in the nostalgic era when one could travel, if one had to—and we had to—on five dollars a day. For years we kept dropping in on the lady, drawn to her and her antique furniture, her garden, and the way she served tea.

There are things one doesn't know one knows. Not until we began this book did we discover that we were enamored of the wench.

We were in love with our eyes open—for this book should leave no one in doubt that we see her faults and have small hope of reforming her.

She is charming and exasperating. But she never palls. Shakespeare saw her in Cleopatra:

> Age cannot wither her, nor custom stale
> Her infinite variety; other women cloy
> The appetites they feed, but she makes hungry
> Where most she satisfies. . . .

England, that half-an-island, is infinitely various. There is not one England; there are as many as you have time and hunger to discover. York, Winchester, Norwich, Bath have in common only their unlikeness. The many cathedrals are not the same cathedral with variations; each has a distinct personality. The truth applies to castles, parish churches, Stately Homes, inns, Tudor houses, hills and dales and streams. Each half-timbered cottage has aged after its crotchety or amiable fashion, leaning and bulging in its own gafferish way.

An American, whose home is a young continent his technology

has largely standardized, is slow to realize how multiplex a nation can be, even one only the size of Minnesota, after men have lived there a sufficient number of centuries. History adds a fourth dimension to geography's three. England's two thousand years have endowed the human landscape with every tint and eccentricity that time can give. A town or village that has lived through Roman occupation and Saxon, Danish, and Norman invasions; that has suffered feudal wars, gloried in the Elizabethans, put up with the Stuarts, flourished with the House of Hanover, and is able to chronicle the defection of its American colonies in a brief line, is bound to have something that Zenith, Ohio, cannot boast of.

George Babbitt's nephew from Zenith says, "Salisbury (or Chester, or whatever) is all right, but I wouldn't want to live there." No one asked him to live there. No one is even so unkind as to remark, "Zenith is a great little town, but who crosses an ocean to see it?"

As with England, so with that concentration of it called London. New York is wonderful; it has better this and greater that, but it doesn't have the Abbey, the Tower, the Houses of Parliament, Georgian squares, Regency terraces, Wren churches, Trafalgar Square, the Inns of Court. There is more than one New York in New York, but they are not as diverse as the Londons that London contains. You can (and you will if you stay with us) adventure at least six different ways out of Trafalgar Square and find yourself in six times six different Londons.

England, thickly populated with the English, with Eric Knight's Sam Small, Housman's Shropshire Lad, and all the people out of Dickens; with parrot-faced dowagers, buxom barmaids, wispy small-town girls, tweedy country gentlemen, Cockneys and bobbies, seedy peers and aristocratic clerks—England (to catch our breath) bears looking into.

If you travel on one of those Europe-in-a-flash tours which devotes three days to England, you may come away disappointed. You ought to. Cleopatra can't be wooed and won in three days. Stay three weeks and you will find her tantalizing and infuriating. Stay three months and you will feel a stab of guilt when you catch a sudden glimpse of the Stars and Stripes over the Embassy in Grosvenor Square.

Enjoy, enjoy! A guilty love is better than none.

# PART I
# WHAT TO EXPECT

# GETTING

# ABOUT

# ENGLAND

It's an easy country to move around in. Road and railway networks cover it. Buses and "motor coaches" (long-distance buses) go everywhere. Off-beat sightseeing can be done by boat on rivers and canals. England is the world's most agreeable country for walking.

The hurried tourist who wants to get a look at Scotland can hop the London-Edinburgh plane.

Tourism is well organized and publicized. The detailed answers to the visitor's wants, whatever they may be, are readily available both on the spot and in the U.S.

## § BY TRAIN

It was an English ex-cowherd who invented the steam locomotive and married it to a road of iron rails. The English were traveling behind locomotives for years before Americans were sure what the new word *rail-road* meant.

Today the only country that surpasses Britain in railroads per square mile is little Belgium. Britain, the size of the state of Minnesota, has 51,100 miles of track and 19,000 route miles of railway. Some eleven hundred million passengers ride the rails annually, using 5200 stations. British Railways, nationally owned since 1947, operates a chain of 38 hotels and 378 refreshment rooms. (Many of the refreshment rooms need a new coat of paint, some gay touches, and refreshments that refresh, but the fact remains that they exist.) The great system is being progressively overhauled. Streamlined coaches and de luxe trains are being added, and diesels are supplanting steam.

Trains are frequent (except on small branch lines and on Sundays). Fares are cheaper than in the U.S. Distances between touristed places are often no greater than an American commuter covers daily between his suburb and the downtown where he works and she shops. There are fast expresses. The London–Oxford express does the 54 miles in 65 minutes. The 103 miles from London to Stratford-upon-Avon are covered in under three hours. The London–Norwich express does the 114 miles in about two and a half hours. The latest crack trains to Scotland—the *Talisman* and the *Fair Maid of Perth*—devour the 395 miles to Edinburgh in 6 hours 46 minutes.

London is the railway hub. Train travel is easiest and fastest when your way runs along one of the spokes. Traveling crosswise is less convenient.

The classes are two, but the difference between them is not great except in price. The upholstery in first may be less worn, and six sit where eight share in second. First class costs about 50 per cent more than second; the chief gain, if you like room and privacy, is that first is thinly populated. We travel first when taking a lot of luggage, for that extra room on the overhead racks.

On the long hauls, sleeping berths are available in both classes. Book in advance.

Seats in certain principal trains can be reserved in advance on payment of a small surcharge. Meals, including afternoon tea, are served in restaurant cars. Some trains carry buffet cars serving snacks and drinks. Packed sandwiches and sundries for eating in your compartment can be bought at station refreshment rooms, if you prefer this to the hearty restaurant-car meal.

You will not find lunch or dinner a gustatory high point in your life; they are average English restaurant fare. You are limited to the table d'hôte, but there's plenty to eat and the bill is modest—about $1.50. Drinks, alcoholic and otherwise, are to be had. There's no dry county in England.

British Railways offers a great variety of special-fare arrangements: cheap day tickets, midweek return, Saturday night holiday return (good for eight or fifteen days), excursion, circular tour, etc. (*Return* means round trip). Station-platform posters carry details. Something to remember is that tickets may be bought and seat reservations made at any terminal station regardless of the London or other city terminal from which the journey is to be made. But you can't do it by telephone.

*Book* in the sense of "reserve" is a survival from early railroad days when you paid the conductor and he entered the transaction in a book instead of issuing a ticket. So you buy your ticket at the Booking Office. That "office" (the station itself) is usually drafty and the ticket window is so low you have to bend down to it. Look at the sign above before you join the queue to make sure it's selling tickets for the class and the station you want. Above all, give yourself extra time; queueing or difficulty in finding the right window or the right platform may make you miss your train. You're not allowed aboard without a ticket.

The coaches (cars) are divided into compartments. On long-distance trains the sliding doors of the compartments open out into a corridor that runs along the windows on one side. Shorter-run local trains have no corridors; the compartment doors open right out on the platform. Opening a compartment door of this kind from the inside is quite a trick. Reach out the window in the door and open it from the outside, but not until the train has stopped. Compartments are marked for smokers and nonsmokers. There's a washroom-toilet on each coach, but no drinking water.

A general slamming of compartment doors heralds departure. The locomotive emits a tiny shriek like a frightened bird, and you are off. Except in local trains, the windows are wide and offer a continuous panorama. The very click of the wheels on the rails is different—this is England!

And here you are, shut up in a compartment with five or seven other human beings who are concentrating on avoiding talk or meeting one another's eyes. Compartment etiquette requires that nobody's privacy be invaded. To the Englishman any stranger is an incipient bore. He prefers to bore himself. His newspaper or magazine is a defense against conversation.

An American can, if he wants to, break the ice with less difficulty than the member of any other human tribe. Try this: get out a map and puzzle over it with your friend or spouse, wondering audibly—but not loudly—how to get from Telscombe Pye to Totterdown or wherever. One of your compartment mates will weaken and take the lure, others will join, and conversation will become general. The English are kindly; they cannot resist giving help. Besides, most of them would like to talk to the American but don't know how to start.

Some DON'TS:

Don't expect to understand the loudspeaker blaring on the station platform.

Don't wait or look for a conductor to answer questions. He may be aboard or not, but he won't come through except on long-distance expresses. Make sure before you board that the train is the one you want, and where, if at all, you have to change. Luckily your fellow passengers talk English.

Don't, if traveling after dark, read a book by the meager, doleful lights of an English coach; you'll get eyestrain.

Don't expect a surge of porters when you get off. At smaller stations you may have to carry your bags. England is enjoying full employment.

Don't look for the club car. You left it back home.

Don't concentrate on the lacks. We have fussed at times, but on cross-examination will admit to more fun traveling by train than by car. You see more countryside. You meet fellow riders. You sit back comfortably and the landscape makes pictures. And there's that Hitchcock–Agatha Christie feeling of being in a story.

A big DO:

British Railways is well organized to serve the tourist. Its staff will map out your whole trip for you, if you need that help. The British Railways office in London is on Lower Regent Street just off Piccadilly Circus.

The *Holiday Haunts* guidebooks published by the British Railways (new issue every year) are big book bargains—about twenty cents for four hundred pages of book with maps, photographs, descriptions of resorts, railway information, and hotel ads. There are five volumes: the west of England and South and Central Wales; Scotland; Eastern and Northeastern England; Northwest England and North Wales; Southern England and the Channel Islands.

# § BY CAR

Great Britain has about 192,000 metaled (paved) miles of public
highway, or more than two miles for every square mile of territory.
The roads are of five types:

| | |
|---|---|
| Trunk roads (national highways) | 8,400 miles |
| Class I roads | 19,400 |
| Class II roads | 17,600 |
| Class III roads | 49,000 |
| Unclassified | 97,600 |

The Unclassified are purely local lanes. The Trunks and Class I
are, on your road map, the A roads; the Class II, B; the Class III, C.

Along this web, eight million motor vehicles travel: 4½ million
private passenger cars; 1½ million "goods vehicles" or trucks
(familiarly called *lorries*), hauling more stuff than the railways
and making more than the usual nuisance of themselves on the
narrow, winding roads; 1½ million motorcycles, motorbikes, and
scooters; and a hundred thousand buses, motor coaches, and hired
cars. All together they give Britain the highest traffic density in the
world. A recent two-year period saw a 21 per cent increase in motor
traffic.

In addition to motors, the local roads are used by herds of sheep
and cows, and by tractors and farm wagons. They're also frequented by cyclists, who often come in groups—an unexpected
traffic hazard for Americans. Yet with all this, and the idiosyn-
crasies of winding roads, high hedges, and hills as steep as 1 in 4,
Britain has a high safety record. Laws are more stringently en-
forced, and the Briton behind the wheel is more law-abiding than
his American counterpart.

If you plan to drive yourself in England, better leave your
supercharged Giganto-Whizz at home and hire a British car which
is smaller, more maneuverable, and has the works on the right side
for keep-left driving. Bring your driving license. The car of your
choice can be waiting for you at dockside or airport when you
arrive. Put it up to your travel agent, or ask the British Travel
Association for its list of recommended dealers. The rates run from

$17 a week plus five cents per mile to $54 plus nine cents, depend-ing on make and size of car.

For our own part, when we don't go by train or bus, or along with a driving friend, we hire a car with a local chauffeur. While he drives we look at England instead of at the road. The best bargain we've been able to strike is 15 cents a mile—far cheaper than the lowest possible drive-self rate.

Of course, such car-chauffeur hire has never been for longer than a day at a time, and mostly for circle tours of the countryside from a town we elected to hole up in. For traveling around England in de luxe fashion different rates come into play because the chauffeur has to be fed and bedded. The going rate quoted by a reliable com-pany for an Austin Princess limousine with driver for one week is $196; for a Humber or Hawk sedan, $176; for a Ford Consul saloon, $157, gas and chauffeur's keep included. You pay extra for every mile beyond 350 for the week. These are the rates at this writing; they will go up.

England's roads and streets are well marked. You will have to learn a few new things, such as the fact that the conspicuous band of black-and-white stripes across a street (called *zebra* with a short *e*) is sacred. The pedestrian who steps on this sanctuary is invio-late, and if you hit him matters will not go well with you.

You may want to try a trailer-camping holiday. Trailer-houses, called *caravans*, are rentable. For information and list of campsites: Camping Club of Great Britain, 35 Old Kent Road, London S.E.1.

If you're planning to drive in England, get *Seeing Britain by Road* (free) from the British Travel Association. In addition to giving you the main rules of the road it contains itineraries for England, Wales, Scotland, and Northern Ireland. Esso Standard also publishes and sells at its petrol stations maps of Britain and Ireland, as well as regional maps of England; price, a shilling or so. It has discontinued its European tourist-advice services in the United States.

You would be wise to take out temporary membership in one of the two British automobile clubs: Automobile Association, Fanum House, New Coventry Street, London W.1; Royal Automobile Club, 83 Pall Mall, London S.W.1. Membership gives you itineraries with road maps, and inspected hotel-and-garage lists. Club scouts are met with everywhere on the roads. They are friends in need.

# § BY BUS AND MOTOR COACH

The bus is a local vehicle. The motor coach is a long-distance bus.

You can see England—all of it—by bus if you've a mind to, provided you carry something small in the way of luggage. Several adventurous travelers have done it, including bus drivers enjoying the proverbial holiday.

Outside London, ninety separate municipally owned systems operate. Another forty-five hundred local bus services are operated by private companies. There's hardly a village so small it isn't on a bus route connecting it with other villages and towns, where there are connections with—on and on, from Land's End to John o' Groat's.

If you're new to England, there comes the day when, out in the country, you see what looks to you like the London double-decker, painted green instead of red, rolling along at a smart pace between the rural hedgerows. The green town-and-country bus is the most obviously standardized object to be seen in England. It goes to little places you can't reach by railway.

Existing for the convenience of the local population, its aim is not to connect the main towns by speedy, direct routes, but to keep the villages in touch with one another and with their market centers. So while it bumps along from hamlet to hamlet, letting the housewives on and off with their shopping and the artisans with their tools and the children with their school kits, it provides the traveler a rambling window on the rural life that most packaged tourists never dream is there.

The fares are as reasonable as they can be. The conductors—often women who mother their busloads—are helpful. Bus stops are plainly indicated along the roads. Centers such as Canterbury and Bath have good-looking and efficient grand central stations with rest rooms and information offices, the routes and schedules prominently posted.

A Green Rover pass costing 70 cents a day entitles one to unlimited travel over 1400 miles of country bus routes.

Bear in mind that wherever you happen to be, you will find buses going to all the nearby elsewheres. As you travel along with us, we will remind you of this where the hinterland is promising.

While the bus is the successor of the streetcar and the suburban trolley, the motor coach has supplanted the old stagecoach—which is why it's called a coach. The London municipality operates the Green Line coaches, which service points in a radius of twenty-five miles from London. In England, about a hundred different private companies operate long-distance coach service in straight transportation from one center to another, with a minimum of stops in between.

In addition, conducted coach tours, local, regional, and all-Britain, from one to eighteen days in duration, are operated by a number of motor-coach companies.

If your time and budget are limited, the guided coach tour is one good way to see a lot of England. But you must be sociable and prepared to suffer gladly the occasional fool—for there usually is a nuisance or two in every party.

We know an American widow, a veteran traveler, who signed up for an eighteen-day round of Britain by Southdown Coach (a private company) out of London, Tour L-16. She let us read the diary she kept. The passengers were twenty-six: seven Americans, five Australians, five South Africans, seven Canadians, two Londoners. There were five married couples and two pairs of sisters. The remaining twelve were unaccompanied—two men and ten women. (Obviously this way of traveling appeals to the woman who is alone.)

The whirlwind tour went London–Canterbury–Tenterden–Lewes–Brighton–Winchester–Salisbury; then along the south coasts of Devon and Cornwall to Land's End, north to Bude and Clovelly; then to Bath and Gloucester, to Chepstow and Hereford, and via Llangollen in Wales to Chester; then up through the Lake District to Scotland; and so down through Stratford-upon-Avon and Oxford back to London.

Phew! We mopped our brows when we digested this itinerary. "Hotels good," our friend reported. "Meals—too much to eat. Schedule—surprisingly restful; leisurely breakfasts and other meals, including stops for tea; no starting out before 9 A.M. or traveling after dark. Good guide and pleasant company. Only drawback—many places where you want to stay longer."

She thought it wonderful, and it was her fifth trip to England. The tour cost her $224, including lodging and meals.

Cook's, American Express, Frame's, and many other travel agents run a variety of tours. The ubiquitous British Railways and London Transport together and separately offer twenty-four different one-day train-motorcoach excursions, detailed in a pamphlet, "Day Tours from London." There are so many coaching companies that you'd do well, if interested, to ask the British Travel Association for its recommendations and get its publication, *Bus Tours in Britain*.

If you'd like a behind-scenes look at guided group tours before signing up for one, read the little book by Guy Abecassis, *Tours and Detours*, the hilarious reminiscences of a tour conductor. Abecassis is French, but his experiences are international.

# § BY WATER

Britain has three thousand miles of inland waterways—rivers, canals, lakes, broads. They are not interconnected. You can embark on river excursion steamers on the Thames, Dart, Wye, and other streams. You can go by steamer to England's lesser islands: the Scillies, Wight, Man, and the Channel Islands. On the Thames, you can have a do-it-yourself vacation, renting anything from a kayak or rowboat to a cabin cruiser; or take any number of excursions by steamer. The Windsor–Oxford trip on the Thames costs about six dollars—which is also the price of a "holiday round-about" ticket on the Clyde steamers of the Caledonian Steam Packet Company of Glasgow, which allows you to make practically unlimited voyages amid the superb scenery of the Scottish lochs and the Firth of Forth.

In this book we confine ourselves to England—but Scotland's water trips are too alluring to ignore. The port of Oban in Scotland's rugged west is the center for exciting boat excursions among the Western Isles and lochs (fjords) of that intricate coast. For details, write Passenger Dept., David MacBrayne, Ltd., 44 Robertson Street, Glasgow C.2.

For under eighty dollars you can make a five-day trip by canal between Nottingham and Boston, stopping at Lincoln, Woodhall Spa, and Newark, and living on board. For about the same amount, you can go from Oxford to Birmingham with night accommodations at first-class hotels.

If you're a fisherman, small-boatsman, or just a landlubber tourist with a yen for water, your first move is to write the British Travel Association for the illustrated free booklet, *Holidays on Britain's Inland Waterways*, a mine of information about routes, boat-hire firms, and types of craft and excursion. Fishermen should also get the Fishing Map of Britain.

NOTE.   Boats go only in season—from April or May to September.

## § *ON FOOT*

Why walk, as if the train and car hadn't been invented?

The answer is that walking is a wonderful way to see England. We know this from experience, not out of a book.

Shanks' mare is of course the cheapest mode of travel, but there's no law forbidding the well-heeled from being well-footed; nor is there any age limit. At seventy, the English travel writer S. P. B. Mais still walks the lanes and footpaths of his green and lovely land.

England is ideal for the hiker. Wipe any American comparison from your mind; it doesn't apply. England is small. The countryside varies from county to county, and its old villages seem to have grown out of the soil like the trees. Public footpaths cut across fields and ramble along streams, and there are narrow lanes where a car is rarely seen. Along the way are inns, small hotels, and bed-and-breakfast cottages. Ordnance maps covering all of England on a scale of an inch to a mile and a half-inch to a mile are guides to the footpaths.

Such a vacation requires, first of all, choosing your territory and laying out a course through it. Devon, Cornwall, the Cotswolds, the Wye Valley and Welsh border country, and the dales of Derbyshire and Yorkshire are, to our mind, the best regions in England for the hiker. To make your decision, read books and study maps.

You determine how many miles you intend to walk in a day. The lusty can do twenty, but sometimes six or seven is all you may care to loiter through. The object is not to devour distance but to enjoy living. You carry on your back in a rucksack what you need for a week ahead, sending replenishments by post or railway to the town you intend to reach at the end of that time. There you get your laundry done and have a little town life before taking to the road again.

You have pleasant little adventures. Unlike the vehicular traveler, you are part of the country you walk through—*on the same level as the inhabitants* and not removed from them by an embankment or plate glass. People will talk to you, and you to people; and this communication is an important reason for taking the trouble to visit a strange country.

If you want to try a walking tour, your first step should be to join the Ramblers Association, 48 Park Road, Baker Street, London N.W.1. Husband-wife membership costs about $1.60 (for those under eighteen, fifty cents), and includes three issues of *Ramblers News*, the *Annual Report*, the *Bed-and-Breakfast Guide*, and the privilege of borrowing, for a small charge, one-inch-scale Ordnance Survey maps. The Ramblers also organize group holidays in Britain and on the Continent. Scotland has its own Scottish Ramblers Federation, 159 West Nile Street, Glasgow C.2. One of its publications, *By Heather Track*, lays out a number of walks through the enchanted country of lochs and glens. To look at one of these route maps is enough to make us want to slip our leash and take off.

Many English counties have their own walking clubs. British Railways helps by publishing handy pocket-size booklets of *Rambles* in Somerset, South Devon, Cotswolds, Wye Valley, and the Chiltern country. These are available from the Commercial Officer, British Railways (Western Region), Paddington Station, London W.2. The other regional branches of British Railways put out their own guides.

London has several walkers' clubs, all of which eagerly welcome Americans. Ramblers Association, Southern Area, 71 Santos Road, Wandsworth S.W.18, organizes Sunday walks during most of the year—out by train to a rendezvous; lunch, walk, tea, walk; and back by another station. London Transport's booklet, "Country Walks, or Out and About in London's Country," is obtainable by mail from the Publicity Officer, 55 Broadway, London S.W.1. A map comes with it.

The least expensive way of seeing England on foot is by youth hostel. The Youth Hostels Association, 29 John Adam Street,

London W.C.2, has almost three hundred dormitories scattered over Britain. They put you up for the night, serve breakfast and evening meal, and provide packed lunches at rock-bottom prices. Details are in the YHA Handbook, which costs nonmembers 15 cents. American Youth Hostels, 14 West 8th St., New York 11, publishes a handbook to the English hostels and a map for fifty cents. The hostels, by the way, assume that anyone traveling on his own feet with a pack on his back qualifies as a youth. A car means age, in their book.

## § *ON BICYCLE*

Hundreds of thousands of English ride bicycles. The bike provides their daily transportation in city and country. The visitor is amused to see the buxom housewife, the bearded university professor, the local vicar, the rural constable pedaling along sedately. On a holiday, not only the young people but the middle-aged and even the elderly go off with a pack on the rack to see yet another part of their land. As far back as 1896 H. G. Wells wrote the classic romance of cycling, *The Wheels of Chance.*

We are prejudiced against the bike as a vacationing vehicle, even though a younger relation joyfully pedaled her way around England and France. Our reasons: steep hills where you have to push the thing and where the descent is like the bat's out of hell; unfamiliarity to an American of British models; traffic hazards. A further reason is that Lawrence has never been able to master the machine.

But the great cycling days are drawing to a close. Why? Because of that statistic we quoted in *By Car*—a 21-per-cent increase in traffic density in two years. Cyclists no longer have long stretches of road to themselves. If you want a bicycling vacation in England, better hurry. The time to do it is now, not later. Helpful address: the Cyclists' Touring Club, 3 Craven Hill, London W.2. Write for its handbook.

# § BY AIR

Pan American Airways jet carries you from New York to London in six and a half hours (it may be even less by the time you read this)—sixteen minutes faster than British Railways' new crack express does the 395 miles between London and Edinburgh. The fastest ocean liner makes the New York–Southampton run in five days. In effect, the air route adds almost nine days to the old vacation time.

Within Britain, London is connected by plane with Manchester, Birmingham, Glasgow, Edinburgh; with the Isle of Man and the Channel Islands; and with Belfast and Dublin. But in England distances between points of tourist interest are so short that air travel plays a very small part.

# § SPECIAL-INTEREST TOURS

In Rome we once met an American widow who, to make good a vow to the Virgin, was visiting a different church each day. She said she had more than a year's occupation before her.

Hers was a special-interest tour.

England has a wealth of special-interest possibilities—literary places, cathedrals, castles, Stately Homes, gardens. On each of these five subjects the British Travel Association publishes a color-illustrated booklet.

Or you can make a round of places with American historical associations; the BTA has a modest booklet on that too. You can line up festivals, from homely village affairs to the big drama and music festivals of Stratford, Malvern, Glyndebourne, Bath, and Cheltenham. You can go in for pretty villages, or golf your way across Britain from St. Andrews to the bottom of Cornwall.

Or perhaps you itch to visit all the six hundred or so places that claim King Arthur? Or fish in every fishable stream? Or travel the route of Offa's Dyke? Whatever the bee in your bonnet, if it's an English bee the BTA will help.

# HOTELS

When Muirhead, usually the reliable British Baedeker, says, "Good hotels are to be found in every part of England," he makes a startling and fantastic statement. England abounds in cities, towns, and villages lacking a hotel that even the most charitable guest could call fair. The gain is that some of the poor ones are picturesque, extraordinary, diverting.

Before descending to cold travel facts, let's prepare you for some peculiarities you may encounter.

*LIGHT*  &#42;  Two young women, one English, one American, checked in at the same time we did at a certain ye olde. Through open doors we heard the English girl call out, "Julie, put on the light, will you?" And Julie's reply: "Beryl, I have news for you. THE LIGHT IS ON!"

In the semi-gloom of our own chamber, we looked at each other and laughed.

The English provincial hotel room is usually equipped with three weak globes. One dangles on a long cord from the ceiling, one is above the washstand, the third is a tiny bedside lamp. Daylight is also restricted by the English custom of blocking the window with the bureau.

*HEAT*  &#42;  In our salad days of travel we scorned Britain as a backward area because it lacked central heating. We sneered at the gas fire and the electric heater. Now that many hotels have put in central heating we are sadder and wiser. They have not put in heating; they have put in radiators. These are seldom allowed to get warm. In a radiatored hotel there is nothing you can do but crawl into bed with a hot water bottle. Most hotels will furnish one on request.

Assume you are lucky enough to get a hotel with the good old-fashioned heating devices. They are metered and you have to feed them with small coins. You never know what denominations you may be needing, but soon learn not to go to your room, which may be three flights up, without a pocketful of meter-fodder. Next you must fathom the mechanism—find the slot, turn the knob, locate the switch. At first-class St. Ermine's in the St. James's region of London, the switch in our room was deep under the bed. One of us had to crouch holding a lighted match for visibility while the other got down on his tummy (to use an English expression), took a sight, got a leverage with his elbow, and gouged the obdurate switch with his thumb.

Electricity is better than gas, which eats up oxygen. Also, when you put your match to the gas heater it often comes on with a fearful explosive bang. Each gas contraption has its idiosyncrasy. One kind ignites with a boom and settles down to a piercing scream. You choke it off and race down for help. The staff knows each heater the way a family knows its dog. "Oh, that No. 22 always screams. Pay no attention. It'll die down."

The heaters are excellent for drying nylon shirts and panties. Only keep the clothes draped on chairs well away from the fire or you'll burn them up, and maybe the hotel too. On our first experience with a heater we came within an ace of burning down Moor Hall in Sussex.

On the subject of what is cold and what warm, either the English are wrong or Americans are. We are prepared to hand down a verdict without waiting for further evidence. On a day in Windsor when the thermometer managed to crawl up to 68, two frail old ladies boarded our bus. "Phew!" cried one, fanning herself with her newspaper, "Isn't it hot!" "Practically tropical, dear," the other agreed. Friends with whom we stayed considered 64 the ideal temperature for the living room.

REMARKS ABOUT THE BRITISH CHARAC-TER * We dislike to go Freudian in this innocent book, but we must assert that the English are masochists. The Duke of Bed-ford recalls of his childhood in his autobiography, A *Silver-Plated Spoon:*

"It was always freezing cold, except for the aviaries full of valu-able birds, which had a tremendously complicated and expensive central heating system. On winter days I used to creep out among the parrots to keep warm." He didn't get enough to eat, either, this heir apparent, and was forced to steal the bread set out for the birds.

It is no secret that the English are more regardful of their pets than of their children. One Molly Turner, in Holyport, Berks., advertises "Individual heated cedarwood houses" in her Cats Inn. A public school that took steps to insure its boys against chilblains would lose its standing.

The English thought Sheraton, the famous chair man, crazy ("his most astonishing fancy" is their circumlocution) because he invented an ottoman with heating urns underneath—"that the seat may be kept in a proper temperature in cold weather."

The masochistic reason why is betrayed in *Tom Brown's School-days:*

"Tom had no legs left at all after the first half a mile on top of the tally-ho. But he found several forms of pleasure in that fact; first, the consciousness of silent endurance so dear to every English-man, the sense of standing out against something and not giving in."

Bernard Shaw put it another way: "An Englishman thinks he is moral when he is only uncomfortable."

Out of the day's London newspaper comes confirmation in the form of a half-page advertisement by Shell-Mex and British Petrol: IT'S NO LONGER WICKED TO BE WARM. The ad goes on: "We've always been tough. A Spartan hillside wouldn't upset the *sang froid* * of the British. But surely the time has come for some good sound sense?"

Shell-Mex and B.P., needing to sell oil, have discovered "sound sense."

It's wicked to be warm, to live in a well-lighted room, to eat well-flavored food, to sit on comfortable furniture, to complain or protest in public about service. An M.P. may ask a question of

* Literally, as you well know, cold blood!

the P.M. in the House, but only a bounder will tell a waiter to take that dish back to the kitchen or insist on pouring his coffee and milk for himself. Bear it, is the Englishman's motto, and nothing said about grinning.

A London Sunday newspaper reported a classic example. A Mrs. Slack, moving into a new council house, asked the gas people to disconnect her cooker and bring it to her new home.

She was forty-eight years old then. After twenty years, they suddenly did it. For those twenty years she had cooked over a coal fire. They asked her why she hadn't complained.

"My husband Joe," she said, "is a quiet man. He doesn't like making a fuss."

But to go on.

*AIR, FRESH* ✻  In England you will never die of suffocation. On the rawest day the room you are shown into will have at least one window thrown wide open and a gale blowing through it. Your first act will be to command the porter to drop those bags and shut that window. He will stare at you slack-jawed, and you may have to spring into action yourself.

The natives are passionate about fresh air. Your bitter nor'easter is their zephyr. When you come down to breakfast in the morning you find not only windows but outside doors flung open, and the staff gives you a sniffly "Good morning." According to the Empire Rheumatic Council, 62 per cent of Englishmen over sixty-five suffer from osteoarthritis.

The condition that to a Briton is most unbearable is "stuffiness." He loves not only fresh air but drafts as well.

No one cares about gaps at the windows and under every door. What a fussbudget you are, complaining that the window won't shut and latch! It's been that way for three hundred years. In all that time the only guests who ever struggled with it were foreigners.

Still, we have fun with those windows. There are many varieties. The best are what we call *Heave-Hos*—windows manipulated by a double set of cords and pulleys, one set for ups, one for downs. One person in good physical condition can work a Heave-Ho provided the window is not very wide.

Window drapes or curtains constitute a problem. In many hotels they are too skimpy to stretch the full width. If they do stretch, they are made of thin material that lets in the light. This you only discover when the dawn wakes you.

DO-IT-YOURSELF TRAVEL KIT * We while away the dull periods by thinking up the contents of a do-it-yourself traveling kit for England.

About those curtains, for example. Include in the kit two yards of heavy dark cloth, and a paper of large safety pins. The two yards will give you only half protection if your windows are almost floor-to-ceiling in one of those high-ceilinged eighteenth-century rooms. For these you need a bolt of cloth and a collapsible step-ladder or a steeplejack's outfit.

There are bed problems. Quilts are covered with some slippery stuff guaranteed to slide them off the bed in the middle of the night. Before retiring, look into drawers and the wardrobe to find where the maids have hidden the bedspreads. Fold these lengthwise (the bedspreads, not the maids), and with them strap down the lower end of the quilt to the mattress. Carry stout twine in your kit in case the maid has hidden the spreads in the hall. You can use the twine anyway, for added safety. Some quilts are more lively than others.

There is also the problem of the second pillow. Hoteliers have invented several tried-and-true techniques for embedding this extra pillow under the bottom sheet. We are trying to counter-invent a pillow-extractor.

What are we to say about the mirror that is set at dwarf height? When you look into it standing up, it cuts you off at the esophagus. If you sit in a chair, you see yourself only from the top of the nose up. To obviate the experience of shaving with knees bent like a diver about to do a half gainer, include a shooting stick in your kit. This is not a gun but a collapsible partial seat at the end of a stick, the other end being a steel spike. It was invented for Englishmen who go on long-trek shooting expeditions with fallen arches. It solves the dwarf-mirror problem, but you must have a rubber tip substituted or it will slide from under you.

The English do not have closets. They have wardrobes. The wardrobe is a huge box which is never wide enough for your clothes and seldom has more than three hangers. The wardrobe is an excellent place in which to hide a body—in old-fashioned plays it served for a couple of centuries for the corpse-concealing and eaves-dropping parts of the action. If you have small children, they can play in the wardrobe. But for clothes, carry your own hangers—and hooks that attach to the wall by suction.

Every English building, from the lowly cottage to Buckingham Palace, has been built for drafts. You can't expect to circumvent the centuries of cunning and craftsmanship that have gone into the creation of those drafts. But if you are traveling with a raincoat (and you should be), topcoat, or shaggy dog, you can lay this out to block the fresh air whistling in under the door.

We thought we had confronted everything and were ready to pin on ourselves a badge of *Nil Admirari* when, on our last day this last trip, we put up at the Royal Hotel in Winchester. An excellent inn-hotel, it gave us something new:

*THE DAVY AUTOMATIC* * Shown into Room 12, we immediately made our usual survey, Sylvia examining the pillow problem while Lawrence studied the heater. We spied by the window a sign in red letters: FIRE ESCAPE. We looked out; there was nothing between us and the pavement but a flagpole. Then we saw that the sign was a box with a latch. Inside were two coils of rope.

When Sherlock Holmes and Dr. Watson stayed in Winchester, theirs was the Problem of Thor Bridge, not of the Davy Automatic Fire Escape. We solved the thing ourselves when we discovered a clue—a card of instructions on the mantelpiece:

1. Release top belt encircling the reeled cable, and drop this reel and cable out of the window.

2. Place remaining belt over your head and under both arms, and tighten the belt slide to body.

3. Clamber out of the window, turning round to face the room.

4. Release both hands, using them to keep the body away from the wall during descent.

As descent is being made the second belt is returning to the window.

Place invalids, unconscious persons or children in the lifebelt and assist them out of the window.

Do not hesitate—it is perfectly safe.

Skeptics are reassured by a photograph of a serenely smiling girl standing on nothing outside a window, with the rope under her arms, and seeming to speak the following:

"The Davy Automatic Fire Escape means certain safety for every occupant. *Numbers cannot daunt it.* Used by Government Departments, over 500 Fire Brigades, and leading authorities all over the world."

Heartening though this intelligence was, it did make us conflagration-conscious. With heightened interest we read on; our Davy —the card warned—was ours in trust only; it had to serve several other rooms as well. Thoughtfully we calculated the distance from our window to the ground. In the corridor were a ladder, too short and innocent of hooks, and an old fire extinguisher with directions to "Drive in Knob by Hard Blows Against Floor." We decided to leave the undauntable Davy to the underprivileged in rooms 6, 7, 8, 9, 10, 11, forget about invalids and children, and make our escape by means of the flagstaff and a ten-foot drop to the sidewalk. As we prepared for bed, we wondered if, as the favored ones, it was right of us to lock our door?

We were still alive the next morning. The Royal had lasted another day in its existence of centuries.

And so will you live through it all, and garner along the way plenty to write home about—which is one of the reasons for traveling. And, like Tom Brown atop the tally-ho, you may learn to get a kick out of fortitude.

## § *PLAINER FACTS*

With few exceptions, English hotels are scrupulously clean. The beds don't have innerspring mattresses but are sound.

Rooms with bath are not common except in London and the shower is unknown. You use the bathrooms and W.C.s spotted along the corridors. Hotels are modernizing but progress is slow. In your room the washbasin with running water represents the last great surge of progress. After all, it was not so long ago that—even in the London hotels catering to the aristocracy—the washbasin with *H* and *C* replaced the porcelain bowl and pitcher. You still find the chamber pot in the little bedside stand.

The toilet paper standard in England is a thin but strong and slick kind of draftsman's tracing paper. We doubt you will be any fonder of it than we are. The soft tissue popular in the U.S. since the outhouse and mail-order catalogue passed into folk history can be bought in a chemist's shop, the English approximation of a drugstore. Kleenex is available too. We carry packets of Kleenex in purse and pocket at all times, and for the hotel we buy the big English box of "man-size" Kleenex, which is stronger and fuller than the small packet and doesn't take up too much room in packing.

Hotel rates, in spite of an irresistible upward trend, remain well under the American. The price quoted for a room usually includes a substantial breakfast. The latest inflationary thrust, as yet confined to a few hotels, is the extra charge for breakfast.

Some places add 10 per cent to the bill in lieu of tips. For the smaller of them this is excessive because there is very little staff.

A negative virtue of the English hotel is the absence of that cynical bird of prey, the American-style bellhop. The English porter hopes to do something for you to deserve a tip, and keeps his palm to himself until he has brought the bags down for your departure.

If you arrive at your hotel in the morning, chances are you will not be able to occupy your room until noon. This regulation is hard on those whose plane deposits them in London at crack of dawn. Noon is checkout time. No matter at what hour you check in, your time is up at noon of the day you are leaving. If you still have sightseeing to do and want to leave later, check your luggage with the hall porter.

Only the larger hotels, and mostly those in London, are outfitted with lobby services. There is seldom a tobacco-newspaper stand, barber shop, beauty parlor, or travel bureau. Many reception desks seem to be staffed by women who have been jilted or have otherwise suffered humiliation that makes them anti-people. It may be that too much work is wrung from them; when you want their help you invariably find them busily posting figures in enormous ledgers. (We have met some memorable exceptions, bless them!) If you have experience of Continental hotels you will miss the omniscient concierge, of whom the English hotel porter is but a poor imitation. Still, although no Jeeves, he can be helpful—within his individual limitations.

Before retiring you tell porter or receptionist what morning newspaper you want, what time you wish to be called, and whether you want morning tea. What is "morning tea?" It is a barbaric custom. The maid raps on your door and, while you struggle up into consciousness, unlocks it with her key and bustles in. She gives you a cuppa along with a revoltingly cheery "Good morning," and proceeds to draw the curtains. We always say (or write; some hotels provide blackboard and chalk): NO MORNING TEA. Sometimes this makes no difference; the maid, balked by a door bolted as well as locked, throws herself against it in a frenzy.

CAUTION.    It is important to book in advance. England is underhoteled. The welfare state has made the English a nation of sightseers in their own country. But whether business is dull or brisk, the English hotel clerk has been brought up to regard it as improper for a traveler to arrive unbooked. For heaven's sake come booked! Some hotels demand not only a written or phoned request, but a subsequent written reply to their reply—a confirmation.

TIP.    Keep in mind that there is no off season for the London hotels. In an emergency, the London Hotels Information Service, 88 Brook Street, phone MAYfair 4514, will tell you where accommodation is available in the London area.

HOTEL LISTINGS  *  The British Travel Association publishes a guide to the hotels and restaurants of the British Isles. The two motor clubs—Automobile Association and Royal Automobile Club—combine to send out scouts, and the hotels that come up to the not-too-exacting standards of the clubs are listed in their guidebooks for motorists—available at approved hotels.

TRUST HOUSES.    With more than two hundred hotels, including historic old inns, this is the largest hotel chain in the country. It keeps up a standard. Its hotels vary in quality and price, as its own reliable booklet indicates by a system of lozenges. The booklet is obtainable at the company's Tourist Enquiry Office in London at 81 Piccadilly, W.1.

THE INN  *  Many hotels outside London are old inns. Where you can, stay in them. The inn is an institution that grew up with the country and can't be found back home. In its humbler and worldly way it is like the cathedral—a complicated structure whose oldest part may go back as far as the fourteenth century, with other parts patched up, remodeled, or added while the centuries wandered on.

Inns vary in size from those with only a few rooms to some with as many as sixty. They vary in quality as well. They have as many (rather, as few) rooms with bath as the more ordinary provincial hotel, and the usual complement of bars, lounges, restaurant, Telly (TV) room. In addition, they have age-blackened oak beams, crooked staircases, undulating floors, furniture of every age they have lived through, grandfather clocks, shining copper, and Toby mugs. Each has its personality, and many have figured in local history.

The best ones—like the Feathers at Ludlow, the Black Swan at Helmsley, the Red Lion at Salisbury, the Lygon Arms at Broadway, and the Great White Horse at Ipswich can't be matched by the ordinary hotel. You will remember them nostalgically after you have forgotten other details of your trip to England.

"BED-AND-BREAKFAST"  *  A less expensive overnight stay is the bed-and-breakfast house, the private home letting out rooms to paying guests. There are thousands of them, and they range from bearable to good. We have made use of them and found them clean. You may occasionally run into a landlady who is a shrew, or one who, as soon as she finds yours a willing ear, will talk it off. You may also occasionally encounter a greasy or stingy breakfast. It's a chancey world, but the odds, from our experience, are very much in your favor.

The personal recommendation is probably the best way to a good b-and-b lodging—asking the railway ticket agent, or porter, or taxi driver, or gas-station attendant. The Ramblers Association (48 Park Road, Baker Street, London N.W.1) publishes a *Bed-and-Breakfast Guide*—a list of places its members have found good.

Still cheaper are the youth hostels; for these see chapter Getting About England, section: On Foot.

# FOOD

To comment on English food is a thankless task. All the best insults have already been hurled, not only by Americans but also by Europeans of every language and cuisine. Among the keenest hurlers have been Englishmen.

A man of Dawlish, Devon, was inspired by a British UN delegate's complaint that New York restaurant turkey tasted like "warm newspapers with gravy" to write the *Daily Telegraph:* "I have always assumed the serving of poultry tasting thus was a closely guarded secret of the English way of life. It is disturbing to think that it has been carried across the Atlantic."

Do not expect to meet that man of Dawlish. The great majority of Englishmen, even those whose travels should have taught them better, think well of their food.

We once shared a compartment on the *Golden Arrow* with handsome young Angus Tudor McGuffey returning from a holiday in Corsica. He lauded the Corsican cuisine. What sauces! What seasonings! What divine cookery! Dinner arrived. He gave one look at his plate and let out the glad cry, "Boiled greens!" The cause of his ecstasy was a soggy heap of Brussels sprouts that filled the compartment with the smell of washday.

But to the facts. The good things first.

English food is filling and nourishing. If you stay long enough you're sure to gain weight on it.

"Upon what meat doth this our John Bull feed?" Lamb and mutton chops, roast lamb and beef cut from the joint, some steak cuts grilled over the coals, ham when from Yorkshire or Wiltshire, breads, pies, cheeses and the biscuits that come with them, are better than you're likely to get in restaurants back home.

There is more drinking of beer and wine with the meal, certainly a better practice than having coffee or Coke.

Many Americans, men mostly, fall in love with savouries for dessert in place of something sweet. Savouries most frequently encountered (always on a square of toast) are Welsh rarebit (the most popular), mushroom and bacon, soft herring roes, prune wrapped in bacon ("Devil on Horseback"), creamed smoked haddock topped with a walnut ("Ivanhoe"), scrambled eggs with anchovies and capers ("Scotch Woodcock"), and liver and bacon ("Canapé Diane").

Americans are not a nation of tea drinkers. But investigation indicates that American visitors become fond of English tea, both the beverage and the afternoon break. To brew a cup of English tea in the U.S. is difficult. The secret is not in the brewing, quality of the water, the temperature or composition of the pot, or the nationality or skill of the brewer. There's no secret at all. The English simply use a tea—full-bodied Indian—which American dealers other than specialty shops do not import.

Another good thing is custard, which we'll go into later.

*THE ENGLISH DIET* * It is heavy on starches. Where else would you find such a passion for the pudding? Where but in England would you find on menus baked beans on toast and spaghetti on toast?

The staple, however, is the potato. An American waiter would be taken aback if you asked for two kinds at a serving—boiled and baked, or French fried and creamed (mashed). The English waiter always brings both and is surprised if you spurn one.

Along with starches the emphasis is on grease—fish and chips (the most popular dish) and the omnipresent roast potatoes, underdone breakfast bacon, breakfast sausages, butter-saturated tea-time toast (which Lawrence always wrings out on his plate before eating, and to hell with manners), pudding which combines both starch and grease while tasting neither starchy nor greasy.

*ENGLISH COOKING* * It is bland. Salt and pepper are the seasonings. Garlic, which much of the world appreciates as the C-major of flavoring, is considered beyond the pale. The onion is only a little less suspect. The one accepted highly flavored dish is Indian curry. Vegetables are waterlogged. The most ubiquitous is green cabbage.

*THE CUSTARD CUSTOM* ✻ Custard is such an inescapable item among the desserts that it demands notice. You will be offered fruit pie (tart), puddings, jello (called jelly), fruit salad (tinned), sponge, tapioca, and so on—all with custard as partner. Sometimes cream replaces custard. Unless you are in Devon or Cornwall where the cream comes clotted (delicious!), reject that cream. It is likely to be out of a tin, a synthetic concoction tasting of the chem. lab. But the custard is far superior to the viscous-rigid American kind. One grows fond of it. Liquid, it is usually freshly made and served warm. Caramel custard is firmer and is one dessert *not* served "with custard." Ice cream is another.

*THE CULT OF TEA* ✻ To the English, tea is more than a beverage. It is what the Wizard of Oz gave the Cowardly Lion—courage, steaming fortitude. It is also a substitute mother, sweetheart, or friend. It is potable hope and charity flavored with the milk of human kindness.

The good life begins for the English with a cup of tea in bed. In many a hotel the maid brings it to you at the hour you have put down to be waked in the morning. If she finds the door barred she tries to batter it down, so firm is the conviction that the stuff must be brought to you at the moment the eyelashes become unstuck. That first cup gives the Englishman the strength to sit up and accept the new day with a stoicism which will have to be reinforced by subsequent infusions.

No English factory could function without a cooker and the makings. Stroll along Holborn or the City at teatime and you will see café hirelings diving into office buildings laden with pots of tea and mounds of bread and butter. To English ears the sound of the kettle on the boil is sweeter than the nightingale's warble, whatever Keats and Shelley may say.

If your reading of whodunits has been as profound as ours, you know how the help rallies round when Sir Reginald is discovered in the library with a sharp instrument pinning him to the carpet. Tea trays are immediately carried to Lady Beryl, the guests, the nurse, the governess and—when they arrive—to the doctor and the Inspector from Scotland Yard—while down in the kitchen the local constable has his cuppa with the cook, who speaks for all: "Well, I always say there's nothing like a good cup of tea."

When the Englishman definitely rules out somebody or something, he says: "He [it] isn't my cup [or dish] of tea."

The brew from "this baleful leaf," as Abigail Adams called it at the time of the Boston Tea Party, frequently gets into the news.

In a court case the wife testified: "When she told me she had been intimate with my husband, I refused to give her tea." The courtroom public probably applauded: "Hear, hear!"

A Bristol husband won a divorce action on evidence that he had found a strange man in bed with his wife, the man being only partly clothed and having tea and scones.

A builder's joiner assaulted his foreman in an argument about whether tea on the job should be taken standing up or sitting down.

English Ford factory managers discovered that striking workers were more concerned for their morning and afternoon tea breaks than about higher pay.

A young farmer won the tea-drinking championship by consuming 534 cups in four weeks, or 19 1/14th cups per day.

Tea-taking has its rules:

1. No tea with lunch or dinner. The workingman has it, but not you; at these times demitasse coffee is served (extra charge), only after the meal and usually not in the dining room but in the lounge. Even in a private home everyone moves to the living room, or if living room and dining room are one, to a small side table.

2. Teatime toast is warm and saturated with butter. Breakfast toast comes cold and dry in a silver hurdle designed to keep the slices from cuddling together to stay warm.

3. Napkins are not forthcoming at teatime when, because of dripping butter, jam, or crumbly cakes, you particularly need them.

4. The brew usually arrives in a "silver" teapot. Test the pot's ear gingerly so as not to get a second-degree burn. You soon get into the habit of wrapping your fingers in your hanky at first sight of a pot.

5. The teaspoon is only for stirring. For tasting, raise cup chest-high on its saucer, raise cup from saucer-platform to mouth, sip. If lips are scalded the tea is too hot.

The four-o'clock-to-five-or-five-thirty tea is the day's climax. The beverage is backed up by buttered bread, buttered toast (or scones or crumpets where available), tiny paste-spread sandwiches on a white bread that looks like pressed cotton, and cakes—usually seed or madeira cake, cup cakes with bilious pink icing, or petits fours. People who have been dull wake up, and conversation may be lively. In tearooms, cafés, hotel lounges, kitchens, drawing rooms, England becomes animated.

Does the magic hour find you in the glamorous setting you have reason to expect, considering the importance attached by the natives to the rite? A cathedral of tea—or at least a grand salon with charming decor, soft lights, gleaming silver, faultless napery, a string orchestra playing Offenbach or Victor Herbert, and dainty waitresses flitting about with delicious morsels on fragile china?

No, it doesn't. *Non, nein, nix, nope, nah, nyet.*

Such tearooms gladden sybarites in Zürich and Montreux, in Frankfurt, in Paris, Monte Carlo, Buenos Aires, Lima. But not in London, not in England. But wait. Let's be just. There *is* one in London, on Fortnum and Mason's fourth floor. And there is one in York, in the North of England—Terry's. And the Chelsea Room of the Red Lion in Salisbury is a pleasant haven. If there are any others, we have missed them and would welcome a post card from discoverers. Most of the tearooms run the spectrum from colorless to grim.

At teatime the hotel lounge comes into its own. It is not beautiful. It may offer nothing better than the tearoom or café, but the shabby upholstery is soft and there's an illusion of drawing-room sociability. The creation of this illusion is the *raison-d'être* of the lounge.

Here's a rite, a cult, whose worshipers have failed to contrive fitting temples for it.

COFFEE  *  It is not as astoundingly bad as the French chicory drink, to our taste, but remains far below the offering at the cheapest American cafeteria chain. To the English, American ways with coffee are as mysterious as English ways with tea appear to the American. Yet here again there is no secret. First, the English have not developed bean-roast-blend finesse. They begin, then, with different raw material. Secondly, they commonly make coffee the way they make tea—dropping the grounds into a pot and adding boiling water. The resulting brew they dilute in the cup with warm milk and sweeten with brown sugar. (There are those who manage the stuff black and unsweetened.)

*Oy!* That chap with contorted features is not about to have a fit. He is merely an American who has experienced his first sip of English coffee. He sets the cup down and pulls himself together. He tries again. It couldn't really have been *that* bad. (Shudder.) It was! It is!

Recent years have shown improvement. Coffee-consciousness is growing. Italian espresso coffee became a fad. Now comes Cona, which is not a superior brand but the name of the glass upsy-downsy contraption in wide use in our own cafés and restaurants. Cona coffee can be good, bad or indifferent, depending on the bean. Evidently a better coffee is also coming in, for one is pleasantly shocked even in the provinces by an occasional happy brew.

If you're used to cream, prepare to do with milk. And if you're used to coffee from the first course on and prepared to fight for it, you're in for lively times.

Breakfast coffee comes in a large cup; at other meals, demitasse. But if you don't mind raised eyebrows, you can get a large cup after lunch or dinner instead of the demitasse. It will taste the same.

*MEALS* * The English breakfast is substantial; the American is patterned on it. Fruit juice (small) is followed by hot or cold cereal (with hot or cold milk, whichever you desire), and choice of eggs with ham or bacon, sausages, kippers, haddock.

Lunch and dinner are also substantial, and of a muchness. The soup is out of a tin (continental Europeans have the right to complain, but not Americans), and the low respect in which it is held is well betrayed by the waiter when he asks if you'll have the thick or the thin. The fruit in fruit cocktails and salads is also out of a tin, just like back home. About the main dish, when you begin to feel overstarched and overgreased, we offer the hint that one standard menu fixture—"ham and salad"—is wise, provided the ham is

York or Wiltshire. Baked ham seems to be unknown. When available, grilled steaks and chops are good.

One problem for the visiting American is the general absence of the snack, the light lunch, the "little something." Few are the cafés or lunch rooms serving freshly made sandwiches, drinkable coffee, and choice of a light dessert. And the quality is N.G.

London has fewer such places than you have knuckles. Those Lyons Corner Houses are depressing in decor and in menu. And consider the offerings at the Kardomah Café in Piccadilly (which prides itself on its coffee, but shouldn't):

> spaghetti on toast
> baked beans on toast
> minced beef with grilled tomatoes on toast
> fish cake with baked beans and potato croquet
> pork pie with beans and potato croquet
> pork sausages with grilled tomatoes (and that blasted p.c.)

The dessert list should include England's celebrated bile beans and stomach powders.

Some pubs serve sandwiches and cold meats; no thrill, but still a possible substitute for the heavy lunch which is identical to the heavy dinner. Since you have to run about looking for the one that has these things, the pub snack isn't a handy answer.

Well, when you can't remold the world to the heart's desire, you adapt yourself to it. The Martin System of Adaptation is to give the standard lunch or dinner an occasional miss and buy fresh fruit and a bar of chocolate, and dine out of the bag while sitting in the park or patroling the sights. This gives the overworked juices a rest and relieves you of restaurant tedium. Another way is to have high tea, if obtainable, as late as possible—about six—and finish up with before-bed grapes, oranges, cherries, or whatever else may be in season in the fruit stores. High tea is usually to be found in cafés. The menu includes ham and eggs, fish and chips, and such odds and ends as we listed on the Kardomah menu.

"WHEN DO WE EAT?" * The approximate feeding hours are: breakfast, 8–9:30; lunch, 12–2; dinner, 6:30 or 7 to 8:30; tea, 3:30 to 5. Chinese restaurants seem to be open all day long and into the night. In London there are restaurants that specialize

in maintaining the feed bag at the ready (with music and/or dancing) until the wee hours.

But for the most part nothing is to be had out of hours. Why?
There is no answer that makes sense. The visitor will find many
natives eager to agree with his strong words on this unhappy situation. Such is a Mr. Beck who went off the deep end in a letter to
his newspaper:

> Sir: Is it not reasonable to expect a hot meal or at least a hot drink
> and sandwich at 8:30 P.M. at a relatively high-class hotel recommended
> by the leading motoring organizations?
>
> This request of mine, made the other day at a hotel near Birken-
> head, was received with almost incredulity by the staff and was politely
> turned down on account of the "lateness of the hour."
>
> The hotel in question will no doubt be aware that I am referring to
> them when they find the empty Spaghetti Bolognese tin and other
> remnants of the meal I prepared on my small pressure stove, left in
> the wastepaper basket of the bedroom. I carry this stove and provisions
> for just these emergencies.

Mr. Beck's sad experience with the hotel staff puts us in mind of
the senior post-office official who declared, "We are not having
anything in the Post Office which smacks of the customers being
right."

The Trust House hotel chain, after years of deliberation, has
initiated an experiment at the Bell Inn, Epping, of a quick-service
restaurant where food may be had outside the classic hours. Let us
pray it is a success, and contagious. Within a decade England may
be an "open society" where you may be able to buy even a glass of
beer or a box of matches at any hour, and where all the shops don't
close down with a bang at 1 P.M. of that purely British institution,
Early Closing Day.

We prophesy that by 1975 it will be possible to lunch at 3 and
dine at 10 P.M., if you wish. The problem will still remain: What
on?

# SPORTS

# AND

# GAMESMANSHIP

We treasure a worn clipping in which this reminiscence appears:

> Sir John Anderson was on board, and we stood together on the bridge and watched the bleak guardian that nightly flashes its warning to the traffic on the sea.
>
> "It wouldn't make much of a golf course," said either Sir John or myself. It really doesn't matter which, because it is the way men of English blood speak when their emotions are roused.

Who but an Englishman could look out over the sea and rate it in terms of a golf course? The simple account outdoes a normally fantastic shaggy-dog story. Yet it's entirely natural that "men of English blood" when deeply moved should think of games.

Sports and gamesmanship are inventions of the English. They created most of the ball games (only basketball is entirely American). They civilized a primitive Dutch club-and-stone affair into golf. They are responsible for cricket, tennis, badminton, squash, volleyball, the two kinds of football, boxing, and the rowing and yachting sports. As far back as the Middle Ages they had made hunting into a rite combining a maximum of physical exercise with a minimum of personal risk. But the extraordinary thing was the feeling they developed for the quarry. It became a good chap who had to be given a sporting chance.

During the passage of centuries, the English evolved an ethical code called *sportsmanship*. One of the great contributions to world culture, this "Is it cricket?" criterion is probably the nearest the human race has come to the actual practice of the Golden Rule.

34

Fundamentally, the Code is that the foul line stays in the same place no matter who is at bat; that the opponent (like the fox in hunting) is a gentleman; and that victory is the secondary reward of a superior performance. Some of the foreign nations who have caught the enthusiasm have yet to absorb the morality. Passed at the net by a brilliant return, an American or Australian tennis star often shows temper. The English player is likely to applaud: "Good shot!"

Asked for a definition of sportsmanship, a British polo star answered: "Win as if you were used to it. Lose as if you enjoyed it for a change."

Admittedly the Ten Commandments are important, but today the English Code is more widely observed. It makes British political life more tolerant than the American. An un-British Activities Committee is unthinkable. There are super-patriots but they do not terrorize the land. By the Code, they would be unsporting.

An incident that got into the *Daily Telegraph* is to the point. In an election campaign Lord Mancroft, chairman of the Conservative Speakers' Association, always brought a flag and a whistle to meetings. When hecklers became a nuisance "he blows the whistle, waves the flag, and shouts: 'Off side! Free kick to Mancroft!'

"Order is unfailingly restored."

In conversation, the Code lays down the principle that each participant has the right to speak his paragraph. Even heated discussion of a highly controversial topic is kept within bounds. An Englishman does not tell that damn fool who doesn't know what he's talking about and hasn't got the brains he was born with to drop dead. To an American who takes no nonsense from anyone and speaks his mind in words as hard as cannonballs, the quiet Englishman counters: "I wonder if perhaps you are not overlooking . . . ?" Belligerence he receives with polite murmurs which lower the temperature. The spectacle may be enjoyed in hotel lounges.

CRICKET  *  Kipling snarled at "the flanneled fools at the wicket." But Kipling was an oddball, and is forgiven because he wrote "If," which is the Code in verse.

Cricket is the national pastime, the most widely played team game. There are some four hundred cricket fields in the London area alone. Every village with eleven men hale enough to heave a ball and swing a bat boasts a team. On reasonably dry Sundays from May to September, greens and commons resound to the mild competition of this bland and protoplasmic ancestor of baseball. Schools and universities play one another, as do towns and counties. World's Series equivalents in cricket are the International Test Matches played between England and other Commonwealth countries.

What is cricket about?

The famous Eleventh Edition of the *Encyclopaedia Britannica* explains it in 11½ pages, 5½ of them in finer-than-fine type—compared to 3½ for baseball. The print is clear, the prose unexceptionable, but the meaning escapes an American.

Cricket is not neatly divided into several innings like baseball, nor is there any obvious point at which it can be said one side is ahead or has won. Play sops up time like a blotter. The village game lasts the greater part of daylight. Major games take about three days. International matches may last five. At the end, the verdict may be "No decision."

Try to imagine baseball with one side batting without stop for nine innings and twenty-seven outs, then ambling out to field while the other side bats its twenty-seven.

The American likes his games plotted and dramatic. For him the bewildering thing about cricket is that most of the time nothing happens. Most pitches (bowls) to the batsman result in no action; the batsman merely blocks the ball defensively. After every six tosses comes an *over*—the men in the field walk across the grass and the game goes on in the opposite direction. A clever batsman may be in for hours, blocking the ball, dumping it, tapping it for a discreet run. When he occasionally lights into it and whales it to the boundary for a 4, the spectators wake up, pat their palms together, and mutter "Well hit, sir!"

Cricket is like polite parlor talk. It goes on and on; it doesn't end but rather peters out, and everyone goes home feeling he's been in good company. Reviewing an unusually active series of test matches, the London *Times* headlined: SEASON TOO TURBULENT TO BE ENJOYED.

But the game should be seen. Being an atheist is no excuse for not looking at Canterbury Cathedral.

Lord's in London is cricket's holy of holies, and the game to see is the one between Oxford and Cambridge. Go as you would to a

theater or a tribal dance. Relax, watch the crowds, enjoy the color
of the awnings, the holiday whiteness of the flannel trousers, the
greenness of the lawn. But don't try to understand it.

We know one Englishman who, when at home, always puts on
his cricket cap to listen to the matches on the wireless. His feeling is sound, for this game's invisible ardor and complications em-
body the Code.

The seriousness with which a true Briton takes his game is revealed in these extracts from readers' letters to editors:

> So long as school cricket is played with a soft ball, there will be
> juvenile crime.

> It was to permit the continuation of such things as cricket that re-
> sistance to the Nazi challenge was worthwhile.

F O O T B A L L  * Soccer—association football—draws weekly
crowds of more than a million during the season, and they can yell
all they want to. Hogarth sketched the lower orders soaked in gin.
If he were alive today he'd have to show them soccer-soaked. The
season begins in the fall and ends in the Cup Final at Wembley
Stadium in April or May. Games are played Saturday afternoon,
and are announced in advance in the newspapers.

Soccer is a professionalized sport. Its fans act more like U.S.
baseball addicts than like the cool spectators at cricket. Its goddess
is money. On these games, through highly systematized betting
pools, something like $215,000,000 is wagered annually. Payoff to
a winner has gone as high as $840,000. About a third of the popu-
lation bets through the pools. The promoters even provide special
envelopes for delicate-minded clergymen to send in their bets
secretly.

But as in baseball, money isn't everything. On a street corner in
some town or village you may see small boys nimbly passing a stone
or tennis ball back and forth or around a circle with their feet.
Behind their total absorption is the vision of such a soccer hero
as the late Duncan Edwards, who stands immortalized in stained
glass in his village church.

Soccer has become the most widespread game in the world.

The other football game, rugby, is parent to the American game.
It was born in a most un-English way. One day in 1815 in a game
at Rugby (where Tom Brown later suffered his schooldays), a boy

*picked up the ball and ran with it.* He should have been disgraced. But important people cried, "How clever!" and "Splendid idea!"— and the school gave its name to a new sport.

Rugby is played in shorts and without benefit of the elaborate mattress-armor and helmet of the American gridiron warriors. Like the American version, it's an autumn game. Twickenham Stadium near London is its chief arena.

GOLF  *  As a tourist, if you find time to play any game at all it will probably be golf. There are 1600 golf links, 260 within a fifty-mile radius of London. The nearer ones will be crowded on week ends. It may not be necessary to carry the membership card of your home club, but it never hurts; the English respect formal material of this kind. Greens fees are modest. Several amateur, pro, and open tournaments are held through the summer.

The weekly *Golf Illustrated* carries much information. The English Golf Union, 34 Aldridge Avenue, Edgware, Middlesex, helps visitors.

HORSE RACING  *  The English are passionate about horse racing, and in the sport of kings the Queen herself is an ardent participant. The great race meetings (as they're called) are a pageant of British social and sporting life. The most famous are the Derby and the Oaks, run at Epsom (Epsom salts came from here), sixteen miles from London, in May or June. Ascot, near Windsor, has the royal and fashionable meeting in the latter half of June. Other near-London racetracks are at Alexandra Park, Hurst Park, Kempton Park, Sandown Park, and Royal Windsor. Two of the most noted in the provinces are Goodwood, near Chichester in West Sussex, and Newmarket in Suffolk. The British Travel Association's calendar of coming events lists forty-nine different meetings around the country for the month of July alone.

Even those who, like Bernard Shaw, have no interest in horse racing because they know well that one horse will be faster than the others, and don't care which, will find a race meeting an occasion on which the Englishman is to be seen at his most vivid and exciting, from the farmer and barrow boy on up to the gray-topper class. The Ascot race scene in *My Fair Lady* was fun but not realism.

*HUNTING*  *  We are on the side of the fox (otter, deer, rabbit).

The addiction to "blood sports" constitutes an area of the English character not easy for the American to find sympathetic. Here the Englishman and his hard-riding mate suddenly become foreigners. We have ourselves followed hunts on foot and have sat around country hotels listening hard, trying to understand the strange passion. Result: it still seems to us absurd, class-minded, and as a sport several degrees below bullfighting, where at least the would-be killer runs considerable risk to his own health.

The hunt is not entirely without danger. Horses occasionally stumble or throw their riders. One accident-prone master of the aristocratic Pytchley Hunt broke his collarbone so often that he finally sent his whipper-in to Northampton Infirmary to learn how to set it.

The Pytchley has seven thousand nonriding financial supporters —an indication of the status value of membership. An ecstatic line in an article about it says, "You ride across oceans of grass, and amazingly, modern farming methods haven't spoiled it." Now you know how fox-hunting ranks with the gentry against raising crops.

At Moor Hall in Sussex we witnessed budding romance when the handsome young man after a hard hunt-day rejoined the charming girl he had left with. Exhausted and mud-bespattered, they had to drink a cup of tea before saying a word. Then he asked eagerly, "Did you kill?"

"No, but it was a jolly good run. And you?"

"Broke a rib, I think."

"Oh? I say, what bad luck!"

A month later the *Times* announced their engagement.

Saturdays from November through March are the hunt days. From cities, towns, and villages the huntsmen converge on the local headquarters of the hunt to which they belong, an inn or country hotel which keeps their mounts and has extras for hire. There they change into jodhpurs, boots, hard hats, and pink (red) coats. (A hunt coat has to be earned; it's not regulation battle dress but the reward of persistence and valor.) Few scenes are more animated than the gathering of a Hunt—riders assembling before the inn or mansion, hounds milling about, yokels gaping, and finally the Master taking a Godspeed posset from Mine Host.

On one occasion we joined the yokels in a laugh when half a couple streaked through the legs of Master and host, straight into the kitchen. He was ejected with difficulty. Yes, "half a couple." In hunt parlance there's no such thing as a dog. Dogs are *hounds.* There's no such thing as *a* hound. There are couples, and one hound is half a couple.

Following the hunt on foot, even in the company of an old gaffer to explain the mysteries, is like getting a yeoman-farmer's view of a medieval battle. The hunt is tootles on the horn, cries from the far horizon, a sudden charge of hounds across a field followed by part of the hunt (others having lost their bearings or gotten mired). You enjoy a jolly good walk, just as the hunt enjoys a jolly good ride, and are back at the inn or hotel to see the return of the bedraggled company (usually foxless) for tea. After dinner these sportsmen, who had appeared too tired to work themselves out of their boots, dance the night away, impeccably groomed.

The point-to-point meetings are more amusing. Taking place during the latter half of the hunting season, these are amateur steeplechases organized by the local Hunt. The entrants are every Tom, Dick, and Harriet who has a horse or can borrow one and cares to risk his bones over a course of about four miles of furrow, thick fence, hedge, and water jump. The finish is at the starting point, where you can usually find a perch from which most of the race is visible. Five or six races are usually run, while the countryside kibitzes and lays bets.

Hunts are little touristed but needn't be. Dotted across the country are the inns and country hotels that are local Hunt headquarters. You can put up at one of them and watch the strange and thoroughly English proceedings, and even participate. Moor Hall in Ninfield, Sussex, is convenient to London and the one we know best. Another is the Manor House Hotel, Castle Combe, near Bath. The British Travel Association has a list.

*PONY-TREKKING* * You may see, as you ride through a picturesque patch of countryside, twenty or so mounted ponies winding over a hill. Pony-trekking is a sport which has taken hold and has a growing number of enthusiasts. Many never had a lesson in posting; such lessons aren't needed.

A pony-trek is a holiday aboard a junior horse, a group trip a little like the one the Canterbury pilgrims had, the host in this case being a professional leader. It operates from a center out into the surrounding hills and dales far from the madding traffic's ignoble smells and hurry. The riders are business and professional people, wives with husbands, children, teachers, students, a Manchester thread tycoon, a Savile Row tailor taking a rest from the right cut of a lapel.

Pony-trekking is fun for all ages and a special treat for children. Information may be obtained from the BTA, and from the Central Council of Physical Recreation, 6 Bedford Square, London, W.C.1. Books, published in England, include *Pony Trekking for All* by J. A. Kerr Hunter; *Pony Trekking* by Glenda Spooner; and *Try Pony Trekking This Way* by Thurlow Craig.

SCOOP  *  An outdoor sport we haven't seen listed anywhere is lovemaking. Years back, a humorous book by a Continental quipped that where other nations have sex, the English have hot-water bottles. This is a gross libel. Wander on a pleasant evening (broad daylight will do) through Hyde Park or Regent's Park, or boat along the Thames near Windsor, and you will see sex play so unabashed that it ranks as a spectacle. Whether for you this would be a spectator or participating sport we hardly know, but there it is.

# THEIR
# LANGUAGE
# AND YOURS

The differences between English English and the home-grown American variety have been exaggerated. You will understand and be understood. But you may have an awkward moment or two, as when you discover that *bug* does not mean "insect" but "bedbug" and is outlawed and that *bloody* is to be avoided in the presence of women.

Englishmen have for so long enjoyed American novels, plays, and movies (the "flicks") that they understand Damon-Runyonese, hillbilly, and horse-opera talk. At the same time, Americans have been so steeped in Bertie Wooster, Lucky Jim, Sherlock Holmes, and other English types that they too can easily fall in step.

With the help of the basic English-American glossary at the end of this section, you will be linguistically at home in England in no time at all.

The matter of pronunciation and enunciation is slightly more difficult, requiring some training of the ear. You may be startled to hear an Englishman speak of the skwiddles in the pahk. A skwiddle is the animal you call a skwurl. Your taxi driver may point out Spaws, the Ahzez of Pahment, and Moblotch, three famous sights of London.

When these oddities become commonplace, you may find yourself unconsciously imitating. Struggle against the tendency. The English expect you to be American. The feeling of triumph, of completion, that comes to you when you hear your first Englishman cry, "Oh, I say!" or "Jolly good!" is the Englishman's when he hears you say, "Well, I guess," or "Heavens to Betsy," or "Good grief!"

There exists across the water a phenomenon of which Americans are innocent—the speech gulf that divides the classes. Shaw dramatized this in *Pygmalion*, and *My Fair Lady* brought Shaw to other millions. It is fascinating to watch two Englishmen, strangers to each other, meet abroad; to observe how they sniff around each other's accents to see if they belong in the same bracket. If the answer is no, they avoid each other, even if (as we witnessed in a hotel in Grenada) the two constitute 50 per cent of the guest total in the hotel. They will drink at the same bar, each as aloof as if the other did not exist. They will acknowledge each other's presence only on an unexpected confrontation, and only by a grunt.

The man who says "The rine in Spine" ostracizes himself in London from the *rain-Spain* people in a way that the New Yorker who says "Joisey City," or "It's a boid, it choips," does not.

U AND NON-U * No language war is fought between Us and Them on any of their levels, but within Britain civil war rages.

Nancy Mitford, an English bluestocking, brought it to a head with a belligerent essay published in a book entitled *Noblesse Oblige*, along with a class-vocabulary study by Alan S. C. Ross, an expert in "sociological linguistics." Evelyn Waugh involved himself with some guerrilla comment. The book inflamed the public. Leaders (editorials) were written, and some letters to editors proved "unprintably violent," according to Waugh. For an American who wants to understand the English, this book contains invaluable information. Here we summarize.

Language divides the English into two camps: U-speakers and non-U. *U* means Upper. The bestower of the epithets shirked calling the other camp Lower; it is non-Upper.

An Englishman who says "Pardon me" when he bumps someone, or belches in company, or fails to understand a remark directed at him, is distinctly non-U. How does the U-man respond? If he happens to burp he lies low and says nothing. If he steps on your foot, he mumbles "Sorry." If he hasn't caught your question he says "What?" His greeting is never "Pleased to meet you," but "How d'ye do?" And only a non-U will answer by telling him how he does.

The U-man says "table napkin." The non-U gives himself away with "serviette." The American comes along and simply says "napkin"—which among the English is quite something else again (see the glossary). But you should worry! Luckily they consider you to be outside this family row. Your diction and pronunciation may be quaint, even horrible, but never non-U.

There's quite a bit about what to call the modern successor to the outhouse. U-speakers call it lavatory (social cowardice, for *lavatory* means, strictly, a place to wash), but the males call it among themselves the "jerry." This is a schoolboy word which indicates the speaker has been to public school—which is, of course, the British term for a private school. Incidentally, the American "john" is not modern, as you may think, but goes clear back to the Middle Ages, probably originating with the French as *le jacques*. The "jerry" was originally the chamber pot—probably still is, in those medieval dormitories of Eton, Winchester, Sherborne, and their cousins. Says sociologist Dr. Ross in a footnote: "But the (recent?) transitive verb 'to pot' is surely non-U?" Don't ask us, Ross; we're strangers here.

According to the expert, the W.C. is non-U. If so, the world has gone non-U, for W.C. is, with O.K., surely the most international of all initials. Non-U kiddies say "dubby" or "dub" because their parents playfully call the letter W dubby-you. The things one learns!

It is non-U to "take a bath"; one *baths*. But at the beach, one "has a bathe."

From signs and notice boards we have learned that a "boy" is a U-youngster. When you hear of a Lads' Club, be sure it is a club of lower-middle-class or proletarian boys. LAD WANTED says the sign in the shop window, never BOY WANTED.

The U-snobs have complicated life to the point of utter absurdity. One problem that plagues them is how to address those among the lower orders one can't avoid speaking to—barmaids, waitresses, salesgirls, telephone operators. Is there any alternative to non-U *Miss?* Yes, says the authority. It is silence.

The U-man seldom gets on a first-name basis. It's a serious matter with him who gets called *Smith,* who *Mr. Smith,* and whose name is never mentioned to his face.

The brainwashing begins at his public school. Here the lads—

sorry, the *boys*—use only last names. If there are two Smiths, they are told apart as Smith Major and Smith Minor. (What happens when a third Smith appears? Crisis. A fourth must be chaos.) Normally the boys don't even know one another's baptismal names. Tutors and masters don't use them. See then how confusion reigns. Jones accepts Smith's invitation to spend the school holidays at Smith's manor, castle, Stately Home, or town house. He arrives. "'Lo, Smith," "'Lo, Jones." The two go on in their usual happy way, until suddenly Papa Smith is on the scene. Great Scott! Holy U! How can Jones call his friend "Smith" in front of Papa Smith? Desperately he ransacks his memory—no, he has never heard his friend's first name. The poor kid is reduced to the utter ignominy of inquiring of the butler or parlor maid.

Apparently these alien people regard first-name calling as a shade effeminate. Only this could explain the meaning of remarks we overheard in the lounge of the Lion in Shrewsbury. One man was saying to another (apparently each had a son at the Shrewsbury school): "In this soccer game David began calling Peter 'Peter,' and Peter was calling David 'David'—y'know, rather like 'darling' and 'dear.' I got the wind up proper, had to take 'im aside and tell 'im boys must not call each other by their first names before other boys."

The use of language to fence people off is an unpleasant aspect of the English character, their brand of apartheid. They buttress it with such physical objects as the old school tie, the tightly furled umbrella, and the school or club blazer—all displays recognized and, alas, accepted by the non-Ughs as signs of the true Ugh.

The Blitz brought the British of all classes together. Holed up in the Underground all night while Hitler blasted their homes from above, they became chummy and discovered their common humanity. Shoulder to shoulder they fought fires, carried away the bodies of unfortunate neighbors, and amid the rubble knocked down the barriers between U and non-U. They are nostalgic about those heroic days. But that togetherness is gone, an un-English episode, a "bright interval." Britain is normal again.

\*     \*     \*

# BASIC ENGLISH-AMERICAN GLOSSARY

| | |
|---|---|
| assurance | insurance |
| biscuit | cracker, not a bun or sweet roll. Ask for a sweet biscuit if you want a cooky |
| bonnet | hood of a car |
| book | as verb: to reserve. Booking office is ticket office or agency. You book a restaurant table, theater seat, hotel room, railway ticket |
| boot | luggage compartment of a car |
| boots | shoes; also the unseen character who blacks (not shines) them if you leave them outside your door |
| braces | trouser suspenders |
| car | short for motorcar (automobile), but not for railway coach, except sleeping car, restaurant car |
| caravan | house-trailer |
| chemist | druggist |
| clerk | office worker, not a salesperson |
| coach | railway car (see *car*); excursion bus, long-distance or cross-country bus. *Bus* is reserved for local service, including suburban |
| corn | cereal grains in general. Our corn they call maize, or Indian maize, although *sweet corn* is coming in |
| first floor | second floor; our first is their ground floor, and so on up |
| flat | apartment; their *block of flats* is our apartment building; their *service flat* is our hotel apartment |
| garters | armbands (they still wear them) when preceded by *sleeve*; for our garters, see *suspenders* |
| goods | freight, as in goods-van or goods-wagon, goods-train, goods station |
| homely | homelike; for *ugly* they use *plain* |
| lift | elevator |

| | |
|---|---|
| lines | railway tracks |
| lorry | truck |
| luggage | *baggage* is edging its way in |
| mad | crazy; never *annoyed* or *angry* |
| metaled road | paved road, hard road |
| motorcar | automobile; may be shortened to *the motor* or *car* |
| napkin | baby's loincloth, diaper. Nappie is *di-dee*. The table item is *table napkin* or *serviette* |
| no standing | no parking |
| paraffin | kerosene |
| pavement | sidewalk |
| petrol | gasoline |
| public con-<br>    veniences | omnipresent genteel for comfort station; synonyms: lavatory, cloakroom |
| public school | a private upper-class school, not state-supported |
| return | round trip |
| sick | not a synonym of *ill,* but used mostly for "in a vomiting condition," as in seasick; the hospital, however, has sickbeds in sickrooms |
| store | department store or warehouse, never small shop |
| subway | pedestrian passage under busy crossing |
| suspenders | garters |
| sweet | as noun: candy; also loosely used for dessert |
| telly | TV |
| trunk call | long-distance telephone call |
| underground | American subway; sometimes *tube* of those lines which are actual tubes |
| van | delivery truck; railway baggage car |
| vest | undershirt |
| waistcoat | man's vest |
| windscreen | windshield |
| wireless | radio |

NOTE. English usage is to treat group nouns as plural: "The government are," "The Cabinet have," "Cardiff (football team) win 3–1," etc.

FURTHER NOTE—KYEW AND KYAW. In Tibet you would have to get used to yak butter, tea bricks, and prayer wheels. In England you escape these, but are confronted with the phenomenon of *Kyew*.

Every time your waiter sets a plate before you, rearranges your eating tools, flicks a crumb from the cloth, takes away the mustard, or is asked for the bill, he says *Kyew*.\* By and by you deduce that he is thanking you, and wonder why, since it is you who are being served. Conscience pricks, and you say, "Thank YOU." This is misguided. It stops him in his tracks, puts him off his game. So to pull himself together he says *Kyew* again.\*\*

The lift man says it when you enter his vehicle and when he lets you out. Do not interfere with the service professions' monopoly of the *Kyew*. Even stout travelers have been known to mutter, then to gibber, declaring that these people carry politeness too far, and that if it goes on they will scream. But this is not politeness. That the expression is a truncated *thank you* is purely coincidental. Theirs is a gesture word designed to cover decently the nakedness of a bare act. When the railway conductor who pops his head in the door of your compartment says *Kyew*, he means "Ticket, please," but doesn't want to be crass or obvious. The waiter's *Kyew* can mean any of several things—"Look out, I'm at your elbow with the soup," "Poddon," or "Well, that's that."

One result of the endless kyewing and kyawing is that the English really lack an expression for *Thank you*.

\* If a tenor, that is. A baritone or bass will say *Kyaw*.
\*\* Or *Kyaw*.

# STATELY

# HOMES

More than five hundred country mansions are open to the public for a small fee—usually about thirty-five cents. An attraction of these sumptuous residences of the highborn is that, unlike museums, they are lived in. They are alive. The present owners of the proud name and elegant pile may have had to crowd themselves into a thirty-room wing, but when all the trippers are gone they issue forth to put the place tidy and count the day's take under the family portraits.

In the 1800s, sentimental poet Felicia Hemans sang:

> The stately homes of England,
> How beautiful they stand
> Amidst their tall ancestral trees,
> O'er all the pleasant land.

These four tra-la lines proved imperishable. Stately Home has become the generic term for the manse of the aristocracy, from the modest manor house to the vast, ornate palace of Blenheim.

Except for Scott's Abbotsford, where she was often a guest, Felicia saw only from a yearning distance the gatekeeper's lodge, the sweeping driveway, and the tall trees in a dreamy park screening the many-chimneyed great house. Deep within the ancestral acres, in hallowed privacy and fabulous splendor, lived the lord and his lady, peers of the realm, contributing in person to History.

Today you can pick and choose among the grandest of the Stately Homes. Dukes and barons beg you—literally—to visit them.

Pinched by taxes and death duties, they are keeping the wolf from the grand portal by opening it to everybody. Their distress is your gain. You see more than your money's worth of marble and parquetry, gilt and brocade, carpet and tapestry, porcelain and gold plate, Old Masters, period furniture, paneling and carving, crystal chandeliers, and miscellaneous knickknacks any of which would fetch the price of a round trip across the Atlantic.

The real estate is magnificent too. The noble house stands in a park often greater in area than a town is able to maintain for its total population. Woburn Abbey, for example, the most popular house on the coronet circuit, is surrounded by three thousand landscaped and lagooned acres. Within roam two thousand animals and, in the course of a year, half a million sightseers. Beyond stretch eighteen thousand acres of Bedford farms worked by tenantry.

In Felicia Hemans' day the Bedfords owned Covent Garden and much of Bloomsbury in London, but the Duke of the time traded these properties for Czarist bonds now about as valuable as Confederate money. That is one reason John ("Call me Ian"), thirteenth Duke of Bedford, spends his days welcoming the crowds to Woburn and his nights thinking up new ways to extract more shillings per visitor.

On our tour of Woburn Abbey, we lingered in the Souvenir Hall while Sylvia scribbled in her notebook. One of the young women behind the counter demanded to know what she was doing. Embarrassed, Sylvia confessed she was making notes.

DUKE'S HENCHWOMAN: You generally secure permission of the Controller of the House to take notes.

SYLVIA (quavering but firm): I generally take notes wherever I please.

HENCHWOMAN: Notes and photographs—special permission!

LAWRENCE: Why?

HENCHWOMAN (unbending): Well, y'know, we must be careful. Other Stately-Home owners come looking for ideas for their own business.

SYLVIA: Spies!

HENCHWOMAN: The Marquess of Hertford came with his whole staff, taking notes. But that was all right—he had permission.

LAWRENCE (chummily): And how is business with the Marquess?

HENCHWOMAN: Quite good—though of course not on a par with ours. All the same, Hartford had a splendid lure all his own this summer of diving into his lake wearing deep-sea equipment. He had a very good press and——

But at this point she broke off, fearful of having said too much.

Competition is keen among the bluebloods. Every year fifty or sixty more great houses join the "open." When the Earl of Pembroke had to shut his house for urgent repairs, his neighbor, Sir Westrow Hulse, had his best year yet at Breamore House.

Lord Montagu of Beaulieu (*Bewly*) Abbey displays a collection of vintage cars as a sideline. One season when it wasn't drawing, he tried a rock-'n-roll session. This almost wrecked the Abbey.

Knole, one of the most beautiful houses, has a dignified ploy—a Connoisseur's Day for those who want to avoid the crowds and will pay five shillings, two more than on ordinary days.

The Marquess of Hertford, after he had reconnoitered Bedford's operation, pepped up his own show at Ragley Hall. After the diving he performed on water skis on his ten-acre lake. Two pros helped with ski acrobatics, and the Marchioness drove the speedboat. Additional inducements for visitors were swimming and sailing on the lake, and cricket in the park.

But John of Bedford, the Barnum among the embattled peers, outdoes them all. He has of course a really great house, and he and his Duchess try to be on hand to chat with the customers. He has enough attractions in his park so that families can put in a full day—zoo, pets' corner, playground, bingo, flower shop, putting green and crazy golf, tuck shop (candy and snacks), restaurant, tearoom, café. It costs 35 cents to enter the park, another 15 cents for the house, and more again to see Their Graces' private breakfast and dining rooms. Souvenir shops are at both entrance and exit, and among the gimcrackery they sell autographed copies of the Duke's sensational autobiography. An engaging sign says in large letters: I HOPE YOU HAVE ENJOYED YOUR VISIT. DO COME AGAIN! BEDFORD.

And by the exit door is the ultimate—a wire-screened chest with a card asking you to toss in your spare change to help Bedford maintain his abbey. We had been sympathetic toward the Duke and his gallant battle for his home, but that chest, the tin cup on a ducal scale, shook us.

We emerged to read this story in the *Daily Mail*, appropriately headlined WOBURN MUGS:

The Duke of Bedford, who is in America, has been giving a dissertation on the souvenirs he sells to tourists at Woburn Abbey.
"They're horrors," he said. "At first I chose only the things I liked. There were few sales.
"Then I chose the things I didn't like, and the people couldn't wait to grab them. There's just no bottom to people's bad taste.
"The Duchess doesn't believe in giving change. Instead, when they've bought two horrible items, she gives them two other horrible items."

Candid chap, His Grace.

The Stately-Homes business has brought fierce argument into upper-class circles: whether to go into it in the first place; and, once in, how far to go. That Honorable Nancy Mitford (daughter of a baron), whom you met in the section on language, is indignant at what she calls the "sad commerce."

"The lowest peasant of the Danube," she wrote, "would stick at letting strangers into his house for 2s 6d, but our dukes, marquesses, earls, viscounts, and barons not only do this incredible thing, they glory in it . . . and compete as to who among them can draw the greatest crowds. It is the first topic of conversation in noble circles today, the tourists being referred to in terms of sport rather than of cash . . . the bag counted after the shoot.

" 'I get twice as many as Reggie, but Bert does better than me.'
"The baiting of the trap is lovingly considered.
" 'Mummy dresses up in her Coronation robes, they can't resist it. . . .'
" 'We've started a pet's cemetery. . . .' "

Bedford has an answer to Miss Mitford: "I have been accused of being undignified. I am. If you take your dignity to a pawn-broker he won't give you much for it."

Most of the bluebloods, however, leave the business to the non-profit National Trust, which conducts it with dignity.

You go through a Stately Home in company with other assembled trippers, mostly British, and usually with a group guide. These house guides are well trained for a difficult job. They must round up stragglers with voice and eye, quell the little old lady who has a mania about ancestral love affairs, scoop up the lively toddler who is trying to crawl under the bed Charles I slept in, see to it that nothing goes into a pocket as unauthorized souvenir. They must talk well and steadily, and be able to answer questions. Most of them are very good.

In the entrance hall you can buy the illustrated booklet about the house. Usually there is a restaurant or tearoom in an outbuilding, and Public Conveniences are convenient.

The very finest treasures of the house and family are on view, not a few of them cleaned or refurbished by experts at great cost, having been discovered in vaults, attics, and cellars where they had lain for generations. The miles of floor and ornate ceiling, carving and gilt, the thousand and one gems, are being housekept for the public as they haven't been since servants' wages ceased being medieval. Each house has a long history intimately illustrated in its architecture, embellishments, furnishings, and portraits. In its Stately Homes, England gives more for less money than any other country.

But you can overdo S.H. visiting. The magnificence becomes oppressive, even tedious. When you find yourself saying, "But I wouldn't want to *live* there!" the time has come to stop.

As we go along in this book, we will mention sightworthy mansions. Here we recommend two, both within easy reach of London, that are rewarding both in themselves and in contrast with each other.

One is Knole in Sevenoaks, twenty-four miles from London—a fifteenth-century archbishops' palace built around an earlier structure and acquiring additions of further centuries as the seat of the Sackvilles. Enormous, it is one of the oldest, most interesting, and most atmospheric of the Stately Homes. It contains, among other things, a priceless collection of early English furniture.

The second is Syon House of the Dukes of Northumberland, in Brentford near Richmond. It was filled by Robert Adam with such a wealth of interior charm and beauty that it might be called an eighteenth-century ducal palace, although its basic structure is much older. There are Adam walls, ceilings, fireplaces, mirrors, carpets, and furniture. The Long Gallery in Syon House is an Adam masterpiece.

Knole is open April to October, and Syon from May to October. Before you go, check days and hours; they are subject to change.

Among the London Transport's conducted coach (bus) tours, No. 5 takes in Knole; No. 9 goes to Syon House and Hampton Court. Fares are under three dollars.

London Transport also offers tours to other Stately Homes, notably Hatfield House, which is worth seeing.

When preparing your trip to England, ask the British Travel Association for its free color-illustrated booklet, *Stately Homes in Britain*. In London, you can buy (for about fifty cents) *Historic Houses in Great Britain and Northern Ireland*, a handsome annually updated publication which gives full details of how to get where, hours, admission fees, whether lunch is served, and so on about hundreds of houses.

About half the open-to-the-public Stately Homes, and most of the best, are concentrated within a fifty-mile radius of London. The standard excursions of London's tourist agents take in several of them. As you travel about England, you will find, posted in your hotel, information about the Stately Homes in its vicinity.

# MOSS IS
# THE STUFF

If you're in London on or about October 21, go to the Law Courts
—located where Fleet Street joins the Strand—to watch a play
highly fantastical—the Quitrent Services.

"*Oyez! oyez! oyez!*" cries the usher opening the prologue. After
preliminaries the presiding personage in a black silk gown, lace
stock, velvet court suit, and full-bottomed wig commands: "Tenants and occupiers of a piece of waste ground called the Moors in
the county of Salop, come forth and do your services!"

A gentleman in a cutaway and pin-striped trousers walks to a
table on which lie two bundles of twigs, a billhook, and a small
hatchet. Solemnly he takes up the hatchet and chops a bundle of
faggots in half. With the billhook he chops the second bundle.

The personage, after a judicial pause, pronounces two words:
"Good service!" The twig-chopper bows and retires amid a relieved
buzz of comment.

But hush! Order in court! Now the personage is summoning
the tenants and occupiers of the Forge in the parish of St. Clement
Dane.

The same man of the cutaway and the billhook responds. He
goes to an adjacent table where he takes up one by one—counting
aloud slowly and distinctly before laying each item down—sixty-
one nails and six oversize horseshoes. When he has finished, the
personage speaks: "Good number!"

Thus, for another year the tenants of the Moors and the Forge
are secure. They have paid their rent. That is, the Corporation of
London, represented by the City Solicitor, has paid their rent for

them to the Crown, represented by the Queen's Remembrancer.

But there are no tenants. The Moors and the Forge don't exist—except in a peculiarly English sort of way.

It's like this:

At some time not known a king of England gave somebody and his heirs for eternity a piece of land called the Moors somewhere in Shropshire for the price, or nominal annual rent, of one billhook and one hatchet, each of which had to be proved of good quality by cutting clean through a faggot of wood. (In time the size of the billhook and hatchet shrank; so did the faggots.)

In the same way, at some other time also unknown but thought to be in the twelfth century, another king of England gave a farrier property called the Forge somewhere on the Strand in return for sixty-one nails and six horseshoes a year. (The shoes were not for a six-legged horse; two were spares. The nails represent ten per shoe with one spare.)

The ceremonies of paying the rent on these two properties were well established by the time royal records began to be kept.

So why not forget the whole thing?

No! This is no ordinary country—this is *England*. The properties and their quitrents are on record. Therefore, they exist. If they exist, they have tenants who must pay the rent. The unknown tenants of these two unknown properties are, by eternally temporary default of flesh-and-blood people, the Corporation of London.

Don't laugh. Remember that this comedy has been played for at least 750 years, which is awesome.

(Those horseshoes, by the way, are outsize because they were made to fit a knight's battle steed, the original farrier having been horseshoer and armor-repairer to the Knights Templar, where the Temple now is.)

About fifty parcels of land are held "of the Crown." They are gifts for some service rendered to a king or queen by a nobleman, a borough, an organization, a favorite. A quitrent was exacted in return. The quitrent could be anything the generous or capricious monarch happened to think of.

A Scottish baron holds his property on condition that he blow three bugle blasts whenever the sovereign hunts the stag on the nearby moor.

The Marquis of Ailesbury, who holds Savernake Forest of the

Crown, must be prepared to tootle on his twelfth-century ivory horn when the sovereign pays him a visit.

The lord of Archer's Court in Kent must accompany the monarch on Channel crossings with a silver bowl in case of royal seasickness.

Kidwelly Castle in Wales must provide the monarch, when he (or she) happens by, the services of a knight in battle dress.

The laird of Dunstaffnage Castle, Scotland, can call his place his own only if he spends one night each year in the roofless castle ruins.

The Duke of Wellington and the Duke of Marlborough must each pay a flag a year for their right to own and occupy the palaces built for their illustrious ancestors by the Crown in gratitude for the victories of Waterloo and Blenheim.

The village of Ketton in Rutland county must provide the sovereign with leggings. It has been doing this since Saxon times— at least nine hundred years.

The Munro of Foulis (Scotland) holds whatever he holds on condition he pay the Crown annually a bucket of snow.

There are many who hold this land or that privilege so long as they pay a rose, or a bouquet ("plucked in midsummer," reads one command), or flags, or gloves.

The official who has to keep the books and collect the tokens is the Royal Remembrancer. He has other chores. For example, he attends the swearing-in of the new Lord Mayor of London. On this occasion his business is to wear a three-cornered hat on top of his full-bottomed wig, to show the Corporation of London that the Crown is supreme, keeping its hat on, by proxy, while everyone else has to take his off. The Remembrancer's office is so old that its origin is lost. He must have been the earliest accountant-royal.

One wonders what his office and staff are like, what sort of books he keeps, what receipts he gives, where he stores the mossy stuff he collects. The Wellingtons and Marlboroughs have together paid him, by now, approximately three hundred flags. What does he do with them? Or with the nine hundred years of leggings? Or the roses and bouquets—are they kept pressed in Gutenberg Bibles?

As to those nails and horseshoes paid by the "tenants" of the Forge—sixty-one nails and six horseshoes per year are bound to create a storage problem after a few hundred years. But it turns out that the same horseshoes and nails have been in use for ages. Every year the Remembrancer takes them out of his files, dusts them off, carries them to the court, and after the ceremony wraps them up and files them away again. So that's all right. But they are a special case. Other things have got to be paid.

What happens if someone neglects to pay, or is unable to deliver, or delays? We see a laird in Scotland, just come into his inheritance, reading the stern note—

To the Munro of Foulis
Sir: I am directed by Her Majesty to bring to your attention the fact that your annual Bucket of Snow is in arrears. . . .

The Munro replies Special Delivery that he dispatched one Bucket of Snow by registered mail in plenty of time, and holds H.M. Post Office receipt No. TX–7782513-stroke 8 in proof withal and therewith.

By return courier OHMS our Remembrancer informs the Munro that investigation reveals a bucket of dirty water received, and calls attention to the terms of the holding which require that the Bucket of Snow be not only dispatched but delivered *as snow,* and reminds his lairdship that there is the Tower. . . .

But there are other traditional survivals less worrisome and more seeable. Every issue of the BTA's monthly, *Coming Events in Britain,* lists festivals and rites on the calendar. Such as

Proclamation of the Beast Mart, Boston, Lincolnshire
Tolling the Devil's Knell, Dewsbury, Yorkshire
Mason's Walk, Melrose, Roxburghshire
Haxey Hood Game, Haxey, Lincolnshire
Annual Dicing for the Maids Money, Guildford, Surrey
Up-Helly-A', Lerwick, Shetland Islands.

For some unknown reason the town of High Wycombe near London weighs its mayor on November 9. The scales are set up in the center of town, and not only the mayor but his lady and the aldermen are—as it were—thrown in.

Hungerford, a fishermen's resort in Berkshire on the London–Bath road, has its Hocktide Festival on the second Tuesday after Easter. This has a slight dash of sex in it, involving two "tutti-men" in top hats and morning coats carrying bouquets at the top of long staves, an orange-scatterer with feathered hat and a sack of oranges, and all the kissable girls in town. The oranges are, in a manner of speaking, a red herring. They are thrown to the men, old women, and children to distract them while the tutti-men go from house to house collecting kisses from the girls. These are supposed to be mere pecks on the cheek, but one never knows. There is neighborly hilarity.

The Olney Pancake Race on Shrove Tuesday is more widely known, since the town of Liberal, Kansas, challenged Olney (pronounced *Oony*) for a transatlantic pancake trophy. Olney's event is first known to have been held in 1445, which is before even Indians came to Kansas. It brings crowds, and publicity. On signal, about a score of aproned women run a course of 415 yards, each tossing a pancake in a pan. The finish is at the parish church, where the verger gives the winner a buss, called for some reason the Kiss of Peace. We like to think the race originated in some forgetful housewife's last-minute dash to the church, frying pan in hand—but obviously it could not have been that simple.

A really ancient affair, about nine centuries old, is the marital-happiness contest for the flitch, or slab, of bacon at Dunmow in Essex. Aspirants must appear before a judge and jury of maidens and bachelors, and prove that their married lives have been un-marred by any "household brawles or contentious strife," and that they haven't, for the last year and a day, repented of marriage even in thought. The trial lends itself to the kind of cross-examination not always easy to keep within bounds. It bowled along hilariously until the press woke up to it. Now it is a self-conscious show.

November 11 is not only Armistice Day; it is also St. Martin's. More than two hundred years ago the founder and builder of the church of St. Martin in Fenny Stratford, Buckinghamshire, left a trust ordaining that six tiny cannon be fired annually to commemorate the church's erection. The cannon, each the size of a quart mug, are known as Poppers and are on view. (Nearby is Stony Stratford, whose two inns, The Cock and The Bull, gave rise to the phrase "a cock-and-bull story.")

On Easter Monday in Hallaton, a village near Market Harborough, Leicestershire, they celebrate "Hare-Pie Scrambling and Bottle-Kicking" Day. After church service a pie, originally of hare but now of beef, is cut up and scrambled for on the rectory lawn. Then is the turn of the bottles—no longer bottles but now small casks filled with beer. And instead of being kicked they are wrestled for. How did this originate? It seems that a village woman was once upon a time attacked by a bull as she was crossing a field. A running hare diverted the bull's attention and she escaped. As a thank-offering she bequeathed a field to pay for these festivities. They don't seem entirely to the point, and must be hard on the rectory lawn.

If you visit Oakham, capital of England's small county, Rutland, you will see—in the hall of a Norman castle—walls adorned with horseshoes, some of enormous size. Every peer of the realm who passes through Rutland has to present a horseshoe to the castle. If he hasn't a spare he must borrow it from his horse. The custom has existed since the Conqueror's day and no one knows how it started. But the castle has a remarkable collection of horseshoes, because Rutland is on the road to one of the great hunting regions. In recent years noblemen occasionally motor that way on purpose with a specially made super-horseshoe.

Customs do change. For hundreds of years the sovereign chose the sheriffs of the shires by marking a list with a pen or stylus. But one time, when the list was brought to Queen Elizabeth I, she was knitting in her garden and no quill was handy. The impatient Queen wouldn't wait; she stabbed holes in the list with her knitting needle. Since then, every monarch uses a knitting needle for the job.

The ceremonial of the King's Champion was the most dramatic of all medieval survivals. After the coronation, the King, newly crowned, sat at the banquet table in Westminster Hall. In came the Lord High Constable, the Earl Marshal, and the Lord High Steward, all on horseback. Hard upon their heels came the King's Champion wearing the King's second-best suit of armor, riding his second-best horse, and carrying lance and shield. A herald blew a trumpet blast and proclaimed: "If any person, of what degree soever, shall deny or gainsay our Sovereign Lord [monarch's name here] to be the rightful heir to the Crown of England, or that he ought not to enjoy the same, here is his Champion, who saith he lieth sore and is a false traitor, being ready in person to combat him."

This was done at three advances to the King's place at table, the Champion each time throwing down his iron gauntlet, *bang!* No challenger ever spoke up. The most difficult part of the Champion's task was to back his horse out of the great hall.

The drama was last played at the coronation of George IV in 1820. It could not have survived Victoria and her times. But in every generation the Dymock family produces, as did the Marmions before, the King's Champion. Now he carries the royal standard in the coronation procession, dressed in a tabard like the Jack in a deck of playing cards, and has nothing to throw.

# ERASMUS VS.
# THE MAN
# FROM UTAH

The man from Utah went to England to see his relations, visit the ancestral places, and look at the society his forebears came from. He was welcomed by his favorite cousin Amy. Two other cousins, her sisters, lived next door.

"When she suggested we call on them, I agreed, thinking we would do as we do in America—walk through the garden, slip in at a side door and say 'Hi!' But I met British formality. Goodness no! We must dress up, don hats and gloves, and walk sedately up that lovely street to ring the front doorbell of the house and be properly introduced."

He did not describe the event further, but we know what happened as if we had been there—as, in a way, we have. Little handshakes are exchanged, little mutters muttered, and after some complicated footwork and self-conscious deferring, all get settled in chairs geometrically laid out. The talk is stiff and correct. The sherry appears, but fails to loosen tongues or erode protocol. The man from Utah (or Tennessee, or New Hampshire) marvels that these people speak the same language as his, that some bear the same name and are nourished by the same blood.

The Englishman and his wife do manage, given time and not pushed, to be at ease with strangers. Even Houdini needed time to work out of the strait jacket and manacles. The English make being human difficult at the very outset by their hats, gloves, and other proprieties. They are fearful of displaying even the minor feelings.

'Twas not always thus. The scholar Erasmus wrote to a friend in the year 1500:

There are here ladies divinely beautiful, the kindest and most fascinating creatures in the world. . . . There is besides a custom which it would be impossible to praise too much. Wherever you go everyone welcomes you with a kiss, and the same on bidding farewell. You call again, when there is more kissing. If your friends call on you, they kiss you, and when they take their leave kisses again go round. You meet an acquaintance anywhere and you are kissed until you are tired. In short, turn where you will, there are kisses, kisses everywhere. . . .

If it were any lesser observer than Erasmus! Yet Sam Pepys' diary and Boswell's writings give a picture of easy social give-and-take, at least among equals. England has changed, has turned topsy-turvy, since Gothic-Stuart-Georgian times. The nowadays Englishman considers a handshake going rather far in familiarity. A hand on the shoulder is in some circles an emotional debauch.

And those "ladies divinely beautiful, the kindest and most fascinating creatures in the world," kissing and being kissed! If the BTA, which can do wonders, could only bring back that old Merrie England!

# MISCELLANEA

## § *YOUR HEALTH*

Consider, if your health is uncertain or if you belong to the senior-citizen class that does a good part of the traveling these days, whether you should have a medical-dental look-over before you go. Your physician will advise you on medications to take along.

Dramamine or bonamine can save you from distress if you are susceptible to motion sickness. Most air and ocean liners carry one or both.

England is a clean country. You needn't fear dysentery. We know from personal experience that British physicians and surgeons are excellent. Should you need one, the manager of your hotel or the American Embassy will recommend one. Major hotels have resident physicians. If you try to see a doctor in his surgery (office) you'll find it crowded with his "panel" patients. It's easier to phone and have him come to you outside office hours.

If you are dependent on eyeglasses, better take an extra pair. A prescription is not as good as an extra because you may have to wait a week or ten days for lenses.

Some American visitors, among them vociferous critics of the welfare state, have taken advantage of it by getting free medical treatment. News of this has got about, not increasing American standing. A de luxe hotel physician charges about nine dollars a visit. In the country the fee is about three dollars. Only a true cheapskate would try to squirm out of paying such sums.

Handy items to take along are Band-aid, aspirin, and a clinical thermometer. They are sold everywhere in England too.

Illness is no respecter of vacations. Many travelers get excited and do too many things. Some begin on the ship by overeating, overdrinking, and overexposure to the sun.

Relax. Take it easy. It's all in fun.

# § *MONEY*

The French Revolution gave the world Napoleon, the Scarlet Pimpernel, Madame Tussaud, and the metric system.

We Americans learned from those antique Reds how handy the decimal system is, and based our dollars-and-cents system on it. Our forefathers, alas, failed to extend it to weights and measures. The English, who still talk weight in "stone," learned nothing. They deserve credit, however, for having abandoned, along with the rest of the world, the Roman notation.

So English money resembles cricket—both are modified chaos. It must be admitted that the actual paper notes (the word *bill* is not used in this connection) *look* more like real money than American greenbacks. The notes of various denominations are of different sizes, which helps an almost blind man who has left his spectacles at home. The coins look like business, too; the half-crown, for example, though it is worth only thirty-five cents, looks more important than a half-dollar.

The money comes in pounds, shillings, and pence, written £, s, and d. £ is for *libra*, a pound; the *d*, which your host country got from the Roman *denarius*, it didn't have the heart to Anglicize. The sum of $34.64 (more or less, and just by way of example) is written £12 7s 5d. (Just for practice, try to figure 15 per cent of the amount, your hired-car chauffeur waiting with impatient palm.)

The pound is currently worth $2.80, but you will get a few cents less. A pound contains twenty shillings, each worth about fourteen cents. A dollar, then, is equal to seven shillings. Twelve pence (not pennies) make the shilling. An English penny is worth a fraction more than the American cent; the four pennies (not pence) the nationalized telephone box swallows up for a local call come to five cents, or half of what the American Telephone and Telegraph Company exacts.

The paper money you will be handling comes in five-pound, one-pound, and ten-shilling notes; that is, $14, $2.80, and $1.40. The coins, from high to low, are half-crown (two shillings six-pence, written 2/6), the florin (two shillings), the shilling, the sixpence, the threepenny bit (or *thruppence*), the penny, and the half-penny (pronounced *hayp'ny*). Certain goods and services are reckoned in guineas, for which no coin exists. The guinea is one pound plus one shilling, or $2.94.

Everyone not British agrees that this nonsystem is a nuisance. Curse it roundly, then learn to live with it.

Warning to belligerent Americans: Don't say, "What's that in real money?"—especially in a pub. Someone who weighs more stone than you do might not think it funny. (Stone? Ah, yes. A stone equals 14 pounds—not the $2.80 pounds but the 16-ounce ones. If you tip the scales at 160 you weigh, in England, 11 stone 6 pounds.)

The end is in sight. The European Common Market has com-pelled the government to consider a revolutionary change to a decimal system in currency, like the American, and the metric system for weights and measures, thereby out-progressing the U.S.A. But such things aren't done overnight.

| BRITISH NOTES | AMERICAN EQUIVALENT |
|---|---|
| £5 (five pounds) | $14.00 |
| £1 (one pound) | 2.80 |
| 10/ or 10s (ten shillings) | 1.40 |

| BRITISH COINS | |
|---|---|
| 2/6 (2 shillings and sixpence, spoken 2 and 6, or half-a-crown) | 35 cents |
| 2s (2 shillings, or florin) | 28 cents |
| 1s (one shilling) | 14 cents |
| 6d (sixpence) | 7 cents |
| 3d (thruppence) | 4 cents |
| 1d (penny) | 1 cent |
| ½d (hayp'ny) | ½ cent |

| AMERICAN | BRITISH |
|---|---|
| $100 | £35/14s/3d |
| 50 | £17/17s/1d |
| 20 | £7/2s/10d |
| 10 | £3/11s/5d |
| 5 | £1/15s/9d |

# § TIPPING

When you visit the St. Cross almshouses in Winchester (more about this later) you will get the Wayfarer's Dole which has been handed out to pilgrims since the Middle Ages. And in no matter what country you may travel, you will be paying out a wayfarer's dole of your own to a long line of porters, waiters, chambermaids, cab drivers, hairdressers, and guides. The situation is at its worst in the U.S.A., probably at its easiest in England.

Tipping is a petty nuisance of travel. (But neither can you escape it by staying in your home town.) St. Cross gives you now a standardized one-inch cube of bread and a thimbleful of ale, but tipping is not standardized any more than it's legalized. "Just whatever you think, sir," says Boots in the hotel. Every occasion calling for *pourboire-trinkgeld* becomes a crisis of your character. How much? You don't want to be a cheapskate. How much, then? Nor do you want to earn the veiled contempt of the servitor by overtipping. Well, how much?

A few hotels try to take the problem out of your hands by adding 10 per cent to the bill. This solves nothing. First, a tip is a reward for service, not an automatic bite. Secondly, a small inn-hotel with a tiny staff (you end up by carrying your own bag down from your room) seldom gives you 10 per cent worth of service. Thirdly, the grand caravanserai de luxe which charges twenty-five dollars a day doesn't give you $2.50 worth of service unless you're a problem guest who has worried everyone sick.

We stick—in principle, for our courage sometimes runs short—to the policy that the tip is not automatic, and that surly or negligent attendance puts the attendant beyond the pale. But we tend to overtip the eager beaver—the receptionist with the genuine smile, the alert and friendly chambermaid, the porter who is quick to make the trunk call and look up the trains.

*Waiter:* Give 10–12 per cent in a modest-priced restaurant, 15 per cent in the higher class. But first see that a service charge is not added to the bill. Wine waiter? You can't take arms against a sea of troubles, but you *can* handle this nuisance. The wine or beer will be on the bill, and you can jolly well tell waiter or wine waiter that this tip includes the drinks.

*Railway-station porter:* A conservative Englishman tips a shilling for one average piece of luggage, sixpence each for additional bags. Size and weight should be considered and also the distance the items are carried. We'd say 1/6 for a single suitcase, sixpence each for the rest, with a bonus of an extra shilling if you like your man. If he takes you to the platform, waits for the train, stows the stuff in the racks, and gives you a smiling "Have a pleasant trip, sir," he should not be short-changed in the coin of the realm.

*Taxi:* Sixpence is the absolute minimum for a 2/6 short-haul fare. Add thruppence for each 1/6 thereafter; roughly, three cents for each twenty. Clear? If your fare comes to 5/6, roughly seventy-five cents, the tip should be a shilling. If your man helps with the luggage he expects a mite more.

*Barber:* England is not Utopia, but it *is* a country in which you can't spend more than five shillings (seventy cents) for a haircut. An American should be so overjoyed that he will be glad to part with a shilling tip. In country towns you will get as good a haircut for thirty-five cents. Sixpence tip should take care of that, but you will add thruppence to it when you think of the boy in the barber shop back home who takes a dime for hanging your coat on a hook.

Although your boat trip over is not our business in this book, we think you might not frown on some words about the size of the ocean-liner gratuity. Many a guidebook says give 10 per cent of your one-way fare. This is making rather free with your money. We are glad to have our own hunch OK'd by the British Travel Association's booklet "Travelers Guide to Britain," page 16: "Take about 7 per cent. . . ." Our practice has been to stand firm on 7½ per cent, and then at the last moment weaken, and put a little more into each envelope. The room steward and waiter should get the bulk. If you have danced and *used* the services of the deck steward a lot, don't forget him and the band.

In favor of plane travel besides its speed is the no-nonsense about the wayfarer's dole. This leaves you free to worry about other matters.

HISTORICAL NOTE. The word *tip* and the odious practice are thought to have originated in the coffee-house craze which struck London in the late seventeenth century. A conspiracy between management and waiters put up a box with a slot in it and letters *T.I.P.S.*, standing for *To Insure Prompt Service*. A few years later there was a bloodless Glorious Revolution, and James II had to flee the country. But there was no revolution against *T.I.P.S.*

# § *THE TELEPHONE*

An American trying to use this instrument in England usually gives an unconscious imitation of Robert Benchley. While a queue forms outside the call box (telephone booth), he fumbles for his pennies, reads the instructions, dials, and then frantically shouts while making grimaces of appeasement at the faces of the waiting public. Everybody knows what's happening and can't understand it. Why doesn't the idiot push Button A? Even a child can do it—an English child.

To begin with, you have to have four pennies. Since you also need pennies for the Public Conveniences, the large coppers you carry at all times present a weight problem.

Well, here you are with your four pennies. You insert them in rapid succession, hear the dial tone that means Open for Business, dial, and are answered. It is at this point that you must push Button A. Otherwise, you can hear your party but he can't hear you. You push B to get your pennies back when there's no answer.

It's simple, but the pushbutton habit can only be acquired with time and practice. The chap at the other end is stupid. When he can't hear anything, instead of saying, "Listen, old thing, just push Button A, will you?" he hangs up.

Most London hotels now have room phones; you pass your communication problem on to the hotel operator. Country hotels are seldom so equipped, and you can't beg Reception to get your number for you. He (more usually, she) can't be bothered with your private affairs. The porter is your man. But too often the porter, just like other Englishmen, can't get it through his head that you require anything further from him than introduction to the call box in the lobby.

For a long-distance (trunk) call, communicate with the operator, who will inform you how much it will cost. You then pop out of the box and try to find the necessary change. You can talk only for the time you have paid for in advance. If you haven't finished, you have to start all over again feeding the coins into the slot.

The system is more cumbersome than the AT&T's—and, as we noted, costs half as much.

WARNING. When Operator on a trunk call says, "You're through," don't hang up! She means, "Here's your party—start talking!"

In London, if you telephone ASK 9211, an excellent clear-voiced recording will give you the day's principal events of tourist interest. That's the easiest way of finding out you've missed the Changing of the Guard at Buckingham Palace—it was yesterday, it will be tomorrow.

WEA 2211 gives you weather forecast for the London area.

# § CLIMATE AND CLOTHING

At both extremes the English climate is milder than the American. Having little experience of 90-degree heat, the English think of a run of warmth in the upper 70s as a heat wave. Having no experience of below-zero weather, they think 33 is arctic—only, with typical understatement, they refer to it as "a bit fresh."

In the summer in England you may get a bout of uncomfortable humidity, but nothing approaching the dog days of back home. In winter, few days are really heavy-coat days; we have managed well enough in a sweater under a medium-weight Burberry. The traveler between October and March should be prepared with woolen underwear in his kit. British interiors are for Americans underheated, and flannels are as welcome indoors as out. (They sell these things in England, by the way.)

Evening dress is not required except for the most formal occasions, which include opera at Glyndebourne and dancing at certain hotels.

Take rainwear.

# § *LAUNDRY*

For the traveler who doesn't stop long in one place, getting the laundry done is a problem. Thanks to the nylon-dacron and the drip-dry, it isn't too serious. Traveling about six months out of the year, we have discovered that the easiest thing is to wash our own. That's where the gas or electric heater in your room helps. Non-drip-dry can be saved up for the longer stops.

There's usually a printed card in your hotel room telling you what to do to get laundered and how much it will cost you. Hotel laundry prices are about the same as in the U.S. Dry cleaning is a bit of a nuisance in a land where rush service is rare, but pressing is quick.

TIP. If you really *must* have something washed and ironed, you'll find a hotel maid willing to do work after hours.

# § *USEFUL ADDRESSES*

For free and unpackaged tourists, the most important addresses are those of the British Travel Association (BTA). Its information centers are staffed by experts who know the answers to your questions—including some you may not think of asking. They hand out advice and literature. The London offices will, if you like, get you an Authorized Guide.

BTA offices in the U.S. and Canada:
New York: 680 Fifth Avenue, New York 19.
Chicago: 39 S. LaSalle Street, Chicago 3.
Los Angeles: 606 S. Hill Street, Los Angeles 14.
Toronto: 90 Adelaide Street West.
Vancouver: 661 Howe Street.
BTA in London:
64-65 St. James's Street, S.W.1, tel. MAYfair 9191.
Australia House, Strand, W.C.2, tel. TEMple Bar 2060.
South Africa House, Trafalgar Square, tel. WHItehall 4488 (summer only).

In London, the American Express Company, at 6 Haymarket, S.W.1, is a good place to make your mailing address. Notify your correspondents to write "Client's Mail Dept." on the envelope. Have your passport when calling for mail. The company maintains clean W.C.'s in the basement, and is one of the few places where you can get a drink of water without trouble. It also sells tickets, tours, and travelers' checks.

The American Embassy is in Grosvenor Square, Mayfair.

The First National City Bank of New York has a handsome branch in Berkeley Square, Mayfair.

Pan American World Airways' office (under one of the largest overhead signs in England) is on the south side of Piccadilly.

Trust Houses, Ltd., which runs 232 hotels and inns, maintains an office at 81 Piccadilly, W.1, tel. GROsvenor 1846, where you can make London and provincial hotel bookings—but only to its own hotels.

Thomas Cook & Son, the world's first travel agency, has its chief office at Berkeley Street, W.1.

British Railways (BR) has a London Travel Center on Lower Regent Street just off Piccadilly Circus. Here you can have a trip laid out for you and get helpful literature.

London Transport (LT), which runs the Underground, buses, and Green Line longer-distance motor coaches, has an information office in the Piccadilly Underground station in addition to its less central Central Office in the St. James's Underground station. It sells many useful booklets and gives away a few.

For various services—baby-sitter, steno, housemaid, companion, apartment, chauffeur, and even guide—try Universal Aunts, 61 Wilton Place, S.W.1, tel. SLOane 5101. If you have a special problem that no other agency seems able to cope with, try the Aunts. It's a profit organization, so expect to pay a fee.

Pharmacies (chemists) in London that stay open all night: John Bell & Croydon on Wigmore Street at Welbeck, an immense place; Boots on Regent Street off Piccadilly Circus.

Physicians: your hotel or the American Embassy will help you. In case of emergency outside your hotel, direct a cab to take you to the casualty ward of the nearest hospital.

Post offices are many. You are never far from one.

If you are armed with some useful addresses of your own, look them up in the phone book before traveling out to them. Even in England people and offices move.

# PART II
# A WEEK IN LONDON

# GETTING

# ABOUT

# LONDON

London Transport (LT) is an awesome municipal institution. It runs what is probably the largest city transport system in the world, consisting of buses, suburban coaches, and underground railways. The only privately owned transportation is in the form of six thousand taxicabs.

LT's operations extend not only to Greater London and its eight million inhabitants, but beyond in a radius of thirty miles from Charing Cross.

LT publishes many handy tourist guides, some free. It issues free maps of all its services, and free leaflets about art galleries, historic houses, museums, and public spectacles. Among its inexpensive publications are:

*Visitor's London*, a guide to places of interest in London and environs, with photos and pocket subway and bus maps.

*Theatergoer's London*, a pocket guide to theaters, with historical background.

These and the others may be had at the main office, 55 Broadway, S.W.1 (the St. James's Underground station), and at the Inquiry Office in the Piccadilly Circus station. The small diagram-map of the Underground may be had from the ticket-seller at any station.

# § *THE UNDERGROUND*

Decibelologists (noise-measurers) estimate that in New York's subway when the express thunders by your local platform the din is that of artillery fire; at the corner of Wells and Lake streets in Chicago, the pounding of the elevated trains overhead is only about one cannon less.

One expert reported that if you had a roaring lion for a seat mate on the Broadway–Seventh Avenue train in Manhattan you wouldn't know it by ear alone. But no self-respecting beast (and a lion *is* self-respecting) would be involved in such an inferno of noise and smells.

There's nothing of this in London. A lion would enjoy the Underground, and so will you. LT's underground system is better than anything in New York, Boston, or Chicago. It doesn't keep breaking down like New York's. Its seats are upholstered and have armrests. The people are better mannered. The coaches are cleaner. In every second coach smoking is allowed. Signs and diagrams tell you where you are and how to get to where you want to go. Stations are clearly lettered. Junction or transfer points are well marked. The escalators move twice as fast as the few and timorous ones in Manhattan. They are wide enough for two abreast; the code is to stand on the right, leaving the left lane for people in a hurry.

Fares are based on travel distance. You state your destination at the ticket window and are told how much, and are given a ticket which you give up at destination. There are seven lines. You don't need a transfer to change from one to another at the junction points, nor do you have to pay another fare.

CAUTION.    Wide-skirted women should watch out for sudden drafts, particularly in the tubes.


§   *BUSES AND COACHES*

Lumbering two-decker buses flow continually through London's streets, well-marked fore and aft. Bus stops are also well marked. You don't compete for getting aboard, you queue up. English buses employ conductors; almost to a man—women. Tell her your destination, for you are charged by length of journey. Upper deck front is a box seat on London. LT's free leaflets tell how to do London by bus: "Hop on a Bus," "London from a Bus Top," and "London's Town Houses." Could any municipal transit system do more? Yes, and this one does. It operates a two-hour circular bus tour of the chief landmarks of London which covers twenty miles of the West End and the City (the financial district). The fare is currently just under fifty cents, children half price. The vehicles leave from Buckingham Palace Road, between Eccleston Bridge and Elizabeth Bridge, every day of the week hourly between 11 A.M. and 5 P.M., except 1 P.M. No seats reserved.

To get leaflets and other transport information, telephone ABBey 1234 giving your name and address; you'll receive them next day.

The technical difference between London red bus and green coach is, besides color, that the coach is a one-decker and goes as far as thirty miles out to the suburbs, taking in such places of tourist interest as Eton-Windsor, High Wycombe, St. Albans, Box Hill, and the Whipsnade (free-ranging) Zoo. Luggage is limited to small parcels (at conductor's discretion). LT publishes route maps and schedules.

EXCURSION TRANSPORT. Cook's, American Express, and other travel agencies operate various See-London tours.

# § TAXIS

A humorous character of New Canaan, Connecticut, bought an old London taxi some years ago and brought it home for laughs. We hope he's caught on to the fact that the joke is not on the English.

The London taxi continues to be better than the American. It is easier to get into and out of, has more headroom, and there's ample space beside the driver for luggage. It can turn on a sixpence. The fares are lower, and tips can be confined to 10 per cent (but not less than sixpence). Figuring the 10 per cent is something you can occupy your mind with en route.

Give your command before you board, for the English love of privacy necessitates a glass partition between you and the driver. This glass wall spares you the heart-to-heart talks New York cabbies are addicted to.

It's no use asking James to go faster than the speed limit no matter how great your hurry.

Unfortunately the cramped sedan-type of taxi is coming into the streets in spite of bitter opposition. Wherever possible, take the old.

## § BY BOAT ON THE THAMES

At this writing, four or five companies operate motor launches on the Thames from April to October. The time span is broadening, the companies increasing in number in this pleasant revival of waterborne traffic. Charing Cross Pier is the main "station," and boats run as far east as Greenwich and as far west as Hampton Court. One service operates every twenty minutes from Westminster Pier. Stopping points are the Tower of London, London Bridge, Battersea Pleasure Gardens, Kew Gardens, Richmond, Kingston, Hampton Court. The Port of London Authority operates cruises to the docks area on certain days of the week. These Thames trips are excellent for an offbeat view of London.

## § ON FOOT

Traffic keeps to the left.

This makes for a tricky little problem. The habit of looking left for advancing traffic when you're about to cross the street is automatic. Now you've got to do the opposite.

WARNING. The greatest risk you run in London (and in England) is stepping off the curb after looking for the traffic in the wrong direction. Develop a new habit: stop at the curb (kerb)— *stop*, not pause—and look *both ways* before crossing.

THE ZEBRA. That broad band of black-and-white stripes you see on a street is a safety lane for the pedestrian. It's called a zebra (*zehbra*, not *zeebra*). When you step out on it to cross the street, the traffic comes magically to a stop.

Before we got used to it, when we saw a car charging up we'd pull up short in the middle of the street—and find ourselves creating a traffic jam in no time at all. The thing works! But as veteran pedestrians, we advise you never wholly to trust drivers, even in England. It will be small consolation to you, as you get picked up and carried off, to know that you were in the right because you were on a zebra.

# LONDON
# HOTELS

London is served by scores of hotels and double-scores of boarding houses and bed-and-breakfast places. The latter are to be found principally in Bloomsbury, Bayswater, and Kensington, but no middle-class residential district is without them. New hotels are being built, but not fast enough. The situation is not satisfactory. Accommodation is difficult to come by even in what used to be the off periods. And what exists is not so good as it ought to be, considering both the price tag and the fact that this is the twentieth century, not the nineteenth.

The de luxe hotels are in the West End, with two exceptions: the old, established Savoy between the Strand and the Thames, which is all suites, and the shining new seventeen-story Carlton Tower on Cadogan Place in Knightsbridge, which is modern American and a beauty. We stayed at this one and thoroughly enjoyed being pampered.

The second all-American is the Westbury on Bond Street. The third, and biggest yet, is the London Hilton on Park Lane at Stanhope Gate, with 32 floors containing, among other things, 540 rooms, four restaurants, five bars and cocktail lounges, and a rooftop night club.

Farther north on Park Lane are the Dorchester and Grosvenor House. The Grosvenor had the honor of denting our pad of travelers' cheques for ten agreeable days. Nearby, on Piccadilly, are the Ritz and the Berkeley, and just off the famous street is the May Fair. Claridge's and the Connaught are two very-English aristocratic hotels near Grosvenor Square, which ironically has become an American enclave.

In the grade below—it has sometimes seemed like two grades, or at least a grade and a half—we have stayed at the "first-class" Mount Royal and St. Ermin's. The first is near Marble Arch, and is a vast tourist-warren with inadequate staff and elevator service. We enjoyed staying there for long spells five or six years ago, but something has happened to it or to us. St. Ermin's we liked as nice-Edwardian in atmosphere, but our unlovely room with the heater-switch way under the bed soon palled as a humorous adventure. Brown's Hotel, Trust Houses' leader, just off Bond Street, is a very English hotel for which we never did succeed in getting a booking; it is very popular and we recommend it. Trust Houses' Hertford, on Bayswater Road near Marble Arch, should be ready when this meets your eye.

Other possibilities in this first-class group are the Park Lane on Piccadilly, the Hyde Park in Knightsbridge, and White's on Bayswater Road across from where Hyde Park merges into Kensington Gardens.

The next class is called "Moderate," and the only hotel of this type that we know intimately is the Cumberland, a British version of a Times Square hotel, right at Marble Arch. If you like to see people, people, people, the Cumberland is your place. Its lobby is one of London's most popular places of rendezvous. It has an excellent grill room and a unique coffee shop. We have fond memories of it because in winter its idea of "well-heated" met ours. Its drawback is that of any nine-hundred-room hotel—you get wholesale treatment. As at the Mount Royal, the staff is too small to handle its chores expeditiously, but the Cumberland is more efficiently run. We have heard Fleming's and the Green Park well spoken of.

Some fairly pampered friends of ours found the Ambassador cheerful and pleasant. This all-rooms-with-bath hotel, at Lancaster Gate, on Hyde Park's north side a little more than half a mile west of Marble Arch, will charge you slightly more than $10 double. A new 422-room hotel, the Mount Pleasant, in Central London (W.C.1), charges a top rate under $10 for double room with bath and breakfast.

The next grade is "Inexpensive," which does not mean that you have hit bottom. We know two hotels in this bracket that gave us pleasanter times than some of the higher-priced ones. The King

Charles in Cromwell Road, Earl's Court, is run by a young couple who take pride in it, and do well by their dining room too. Tennis stars stay here during the annual Wimbledon struggle, and we figured that what was good enough for them was good enough for us. It is handy to the Earl's Court Underground and its rates are about half those of the Mount Royal and Cumberland.

The other Inexpensive is one we stayed in a couple of decades ago. We passed its façade the other day and were glad to see it still looking young and fresh: White Hall in Montague Street, Bloomsbury. It overlooks gardens and probably still caters mainly to schoolteachers, researchers, students from abroad.

We like the look of Durrant's in George Street near Manchester Square, a cut above the Inexpensive.

Hotel lists, more or less approved, are provided by several organizations. BTA sells an annual, *Hotels and Restaurants in Britain*, and if coaxed may even make a recommendation. If you take out temporary membership in the Automobile Association or the Royal Automobile Club, you can get their list of inspected hotels. If you find yourself roomless, call London Hotels Information Service, 88 Brook Street, W.1, telephone MAYfair 5414, or the organization used by hotels, HOTAC (Hotel Accommodation Service), 93 Baker Street, W.1, WELbeck 2555.

We wish we knew a cozy, efficient, *gemütlich* hotel in the center of everything, yet quiet; unshabby, yet inexpensive. We know such a hotel in Zurich, in Taormina, in Salzburg and Vienna, in Amsterdam, in Rabat—but not in London. In fact, we seem to be in the same dilemma as when we were new to the big town. If you happen to know of such a hotel in London, will you tell us?

# LONDON

# RESTAURANTS

Recommending restaurants is tricky, like bringing together two friends you think are made for each other. Worse. For restaurants change hands or their names or—worst of all—their chefs. Or they move, or close. Finally, tastes differ; a truth known to the Elizabethan dramatist who wrote, "What's one man's *poisson* [or was it poison?], Signor, is another's meat."

Bear in mind this escape clause as you read. Bear in mind also that in London it is a long-established custom to book a table beforehand for dinner.

We are fond of *Simpson's* at 100 The Strand—just east of the Savoy Hotel and Theater and three-eighths of a mile east of George Washington's monument in front of the National Gallery. Simpson's is the old, the honest-to-real English. For well-nigh thirty years it has never failed us, not even when our favorite headwaiter emigrated to Australia. Atmosphere Edwardian, service excellent, prices so reasonable you may inadvertently raise your eyebrows and let your monocle fall. We always go for the roast mutton or the roast beef sliced from the joint, and for dessert, the apple-and-blackberry pie (when at hand) with ice cream. The curries and savouries are also good.

When we say mean things about English food we always feel guilty, because there is Simpson's to give the censorious the lie. Holmes and Watson used to eat here. In fact, they ate at Simpson's twice while unraveling the Case of the Illustrious Client.

*Simpson's* in Piccadilly is no relation. This is a lunch place and snackery in the department store of the same name. Popular, usually crowded, not open for dinner.

A block west of the Piccadilly Simpson's is *Fortnum & Mason*, the eye-satisfying department store, on whose ground floor on the Jermyn Street side is the most attractive tearoom in London, with counter as well as tables. On the fourth floor the restaurant (lunch and tea only) is less crowded, the prices higher. This dining room is in exquisite taste and offers lighter and tastier dishes than most. The entire store is handsome, and for women who love shops it may well rank as next in interest to Bond Street and Westminster Abbey. A place a husband could treat his wife to, or a nonhusband his to-be, for while lunch or tea goes on, models stroll about with the latest froufrou. Book in advance.

Whenever we explore the City (the financial district), we make it our business to be there for lunch. Many eating places here have just the right English atmosphere and food. There's no decor nonsense (unless it be at *Ye Olde Cheshire Cheese*, Wine Office Court, 145 Fleet Street), nothing but grilled steaks and chops done to a turn for stockbrokers, financiers, and other men of business who come to eat well. Note the costume of the financial community, the bowlers, pin-stripe trousers, tightly furled umbrellas. You will be dividing your observations between the eaters and the chef, whose technique at the open charcoal grill is fascinating to watch.

We have particularly in mind that old tavern, the *George and Vulture*, patronized by Dickens, but the description will fit half a dozen others as well. The G. and Vulture may be found at 3 Castle Court, if you can find it. It's just behind the Royal Exchange, between Lombard and Cornhill streets, down some alleys, courts, and passages. Across a narrow passage is its almost-twin, *Simpson's* (no relation to the other two). The way to find both is this: walk a hundred yards past the Royal Exchange, then stop and ask the first financial-looking person to direct you.

Of the same kind is *Williamson's*, Groveland Court, Bow Lane, Cheapside, in the neighborhood of the Guildhall. It is early seventeenth century, has a mummified cat, and is favored by textile men. When finished with your lunch, look at Bow Church, which is just outside somewhere.

Then there is *Sweeting's*, famous for fish, at 39 Queen Victoria Street, south of St. Paul's; the Lucullan *Lucullus*, Plantation House,

Mincing Lane, between Fenchurch and Great Tower streets; *Cock Tavern*, 22 Fleet Street (historic; Dickens, Grinling Gibbons, et al., ate there; Gibbons, greatest of wood carvers, did the sign of which the one swinging above the place is a replica).

This is only a sampling. The City has more good lunch places than you can shake a bread-stick at: businessmen's, lawyers', newspapermen's haunts. But the City is dead at night; no dinners here.

Soho is a rabbit-warren of tourist dives and foreign cuisines. It has restaurants that take pride in their offering and others merely in business for the hit-and-run money.

If you feel like having a smörgasbord, try the *Three Vikings* at 84 Brewer Street, an interesting thoroughfare which you enter from Regent Street at the Aquascutum department store. Regular meals on ground floor, smörg on second floor; $1.50 for what costs considerably more back home. Get there early before things begin to look wilted.

Soho eating places that have upheld good reputations for many years include *Romano Santi*, 50 Greek Street; *Kettner's*, 29 Romilly Street; *Isola Bella*, 15 Frith Street; *Gennaro's*, 44 Dean Street.

Above Oxford Street and just west of Tottenham Court Road, across the border from Soho but counted gastronomically part of it, is the good *White Tower* (Greek), 1 Percy Street, and *Bertorelli*, 19 Charlotte Street. Schmidt's, farther up Charlotte Street, we won't recommend because of a meal they served under the guise of chicken just after the War. And, speaking of disappointments, the BTA-recommended Balkan Grill on Baker Street did not do us well in either food or service. And speaking of Baker Street—on Wigmore Street just east of Portman Square (which is bounded by Baker Street) you'll find some fairish restaurants, among them the modest *Wivex* (Danish).

For dining expensively (the bill approximating that of New York's best) in a fashionable setting, there are *Prunier's* on St. James's Street, a sort of branch of the Paris Prunier; *L'Écu de France* on Jermyn Street; the *Society* in Prince's Arcade, just off Jermyn Street; the *Colony* in Berkeley Square; the *Ritz Hotel* and *Hatchett's* in Piccadilly; the *Hungaria* in Lower Regent Street; and the *Coq d'Or* in Stratton Street.

For knock-your-eye-out decor and Gallic cuisine, try the new Persian Room of the *Empress Club* in Berkeley Street, about halfway between Berkeley Square and Piccadilly. Persian friezes, rich ceiling fabrics draped to give a tented effect make the customer feel he has somehow got into the Shah's royal *yurt*. Dancing later in the evening, and after-theater supper. Although it's a "club," foreigners don't have to join or pay an entrance fee; just call MAYfair 6126 and book.

In the Piccadilly Circus–Leicester Square vicinity are some good restaurants and some horrors. The horrors, luckily, are apparent to the naked eye.

The kingpin, famous for almost a century as the haunt of writers and artists, and called by an expert "the *doyen* of the great restaurants of London," is the *Café Royal*, a hop-skip-jump from Piccadilly Circus. The Royal is a notch less expensive than the swanks. In addition to its fourteen-crystal-chandeliered DuBarry Room it has a less dazzling grill and has converted the balcony of its Brasserie into an after-theater supper-snackery with music. Certainly one of your meals should be taken at the Royal.

*Scott's*, Coventry Street just off Piccadilly, has been pleasing food-fussy diners since the 1850s. It ranks among the best sea-food restaurants, and is expensive.

Near the Oxford Circus end of Regent Street, *Verrey's* is a proven eating place whose class is higher than its price. It has style. The main restaurant is downstairs.

Dropping down a rung or two in price, you find in this "Times Square" neighborhood the *Comedy* on Panton Street off Haymarket, red plush and "Continental" food; *Snow's Chop House*, 5 Sherwood Street, traditional John Bull; and *Trocadero* in Shaftesbury Avenue, for those who like dancing with their food. The *Pancake* in Bear Street off Cranbourne is a help-yourself oasis claiming to produce ten different kinds of pancake until midnight; other dishes available. Try at your own risk. *Gow's* at 37 St. Martin's Lane is grill-famous; *La Coquille* in the same street has a good French accent, and the same goes for *Le Perroquet*, 31 Leicester Square. While we never tried it, the *Seven Stars*, Coventry Street, has been praised to us by fellow Americans for good English food and service, with moderate prices. Try to get in a meal at *Rule's*, 35 Maiden Lane, long a colorful hangout of theater people.

In the Marble Arch sector, the *Cumberland Hotel Grill* is spacious and offers a generous *à la carte* menu at reasonable prices.

We usually go there for the rainbow trout and the curries. For dessert we order vanilla ice cream and hot chocolate; pouring the second over the first, we get a hot fudge sundae. There is music. On its lobby floor, the Cumberland has recently put in a *Jardin*, which offers good lighter-than-usual lunches and suppers, and we liked the coffee there. But it's crowded.

Facing Big Ben and his clock in the tower of the Houses of Parliament is *St. Stephen's*, a good workaday lunch place handy to your explorations of the Westminster part of town, where you're not unlikely to see M.P.s gnawing a bone. St. Stephen's has a direct wire to the House. There's a chance that while you're worrying a bone of your own the little bell will ring, causing several political types to drop their napkins and make for the door. The signal warns that a "division" or vote is about to be taken.

*Tate Gallery*, on the Thames beyond the Parliament and Lambeth Bridge, has a basement restaurant (murals by Rex Whistler) open 10:30–5:30 weekdays, 2:30–5:30 Sunday.

The Knightsbridge–Belgravia–Kensington–Chelsea west end of the West End, beyond Hyde Park Corner, has good eating places and some oddities. Take the oddities first. One is the *Aragona*, a "Spanish" restaurant on the borders of Chelsea (King's Road), owned and chefed by a Greek who once spent a month in the Balearic Islands and prefers Spanish dishes to Greek. His Chicken Aragona we found an acceptable variation on the *arroz con pollo* theme. Another curio is *El Cubano*, 171 Brompton Road, near Harrods. It has a ground-floor dinery, but the main dinner spot is below in the Roman Room, very Ancient Rome in decor with busts of the Caesars snooting the diners—and the waiters wearing togas! We counted two Latin-American dishes justifying the Cuban tag; the stock in trade is Italian.

For something to write home about, dine off the Elizabethan Feast of the *Gore Hotel* restaurant, 189–91 Queen's Gate, Kensington. You can order boar's head, peacock, roast swan, salmagundi, syllabub, and other costume-novel dishes, in Elizabethan surroundings (but no lusty oaths, please) to the sound of lutes strumming "Greensleeves" and the mob-capped service of Elizabethan II wenches. You drink honey mead and sack. You can spend the entire evening here (it's a package bill), smoking a long pipe while recalling that Sir Walter Raleigh has just brought the first shag over from Virginia, watching the revolving spit before the fire, and chucking cute Doll Tearsheets under the chin. The only jarring notes, Gadzooks, will be furnished by your fellow diners—not a ruff or slashed doublet among them.

The *Rib Room* of the *Carlton Tower Hotel* in Cadogan Square is a triumph of colorful furniture and fixtures, a cheerful place to go if you are in the dumps, and the roast beef and steaks help.

The *Shorthorn* in Chelsea Cloisters, Knightsbridge, is a steak house which also does good things with fat hens. In Chelsea at 353 King's Road the *Ox on the Roof* is not on the roof but on the ground floor, across the street from the Aragona. *Charco's*, 1 Bray Place near Sloane Square, dines outdoors when weather permits. These last two also specialize in steaks. The *Scholar Gypsy*, 119 Sydney Street, opposite Chelsea Town Hall, is an attractive place with "Continental" cuisine, plus barbecue in the little court of its Georgian house. The *Barbizon*, 132 Cromwell Road, near the West London Air Terminal, has French cuisine, combines a pleasant air with reasonable prices. At 29 Kensington High Street the inscrutable *Fu Tong* runs what is said to be the most recommended chopstickery in London. This claim is also made on behalf of *Lotus House*, 61–69 Edgware Road, beyond Marble Arch.

Should you visit Hampstead, London's most interesting residential quarter, you'll find some good little restaurants, among them *Spinning Wheel* at 1 Perrings Court (Hungarian) and *Cresta* at 102 Heath Street (Polish).

A mystery we have never solved is why restaurants and tearooms playing to standing-room-only business suddenly fold their tents like the Arabs. Gone is Frascati's, leaving mourners behind, and the Holborn, one of London's best lunchtime grills. Gone are Sherry's, the fashionable tearoom near Grosvenor Square, and Gunter's off Berkeley Square.

London has hundreds of restaurants, scores of them good and better than good. It is beyond the powers of these reporters to eat in them all.

Coffee-bars are by no stretch restaurants or even cafés. But one must speak of them somewhere, for they are a relatively new phenomenon and spawning like rabbits, not only in London but even in quiet cathedral towns. On an evening walk in Earl's Court we counted eight within half a mile, each crowded to the plate glass with intense and haggard young men and women, many dressed as if they had charge accounts at the Salvation Army. For these are the babbling grounds of beatnikery. We've never had the courage to join the mob, although dying to know what they talk about and if coffee in England has suddenly become that good.

Most of the coffee-bars and cellars are concentrated in Soho; some are naughty, with amateur strip-teases. A change is coming over England and the trend is not merrie, for while coffee-bars multiply, pubs decrease. While the pub has an air of homely neighborhood jollity about it, the coffee-bar and its habitués are something out of Dostoievski or Arthur Morrison's *Tales of Mean Streets*.

# THE PUB

The Englishman's drinking habits center on the public house, or pub, also known as "the local." No visit to England can be considered complete unless you have bent the elbow in a few pubs. They're not difficult to find, some 72,000 being in business by the latest count. A woman alone need feel no qualms about entering a pub, but if a tourist she is expected to go to the saloon part of it.

Pubs are divided by a partition into two sections. The public bar is for run-of-the-mill folk, usually the working man. The saloon bar is for the quality—or those who think themselves such. But there is no law to keep them apart. The American in England is not considered out of place in either bar; we have been as welcomed and as ignored in one as in the other.

For the tourist the public bar is likely to prove the more interesting. The local characters are there. It functions also as a games room. A darts board hangs on one wall. Cribbage, shove ha'p'ny, draughts (checkers), and dominoes are played. Shove ha'p'ny, by the way, is a game compared to which tiddledywinks is a wild encounter.

The same drinks can be had at either bar, served by the same barman or -maid. They cost a few pennies more in the saloon, which is more plushily furnished. Some pubs have a third room, a lounge.

The barmaid is a charmer only in fiction. She is one of the characters, a respectable, hard-working woman with the gift of cliché and repartee. Don't try to banter with her unless you know your way about in English-style gaggery. A barmaid in apparently exclusive intimacy with a lone male customer is merely lending a matey ear to the woes of a lonely commercial traveler well known to the house. One day pubs may wake up to the fact that tourists too can use a smile as well as a drink.

Some pubs sell sandwiches and cold meats, light lunches and suppers. Some may have a couple of rooms to let. A pub with food and rooms may seem no different from an inn, but its main business is drink; the inn's main business is lodging.

There are no dry shires or counties in England. But there are dry hours.

Pubs are open nine and a half hours a day Monday through Saturday, five or six hours on Sunday. Exact hours vary with the locality and the local. Usually they open at 11 A.M., close for the night at 11 P.M., and take their compulsory siesta from 3 to 5:30. Up and down the land from the Channel to the Roman Wall, at five minutes before zero hour, the barkeep's mournful cry rings out: *"Time, gentlemen!"* It stops the funny story in midcourse, stills the chatter, turns the tankards bottoms up, brings out handkerchiefs for a final mustache-wipe. There is nothing more English than that cry—*"Time!"* You can no more argue with it than you can with Big Ben.

Pubs also serve soft drinks: ginger ale, Cokes, fruit squashes, cider. The genteel sherry, and gin-and-tonic or gin-and-lime are also popular. Whiskies and liqueurs are available. Cocktails are little known outside tourist haunts. Beer is the main tipple.

To the American gullet English beer tastes odd. The nearest to the American version is imported Danish lager—Tuborg and Carlsberg—costing only a trifle more than the local product. The native lager is next best. Only lager is served cold.

Besides lager, the beer comes in varieties called mild, bitter, half-and-half (*ahf-n-ahf*), ale light or brown, porter, and stout. Bitter beer differs from mild in containing a larger percentage of hops. Half-and-half is a fifty-fifty mixture of mild and bitter. Ale makes up for having less of the hop by an infusion of top-fermentation malt. Porter is a dark malt liquor heavier than either ale or beer. It received its name from having been ages ago the popular drink of porters and other hard-working people. Stout is extra-strength porter.

A beverage that finds favor with the ladies (and with not a few men) is shandy or shandygaff—ale mixed with fizzy lemonade. It tastes better than it sounds and is an excellent warm-day drink.

Lawrence, sampling the East Anglian bitter in an Ipswich pub, explained to a man how refugee weavers fleeing religious persecution presented England with something better than medieval near-beer. From the Low Countries they brought the idea and the talent for making a drink from hops. They also, he remarked, brought canaries and the art of breeding them.

The man said, "You can't drink a canary."

*SOME NOTABLE LONDON PUBS* * A tourist endowed with time and a consistent thirst can make a special-interest tour of London's more celebrated pubs. Among them are:

The Prospect of Whitby, on the Thames at Wapping Wall, East London.

The Tiger Tavern, opposite the Tower.

The Coach and Horses in Covent Garden.

The Hoop and Grapes on Aldgate High Street near Petticoat Lane market.

The London Apprentice, eighteenth-century riverside house on the Thames at Isleworth.

The Champion in Wells Street just south and east of the crossing of Great Portland Street and Euston Road.

The Sherlock Holmes, at Northumberland Avenue and Northumberland Street, near Trafalgar Square.

Louis Stanley's *Old Inns of London* gives names, descriptions, and histories of a hundred old-time pubs.

# ENTERTAINMENT

*THEATER* ∗ Why is going to the theater in London so exciting? Because the familiar is tinged with the strangeness of being abroad? Because the London theater has a long and glamorous history—from Shakespeare to Shaw, from Gay to Osborne?

That may be a mystery, but here is an agreeable, solid fact: theatergoing in London is inexpensive. Even off-Broadway is high by comparison. On Broadway, what you pay for a gallery perch buys you the best seat in the stalls (orchestra) at a hit show in London. Ticket agents' fees are correspondingly low.

You don't get a free advertiser-sustained magazine by way of a program; instead, a sheet containing the essential information, which costs some seven cents. The usher will ask if you want tea, and during the interval (intermission) trays are rushed down and passed along the aisles. In some theaters smoking is permitted, and many have bars.

Thirty or forty theaters are in action throughout the year. They advertise in the daily press, and, with other forms of commercial entertainment, in the weekly *What's On in London*. The standard is generally high. You can often catch up on American plays you missed; American musical comedy is a popular import. Evening performances still begin at seven-thirty (originally a wartime measure), making dinner a problem, but public sentiment may bring about a change.

Keep your eye on what is being offered at Sadler's Wells, and be prepared to leap for tickets. This theater is a must for the lover of opera, operetta, and ballet. Some three centuries ago a mineral spring was discovered where the theater now stands, and one Sadler organized musical entertainments for those who flocked to take the waters. That spring still burbles, forgotten, under an aisle in the stalls. And Sadler's Wells has become a fountain of music. It is a magnificently competent company—or rather two of them—consisting of altogether four hundred people, playing classics and introducing new plays. Each company has its orchestra. The singing-dancing actors are multitalented. We saw the production of Offenbach's *La Vie Parisienne*; it was one of the most memorable nights we ever enjoyed at a theater, and our excellent first-balcony (dress circle) seats cost $2.45 each. Sadler's Wells publishes its own illustrated paper, *Repertoire*.

This theater is in E.C.1, just beyond Finsbury Town Hall, well outside the theater district, but is easily reached not only by taxi but by buses 19 and 38 from Piccadilly Circus. Arrive at least half an hour before curtain time and have a light supper in the refreshment rooms. The after-show dispersal of people and taxis is so swift you may be left standing at the curb, practically alone in nowhere. The dilemma is resolved by crossing the street and boarding a bus for Piccadilly.

The Royal Opera House, more popularly known as the Covent Garden Theater, is another with a long history. The present theater, the third on the site, was a hundred years old in 1958; the first opened in 1732 with Congreve's *The Way of the World*, followed on the next night by John Gay's *The Beggar's Opera*. The great crimson-and-gold opera house offers more conservative and less ebullient fare than Sadler's Wells. And where but in England will you find a grand theater, greeting you with bewigged footmen, tucked away in a corner of a vegetable-and-fruit market? The house is an endearing period piece, and an evening here, particularly a gala for a state occasion, is a scintillating event. The royal family is on hand, and evening dress is the thing at such times.

There's a theater in Sloane Square just upstairs from the Underground station that is worth attending no matter what happens to be on the boards. It was at the Royal Court that young maverick Bernard Shaw was first presented to a hostile world. More recently it launched John Osborne, the *Look Back in Anger* man, and another angry one, Angus Wilson. It concentrates on the modern and on discoveries foreign and domestic, but also presents exciting revivals. The company is first-rate.

Another, even more experimental, is the Mermaid on Upper Thames Street at Puddle Dock, just beyond Blackfriars Underground station. This extraordinary little theater, the first erected in the City since Shakespeare's day, was built by contributions (including labor) in the shell of a bombed-out warehouse on the river's brim. It has built-in stereophonic sound, the first such in Europe, and a popular restaurant overlooking the river. Besides its unusual stage fare (it did some medieval "mystery" plays, for example), it has winter lunchtime showings of unusual films. The Mermaid has a keen following and plays to full houses.

The best-known name among the theaters is that of the Old Vic, as the Royal Victoria is always called. Founded in 1816, it first won fame of a sort for its melodrama. Since 1880 it has won a name for its productions of Shakespeare and other classical plays at popular prices, and now has a junior company as well. You'll find it on the other side of the Thames on Waterloo Road, just beyond Waterloo Station.

VAUDEVILLE  *  Variety, moribund in the U.S., flourishes in London. Its principal haunts are the Palladium, the Prince of Wales, the Windmill, and the Victoria Palace. The prices are as low as the humor—but there's a place for low humor in anyone's life. Whether you're amused or not, the music hall is the place to find the Cockney enjoying his leisure with his wife or his girl. It is also the place to test your comprehension of English slang and colloquialisms delivered rapid-fire. (Don't take a prissy maiden aunt to the Windmill.)

CONCERT HALLS  *  The Royal Albert in Kensington and the Royal Festival Hall across the Thames at Waterloo Bridge are the two great ones. The Festival Hall is new and acoustically famous, and an exciting place, especially when Sir Malcolm Sargent conducts a pops concert. It has a river-view restaurant.

OPEN-AIR ENTERTAINMENT  *  The Open-Air Theater in Regent's Park plays Shakespeare and other bards, June–September, retreating under cover when rain falls. Concerts are held in a number of parks. The best are at Holland Park in Kensington, at Hampstead Heath's Kenwood Lake, and in the Festival Pleasure Gardens, Battersea Park on the Thames' other bank.

In addition to *What's On in London*, you can consult the *London Theatre Guide*, free at main hotels, restaurants, and railway stations.

*DINING-DANCING* ✳ The top hotels let you dance while dining from about 9 P.M. Among the better nonhotel dine-and-dance restaurants are the Colony, Pigalle, and Talk of the Town, the Pigalle being the least expensive of the trio. Quaglino's and the Allegro, which also offer cabaret, occupy the same building at 16 Bury Street. The Allegro is gay, informal; Quaglino's elegant and formal.

There are a score of good dine-and-dance restaurants. In all but a few you needn't bother about evening dress. To be safe, inquire when reserving.

Tour agencies offer night-life tours.

The time has come to confess that we are personally allergic to the synthetic *joie de vivre* of London nighteries. They offer nothing not to be found in similar places in New York and other American cities. Why cross an ocean for an inferior product?

There is an exception. On Greek Street, Soho, in an abandoned strip-teasery, The Establishment features satiric skits that comment on the problems and personalities of the day in a clever, highly literate style. The Crown itself is not immune. The Establishment is a "club," membership for a year $9, and its dinner bill (jazz band with food and dancing downstairs) comes to about $6. For the politically sophisticated couple's night out it is a lively haunt.

# SHOPPING

# IN LONDON

You do most of your shopping in London. Except for antiques there's little to be had outside the capital. Where we have found a tourist-worthy shop in the provinces, we mention it.

Shops close in London on Saturday at 1 P.M.

RULES AND REGULATIONS * By U.S. law you are permitted, duty-free, a hundred dollars' worth of purchases for personal use or as gifts.

If you live in a dry state, don't try to bring liquor home.

Some stores in England participate in the voluntary *Personal Export Scheme.* This scheme permits you to buy articles of fourteen dollars or more free of purchase (sales) tax, provided you have them sent to your boat or plane, or to an overseas address.

The tax is not uniform. On some items, such as wearing apparel, it is not high enough to be worth considering. On others, notably china, it is worth your while to buy only on the Personal Export Scheme. Most of the department stores in London participate in the plan; smaller shops that do so usually have a sign in the window.

If you're having something sent, check with the sales person (a "clerk" works in an office; there's no such thing as sales clerk in England) as to whether the mailing or shipping charges are greater than the tax. If they are, you might as well pay the tax and carry that item with you.

Do you want something, or are you just looking?

If you're just looking, there are no problems. Walk up and

down Bond Street (New and Old), then on Piccadilly to Burlington Arcade, and finish by going through Fortnum & Mason's
hard by the arcade. This is the way to avoid excessive fatigue
while passing in review much of London's discreetly glittering
wealth and quality. *Fortnum & Mason's* is the stroll's logical end.
It's a luxury department store of unique charm, full of costly
things you don't need. The ground-floor staff wear tail coats and
boutonnieres—they are customers' gentlemen. You can lunch there
(book in advance) or have tea or a soda.

If you are more serious, widen the territory to take in everything
within the rough square formed by Oxford Street, Regent Street,
Piccadilly, and Park Lane. This is Mayfair, and in it *Liberty's*
department store is to Regent Street what Fortnum & Mason's
is to Piccadilly.

Then hop out of the rough square to Knightsbridge. Here in
another shopping area is *Harrods* department store, home and
mother to the western West Enders. Nearby is a fashionable region
of specialty shops.

Finally, come back to take in *Selfridge's* on Oxford Street. This
is a step down. Oxford Street is definitely middle class, like 34th
Street in New York, and Selfridge's is London's Macy's. We don't
know why you should want to go there. To an American it has
no novelty. However, we know a Westport man who plunged in
and came out hours later battered but triumphant; his purchase—
a catnip mouse. He said, "My wife would never forgive me if I
didn't bring her something from Selfridge's."

For the rest, the shops are scattered all over London's confusing
map. Canny tourists come with lists. We had a list once. It took
us days to find the shops. Each day we wound up we knew not
where, right in the middle of the taxi-taken rush hour. With two
hours to spare before plane time we shot out by the Underground
to *Heal's*, the home-furnishings store on Tottenham Court Road,
and invested in Irish linen dishtowels. Keep them in mind in case
you're up against it. They're not any old dishtowels. They're called
*glass cloths*, their lovely colors and designs are by individual artists,
and their price is sixty cents apiece. Our friends who received them
appeared pleased.

Another place for that last-minute dash is *Liberty's*, where you load up on Liberty silk scarves. Their knowing scarf department is handy for that purpose, right off the street.

What are you looking for?

If it's quality and at a substantial saving, the best buy is in bone china by Wedgwood, Doulton, Worcester, Derby, Spode, Minton, and the like. In the U.S., protective tariffs raise them to the price category of heirlooms. In England they sell from a half to two-fifths as much—one example, U.S. $38 as against England $16.50 for a five-piece setting. Even with the cost of shipping tacked on (about twenty-five dollars for a full dinner set), you save.

If it was you who broke Aunt Dodie's Spode sugar bowl ten years ago, now is your chance to make it up to her. But be certain you have the name of the pattern. A pitiful sight is the tourist in the china shop, eyes as glazed as the unwinking display, saying brokenly to the weary clerk, "I think it had flowers on it."

In style, bone china remains traditional, highly conservative, unchanging. But something new has recently been added. Doulton is producing a translucent line which is cheaper and an excellent buy. It is carried by *Lawley's* on Regent Street.

Each of the famous producers has many lines in a varying price range. No single shop can carry all the lines of even one of them—there isn't room. Some concentrate on the lower price ranges, some on the higher; some make a specialty of one or two producers.

*Harrods* china department has good variety and knowledgable clerks. *Liberty's* has less variety but its china department is pleasant. *Lawley's*, 150 Regent Street, carries Doulton, Worcester, and Wedgwood in a medium price range. The shop called *Burlington Glass* in the Burlington Arcade specializes in the finest Minton and also has some Doulton. Across the street, *Gered* in Piccadilly Arcade specializes in Spode and Wedgwood, and has some Worcester. *James Leather*, 59 Piccadilly, specializes in Royal Crown Derby.

China dealers also carry glassware. Hand-cut crystal is a good buy.

Doulton figurines are everywhere. If you want some of those, buy early or you'll get sick of seeing them around.

Sweaters are the next most popular item. There's a saving of at least seven dollars on the big-name cashmeres—Ballantyne,

Pringle, Braemar, and so on. They are carried by the better department stores and by specialty shops. Try *Burberry's, Harrods,* or *W. Bill* of 12 South Moulton Street.

Materials by the yard—tweeds and woolen suitings—are snapped up by tourists. We presume that each of them knows at home the priceless but reasonable tailor we have looked for all our lives and never found. *Hunt and Winterbotham* at 4 Old Bond Street and *Allan* of Duke Street have the largest selection. *N. Peal* of Burlington Arcade is also good.

London is full of antique shops of every imaginable specialization—from old coins to fireplaces. But the best way to shop for antiques is at the annual shows. Come in time for the Chelsea Antiques Fair in the spring and autumn, but particularly for the delightful Kensington Fair in late August or early September. For an experience, attend the auctions at *Christie's* and *Sotheby's.* For another, go to the *Cameo Corner,* 26 Museum Street (near the British Museum), a curio shop for antiquarians.

Books are among England's bargains for the American. The *Times Bookshop,* 42 Wigmore Street, is our first choice, closely followed by *Hatchard's* of 187 Piccadilly, and *Bumpus* of 8 Baker Street. No, not Foyle's; the "world's largest bookstore" is a chaos and a bedlam. For rare books, the great place is *Maggs,* 50 Berkeley Square. Charing Cross Road with its secondhand bookshops and stalls is the beat of browsers.

*SHOPS HERE AND THERE* ∗ *Burberry's* in the Haymarket. The name is a synonym for weatherproofs (raincoats), but they also have a full line of men's and women's wear, including leather and suede jackets or coats. On the woman's floor we liked their reversible rainproof capes in tweed and tartan, and the coats of their own "saddle tweed." Their sweaters were superb. Burberry's has a solid English tone of understatement that makes the word *fashionable* seem shallow. Their styling is classic, the workmanship impeccable.

*Aquascutum,* 100 Regent Street. This is the second big name for raincoats, and they too have men's and women's wear.

*Simpson's* in Piccadilly has the Daks line in men's and women's wear. It's particularly good for sports equipment.

*Pollock's Toy Theater and Museum,* 44 Monmouth Street,

carries on the firm that invented the toy theater in 1808. The cardboard do-it-yourself theater used to sell for "penny plain and tuppence colored," as Robert Louis Stevenson fondly recalled. One dollar buys you a "tuppence colored" now. Pollock's is fun to visit and often has amusing exhibitions.

*Craftsmen Potters' Shop*, 3 Lowndes Court (off Carnaby Street, which is somewhere behind Regent Street). In this hard-to-find shop potters from all over the country display and sell their work.

At *Edouard and Butler* of Clifford Street, gentlemen, maharajas, and discriminating tourists have ties made to order. At *Wilkinson Sword* on Pall Mall you can order a bulletproof vest or a scimitar, and from *H. Potter* on West Street a military drum. *Perkins & Co.*, chemists of Piccadilly, specialize in pick-me-ups for the morning after. *Norman Newton* of Shepherds Market specializes in model soldiers. *Daniel Neal* in Portman Square is a department store for children. *Hanley's*, 200 Regent Street, is a department store of toys. If you're a medical student you can buy a skeleton from *Adam Romilly* of 18 Fitzroy Street. *Paris House*, 41 S. Moulton Street, beltmaker to H. M. the Queen, is also the top handicrafter of costume jewelry and will make to your design. *Smythson* of Bond Street is the place for stationery, diaries, account books. *Finnigan's* of Bond Street is the great place for leather goods, if you can afford them.

*What's Where in London* by Denys Parson is a paperback shopping guide selling for about a dollar. If your problem is where to find an unusual gift or a useless but irresistible object for yourself, the answer, if it exists, is here. The book also lists people who render out-of-the-way services.

ABOUT GIFTS  *  When you buy Great Name items for others, ask yourself whether they know the Great Names. If they don't, will they appreciate the gift?

MEN ONLY  *  Handy for tobacco and pipes because it is situated on the Haymarket near the American Express is *Fribourg and Treyer*, which has been doing business behind the same bow windows since 1720. A branch in Burlington Arcade sells pewter also. (Prices of tobacco are so high, because of taxes, that sellers are adding gifts to their slow-moving stock.) There are a number of first-class tobacconists in Jermyn Street, which runs parallel to Piccadilly one block south. (Dutch cigars are available, but no American, Swiss or Danish.) Jermyn is a male shopping street, and here without lingering you can see British types out of Noel Coward and P. G. Wodehouse.

Superior barber-shop treatment is to be had in the basement of *Austin Reed's* on Regent Street. Book in advance.

CAUTION.   Are you having a suit made? English tailors just now are cutting-fitting Italian style. Your suit will be beautifully made but will probably be tighter than you're used to. Travel at own risk to *Allan* of Duke Street, *Gieves* of 27 Old Bond, or *Hawkes* of 1 Savile Row.

# GETTING
# YOUR
# BEARINGS

Lawrence said, "First thing we have to do is study the map."

Studying, Sylvia followed his index finger as it journeyed over London while their ship ploughed the ocean. The Thames, the City, Piccadilly Circus, Marble Arch, Hyde Park—they were there. It was easy.

"A map," Lawrence said, "is a portrait of what you are going to meet. To wait until you're there is like postponing the loading of your gun until you come face to face with the lion."

He frowned. "Where's Bloomsbury? I had it a second ago."

"Isn't that it under your elbow?"

London is large and complicated. Having arrived and carefully oriented ourselves before walking out of our hotel bound for a certain publishing house, in no time we were hopelessly lost two turnings from Trafalgar Square in a maze of tiny streets which, by all that was holy and our map, had no business to be there.

By the time we found our street we were late for our appointment. Our sigh of relief was premature. We couldn't find the number. It turned out after further study that the numbers on that street ran down one side and then up the other.

The next day, after tramping the Holborn district looking for the Old Bailey, we pocketed pride and approached a bobby.

"Old Byly?" He peered at us from under his bushy eyebrows and inverted coal scuttle of a helmet. " 'Ullo! Oo's leg might you be pullin'?" It was right across the street.

When we leave our map in the pocket of the other suit we bog down in Petty France, mire in Soho, go adrift in Mayfair. Study the map—that's essential. How else will you learn, if not London, humility? And, having studied the map, carry it with you.

London is a crazy quilt of towns, hamlets, and villages that grew separately and into one another while refusing to give up their identity. But the terrain must have been bewildering to begin with. Even the disciplined Romans couldn't make the grid or checkerboard so dear to their hearts out of what they found and built upon here. They ran broad straight roads across miles of twisting country, but they couldn't straighten London.

Since their time it has gone its merry way, forming in unconformity what William Blake called "a human aweful wonder of God!" That was more than a century ago, when it was less awful than it is now.

The confusion is abetted by the Thames. After following a fairly east–west course, it suddenly dives at Waterloo Bridge, curves, and is a north–south river at the Houses of Parliament. The streets follow it, tumbling south and west like the spill of a mighty waterfall.

In New York the Empire State Building, in Paris the Eiffel Tower are tried-and-true landmarks. In London nothing stands out in the architectural mélange of Gothic, Jacobean, Georgian, Victorian, Edwardian. Something may, in good time. For alas (or is it hurrah?) under Elizabeth II a skyscraper metropolis is taking shape around, between, and on top of everything else.

Meanwhile, some plan of action must be adopted to master the chaos. We have one for you. Its simplicity astonishes us. We can't understand why it took us years to figure it out.

*THE PLAN. PART I: ORIENTATION*   *   Only a small part of what Dr. Johnson called "the wonderful immensity of London" matters to the tourist. It forms, roughly, a triangle between Knightsbridge and Marble Arch on the west and the City and Tower of London on the east. The broad base is on the west, the almost-point or narrow end in the City—financial London. Its length is about four miles. If you want to be more generous and take in Kensington Palace and the Victoria and Albert Museum, add two miles more.

Two main west–east avenues traverse this visitor's London. They are three-fourths of a mile apart at the western base. Each keeps changing its name as it goes along—an old English custom. Here they are, moving from west to east:

1.  The northern one starts at Kensington Gardens as Bayswater Road. At Marble Arch it becomes Oxford Street, then New Oxford, Holborn, High Holborn, Holborn Viaduct, Newgate Street, Cheapside, and Poultry. Then it bifurcates into Lombard Street and Cornhill. Simple.

2.  The southern artery starts at the southwest corner of Kensington Gardens, where it sets out at a smart pace as Kensington High Street, becomes Kensington Road, then Knightsbridge, whirling into traffic-mad Hyde Park Corner and coming out as Piccadilly. At Piccadilly Circus (careful here, the statue of Eros presides over bedlam) following the mainstream of traffic it turns down Haymarket, swirls around Trafalgar Square and into the Strand, enters the City as Fleet Street, becomes Ludgate Hill, Cannon Street, and East Cheap, and finally runs into the Tower as Great Tower Street.

Map-scanning is passive. Our conquest of London began when we thought up a do-it-yourself supplement to it. You draw on a piece of paper, guided by your map, two long lines to represent these two mainstems, these twin spines. Mark each with its names. Add the main north–south connecting streets: Park Lane, Bond Street, Regent Street, Charing Cross Road, Kingsway, and—in the City—Chancery Lane. You now have a considerable part of tourist London taped in a crude version of the lines of latitude and longitude on a globe. Armed with this barest of diagrams, you can get a general idea of where you are at any given time, provided you're in or just outside the triangle. When thoroughly lost, present the paper to a bobby or a helpful-looking native and ask him which of the names you're nearest to.

After trying this scheme on ourselves and finding it worked, we passed the idea on to a friend who was going to London for the first time. She took to it and, being an artist, began sketching in the Corners, Squares, Circuses, Palaces where they belonged. She presented the finished job to us as a souvenir, which we treasure.

THE PLAN. PART II: ACTION  *  London has no one center. It has several: Hyde Park Corner, Marble Arch, Piccadilly Circus, Trafalgar Square, the Bank of England. Everyone chooses his own, directed by routine, convenience, affection, or fancy. We choose Trafalgar Square, Britain's heart and London's most interesting open space. From there we will take you out on six radiating tours encompassing all the major and most of the minor sights.

So get into your easiest shoes, slip the Orientation Paper into your pocket, grasp your neatly rolled English umbrella, and meet us on the north side of Trafalgar Square. You will find us sitting on the stone parapet alongside the National Gallery under the statue of George Washington.

SOMETHING TO REMEMBER. London took a terrible beating in World War II. Bombs rained down upon it, fire raged through the streets. Sirens wailed. You heard the putt-putt-putt of the nearest buzz bomb, listened for the cutout, the hush that meant it had gone into its dive—whose number was up this time? Your own? You worked, fell in love, married, had children, with the sound of death in your ears, the smell of it in your nostrils, the ghastly sight of it before your eyes. You fought fires and dug neighbors out from under the hot smoking rubble that a few moments before was a home.

When it was all over, London was a city to weep over—a broken body pitifully alive. It still bears the scars. It is still rebuilding. From its ordeal it emerged sane, strong, free.

# § *TRAFALGAR SQUARE*

Of all London's open spaces, Trafalgar Square looks most like the capital of Empire.

Ranged round it are Canada House, Norway House, South Africa House (where in summer the BTA maintains a tourist-information office), steamship companies, the Admiralty Arch, the National Gallery, and the church of St. Martin-in-the-Fields—a name that tells you this was once out in the country.

St. Martin, designed by James Gibbs, a protégé of Christopher Wren, is the oldest structure hereabouts and the most pleasing. Enter; the eighteenth-century interior is restful. As the parish church of Buckingham Palace, it contains the royal pew. Nell Gwyn, Charles II's mistress, was buried in the churchyard, but 130-odd years ago Duncannon Street was run through it and her. See the crypt, reserved as a nightly shelter for the poor and homeless. Who knows but that some night when you arrive without hotel space——?

The square is dominated by Horatio Nelson, hero of the naval victory of Trafalgar off the coast of Spain (1805), in which he died. The enemy was France, the villain Napoleon. The Nelson Monument is a column 167½ feet high with a 17½-foot Nelson on top of it. He looks undersized. The mere thought of standing on such a height would have made the Admiral ill. He was the sickest hero history ever clutched to her bosom. Accident- and disease-prone, he suffered from several chronic ailments, of which the least was seasickness. Up there he symbolizes not only national victory, but also man's triumph over a frail body.

Landseer's famous bronze lions at the monument's base are a perch for orators, children, and pigeons. Here and there stand the statues of lesser heroes. Fountains play. Flower beds line one side. There are seats for the weary.

Sitting with us on the parapet, you enjoy an exciting view across the square south down Whitehall to the Parliamentary clock tower from which Big Ben's familiar notes bong the hours. Then, reining in your eye, find the bronze horse with a rider aboard immediately south of the square at the head of Whitehall. That small open space, called Charing Cross, is important. (Don't confuse it with Charing Cross railway station or Charing Cross Road.)

Charing Cross bore a cross—the last of thirteen set up by Edward I to mark the places where the body of his queen Eleanor rested on its journey from Nottinghamshire to Westminster Abbey. There it stood from 1291 until 1647, when Cromwell, an anti-cross Christian, had it removed.

"Sir," declared Dr. Sam: Johnson, squelching an extoller of Fleet Street, "the full tide of human existence is at Charing Cross." And the poet Francis Thompson sang of the "shining traffic" of Jacob's Ladder "pitched betwixt heaven and Charing Cross." In Dr. Johnson's day Trafalgar Square didn't exist. In Thompson's day it was too new for poetry, but Charing Cross was to an English poet the hub of the universe.

This equestrian statue, considered the handsomest in London, is of Charles I. He is looking toward the spot where he lost his head in 1649—a platform in front of the Banqueting House on the left-hand side of Whitehall. He sits above a revenge spot; here after the 1660 Restoration several of the regicides were in their turn beheaded. History is a long feud, blood-bespattered, and the end is not yet.

Before Charles' bronze, new-cast, could be erected, the Civil War broke out. Cromwell's Roundheads sold it to a bronze-worker named Rivett to be scrapped. Brother Rivett had other ideas. Secretly burying it, he proceeded to sell bronze "relics" to the Royalists and "souvenirs" to the Roundheads. When monarchy triumphed again, he dug it up and presented it to Charles II. That too was good for business. Rivett deserves to be immortalized in the English language like the Hobson of "Hobson's choice." A *rivett* would verbalize the successful deal with two opposing sides.

Behind Charles I a plaque marks the spot where the original cross may have stood. From this plaque all distances from London are measured. Officially, it is the center of a metropolis whose extent and confines are vague.

Few Londoners are aware that embedded in the pavement on the square's north side are the Standard British Linear Measurements: inch, foot, yard. Bring your tape measure and see if it checks.

In the northeast corner observe an oddity—George IV riding bareback and in stocking feet. It is said that, money running short, the statue had to be skimped of shoes and saddle. That such ignominy should happen to Prinny, the "first gentleman of Europe"—who wouldn't have been caught dead, let alone immortalized, unsuitably horsed and clothed!

The National Gallery, behind you, has one of the world's great collections of paintings. The sidewalk in front of it attracts a kind of professional artist, the war veteran who draws his perishable works in colored chalks alongside the legend * My * Own * Work. * Battered caps for pennies and sixpence line the gutterside gallery. George Washington, the eagle, and the Stars and Stripes are favorite subjects, for Americans are generous.

The square is a favored place for mass protests and demonstrations, ranking with Hyde Park as a safety valve of minority indigna-

tion. Much is made of this aspect of British tolerance. But sometimes—as in the case of Bertrand Russell and his fellow protestors
against nuclear snowballing—Authority feels that freedom of protest may become awkward, and calls out battalions of police with
paddy wagons.

Those who clock such things say that seventy thousand vehicles
go round Trafalgar Square in the busiest twelve hours of a working day. Hyde Park Corner ranks first, with eighty thousand.
You'll never miss that ten thousand.

No one has ever attempted to count the square's pigeon population. Only determined tourists escape having themselves snapped
by photographers armed with pigeon-feed to attract the standard
halo of gluttonous birds.

What with the traffic, pigeons, photographers, fountains, star-
lings, and crowds, there's not a dull moment. We dote on Trafalgar
Square at any hour of the day. It is romantic by night. But its
climax is the evening rush hour. Then the large soul of Samuel
Johnson joins us on the parapet to savor "the full tide of human
existence."

Trafalgar Square is the scene of a shaggy-pigeon story. Pigeons
Bert and Gwen were deeply in love. He lived up at Nelson's left
boot, she on a cozy cornice of St. Paul's Cathedral. They met,
alternating between his roost and her ledge, every noon. One day
Big Ben boomed twelve, and no Gwen descended out of the rare
blue sky. The minutes wore on, and a distracted male bird paced
the top of the Admiral's hat, scanning the horizons. At last—oh
joy!—he spotted her walking on our parapet. With a sob of relief
he swooped down to her. "Gwen! Gwen! I've been so worried.
Whatever——"

"Bert, it was such a lovely day I thought I'd walk."

And so should you.

# ROUTE ONE

## To Buckingham Palace
## and St. James's,
## and on to the
## Tourist Far West of Kensington

Leaving the pigeons and Landseer's relaxed lions, cross Trafalgar Square to its southwest corner and advance with stately tread under Admiralty Arch. It is only right to start from Admiralty's square— Trafalgar—to the Admiralty itself, and then go on to Royalty. The Mall makes the clear connection.

At the Arch the Royal Navy, so long the instrument by which Britannia ruled the waves, has its administrative buildings and naval library. Before you stretches the broad tree-lined Mall, running three-quarters of a mile straight to Buckingham Palace.

This is the grand boulevard of royal pageantry. Britain's kings and queens are driven along it in ornate coaches from the palace to their decorative chores at Westminster Abbey, Parliament, and the City. The Mall, like Pall Mall which parallels it on the north, takes its name from *paille-maille,* a French form of croquet which became the rage in the seventeenth century and was played here.

Walking along the Mall, the line of porticoed mansions you see on your right is Carlton House Terrace. It replaces a house of that Prince of Wales (Prinny) who was later George IV. You saw him riding bareback and shoeless in Trafalgar Square.

Prinny had a passion for building in the latest mode, but couldn't meet the bills. To get his Carlton House debts paid, he gave in to his father's choice of a bride for him. At his first sight (and smell) of the German princess, he reeled back and called for brandy. Since he was already secretly married and therefore about to commit bigamy, he needn't have been so fastidious. His Carlton House was soon pulled down, and the Terrace, designed by John Nash, Prinny's favorite architect, took its place. Most of it is now used by government offices.

At the time Prinny was playing with Carlton House, Buckingham House (now the palace) had been bought as an informal town residence for his mother, the queen of whom a wit remarked on her fiftieth birthday, "I do believe the bloom of her ugliness is wearing off."

The stairway down to the Mall which interrupts the Terrace is the Duke of York Steps (you'll be coming back that way), decorated by a tall column surmounted by a statue of the duke, one of Prinny's shoddy brothers. The youngest and shabbiest of them became the father of a girl named Victoria.

Thus the Mall provides a glimpse into the affairs of an important, foolish, unhappy, historic, and vividly human royal family about whom there is a wealth of anecdote, scandal, and gossip.

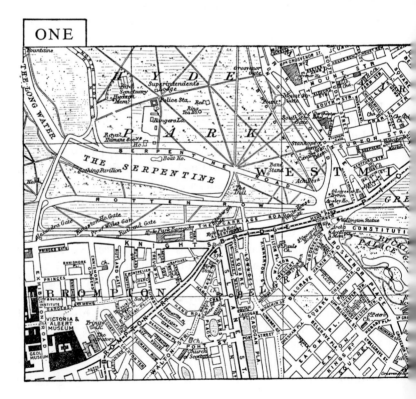

It is the family of George III, the king who lost the American colonies; the dynasty under which Georgian architecture developed.

The short road opposite the Steps goes to the Horse Guards Parade, where the brilliant ceremony of Trooping the Color takes place on the sovereign's official birthday, about June 6.

St. James's Park is on your left all the way to the palace. If you have your Orientation map with you, why not add the park to it? At once intimate and aristocratic, it is the most beautiful of London's parks and an ideal resting place for the weary of foot or spirit. John Nash created the lovely lagoon populated by ducks, swans, and pelicans. They are descendants of birds settled in the park by Charles II. The first pair of pelicans was a gift to him from the Russian ambassador.

The best entrance into the park is the mid-Mall path you should now have reached. It takes you to the bridge over the lagoon, with

↓ *Trafalgar Square*

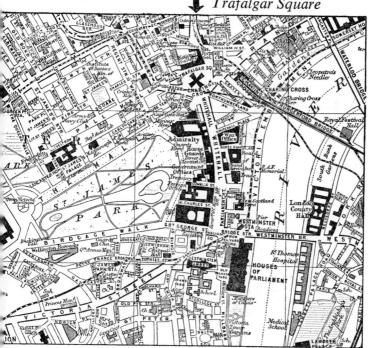

views of Buckingham Palace on one side, Whitehall on the other, and the royal birds sporting below. That tall narrow tower directly to your south is Westminster Cathedral, England's principal Roman Catholic church, a rich edifice in a Byzantine style completed in 1903. A lift will take you up; view is extraordinary.

Some day when you want to extend this walk, cross the park and come out on an old quarter whose aristocratic former character is hinted at in names like Petty France, Queen Anne's Gate, and Birdcage Walk. Milton began *Paradise Lost* in a garden house in Petty France, later occupied in turn by Jeremy Bentham and William Hazlitt. The house is gone, and the area is much eaten into by unlovely blocks of flats. A few fine eighteenth-century houses survive—the Blewcoat School in Caxton Street, for example—and Queen Anne's Gate is a small eighteenth-century close.

But you have other fish to fry just now, so return to the Mall. Swing round the Victoria Monument—Prinny's niece grown up and a mediocre subject for statuary—and you come up against the high ornamental iron fence of the Palace, which an insider tells us the royal family call Buck House.

It became the sovereign's permanent London residence when Queen Victoria, a mere girl, moved into it immediately after her coronation in 1837, to get away from her mother in Kensington Palace. Although millions had already been spent on it, it was— and until recently remained—one of England's least comfortable homes. It was chilly and drafty, the W.C.s went out of order, doors wouldn't shut, chimneys smoked, bells and drains failed. The Empire's Queen had to bathe in a tin tub. Yet to Victoria it was heaven. She had escaped from Mother.

It was only half its present size then. Royal levees and other affairs were held in nearby St. James's Palace. The first royal occupant, George III's queen, named rooms after the color of their furnishings, beginning a custom which was adopted for the White House. King George met with his privy council in this Buck House; among the problems they took up was the stubbornness of the American colonies. Longfellow called George the "lazy old drone of the German hive." Whatever else he was, Prinny's father was not lazy. But then, the poet was off about P. Revere too.

It doesn't make sense to be here at any time other than when they change the guard—at 10:30 A.M. Monday through Friday,

April 1 to September 30, if the Queen is in residence. Buck House doesn't look very palacelike. The public is not admitted to any of its 602 rooms (many of them offices). The best part fronts (or backs) on forty acres of lovely, royally private garden. All you can see between the bars of the fence is the undistinguished façade and the bare, graveled entrance yard.

But wait! An exception has lately been made. On Sylvia's birthday in 1962 Her Majesty opened The Queen's Gallery in a new building on the site of the royal chapel destroyed by Nazi bombs. It houses changing exhibitions from the royal collections, one of the world's richest private art hoards. Four centuries have accumulated 4,500 paintings and 20,000 drawings. They are shown in a non-museum ambience. Entrance on Buckingham Palace Road; small admission charge.

The Changing of the Guard is a standard tourist thrill. To be sure it's scheduled for the morning you plan to see it, call ASK-9211, which gives information on the principal tourist events of the day. We were disappointed in it because we had seen the same ceremony at Windsor Castle, where it isn't fenced off. We'd advise you to skip Buck and see the show at Windsor if it weren't that it's the Thing to Do.

The iron fence deserves a tablet if the story is true that England's first cup of tea was brewed and sipped in Goring House, which occupied its site. It is claimed that the pioneer pound of leaf cost ninety dollars in today's money, and that the event took place in the 1670s. A pretty tale! Samuel Pepys on September 25, 1660, drank a "cup of tee, A China drink, of which I had never drunk before." Further sniffing along the tea trail uncovers a London newspaper of 1658 carrying this ad: "That excellent and by all Physitians approved China Drink called by the Chineans Tcha, by other nations Tay alias Tee, is sold at the Sultaness Head, a cophee-house in Sweetings Rents, by the Royal Exchange."

Now go back down the Mall a way and take the third passage on your left, which passes beside red-brick-battlemented St. James's Palace. You will come out on Cleveland Row, the dead end of Pall Mall. The palace may disappoint. There's something of the large toy or stage-set about it. But it grows on one, it is so Tudor. Wooden-soldierlike are the scarlet-uniformed guardsmen who pace back and forth between the sentry boxes, pop in, pop out, and go through synchronized arms drills. They about-face with mechanical stamping. "Oh, their poor feet!" cried a motherly tourist.

This Tudor leftover of a palace is still in use. The kings and queens have lived in Buck House for more than a century, but ambassadors are still accredited to the Court of St. James's. Elizabeth, when she was a princess, and her sister Margaret lived in the more modern part of it, Clarence House, which is now the London residence of the Queen Mother. Royal uncle the Duke of Gloucester occupies an older part. It is also the headquarters of the Yeomen of the Guard, the Beefeaters. (Those chaps at the Tower are Yeomen Warders.)

Henry VIII, needing a palace, chose a stretch of swampy meadow with a leper hospital on it. Only four leprous females lived there. He had them pensioned off, goodness knows where to. You'd think a superstitious sixteenth-century king would have shunned the place. The hospital was dedicated to St. James the Less. The name stuck to the palace and in time infected the entire area. Henry had the swamp drained and laid out a deer park—now St. James's Park —behind his new home. But he never lived there; Anne Boleyn didn't care for it. (A man like bluff King Hal will give in to a woman's whims just so long, then chop her head off.)

Here, in time, three kings and two queens were born. On a morning in 1649 Charles I talked to his God for the last time here in the Chapel Royal and was then escorted across the park to the block. The chapel is in Ambassadors' Court, and from mid-October to Palm Sunday visitors may attend Sunday services.

Little Sam Johnson, two and a half years old, was carried to this palace by his mother to be touched by Queen Anne for the King's Evil (scrofula), but she failed to effect a cure. The queen, who was born in the palace, had a great row with Sarah, Duchess of Marlborough, her Royal Housekeeper and next-door neighbor (Marlborough House). Sarah was a great lady, born to dominate, but the queen finally decided she had been pushed around enough. "Who's queen around here?" she demanded (in effect), and ordered the duchess to give up her keys, the signs of office. In retaliation the duchess went off with the palace doorknobs. At the time, the nation was building the Duke of Marlborough the vast palace of Blenheim, and the queen, slow to anger and slow to cool, for some time held back money for finishing it.

Nell Gwyn, who was not only Charles II's mistress but wanted the world to know it, popped in one evening after the theater (she was an actress, too), and being begged by the courtiers and their ladies to display the underwear for which she was famous, obliged by raising her skirts and letting the ladies finger her petticoats, layer on layer, her green stockings, and diamonded velvet garters. The gentlemen too were impressed. The French ambassador, soberly reporting to his Foreign Office, described the scene, but unfortunately was attacked by un-Gallic reticence, and history has lost a sexy tidbit. Still, the incident was a scandal of 1675.

When you turn your back on the palace and its wound-up sentries, you look up St. James's Street. Its four short blocks are lined with buildings that have seen a deal of high-life gambling and revelry. On the right, as you go up toward Piccadilly, are some eighteenth-century shops. A narrow passage between two of them takes you into Pickering Place, a tiny courtyard. Those solid, mansionlike buildings you see on both sides of the street are the famous clubs, too lordly to identify themselves: the Union, the Bath, the Carlton, Brooks's, Boodle's, White's, and the Devonshire. Some were fashionable gambling hells. White's, at No. 37, is the oldest. It began in the seventeenth century as a coffee house. The twentieth-century visitor's friend, the BTA, is at 64–65. Christie's auction rooms are in King Street, just off St. James's. More about Christie's in the section on Route Six.

Coming back, turn into Pall Mall. Named after the French game of *paille-maille*, as noted earlier, it is Englished as *pell-mell*, but you will find it as often pronounced *pawl mawl*. At the corner of St. James's and Pall Mall, Jonathan Swift used to collect his letters from his dear Stella at the St. James's Coffee House (long gone); the post office across the way wasn't in existence then. Alexander Pope, and John Gay who wrote *The Beggar's Opera*, knew the street well, this other broad street of clubland.

The St. James's part of town was built up early in the eighteenth century, and ever since has been preeminently the fashionable male quarter. In their *Tatler* and *Spectator* (you had a dose of them in your high school or college Eng. Lit., remember?) Addison and Steele wrote of and for the coffee houses. Jermyn Street with its elegant men's shops runs parallel to Piccadilly and just south of it. Pleasant St. James's Square lies just north of Pall Mall. From No.

31 at the southeast corner (Norfolk House), General Eisenhower
and his Allied commanders launched the Normandy invasion.
Many homes carry tablets; plaques are thick all through this district.

Pall Mall sports as many exclusive clubs as does St. James's
Street. The most famous is the Athenaeum, Britain's leading literary club, that white palace with the Greek frieze above. This stands
at the corner of Waterloo Place, from which Lower Regent Street
runs up to Piccadilly Circus. Most of Waterloo Place's monuments
and memorials, including the Florence Nightingale statue, have to
do not with Waterloo but with the Crimean unpleasantness of a
century or so ago. The Place ends in the Duke of York Steps,
going down to the Mall, on which you can return to the parapet
on Trafalgar Square.

Why does the Duke of York deserve a monument that for height
and site ranks him with Nelson? He happened to be Commander-
in-Chief of the Army. The monument is really a tribute to the
British soldier, who was docked a day's pay toward its cost. It's
strange they didn't reserve the top for Wellington, the hero of
Waterloo.

*ROUTE ONE EXTENSION* ✳ The ramble, so far, is
hardly a day's work. If your curiosity about London has merely
been whetted, explore the Far West of the tourist's London.

From Buckingham Palace the street called Constitution Hill goes
to Hyde Park Corner, running between Buckingham Palace Gardens and Green Park. There's little to be said for Green Park. It
is *not* the garden of the Ritz Hotel, which is alongside it on Piccadilly. In the 1700s this was a desolate space and therefore a favorite
dueling ground. When Mayfair began to bloom, the park was
brushed and combed and became a promenade—the dueling
ground of fashion. Now it is an expanse of tended grass that helps
keep the West End fresh.

Hyde Park Corner with its Wellington Arch is the main traffic
torrent of London. In the rush hour it is a place to stay away from.
Piccadilly ends here. Its last building before the Corner is Apsley
House—No. 1, London, an address of distinction awarded the Iron
Duke; he lived there after Waterloo had made him the man of the
century. The house is now a Wellington museum. Wellington rides
his horse Copenhagen on an island in front of it.

Hyde Park Corner is the classic gateway into 360-acre Hyde Park and famous Rotten Row. Add Kensington Gardens, which adjoins on the west, and you have more than 600 acres of landscaped greenery with an artificial lake.

Belgravia is a fashionable residential district south of Hyde Park Corner, named after Belgrave Square, one of London's finest. Aristocratic buildings in the Regency style surround it. Three dukes used to live here: Kent, Norfolk, and Bedford. The district has a wealth of Georgian and Regency houses.

Next west is Knightsbridge, a bustling district named after its main thoroughfare. It contains specialty and luxury shops and Harrods, the upper-class Selfridge's. Scan the horizon to the southwest and you should be able to make out the eighteen-story Carlton Tower hotel on nearby Cadogan Place, a recent American de luxe contribution to London hoteliering. The lobby is a work of art; the colorful Rib Room is an excellent place for lunch. Cadogan Place is London's largest square (oblong).

South of Knightsbridge, between long, broad, imposing King's Road and the Thames, lies the interesting quarter of Chelsea, which has kept its distinct character of a small town within the metropolis. Long favored by writers and artists, it has handsome and quaint old houses, many of which bear plaques, for within lived such creators as Thomas Carlyle and his Jane, Leigh Hunt, the painters Whistler and Sargent, Oscar Wilde, George Eliot, Dante Gabriel Rossetti, Henry James, Tobias Smollett, Mrs. Gaskell, and Ellen Terry. By all means stroll the Chelsea Embankment. It extends from Chelsea Bridge to Battersea Bridge, and its best stretch is Cheyne (*Chaney*) Walk, with delightful houses. Others stand in Cheyne Row, Upper Cheyne Row, Tite Street, and Lawrence Street.

Visit the Carlyle house at 24 Cheyne Row. The National Trust keeps it as it was, with the Carlyles' furniture and even the makeshift shower Carlyle rigged up, the kitchen where Carlyle and Tennyson spent hours in talk, and the garden. It's open weekdays 10 to 6 or until dark, whichever comes first.

The easiest way into and out of Chelsea is the Sloane Square Underground station. Above ground at that point is the Royal Court Theater, a shrine for drama lovers because here Harley Granville-Barker produced the early Shaw plays. Chelsea Royal Hospital, with colorfully uniformed pensioners to take you round, is south of the square on the Embankment.

Those two new fourteen-story apartment buildings you can't avoid seeing are barracks—yes, of the most *moderne*—for the men and families of the élite Household Brigade and its bands. They're the olde-uniformed chaps who guard Buckingham Palace and other royal institutions, and make London parades a joy to behold.

West of Knightsbridge, to return to our main axis, you enter the upper-middle-class residential areas of Brompton and South Kensington. As you come to the end of Kensington Road and the beginning of Kensington Gore, you may be startled by the fantastic canopied Albert Memorial honoring that Number-1 Victorian, Vicky's husband, the chief spirit in developing this area devoted to the arts and sciences. On the south side of the road is the Royal Albert Hall, where concerts and large meetings take place practically every day of the year. South of that is the Victoria and Albert Museum, a vast building containing one of the richest hoards of significant objects in the world. Round about are other museums, the Royal College of Music, and the Royal Geographic Society. The Brompton Oratory, of special interest to Roman Catholics, is a church in ornate Italian Baroque style.

Here you are, then, on the western frontier of the stranger's London, with London Airport beyond, across the desert of residential quarters. The lure, aside from some pleasant squares, is at the west end of Kensington Gardens: Kensington Palace.

William of Orange (William III of Britain, called in to take over when James II had tried the British too far) liked open spaces and comfort. He suffered from asthma. Kensington was his choice —it was far more open then, late in the seventeenth century—and his palace was built around a country house he bought from an earl. His successors, Georges I and II, lived there. George III moved the royal nest to Kew Gardens, and commuted between that and Buckingham House. Then his fourth son, the Duke of Kent, Prinny's youngest brother, came home from a Continental junket with a pregnant wife and empty pockets. The couple arrived breathless—hurry, hurry, so that the child will be born in England, and so insured of its possible succession to the throne. They were hastily moved into Kensington Palace.

That is how a girl-baby named Alexandrina Victoria came to be born here in 1819. It was here in her bedroom eighteen years later that she wrote in her diary in a neat round hand: "20th June.—I was awoke at 6 o'clock by Mama. . . ." She was hustled downstairs in her dressing gown to be informed "that my poor uncle, the King, was no more, and had expired at 12 minutes p. 2 this morning, and consequently that I am *Queen*."

The Archbishop of Canterbury and the Marquis of Conyngham had leaped into a landau and driven at breakneck pace through London to Kensington, arriving at the palace at five in the morning. They almost broke down the door trying to get in, and once in had to wait. A severe maid told them that the princess was in a sweet sleep and could not be disturbed. Two old gentlemen making a great clatter and a scene to get a girl up at five o'clock in the morning! Really! But after an hour's expostulation they had their way, and by that time Vicky had probably had a chance to wash her face, brush her teeth, comb her hair, and put on her very best *peignoir*. Thus began a long and momentous reign of sixty-four years—during the first day of which, by the way, the Queen's style was Alexandrina Victoria. After twenty-four hours this was changed to plain Victoria, and all the oaths and paper-work had to be done over again.

Her bedroom and staircase are in the part of the palace today given over to the London Museum, and in what is now the museum's entrance hall she held her first council of ministers.

Various royal relatives occupy apartments in Kensington Palace. The two lower floors, which in their time were granted to the impoverished parents-to-be of a great queen, are occupied by the London Museum. Admission is free. Above them are the old state apartments designed by Wren.

The museum's exhibits tell the story of London life from prehistoric times to only yesterday. It is an intimate museum filled with objects of everyday use—toys, beer mugs, jewelry, sedan chairs, early bicycles and telephones, and period costumes. There are also royal robes and wedding gowns, and a twenty-seven-foot diorama of London as seen from St. Paul's. You can visit the state apartments and, greatest treat of all, Victoria's anteroom, nursery, and bedroom. The gardens are formal, but lovely.

# ROUTE TWO

Whitehall,
the Houses of
Parliament, and
Westminster Abbey

Down Whitehall from Charles' bronze horse in Charing Cross to the bottom of Parliament Square, is half a mile—a tremendous 880 yards, climaxed by the Houses of Parliament and the Abbey. Few inhabited places have seen so much or mean so much.

Whitehall takes its name from a forgotten royal palace. When Henry VIII seized Wolsey's York House for himself and Anne Boleyn he built a grand and complex palace all round it and called it Whitehall. In it he was married to his "darlyng"; in it he died. In 1619 a careless laundress set off a fire that burned much of it to the ground. In 1698 another fire finished what the French diarist Saint-Simon called "the biggest and most hideous palace in the whole of Europe." He added, "The kings are now lodged pretty miserably in St. James's Palace." Of Whitehall is left a building, Inigo Jones's Banqueting Hall (now the United Services Museum, and visitable), and the names and locations of the Horse Guards and Scotland Yard.

This half-mile is the Pennsylvania Avenue of nation, Empire, and Commonwealth. The view down it is crowned by the great parliamentary clock tower. Visitors are drawn to the Horse Guards, and as long as daylight lasts the cameras click as the helpless, gorgeously uniformed Guards sit their sleek horses, motionless as statues. What if a fly alights on a nose, a leg gets pins and needles? Daily at 11 A.M. (10 on Sunday) you can watch their Changing of the Guard; dismounted inspection comes at 4 P.M.

A second attraction is Downing Street. The Prime Minister's home and office at No. 10, the Chancellor of the Exchequer's at

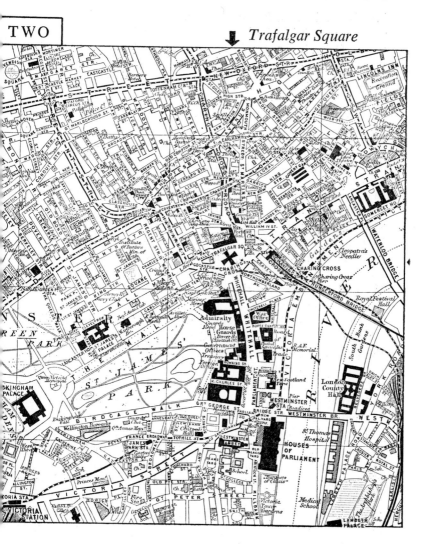

## TWO

*Trafalgar Square*

No. 11, and that of the Government Whip (a sort of majority leader of the Commons) are very casually guarded by a constable or two. Not much to see except Georgian façades.

Technically Whitehall ends here and the rest is Parliament Street. Islanded at this point stands the Cenotaph, commemorating the servicemen, known and unknown, who died in the two world wars. It is inscribed simply *To the Glorious Dead.* Reference to the Deity is omitted in deference to the variety of religions among the peoples under British rule.

New Scotland Yard looms through Derby Gate opposite King Charles Street. This is Metropolitan Police headquarters—not only of detective inspectors of the C.I.D. but also of the rank-and-filer, the bobby—

> The finest thing in London is the bobby,
> Benignant information is his hobby.

We didn't list him under Useful Addresses because his office is wherever he happens to be, under his helmet. He is not weighed down by armaments like the American city cop. Over the years we have encountered only two bobbies who were gruff. The second time was when we asked one near the Tower what the crowd and excitement were about and he said it was none of our business. We said, "Whatever is the world coming to?"

"What do you mean?" he asked heavily.

"That we should encounter a London bobby who was rude."

"*Awr!*" he growled, and turned away—to hide his confusion, we think. Having hid it he turned back. "It's the Duke of Gloucester come to open somethink," he said. We thanked him kindly.

Oh—why *Scotland* Yard? Because in Whitehall Palace days here was a subpalace used by Scottish kings when they visited London. In England a name is pretty much for keeps.

To your left, Westminster Bridge spans the Thames. You may like to go part-way across for the views, especially that of the river façade, about 890 feet long, of the Houses of Parliament.

Many assume that these glorious buildings (their official name is New Palace of Westminster) are ancient. They are in fact weathered Victorian, slightly more than a century old. Whenever one feels like sneering at the Victorians—and they did create some ugly structures—one should remember that they managed this. Compare the County Hall on the opposite bank of the Thames, a job in Contemporary Nameless.

The parliamentary complex stands on the site of the medieval Palace of Westminster, home of sovereign and court from the time of Edward the Confessor (eleventh century) until restless Henry

VIII moved to Whitehall. Then the Lords and Commons were permitted to use it. Incredible it seems, but the ancient palace was there until 1834. In that year a workman assigned to burn old tax receipts let the job get out of hand, and that was the end of it.

But not entirely. As you approach from Whitehall the first building is Westminster Hall, put up in 1097 by William Rufus, the Conqueror's son. It was the great hall of the palace where important affairs were transacted, such as state trials and coronation banquets. The most historic structure in England, it has borne a charmed life, spared not only by fires but by the Nazi bombs that demolished the House of Commons. Other survivors are the crypt of St. Stephen's chapel and a part of the cloisters.

Westminster Hall is grand and awesome. It is part of the Houses of Parliament guided tour, Saturdays ten to four. The guides are excellent. But you can visit the great hall by itself between 10 A.M. and one hour before Parliament sits (which generally means Monday through Thursday, ten to one-thirty), and from ten to four when it is not in session.

One other piece of old Westminster Palace survives: the Jewel Tower, across the street from the Parliament entrance and next to the Abbey. It has been altered and can be skipped.

A pier on the Embankment by the bridge is served by Thames sightseeing steamers.

From the north side of Parliament Square, that green rectangle, the view is one of the finest in London, or anywhere. Whitehall is behind you. On your right (you're facing south) you see Middlesex Guildhall and beyond it St. James's Park. On your left is the bridge. Directly in front of you is St. Margaret's, church of the House of Commons and a good place to rest the feet. St. Margaret's has for centuries been London's fashionable church for weddings: Pepys, Milton, and Winston Churchill were among those married there. Behind it looms Westminster Abbey's northern length. Very close to you should be the replica of St. Gaudens' famous statue of Abraham Lincoln, the original of which stands in Chicago's Lincoln Park. On your left rise

## § *THE HOUSES OF PARLIAMENT*

There are eight acres of buildings grouped around eleven court-yards. Inside are nearly eleven hundred rooms, a hundred staircases, and two miles of some of the draftiest corridors in England. Not even long-time inmates are familiar with the maze. An M.P. of thirty years' service was astounded one day to see a workman come out of the woodwork. There was a hidden door in the paneling. Besides the chambers of the Lords and Commons there are offices, service rooms, committee rooms, interviewing rooms, dining rooms, libraries, bars, lobbies, and galleries.

About Big Ben (if you want to be one up on people): it is nei-ther the clock nor the tower. It is the 13½-ton bell whose toll, opening the BBC's "This is London calling" all through the Blitz, symbolized Britain's fortitude. You'll also be one up on the local wits who have named the still larger clock of the Shell-Mex build-ing on the Embankment "Big Benzine."

The Houses of Parliament suffered fourteen direct hits in Nazi air raids, plus one bomb that crashed into the House of Lords but failed to go off. Damage has been repaired.

Excellent as the guides are, they can't tell you all. So we give you some

*FACTS PLAIN AND FANCY* ✳ There are interest-ing differences between the Houses of Parliament and the House and Senate of the U.S. Congress. First, the House of Lords.

The peers of the realm, at this writing, number 883, of whom 850 have a right to sit in the chamber. From fifty to seventy actu-ally exercise this right, and only about twenty-five or thirty attend faithfully. Three constitutes a quorum. The Lords receive no salary but are paid the equivalent of about nine dollars for expense money when attending, plus transportation. A peer who lives in London can collect thirty cents' fare for the Underground.

In robes, blazing orders, and coronets the peers make a brave show when the monarch opens Parliament, but little voice in gov-erning remains to them. When an M.P. is awarded a title, he is thought to be kicked upstairs. M.P. Anthony Wedgwood-Benn put up a fight *not* to inherit his father's title because it automatically excluded him from the Commons.

Alas, the romance has gone out of the peerage. About a third of the existing titles were created since 1900. Baron Adams, ennobled in 1949, chose *Labor Conquers All* (in Latin) as his motto under heraldic arms of cogwheels rampant, a miner holding a lamp and pickaxe, and a pitchfork-wielding farmer. A former official of the Northern Gas Board, he is a far cry from A. A. Milne's Sir Brian who had "a battle-axe with great big knobs on, and went among the villagers and blipped them on the head."

There may not any longer be enough blue blood among the Lords to create a blueblood bank. But they have a fine, cavalier-like rule for stopping a bore. Any lord can rise and move "that the Noble Lord be no more heard."

They open debate obliquely. Someone moves for "the papers." That starts things. The papers never appear. There are no papers.

Since the Prime Minister is the rough equivalent of the American President in addition to being the responsible head of the legislative body, it can be said that the House of Commons pulls more governmental weight than Congress does.

Most national legislatures meet in amphitheaters; the party designations *Right*, *Center*, and *Left* derive from the seating in such semicircular bowls. But in Britain the M.P.s face each other, the party in power on one side, the opposition on the other. The Speaker, presiding officer and umpire, sits high up between them like an officiating priest. The arrangement is said to derive from the time when the Commons sat in St. Stephen's Chapel, in the choir.

Parliament is rife with cultural hangovers or fossils. Moss is the stuff that keeps England green and wonderful.

Note the red line that runs along the floor beside the two front benches. An M.P. who steps over his red line commits a foul. It seldom happens, and then by accident, but when it does the other side cries "Order! Order!" The culprit (he may be the Prime Minister himself) becomes rattled, wonders what he has done, is told, pulls his foot back, and apologizes.

The lines are two swords' lengths apart, and they were fixed in days when gentlemen wore swords and might become so emotional as to pink one another in the heat of debate. In the French and Italian assemblies—and even in Congress—legislators have assaulted one another, but it isn't any longer the done thing in Parliament.

And, although swords haven't been worn for almost two centuries, the pegs in the Commons' cloakroom still bear looped red tapes from which the swords, when no longer allowed in the chamber, were suspended.

Even verbal assault is restricted. A guide to parliamentary usage lists the forbidden epithets. Among them are *ruffian, villain, windbag, Pharisee, hypocritical lover of liberty, hooligan, blackguard,* and *slanderer.* Among new ones added since the war are *cheat, stool pigeon, bastard,* and "not a damned one of you opposite." Each of these was ruled out by the Speaker when first uttered. When the Speaker decides that a member is abusive, he calls him to order. If the member refuses to withdraw or apologize, he can be shut up in the clock tower.

A certain dignity characterizes parliamentary debate, punctuated with passages of high emotion or hilarity. A member, even when cutting the opposition to ribbons with the rapier of his tongue, refers to him as "the Honorable gentleman." A lawyer is Honorable and learned; a soldier or ex-soldier, Honorable and gallant. "Sir" often crops up, and refers to women as well as men. When Dr. Edith Summerskill, in the Labour cabinet, playfully objected to being sirred by Churchill, he honorably and gallantly acquitted himself with "Man embraces woman."

Princess Margaret used to visit the House to listen and watch from the gallery. The Glasgow *Bulletin* reported her as declaring that the House gave her a chance to see human nature in the raw!

Remember when in the Commons that you are where the monarch may never set foot. The last one to do so was inept Charles I. Storming in to demand that five censorious M.P.s be turned over to him, he laid violent hands on the Speaker and usurped his Chair. Where were the five?

Mr. Speaker, kneeling to his king and wondering if his last hour hadn't come, replied that he was blind and deaf to everything but the dictates of the House.

The five had meanwhile got away to the City by boat. Charles, in pursuit, burst in on the Lord Mayor and Council at Guildhall.

The City fathers heard him respectfully—and replied with silence, utter and profound. Charles went away fuming. It was the beginning of his end. He had shown himself incapable of understanding that an English king could no longer be a tyrant.

The story is recorded in a mural in the central lobby.

Mr. Speaker is a very important person. He must be impartial, and his decisions are final. The Commons elects him from one of their number. When nominated, he rises and shakes his fist at nominator and seconder, indicating clearly that he doesn't want the post. Each then takes him by an arm and conducts him to the Chair.

This sham reluctance goes back to those days of Charles I, and earlier, when being Speaker was dangerous.

The ceremony surrounding the man and the office is something we hope you'll have a chance to witness. You are standing in the lobby when a constable on duty shouts, "Mace! Hats off, strangers!" In marches a Messenger of the House wearing tails, a chain of office, and a medallion of Mercury. After him comes the Serjeant-at-Arms in silk court dress, carrying the famous fourteen-pound silver-gilt mace on his shoulder. Mr. Speaker follows, dressed in gown, full-bottomed wig, knee breeches, and buckled shoes, and attended by his train-bearer, chaplain, and secretary. When Parliament is in session this happens at the opening of each day's sitting, just before 2:30 P.M. Monday through Thursday, and 11 A.M. on Friday.

The mace is the symbol of the Commons' powers. In the House it must rest on its rack on the central table. If it's not there no business can be done. Once a member who wanted to stop debate, effectively did so by seizing the mace and running off with it.

About 10 P.M., except when the business is extraordinary, the House begins to adjourn. A Government leader rises to move "that this House do now adjourn." If you think the members will now get up and head for the door, you haven't learned about moss. This is only a signal opening a new phase of debate. After about half an hour of this, Mr. Speaker declares the House adjourned, and it finally is.

Instantly the light in the clock tower is switched off, informing London that the great talk-shop has put up its shutters. Inside, a constable on duty shouts, "Who goes home?" a cry that has been heard here for almost three hundred years and tells of times when streets were unsafe and citizens out late traveled in groups and often with an armed retainer as protection from Mack the Knife and other cutpurses and cutthroats.

The opening of Parliament in November is a royal pageant. As the Queen is not allowed in the Commons' part of the building, the scene is the House of Lords. It is a beautiful sight. The peers (even those who don't bother to attend sessions are here for *this*) are in full court dress, ablaze with decorations and orders. The ladies wear their finest gowns and all the jewelry they can hang on or pin up. The bishops and judges are robed. The ladies-and gentlemen-in-waiting and the gentlemen-at-arms make a brave show, and the heralds of the College of Arms are conspicuous in their scarlet tabards.

The Lord Chancellor in black and gold kneels and hands Her Majesty her own Gracious Speech from the Throne. This message was written by the Commons, by the leaders of the party in power.

Her Majesty looks at her Message and requests that her Honorable and Loyal Commons be summoned.

The Gentleman Usher of the Black Rod leaves the Lords and walks along the corridor to the Commons. When he is near enough, the Honorable Commons slam the door in his face. They have been keeping it open in order to accomplish this. Black Rod taps the door three times. (Note Honorable bruises on door.)

A little window opens in the door; the Serjeant-at-Arms verifies that Black Rod has brought no soldiers with him and is unarmed. The wicket closes, the door is opened, Black Rod enters, bows to Mr. Speaker, then to left and right, and delivers his message. The Serjeant takes the mace and leads the way to the Lords, the Commons marching two by two, headed by the Prime Minister and the Leader of the Opposition. As many crowd into the Lords as can find room—not many, since the place is already almost full. The rest go to the Commons smoking room and listen on the public-address system.

When the Queen has read the speech, the Commons troop back to their own House where, just to show the Crown that they don't have to obey, at least not right away, they take up a meaningless, long-dead document, the Clandestine Outlawries Bill. The point having been made, Mr. Speaker informs the House that "for greater accuracy" he has obtained a "copy of the Royal Speech," and reads it. It is now official. The House adjourns; the fireworks of debate will begin the next day.

The caution over the approach of Black Rod, like the sham shyness of Mr. Speaker on his nomination, points back to dangerous times when a slow revolution was taking place, the merchant class cutting down the privileges of the Crown and nobility and beginning to take over the running of things. The fuss about the mace, Mr. Speaker's processional, the costumes, bowings, and other ceremonials, are survivals of attempts to invest the New Men with an aura of dignity and respect to parallel that of royalty.

Lockers line the corridors of the House of Commons. Every M.P. has a locker—his very own!—2'6" by 1'3" by 1'. This is his office. But he can't fit his visiting constituents into it. He sees them in one of the interviewing rooms; when these are occupied, he talks with them on benches in the central lobby. He reads up on bills, prepares speeches, and dictates his letters wherever he can find room, sharing a stenographer with one or more members.

Compare the American legislator's high standard of living. He occupies a suite of five rooms (six, in the new marble Senate Office Building—which cost $24,500,000) with telephones and two or three lavatories. The Honorable Senator drinks bottled water (Uncle Sam picking up the tab) and can get out of air-conditioned coolth to a sun roof equipped with showers.

An M.P. queues up for the lobby or smoking-room telephones. For air-conditioning he has the drafts. But he has the boon of the Thames-side terrace; the greatest treat he can offer an important visitor is tea on the terrace.

The congressman's telephone and telegraph bills are paid, his mail goes out postage-free, he has a $1200 allowance for stationery and office expenses, and $20,000 a year for office staff. On this payroll he may (and ninety congressmen did, on last count) include relatives. The M.P. gets a petty income-tax allowance for postage and secretarial help.

When an American congressman travels, not only to and from Congress but also on investigative and other chores, the government gives him forty cents a mile. The M.P. gets a round-trip ticket on the railway: one per session.

The congressman's salary is $22,500 a year; the M.P.'s $2800.

You can estimate, conservatively, that in salary and perquisites the statesman of Capitol Hill receives well over ten times as much as his British cousin. Recently a congressman collected $6,082 for expenses on a thirty-eight-day tour abroad—$160.05 a day!

Interesting to a tourist-taxpayer, isn't it?

# § WESTMINSTER ABBEY

Once long, long ago, the Thames, along with the Tyburn, the Fleet, and other lesser streams now well underground, made marsh-lands all the way to St. James's Park. A heavily used road ran through the marshes and right into the Thames where it happened to be shallow. The road emerged to cut across a large island —Thorney Island it was called—and then went into the shallow river again; on the other side it continued as the Roman road to Dover. This was a very important place, because it was the only spot at which the unbridged Thames was easily fordable.

The island had a church as far back as anyone knows. A church and a monastery at a ford was a resting and thanksgiving place for travelers—a holy hostel.

In time the Thames was banked and narrowed, the channel deepened. The marshes dried up and the island became part of the mainland. By then a Benedictine abbey with church was well established. Its domain was called Westminster; that is, West Monastery, the monastery west of the City of London. Westminster was the first part of London to grow up outside the City walls. It is thought to have had a royal palace as well as an abbey in the time of King Canute. Certainly there was a palace in the first half of the eleventh century, for Edward the Confessor died in the "painted room" of Westminster Palace.

The pious Edward was a Saxon king, but he had been brought up in Normandy. His mother was Norman. About 1050 he had the old buildings pulled down, having imported Norman masons to build a church that would rival Normandy's cathedrals.

He finished it just in time for his burial in it and for William the Conqueror to be crowned in it. As the first great Norman-style church erected in England, it helped inspire the fantastic building boom in monasteries and cathedrals. But it was almost entirely rebuilt in Early English Gothic in the thirteenth and fourteenth centuries, and this is the abbey church one sees today.

All but two of the British sovereigns from 1066 (William of Normandy) to 1953 (Elizabeth II) were crowned in the Abbey. Almost every sovereign, from 1272 to 1760, is buried (with his consort, if any) in this most considerable royal burial ground in the world. As for lesser folk, to be buried here has been from time out of mind the greatest posthumous honor the nation could bestow.

Babes royal were christened, and later married, here. The wedding of Princess Margaret gave the TV-watching world a chance to see the Abbey in its glory.

It's a magnificent church. That is the impression you are bound to have as soon as you step inside and look down the length of the nave. But the impression will fade. The first monument your eye meets begins the process of erosion. It's the Tomb of the Unknown Warrior. The inscription is wordy; in contrast to the chaste Cenotaph in Whitehall, which respects the possibility that the anonymous soldier may have been Moslem, Jew, Buddhist, or Zoroastrian, this tablet is exclusively Christian.

To your right and left the tombs march—field marshals, statesmen, missionaries, empire-builders, an admiral, Major André, assorted earls. You stumble along, and it's not the Abbey you're seeing but tombs and *In Memoriams*. Aisles, chapels, nave, and sanctuary, floors and walls, are cluttered, as if in a stone-and-marble museum of obituaries. Everybody who was anybody seems to be here. And others too. In former times a comparative nobody could have a tablet in the Abbey if his status-seeking heirs paid the fee.

Westminster Abbey is a vast intramural cemetery.

It is these tombs, and especially the memorials in the Poet's Corner, that draw the crowds. Chaucer's is a fine one, but a Duke of Argyll has intruded with a rococo monument outshining that of "Guglielmo" Shakespeare a few yards away. (Why that Italian rendering of the good English *William?*) Walter Scott's bust is almost hidden behind a legendary figure on Argyll's reredos. But Scott wouldn't have minded; that man loved a lord.

"Look out. You're standing on Dickens!"

"Look out yourself, you're on Thomas Hardy."

Longfellow, represented by a bust, is the only American.

Shakespeare had to wait 124 years to achieve his monument. On his marble scroll some words of his speak out with uncanny pre-science of our own fissionable world:

> The cloud-capt towers
> The gorgeous palaces
> The great globe itself
> Yea, all which it inherit
>        Shall dissolve
> And like the baseless fabric of a vision
> Leave not a wreck behind.

Tomb-shopping is interesting while the feet hold out. Before yours give way you'll want to find:
The shabby Coronation Chair with the Stone of Scone under it.
The Henry VII Lady Chapel with its superb fan-vaulting.
The chapels on each side of the Henry VII, with Elizabeth I on the north and Mary Queen of Scots on the south. Mary has a mar-velous lion at her feet, providing humorous relief from the stony landscape's funereality. He's a small red beast, erect, pugnacious, and grand, sitting on one crown and wearing another. His tail is draped over a thigh. For a mane he has a wealth of gold tresses. A cross hangs down to act as a figleaf. He holds a sword in one paw, a fleur-de-lis in the other. His leonine face is so fierce, and he's so very red-and-gold, that we wonder red-haired Queen Elizabeth didn't filch him for her own.

Mary's lion is our favorite discovery. Like everyone else, you will have yours. Here's another we fancied, an *In Memoriam:*

Dame Grace Gethin, wife of Sir Richard Gethin, who being adorned with all Graces and perfections of mind and body crowned them all with exemplary patience and Humility and having ye day before her death moft devoutly received ye Holy communion w'ch fhe faid fhe would not have omitted for ten thousand words fhe plainly evidenced her sure and certain hope of future blifs and thus continuing fenfible to the last fhe refined her pious Soul to God in fervent transports of Spiritual ioy and comfort for her neer approach to the Heavenly Glory. 1697. 21 years old.

The largest tomb is the ugliest: the multiple Hunsdon. It has drums, spindles, halberds, spears, corselet, complete suit of armor, tassels, feathers, caduceus, fruit, two nude female torsos, assorted shields, helmets, obelisks—all gilt and silver, marble and stone. "How do you like your vulgar blue-eyed milords, Mister Death?"

Every time we've dropped in, Abbey housekeeping was going on. Workers on scaffolding clean years of grime from upper stonework. Overalled men tote wheelbarrows of boards and props. An immense roll of red carpeting is swept for some grand ceremony. A smocked artist renews with a fine brush the black lettering on a fading monument. The contrast between scrubbed and grimy is startling.

NOTE. If you are more than tomb-serious about the Abbey, buy Westlake's "New Guide to Westminster Abbey," on sale just outside. Its floor plans are a great help.

Leave the church by the south aisle, go along the east cloister walk, and turn sharp left for the Chapter House. At its door you don felt slippers over your shoes so as not to subject the tiles of A.D. 1250 to wear. The octagonal chamber is beautiful. The Commons met here before moving to St. Stephen's Chapel.

Then back to the east cloister, along a few steps, and into the Chapel of the Pyx. Pyx sounds mysterious, but it's only an old word for box or chest. Here it meant the treasure chest where the standard coins and their dies were kept. The room and the adjoining Undercroft (small admission charge) are the oldest parts of the fabric—early Norman. The Undercroft is a museum of fascinating old wax and wooden effigies of kings and queens.

From the Undercroft you can go on to the eleventh-century Little (or Dark) Cloister, which leads into the yard of Westminster School, a public school using the patched-up old monastery buildings. Where Eton has its annual muddy wall game, Westminster's traditional scramble concerns a pancake. On Shrove Tuesday the cook tosses a pancake among the boys and the one who emerges with the largest fragment gets a guinea from the Dean. Among the famous who as youths fought the pancake fight are Hakluyt the geographer, Ben Jonson (now in Poet's Corner), many other poets, Warren Hastings, Gibbon the historian, and Charles Wesley the composer of Methodist hymns.

Wander about the Abbey precincts: the Great Cloister, Abbot's Courtyard, Deanery, Jericho Parlour, and Dean's Yard. You can hardly hear the reverberations of Parliament Square's traffic. It is here, in these quiet spaces and odd passages, that you begin to understand that Westminster Abbey was a monastery. The church is not the Abbey, but the Abbey's church. All monasteries were dissolved—the Dissolution, this is called in English history—by Henry VIII and put to various secular uses. So now the tail wags the dog; when one thinks of Westminster Abbey, it is of the church.

## § ODDS AND ENDS

Aside from St. Margaret's church and the Jewel Tower, there is the Middlesex Guildhall, a minor sight. It's a modern building in Renaissance style with some interesting rooms and a history. A folder sold within tells all about it, with illustrations.

A final item:

The Tate Gallery is handy—on the Thames between the Lambeth and Vauxhall bridges, south of the Abbey and Parliament. It has an outstanding collection of modern and contemporary painting and sculpture; it is open, free, weekdays 10 to 6, Sundays 2 to 6. Its restaurant has colorful murals by Rex Whistler; lunch from 12 to 3, snacks earlier and later.

# ROUTE THREE

## The Strand,

## Fleet Street,

## St. Paul's

With palaces and Parliament tucked away, you are now ready for the London that requires an effort of the imagination. From the rear of Charles I's horse in Trafalgar Square, take the wide street off the southeast corner, called the Strand.

Before setting out, however, there's something you need to know.

Old London—the London of Elizabeth I and Shakespeare, and of much earlier times—consisted of two separate entities. The first, with a simplicity that underlines its preeminence more than anything else could do, was "the City." A rabbit-warren of timbered, gabled houses and shops on narrow, jumbled streets, alleys, and lanes, it followed the river in a solidly built-up arc from the high, stony castle called the Tower. It was a vigorous, hard-working port town and mercantile center. Its most distinguished citizens were its merchants, who governed through a lord mayor and aldermen and through the guilds of their trades. It stopped where the Thames begins its broad bend.

The second—Westminster—lay on the curve and dived south with the river. More open, with its parks and gardens and leisured elegance, it was populated by courtiers and a multitude of royal servants and hangers-on. This was the royal and noble town outside the City's ancient walls. Your starting-point of Trafalgar Square used to be occupied by the royal mews, the stables of the king's thousand or so horses.

One street, the Strand, connected the two towns, changing its name when it entered the City. The leading noblemen had their town houses on the south side, with orchards and gardens running down to their private river steps where their canopied barges lay. The river was the important thoroughfare. At the bottom of lanes public watermen waited for fares, like taxis at stands today. The names of the side streets remind one of the ducal past: Lancaster, Somerset, Norfolk, Arundel, Essex, Villiers.

Today's Strand is only a busy modern street; its architecture has no distinction or unity, and it is certainly shabbier than it was in the Gay Nineties and Edwardian times, when hansom cabs plied among its theaters. A few theaters still linger. In one of them, the rebuilt Savoy, the Gilbert and Sullivan operettas enchanted Londoners and gave the company the name *Savoyards*.

There's a lot of Savoy here. The celebrated Savoy Hotel is next to the playhouse. A Savoy Street descends to the Embankment. On it is the royal heraldic Chapel of the Savoy, dating from 1505 but rebuilt in Victorian times after a fire. You might just look in. It is left over from a thirteenth-century palace Henry III gave to his wife's uncle, Count of Savoy (in what is now France). The chapel alone remains, but the name has stuck. Chaucer was probably married in the chapel. Wyclif preached in it.

Note Southampton Street opposite the hotel. Its two short blocks bring you to Covent Garden, the famous fruit-vegetable market (early morning visit, if any), the Covent Garden Theater, and the actor's Church of St. Paul (*not* the cathedral), backdrop to the street scene of Eliza Doolittle's first encounter with Professor Higgins (*Pygmalion, My Fair Lady*). When Covent Garden was laid out as an elegant square about 1632, it became the focal point of the first great fashionable exodus out of old London into what became the West End.

On the Strand the huge office block of Somerset House replaces the mansion of the villainous Duke of Somerset who got control of the royal children when Henry VIII died. Durham House, willed by Henry to Princess Elizabeth for her town house, must have stood next to it. Somerset took it, but his enjoyment of it terminated abruptly with the loss of his head. The present Somerset House is the government office of vital statistics and records. Here the Scotland Yard man comes to look up the marriage and birth certificates that identify an unknown heir and the murder motive;

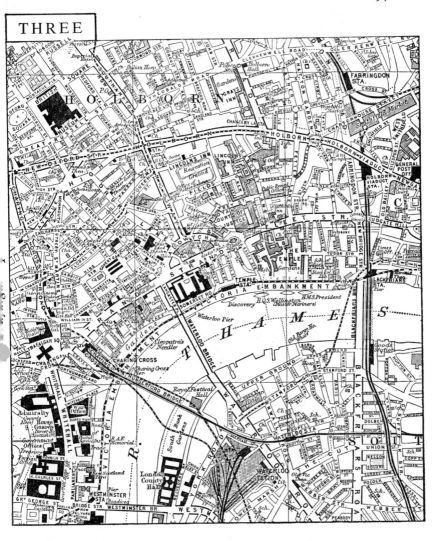

here comes the scholar to see with his own eyes the will in which
Shakespeare left his wife his second-best bed.

By now you know what you're up against. If they are themselves
without visible distinction, things that stand "on the site of" are
only palely interesting. So what you keep firmly in mind as you

go along is old London and the fact that you are walking from town No. 2 to town No. 1 on the above-river road used by centuries of Londoners before you.

Two churches islanded in the street should claim your interest. The first is St. Mary-le-Strand, done by Gibbs, the same Gibbs who made St. Martin's off Trafalgar Square. The second is St. Clement Danes, a little thing Wren tossed off. Sore damaged by Hitler's obliteration squads, it is now restored—in revenge?—as the Royal Air Force church.

"Oranges and lemons say the bells of St. Clement's." This is the church of that famous peal. All the bells but one were cracked when a bomb jolted them to the ground. They have been recast by the same bell-founders, Meers and Stainbank, who in 1588 (the Armada year) cast the bell that was undamaged. There's continuity for you! St. Clement's was Dr. Johnson's church; his statue is beyond its east end.

A bit farther on the Strand becomes Fleet Street. The considerable pseudo-Gothic building is the Law Courts. That column with a griffin on top is there to let it be known that Westminster ends with it and the City begins. It is Temple Bar. *Bar* is an old word meaning gate. The City gate here was called Temple Bar after the Knights Templar built their temple (and much else) outside it in 1185. When they were expropriated and expelled in the thirteenth century, the lawyers moved in.

Now here is where you particularly need imagination.

In old London a space of a mile separated the City from Westminster. Across that space the two towns regarded each other with mutual distrust. The Temple stood between them—"a geographic position," says the historian Trevelyan, "that helped the English lawyer to discover his true political function as mediator between Crown and people."

Temple Bar was the gate most jealously guarded against the encroachments of Westminster upon the independent City. At some time unknown it was established that the sovereign must stop at Temple Bar for permission to enter the City. When the walls were torn down, a symbolic gate was erected. The column called Temple Bar is a symbol of the symbolic gate. When the sovereign enters the City on state occasions, the Lord Mayor is on hand at the Bar. He presents the City Sword. This is promptly returned, with thanks, and is carried before the sovereign so long as he or she is within the City's bounds.

The idea that Temple Bar stands for—that the monarchy has its limits—was carried across the ocean in the minds of the colonists, and in 1776 resulted in a republic. It must be remembered, however, that it took a strong gate to hold back a king. The strength of London lay in its control, amounting to monopoly, of England's commerce and money. Kings who forgot this (Charles I is the saddest example) came to a sticky end.

§ *THE TEMPLE*

Two Temples they are, side by side—Middle and Inner, divided by Middle Temple Lane. These are the greatest of the Inns of Court. No one—certainly no vacationing lawyer—should miss the Temple, if for no other reason than that here lived the Blackstone of the *Commentaries.* For six centuries it has been the general headquarters, school, library, offices, and living quarters of the men of law.

These walks and buildings have known famous men, among them Raleigh, Congreve, the diarist Evelyn, bloody Judge Jeffreys, Fielding, Sheridan, Cowper, Boswell, De Quincey, Lamb, Goldsmith, Thackeray, Dickens. Also Dr. Thorndike, Austin Freeman's fictional jurisconsult-detective.

Built around courtyards and gardens, the Temple is a sudden oasis on the borders of the Strand's chaos. Some of the eighteenth-century houses are very handsome. The Round Church is all that remains of the Knights Templar. In Middle Temple Hall Shakespeare's *Twelfth Night,* written on order for Queen Elizabeth for a state occasion, had its first performance, the Bard himself probably acting in it.

The Lord Mayor, who stops kings and queens at Temple Bar, cuts no sort of figure in the Temple. He can walk in just like you and us if he comes in his ordinary business suit, but let him try to call as Lord Mayor, with sheriffs, serjeants, mace, and mayoral robes, and he may touch off a riot. It happened in 1669, when the then Lord Mayor, invited to dinner, thoughtlessly came in state. He got inside before he was stopped. The benchers pushed him out. A serious town-gown riot was nipped by the City train-bands (militia). It happened again in 1961. Both times, His Lord-ship had to retire to Mansion House dinnerless.

You come out of the Temple into Fleet Street, named after a river that has gone underground. This was old London's street of mountebanks and Barnums. Then it became the "Street of Ink," but most of the newspaper plants are now off on side streets.

No. 1 Fleet Street is Child's Bank, London's oldest, founded in the seventeenth century. Here royalty and its mistresses banked. It had hardly opened its doors when Samuel Pepys dug up his money and valuable plate from his cellar and deposited them with Mr. Child. Before that, every time he heard a movement in the garden or a cat on the leads (tiles) he had started up in mortal fear of robbers and a cut throat.

Fleet Street's north side has since the Blitz undergone so many changes that its whole wonderful character is gone. It was a maze of lanes and passageways, surprise turnings, tiny courts. But Dr. Johnson's house in Gough Square survives. To find it you have to creep under the new Hulton Press building and look about for a sign; or ask a passing clerk or errand boy. The house is open and can be visited for a small entry fee. It looks old and nostalgic in the nonresidential City. Ye Olde Cheshire Cheese in Wine Office Court is nearby and equally hard to find. This done-over and much-touristed seventeenth century tavern-restaurant is either where the Johnson-Boswell-Garrick-Goldsmith-Reynolds set ate and talked or a reasonable facsimile.

Beyond the ancient church of St. Bride's, Fleet Street becomes Ludgate Hill and comes bump against the great portico of St. Paul's, the Cathedral of London.

# § ST. PAUL'S

The cathedral was the heart of the City, dominating the gabled houses and lesser church spires. The first Christian church known to have been here was a Saxon one of A.D. 604, and Saxon kings were buried in it. This was destroyed by fire; so was its successor. Still another was built. Lightning toppled its 500-foot spire, leaving it with a spireless great square tower 265 feet high. That cathedral was even larger than what you see now. It was one of the largest churches in the world.

When Henry VIII took England out of the Roman Catholic fold, Old St. Paul's was whittled away. The Duke of Somerset tore down the cloisters to get stones for his Strand mansion. Merchants did business in the nave and aisles, using the font as the money counter. Each pillar was an address of distinction where lawyers met clients. Out-of-work servants had a bench where they waited to be interviewed for a job. Fashionable gentlemen came to be seen, or to meet questionable women, and tailors lurked making notes of what was the rage that season. It was the place of rendezvous: "Meet you at S'Paul's." (The taxi driver now says *Spaws.*) Shakespeare was often here, sometimes on business (he dabbled in real estate), sometimes because here in his day was "the high tide of human existence."

A hundred years later the fire that started quietly in Pudding Lane ate its way west and overwhelmed St. Paul's. The present church is the work of Christopher Wren—first stone laid 1675, last stone 1710. While it was still a-building, Wren laid down a strict order forbidding anyone to use the new cathedral for profane purposes. The only profane purpose for which it is used nowadays is city clerks resting away part of their lunch hour on the west steps.

Those old Londoners must have been taken aback by Wren's stricture, but they obeyed. They were proud of their cathedral. They still are. St. Paul's means more to them than any non-Londoner can understand. During the Blitz, volunteer fire-fighters risked their lives to save it. They worked the miracle of December 29, 1940, when bombs and fire leveled acres of the City. By dawn's early light when the smoke had cleared, sooty St. Paul's was visible as never before, standing alone amid a sea of rubble. It was subsequently damaged, but not seriously.

Even to the unschooled eye it is apparent that St. Paul's belongs to an epoch and style of mind entirely different from the Abbey's Gothic. Here is a balanced, secular style, composed, cool, speaking of no great hopes or fears of the Cosmos. Religious ecstasy would be out of place in what looks more like an ecclesiastical palace than a church of God.

But it isn't Wren's fault that St. Paul's is also a pantheon of patriotism, crowded with tombs and memorials to war heroes, admirals and generals from Nelson and Wellington on. Interesting is the tale of Nelson's sarcophagus. Originally made for Cardinal Wolsey, it was appropriated by Henry VIII for his own last sleep, but, well—Nelson occupies it. What Henry occupies we can't say; he lies under the floor of St. George's Chapel at Windsor.

Lord Byron, that angry young man, insulted both St. Paul's and London in two lines of *Don Juan*:

> A huge dim cupola, like a foolscap crown
> On a fool's head—and there is London town!

Byron's and our lack of enthusiasm for St. Paul's is a matter of personal taste. The cathedral is one of London's major sights and an architectural triumph, Renaissance style.

# ROUTE FOUR

## By the Embankment
## to the Tower of London

Northumberland Avenue runs from the bottom of Charing Cross to the Victoria Embankment on the Thames. The Embankment is a pleasant promenade. On the way to it, where Northumberland Avenue meets Northumberland Street, is the Sherlock Holmes Tavern. Here in the fictional detective's day stood the Northumberland Hotel, where Sir Henry Baskerville was staying when he received the mysterious letter which started Holmes ("Quick, Watson, the game is afoot!") on the trail of the phosphorescent hound. On this foundation the Whitbread brewers' firm recently converted its old Northumberland Arms tavern to the Sherlock Holmes, fitting it up as a shrine of Sherlockiana. Drop in; the atmosphere is right.

At that corner, Craven Arches leads to Craven Street, where Benjamin Franklin lodged for all but two of the fifteen years between 1757 and 1772, working hard to mollify George III's stand against the American colonies and failing. No. 36, where he lived, is now—by way of penance?—the British Society for International Understanding.

Under the railway bridge on the Embankment is a pier where excursion steamers stop. The schedule is posted. They go to the Tower by water, as they did in ancient days.

But the Embankment is also for strolling. There are gardens, the Shell-Mex's Big Benzine, the Savoy Hotel. Cleopatra's Needle may startle New Yorkers, for it is twin to the obelisk which stands behind the Metropolitan Museum in Central Park. Each is about thirty-five hundred years old and suffering from the damp climate of the north.

One ship moored in the river is HMS *Discovery;* the polar research vessel of the heroic Captain Scott is now a naval training ship, but you are allowed to visit Scott's cabin. Next is HMS (Her Majesty's Ship, in case you're a landlubber) *Wellington,* which now belongs to the Honourable Company of Master Mariners. Then come two more navy training ships.

That ultramodern building across the river is the Royal Festival Hall, famed for concerts and acoustics, with a café and a restaurant on the river.

The Embankment ends at Blackfriars Bridge, just over a mile from where you started out. But if you go along a little farther, on Upper Thames Street you will find the Mermaid Theater at Puddle Dock, the only theater built in the City these last 250 years.

## FOUR & FIVE

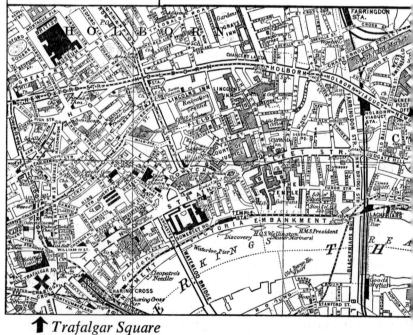

⬆ *Trafalgar Square*

The gayest way to arrive at the Tower is by boat, but you can also reach it by Underground (Tower station) or by bus.

## § *THE TOWER*

To clear up possible confusion: the Tower, the Tower of London, and London Tower are one and the same. The complex of moats, walls, bastions, baileys, towers, barracks, and other buildings should really be called the Castle of London.

It's all very well to be told that the little princes were murdered in the Tower, that Raleigh was imprisoned there for years and years, that Lady Jane Grey spent the nine days of her queenship in the Tower, and so on. When we first got there we kept asking, "Which tower of the Tower?"

After a while we didn't care. It was enough to sit on a bench

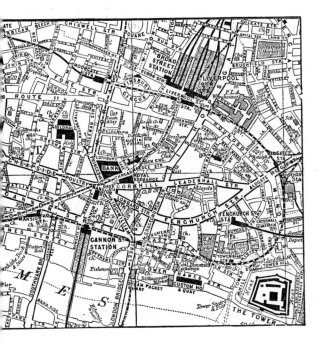

in the watery sunlight watching the ravens hop about on Tower Green, thinking shudderingly of the block and the axe (the site is marked)—except that on Anne Boleyn, by special courtesy, the two-handed sword was used; the axe was the clumsier weapon. "I have such a little neck," says Anne, and bursts into shrieking laughter. Lady Jane looks out the window and sees her husband's severed head going by in a cart. Sir Thomas More lays down one gold angel, a handsome tip, for his executioner, before giving up his life to him.

During the war the Tower suffered one casualty—a raven. These legendary, literary, sinister birds hold the eye the way flames do on the hearth. Poe was right; if they could talk, they'd say "Nevermore!" There are six ravens in the charge of a Raven Master, who sees that they eat regularly and have nothing to complain of. The Crown foots the bill, twenty cents per week per raven.

The Tower is peculiar. A castle and a town usually grew up together as protector and protected. In London this didn't happen. The town was first; the castle intruded.

When William the Conqueror came to London, the City—which was the whole of London—looked impregnable. It was a fortified town enclosed in walls built by the Romans, but strengthened and kept in good repair. Its citizens were independent. They hadn't bowed to lords spiritual or temporal. When Pope Gregory the Great in 597 sent missionaries the people proved so unruly the Pope decided on Canterbury for the church capital. Edward the Confessor lived in a palace outside London while getting his Abbey built, but his capital was Winchester.

The tale of the Tower rightly begins with that Edward. He was a Normaniac. He loved all things Norman, and during his reign imported Normans in considerable numbers for important posts. When William the Conqueror arrived before London, these Normans housed in the City became his fifth column. He didn't need to infiltrate; the City was already honeycombed.

When William and his men knocked on the City gates, some fearless citizens sallied forth. There was a skirmish, and then William crossed the river and burned Southwark to give the Londoners something to ponder. In due time a deputation came and invited him to be king. He had himself crowned in the Abbey, then dashed to Winchester for a second coronation. He was not a man to overlook the fine print on a legal form.

However—no king made London. London made a king.

The Tower was built to keep the Londoners from changing their minds. It was a branch of Westminster in the City. The Londoners probably tolerated it because William left them out of the Domesday Book—he exempted them from taxes. And he didn't force them to accept Norman masters. Instead, he gave the City a charter reaffirming rights it had long enjoyed.

As a royal castle royally garrisoned it was also a royal residence with state apartments in the keep or White Tower. But no king could feel comfortable there. The Tower was isolated; the whole City lay between it and Westminster. Also it was cramped, with not room enough for the royal elbows. So no attempt was made to convert the Tower into a real palace.

By Tudor-time, peaceful coexistence had been established between City and monarchy—between budding capitalism and the remnants of feudalism. The monarch spent the night before his coronation in the Tower, and rode from it through the City to the ceremonies in Westminster Abbey.

That is how Jane Grey happened to be there. She went to the Tower as queen, to make ready for her coronation. She never left it, and went instead to the block. But before that she was hurriedly moved out of the White Tower to the Yeoman Gaoler's house, the Beauchamp Tower being already occupied by her husband and kin. All these state prisoners probably watched while Mary Tudor, soon to be abominated as Bloody Mary, was escorted across the Green to the White Tower for the coronation that was to have been Jane's. Among Mary's attendants was her half-sister, Elizabeth.

So it happened that three women, queens, were for some days all together in the fortress, preparing for separate destinies. Three personalities so vivid that they live for all time—even the young, fatalistic Jane Grey, whose historical life was so brief.

Soon after, Princess Elizabeth was brought by barge, entering with furious protest by the water gate, called the Traitor's Gate—her sister's prisoner. She was lodged in the Bell Tower, and was so certain of execution that she debated sending word to Queen

Mary begging that a sword be used, as with her mother Anne
Boleyn, instead of an axe.

And then you see her returning in triumph, visiting her cell
before going to the White Tower; and at last she comes, in gold,
crimson, and ermine, through a cheering, adoring City to be
crowned in the Abbey. It may have been the City's powerful
affection that saved her from Jane Grey's fate through her perilous
youth. When Henry VII, the first Tudor king, borrowed money
from the City, he *paid it back*. This sensational departure from
royal practice was the beginning of a love affair between the City
and the Tudors.

You enter the Tower by the Lion Gate—so called because the
place once had a zoo. It began with Henry III in the thirteenth
century receiving a gift of three leopards, his coat of arms. Where
to stow them? The safest place was—the Tower.

Other animal gifts followed as the centuries rolled by, among
them a camel and an elephant, an alligator from John Smith's
Virginia, and several lions. The lions flourished, and some of their
descendants may be in Regent's Park or Whipsnade today. Sam
Pepys records in his diary on May 3, 1662, how he took a friend's
children to the Tower to see the lions.

The Tower has two rings of walls forming the two baileys or
wards, inner and outer. The uniforms of the Yeoman Warders
enhance the medieval effect. People confuse them with the Yeomen of the Guard, or Beefeaters, who are attached to St. James's
Palace. The Tower's Warders are a separate corps of about two
score war veterans, among whose functions is that of guiding
tourists. The Yeoman Gaoler is one of them. He has had no
clients since Rudolph Hess boarded here during World War II.

The Tower once housed the royal mint and archives, among
other things. It has had a garrison for nine hundred years without
a break.

The White Tower is what everyone heads for first. It will disappoint. Instead of seeing it as it was in its heyday—the oldest and
strongest part of the castle, bristling with armaments, the royal
apartments always ready for the sovereign—you see a museum. The
only part which remains as it was is the Chapel of St. John. This
is pure Norman, simple and strong. If one could only have it to
oneself for five minutes—but no, there are crowds.

The royal living quarters were at the top, where the museum of armor is. Note, by the way, that the spiral stairway winds to the right, so that mounting attackers would be at a disadvantage—unless they were left-handed!

Some relief from armor, weapons, war trophies, executioner's axes, instruments of torture, and other knickknacks of battle, murder, and sudden death is afforded by three grotesques. Two are the carved figures known as Gin and Beer, which were originally in Greenwich Palace. The third is a Venetian lion with hanging jowls, oh-so-golden wings, and silly pop-eyes raised to heaven.

Where you see a long queue shuffling and shifting from one foot to the other, that's the lot for the Crown Jewels, and you'll probably be joining it. The baubles are on display, heavily guarded, in the Wakefield Tower, in the room where Henry VI is thought to have been murdered. This magnificent collection of precious-historic stones, crowns, scepters, orbs, and et ceteras has been taking in visitors' pennies since 1660, when the penniless spend-thrift Charles II mounted the throne. Several pre-Charles monarchs hocked various gems with London merchant-bankers to raise a bit of the ready.

Raleigh was imprisoned in the Wakefield. It's in the Bloody Tower that the two princes were put to death on order of their uncle, Richard III, in 1483. So tradition says; history is less sure whodunit.

*BARGAIN TICKET* * The Ministry of Works of the British government has introduced a season ticket for entry to historic buildings it controls—and they total hundreds, scattered over England, Scotland, and Wales. For 7s 6d ($1.05) this gives you entree over a period of twelve months to the Tower of London, Edinburgh Castle, Dover Castle, Tintern Abbey, Rievaulx Abbey, Caernarvon, Carisbrooke, and Kenilworth castles, Hampton Court Palace, Households Roman Fort (at the Roman Wall), and scores of others. For anyone spending a few weeks in England this should be a money-saver. Buy the ticket at the British Travel Association's office, 64–65 St. James's Street, London, and be sure you get with it a list of the properties it covers.

On leaving the Tower, visit All Hallows Church, near the Tower

Hill Underground station. Pieces of the original church, founded about 675, still exist in the fabric of this one, which is being painfully restored after bombing. Here John Quincy Adams, intended by destiny to be sixth president of the U.S., was married in 1797. Here William Penn was baptised.

St. Olave's is nearby, to the north. Pepys and his wife worshiped there, he more with an eye to pretty women than to the service. Both are buried there. He outlived her for many a year, and commissioned and erected the bust of her that you will see.

One can't talk about old London without bringing in Pepys. Take his *Diary* with you, or perhaps even better, Cecil Abernethy's *Mr. Pepys of Seething Lane* to read in St. James's Park, where he used to walk.

# ROUTE FIVE

## By Way

## of Holborn

## to the City

You have already been in the City to see two of London's greatest showpieces—St. Paul's Cathedral and the Tower. This time your objective is the City itself. You will pluck a flower or two as you go by way of the northern of the two Orientation arteries: the Oxford Street–Holborn axis.

Rise from the Trafalgar Square parapet where we meet again and round (left) the National Gallery, passing the National Portrait Gallery, glancing at the statues of Nurse Edith Cavell ("Patriotism is not enough") and Sir Henry Irving. On your left you see ahead an open green space. It's the Leicester (*Lester*) Square which figures nostalgically in the Tipperary song of World War I.

London developed through its squares. As late as Shakespeare's time everything around where you now stand was country. Haymarket really was a hay market, and Piccadilly a muddy road to Reading. But the two Londons of the City and Westminster were expanding. In 1632 the Duke of Bedford plunged into the real-estate business. He laid out a square on land he owned and surrounded it with fine houses. That was Covent Garden, and it was immediately fashionable.

"My dear," a Countess said to her husband one day, "we really must have a proper town house. It wouldn't cost anything if you laid out a square, like Bedford's, and rented the houses, reserving for ourselves the sunny side. Squares are the coming thing. It would be too, too enchanting!"

It may not have happened exactly that way, but four years after

Bedford did Covent Garden the Earl of Leicester made *his* square. And this kept on, square after square, for some two hundred years. The architects did not design individual houses—the entire square was regarded as a single composition, houses and all.

Like Covent Garden, Leicester Square rapidly degenerated as London swamped it. It became a hangout of gamblers, roués, pimps, and harlots. In decorous Victoria's reign Kate Hamilton, queen of the madams, had her "palace" on Leicester Square. She received sitting on a bejeweled velvet throne with her "maids of honor" around her. When the Shah of Persia was a state guest at Buckingham Palace (Queen Victoria having retired to Windsor) he liked to visit Queen Kate.

Leicester Square today is honkytonk but quite respectable. It has cinemas and restaurants and is part of the entertainment district. You will find that West Enders have moved out of most of the other squares in the last thirty or forty years, leaving what were once the town houses of nobility to insurance companies, learned societies, lawyers, and the like. Some are still handsome, but Leicester Square has nothing of the old but good proportions and memories.

Go east now to Charing Cross Road, a shabby street with secondhand bookshops on it, taking it to New Oxford Street. You're now on the northern main stem; in old days, the road to Oxford.

Just above, in Bloomsbury, is the British Museum, one of the world's greatest treasure houses. It will exhaust you long before you exhaust it. Among other things, it displays the Elgin Marbles, priceless friezes and statues from the Parthenon.

The easiest way to do the Museum is to join one of the free lecture tours. They start off from the main lobby on weekdays at 11:30 and 3. On Sunday the Museum is open 2:30 to 6; no guided tours.

It's a pity they don't let you see the library, called the Reading Room. The great circular, book-lined hall is beautiful, and eminent intellects have sat and worked at the desks which branch out from the central catalogue like spokes of a giant wheel. The Museum should erect a glassed-in gallery from which you could overlook the big round busyness where Karl Marx put together *Das Kapital* and George Bernard Shaw wrote his first play, *Widowers' Houses*, from a plot he begged from a theater critic. Even the Martins have toiled here.

"And who is the distinguished man in the French beret?" a tourist inquires of the attendant.

"That is an American gentleman who, with his wife, is writing a book about England. However, it is not a French beret he wears but a Basque *boina*."

"Ah! Why does he wear it? Is it a mark of distinction?"

"No, Madam. Being an American, he has a head too weak for the drafts which circulate within."

"And the charming little lady who follows him, carrying those large books?"

"That is his wife."

Out you go now, back to New Oxford Street, then east, noting that the street has become High Holborn. At the major crossing just ahead, turn right into Kingsway, and off it into Lincoln's Inn Fields, an attractive open space with Lincoln's Inn beyond it. On the square's north side, at No. 13 of a row of Regency houses, is the Soane Museum in what was the house of Sir John Soane, a fashionable architect and avid collector. Go in, if only briefly, to see how a gentleman of the times lived. The most important part of the collections are the Hogarth originals. Look at the Gothick Fantasy, and the tomb of the Soane pet dog: "Alas, poor Fanny!"

Lincoln's Inn dates from about 1420. Stroll about the lovely quadrangle and gardens. The law library is London's largest. You are admitted to it and to the chapel and halls on application to the Porter's Lodge on Chancery Lane, and your best bet is on Saturday or Sunday. If the porter obliges, remember the gratuity.

(The fourth of the four Inns of Court is Gray's, north of Holborn on Gray's Inn Road, entrance through a gateway on Holborn. Skip it unless your interest is special.)

Leave Lincoln's Inn by the main gate on Chancery Lane, a very legal street. The Victorian Gothic edifice on your right will be the Public Record Office, which has a small museum of documents: Domesday Book, Magna Carta, medieval letters, petitions, royal autographs, and some items of Americana including Washington and Franklin letters. It's a marvelous collection of priceless papers.

Chancery Lane runs south to Fleet Street and north to Holborn.

Your way lies north, and on Holborn to the right. Two small stone obelisks, the Holborn Bars, here mark the entrance to the City. The half-timbered gabled façade is Staple Inn, the only timbered house surviving the Great Fire of London.

We came upon it by accident the first time, and could hardly believe our eyes.

Staple Inn was a fourteenth-century "hotel" for merchants in wool (staple) coming to the City on business. It became a subordinate Inn of Court and went on to a varied history. There isn't much to the place but you can go into the courtyard, look around, and try to imagine the entire City thus timbered and gabled—and while trying, dodge the clerks, office boys, and stenos who shoot in and out in an un-English hurry.

§ *FIRE! FIRE!*

September 2, 1666. This night, about ten o'clock, a fire started up in Pudding Lane, one of the City's narrow streets near London Bridge. At 2 A.M. all the neighborhood was watching Mr. Farynor's bakeshop burning. The Farynors watched too. They had got out in time. Across the street the Star Tavern, filled with night-clad spectators, was doing a fine business.

Fires were frequent, and no one was alarmed. But it had been a dry summer, and a strong wind was blowing. Suddenly the wind caught up flaming fragments and flung them into the piles of hay in the tavern's stable yard. The next minute the Star was afire. At the same time the houses on each side of the bakeshop began to burn. People shrieked and ran, knocking at shutters to arouse sleepers. In the church of St. Clement's the sexton rang the bells, but few heard. The clamor was carried away by the wind.

Along the water by London Bridge the wharves were piled and the warehouses packed with naval supplies—oil, hay, pitch, tar, timber, hemp. And all through the City, because of the summer drought, the old timbered-and-thatched houses were as dry as kindling.

In the morning, Samuel Pepys, who lived in Seething Lane near the Tower, flung on his clothes, ran up to the old fortress and climbed the Bell Tower. All he could see was billowing smoke.

He came down into panic. People were running about madly, moving their possessions from house to house as the fire traveled.

Pepys found a waterman who took him to Whitehall. There the air was clear, and people were strolling in the usual mannered grace of the court. Smoke in the City? It was only another fire. Ho-hum.

Mr. Pepys managed to get the ear of the king. Charles II was an indolent monarch, but to everyone's astonishment he leaped to action, calling out the guard and commandeering firehooks for pulling down houses in the path of the fire so that it would have nothing to feed on and burn itself out. He sent Pepys back in a coach with instructions for the lord mayor.

The coach raced along the Strand and Fleet Street, but was halted at St. Paul's Cathedral. The entire area was jammed with terrified people, the cathedral bells were pealing, and through their din and the shrieks and wails could be heard the roar and crackling of the fire.

Fighting his way through on foot, Pepys came upon the Lord Mayor standing in a street, shouting hoarsely and unintelligibly, a man half demented and utterly useless. He found other City fathers on a wharf arguing about whose house should be torn down and whose spared. Pepys ran home to save his wife, servants, and possessions.

The fire, as if demoniacally possessed, turned back *against* the wind to devour streets it had bypassed. Lombard Street and Cornhill glowed and broke, their ashes flying high.

Next day the fire was still raging, moving slowly but inexorably up Ludgate Hill. The lead sheeting on the roof of St. Paul's melted and ran down, the stones calcined. The great cathedral was doomed. Houses were now being pulled down, but never fast enough. The flames leaped the gaps. At last dynamite was used to blow up whole streets of houses. But it was late, very late.

The fire burned for four days. Many days later it was still spurting up in smoldering corners. Homeless Londoners camped desolately in the fields—oddly enough, there had been few casualties. The Tower still stood. But most of the City, from the Tower to the Temple, was gone.

Many plans were drawn for a new City. None could be adopted because the City clung to its old streets and byways. But among the planners was a brilliant and personable man of thirty-four, a mathematician and astronomer who had a high clerkly post in Westminster. He had begun to study architecture in books only four years before the Great Fire. His name was Christopher Wren.

Later a stupid and spiteful rumor circulated that Christopher Wren had set the Great Fire. On crime-novel reasoning Wren was suspect, for he gained most by it. The fire made him a full-time architect and gave him more work than he could handle. By the time he died he was universally acclaimed. He was buried in his largest creation, St. Paul's Cathedral, the first man so honored.

# § *THE CITY TODAY*

After the Great Fire the City rose in brick and stone, keeping the memory of its old self in twisting streets, narrow passages, and courtyards, its new look ornamented by Christopher Wren's small but lovely churches that do not age. Many of these were blasted in the Blitz.

The word *City* never refers to London as a whole but only to this "square mile" which has its own mayor, aldermen, common council, and police force, and is the cradle of democracy in England.

The City today is

1. The center of finance, shipping, insurance, banking.
2. Ancient and medieval London.
3. A political oddity, a city within a city.
4. A geographical oddity, its area less than one square mile—about 1/700th of Greater London.
5. A population oddity. Its population during working hours is about five hundred thousand. After the evening rush, five thousand stay on—guards, watchmen, and a few residents. And many cats.

Having left you at Staple Inn, we now hurry to your rescue.

Come out and continue on Holborn Circus, cross it to Charterhouse Street, and dart for a moment's peace into Ely Place.

This curious blind alley is an enclave in the City. Once the

Bishop of Ely maintained a town house here which was granted a "Liberty," placing it outside the control of anyone but the episcopal authorities. Ely Place still has its Liberty. It cuts itself off at night by locked gates, and is patroled not by City police but by its own beadle in a long coat and silk topper. The annual rent since Elizabeth I's day has been £10, ten loads of hay, and a red rose (white won't do) plucked in midsummer.

Ely Place has some handsome late-eighteenth-century houses and an interesting crypted chapel, now a Roman Catholic church.

Carry on with Holborn, which becomes in turn Holborn Viaduct, Newgate Street, Cheapside, and Poultry. The large church on the left as you go along is St. Sepulchre's, originally a Crusaders' church but much rebuilt. A tablet to John Smith, who's buried in the aisle, east end, salutes him as Governor of Virginia and Admiral of New England.

Grim Newgate prison stood on Newgate Street. In the days of public executions the condemned man walked from there all the way to Tyburn, about where Marble Arch now stands. As he passed St. Sepulchre's, which tolled its bells for him, he was handed a little sweet-smelling bouquet. (There's something peculiarly horrible in that touch of kindness.) Old Bailey stands in Newgate's place, its correct name the Central Criminal Court. You can sit in on a trial, but if it's a dramatic case hundreds will be waiting to get in.

The area between Newgate Street and St. Paul's was bombed out. A beautiful steeple rises—all that's left of Wren's Christ Church.

As you pass the General Post Office, reflect that within is the world's longest counter, 150 feet of it. And that if you had applied at least three weeks beforehand to the Regional Director, London Postal Region, E.C.1, you'd now be taking a two-and-a-half-hour GPO tour, its highlight the underground automatic railway which transports more than forty-two thousand sacks of mail a day across London, one train every ninety seconds.

Near the bottom of Cheapside stands the church you want to visit—St. Mary le Bow, of Bow Bells fame, the one that you're a Cockney if born within sound of. It's a Christopher Wren church with a Norman crypt, and is now almost entirely restored, triumphant on a modern square which has a statue of Captain John Smith, not governor and admiral this time but "citizen and cordwainer."

For twenty-two years—since the Bells were shattered—technically no Cockney was born. On December 22, 1961, thirteen minutes after the new Bow Bells began tolling, a little girl was born within a mile of the church. Cockneys are once again in production, and all is well with London.

Cheapside, as we remarked, goes into Poultry, which opens into the great eight-street crossing known as the Bank. This is the City's heart.

That Corinthian-portico building in the wedge is the Royal Exchange. (We've got news for you—here's the Duke of Wellington again.) To its left is the Bank of England, "the little old lady of Threadneedle Street." That almost good-looking eighteenth-century structure on the right is Mansion House, official residence of the lord mayor.

In the Royal Exchange, all there is to interest you is the central court, if it is still housing temporarily (as it has for about seven years now) the Guildhall museum of Londoniana.

About the Bank—enter with courage. Ushers in top hats, pink coats, red vests, will ask what you seek, and when you confess you are an American just looking, will let you stand in the hall and peep into the gardens, but warn you against going out of bounds. This is the banker to the government and to banks—no common business is done here. It is money's mighty fortress.

Now walk a block on Threadneedle Street to the Stock Exchange. Around to the north at No. 8 Throgmorton Street is the entrance to the public gallery from which you can watch the antics on the floor. It closes at three-thirty, but curbstone buying and selling go on in Throgmorton and immediate neighborhood.

From 10:30 to closing you will be greeted by pleasant young women who show you a color-film and then take you to the visitors' gallery and explain things, including who those men are in the gold-braided top hats.

And now for a while you're on your own to wander up and down the mercantile and financial streets of Cornhill and Lombard and the curious passages between them. You keep meeting old churches. One of them, St. Peter-upon-Cornhill, has a pretty courtyard with seats and plane trees and tubbed geraniums. In Abchurch Lane the old burial ground of St. Mary Abchurch has been similarly transformed. The seventeenth-century taverns are now chop houses, charcoal grills their specialty.

Easiest way to find the Guildhall—and you do want to find it— is to get back to the Bank and ask. It's the City's city hall, and parts of it are early fifteenth century. It was damaged in the Great Fire of 1666 and in that terrible December 29, 1940 air raid. Again it emerges, new-old. See the Great Hall with Gog and Magog— figures more than nine feet high once carried in medieval pageants. These are modern copies. The originals, after standing for 232 years, were liquidated at long distance by Hitler.

And—how could we forget this?—you ought to work in a ride on the Trav-o-lator, which you'll find in the Bank station of the Underground. It's a moving footway 104 yards long connecting the Bank and Waterloo stations.

Before the Lord Mayor inaugurated it in September 1960 by turning a gold key and being borne out of sight by 3904 invisible wheels, some twenty thousand City workers had to climb up (and down) a tunnel they called "the Drain" on a killing grade of 1 in 7.4, shuffling along like stockyard-bound cattle. The moving sidewalk slides along at 180 feet a minute. It took three years to make and cost about two million dollars.

Part of the fun is the utter sobriety and dignity of the passengers. The first day saw smiles and jokes and elbow-digs. Cheers were cheered, decent excitement prevailed. The novelty of the thing was exhausted by the end of the first week.

What is it that's always like that? Life!

# ROUTE SIX

## Soho, Mayfair,

## and North

This time you take off from George III, who sits only a hundred yards away from George Washington in the open triangular space where Cockspur Street begins, due west from the National Gallery.

Cockspur Street, once busy with shops that made spurs for fighting cocks, carries you into Haymarket, a broad short thoroughfare along which one-way traffic charges from Piccadilly Circus into Trafalgar Square. Many a tourist knows Haymarket before anything else in London because he makes a beeline to it for the American Express for his mail. Haymarket also has theaters, the Design Centre, Burberry's, and Fribourg and Treyer's with the same bow windows as when they opened their snuff shop in 1720.

At the top of Haymarket bear left to be swallowed in the maelstrom of Piccadilly Circus. Somewhere hereabouts, three hundred years ago, a fashionable tailor skilled in making piccadils, the seventeenth-century ruffs, retired to a fine country house which everyone then called Piccadil Hall.

A Circus is a circular "square," like the *rondpoint* of Paris. Piccadilly Circus disappoints; it's a mess architecturally, with a rash of advertising signs. But it's the gateway—several gateways— into fun, high class and low: theaters, movie houses, Soho joints, eating places (from fish-and-chips to the eminent Café Royal), Mayfair shops and hotels, and the clubs of Pall Mall and St. James's. Londoners have a special affection for it, and for its inadequate Eros who is poised on one leg on the bronze fountain. Few know that he's supposed to be a respectable Christian angel of charity, a tribute to the philanthropic Earl of Shaftesbury.

The Underground station, said to be the busiest in the world (thirty-three million passengers yearly) is also a circus in form, with shops and an LT information office where maps and literature may be had. Above it fifty thousand vehicles whizz or crawl by each working day. Deep down below on the station platforms four thousand persons spent the nights during the Blitz.

Problem: you can't go two ways at once; shall it be Soho or Mayfair? We suggest Soho as being more quickly done.

The easiest way to cross Piccadilly Circus is to pop down into the Underground and locate the street you want by the signs over the seven or eight radiating exits. For Soho take the Shaftesbury Avenue, and at the top turn left into Wardour Street, Soho's main stem. Then amble about, as you would in Manhattan's Greenwich Village or New Orleans' French Quarter, eating here, drinking there, and trying to distinguish between the real and the phony.

Soho is a muddle of little streets between Regent Street and Charing Cross Road, bounded on the north by Oxford Street. It's the foreign quarter. We used to buy strange items from Little Pulteney Stores on Brewer (an interesting street). Once we tried to make a list of what they stock: breads of every nation arriving daily from the Continent; sausages Algerian, Polish, Swiss, and several others; Chinese salt fish; Spanish dried apricots; Italian pastas, melon, and blue poppy seeds; French crystalized cake decorations; dried cod, sweetwood, cummin seeds, *hoobergritz*, Indian *basmati*, Turkish *lakerda*, *farfel*, smoked roe, Greek and Albanian cheese—but we had to give it up.

On almost every other street you see a "club." This is clubland too, with a difference. These clubs anyone can join for three dollars or less. Frank and interesting photos outside tell you what you get for your money. The female corpus is the attraction, and we hear that more is taken off than in American burlesque. It's not excess of moral rectitude that has kept us from inspecting the fleshly treasures within; we always seemed to have something more important to do. Once we did get as far as searching for our money at the ticket desk, but we didn't like the shifty-gangster look of the chairman of the club's membership committee.

The better clubs are more like the American night club, and you can tell them from the strip-teaseries by their smarter appearance and higher fees. That membership fee is good for a year, but it does not pay for drink or a meal. Since it isn't likely that you'll be going into one of these clubs more than once, regard it as a cover charge.

Soho is to be prized for the relief it offers from the limitations of the British cuisine. Many of its restaurants are run by people who love food and prepare it well.

Upper-class Mayfair, Soho's neighbor on the west, is territory bounded roughly by Regent Street, Oxford Street, Piccadilly, and Park Lane. Roughly, because it's a concept. Some would extend it to include the St. James's Square area. The name comes from a May fair held some centuries ago at Shepherd Market but suppressed when it became bacchanalian. Recently it has been sedately revived.

Mayfair is as mazy as Soho, but more spaciously so. Bond Street, divided into New Bond and Old Bond, is its only north–south through street and its shopping glory. The name is known the world over, the label lends distinction. When it was more residential than it is now, many a famous man lived here: Swift, Sterne, Johnson, Lord Cornwallis, Boswell, the painter Thomas Lawrence.

One of London's best-known addresses is 34–35 New Bond Street—the door bears the Egyptian sculptured head of Sekh-met. This is Sotheby's, the world's oldest auctioneers, founded 1744. Christie's at 8 King Street was established in 1766. Auctions go on daily in both, and they are something worth beholding.

If you have time to treat yourself to a seat at an auction and want to know what's going on, proceed thus:

1. Look in the *Sunday Observer*, the *Sunday Times* or the Monday *Daily Telegraph* for the Sotheby and Christie announcements.

2. Buy the catalogue.

3. Attend the preview of the objects to be sold. They're on display for the three days before the auction.

4. Go.

You may even fancy something and plan to put in a bid. But if you're only looking, sit quite still. Don't clear your throat, don't jump up, don't throw up a sudden hand to pat your hair or scratch your ear, or you may find yourself stuck with £20,000 worth of Picasso.

Some who come with serious intent are modest collectors eternally hopeful of picking up something rare and beautiful for less than a king's ransom. And a king's ransom the knock-down price often is. On a day in June 1959, Sotheby's sold Rubens' *Adoration of the Magi* for £275,000, until then the highest price ever paid for an auctioned canvas. Another spectacular was the sale of the Beverley Castle silver service for £207,000 in the record time of two minutes twenty seconds.

We found ourselves on Bond Street one Saturday afternoon, when Sylvia suddenly exclaimed, "Why, it's beautiful! Why didn't they tell me? Don't they know?"

"They" probably referred to the writers of travel guides. What they had kept secret was that the street is worth seeing for itself, and that you can see it only after the crowds and autos are gone. Then the varied façades, the intimate eighteenth-century scale of things, the details of shining plate glass, polished woods, gilded signs, and brass name-plates, and the quiet pride and dignity combine to make this the handsomest commercial street in London.

Piccadilly is second best, too wide and long to be taken to one's heart, too pockmarked with brash signs and slicked-up façades. But off it, just east of Bond Street, you will find Burlington Arcade on the north side and, across the street, Piccadilly Arcade. Burlington is longer and better known and still pretty much as it was in Regency times, with its top-hatted, long-coated beadle to keep law and order and lock the gates at night. It is estimated that the seventy-two shops along its 588-foot length pay an annual rent of $150,000.

Other Piccadilly ornaments are the Albany, famous for bachelor flats, set back in its courtyard; palatial Burlington House, containing the Royal Academy of Art with modern exhibitions; and fashionable St. James's Church and garden. A mixed-up thoroughfare, Piccadilly is almost a mile of fascinating shops, restaurants, and hotels. Here too are the central English offices of Pan American World Airways.

Mayfair's squares are Berkeley, Grosvenor, and Hanover. Hanover still has old-times grace in spite of some modern building.

Berkeley (*Barkly*) once the most atmospherically eighteenth-century, is now bordered by office blocks. The First National City Bank of New York has an attractive modern branch here.

Something almost as sad has happened to once-proud Grosvenor Square. It has become practically an enclave of the United States of America. The square was hardly fifty years old when in 1785 the infant U.S. got its foot in the door—John Adams, first American minister to the Court of St. James's, settled down in No. 9 at the northeast corner. Since then the U.S. has been eating its way round the Square. For decades it inhabited a fine Georgian building for its embassy, but outgrew it, and Uncle Sam is now installed in a heavy, costly, almost brutally modernistic structure occupying the west side of the square. Controversy has raged round this building, and especially over the far-spreading, aggressive eagle at its top. The ensemble makes us say "Ouch!" and reminds us that we owe Internal Revenue another quarterly payment. Mutilated as it is, Grosvenor Square is still imposing, and we hope you will agree that the statue of Franklin Roosevelt on the green, Britain's tribute to his memory, in the heart of America-in-London, is a fine thing.

At No. 44, Lady Illingworth throws open her town house Thursday afternoons during the summer, for a small fee which goes to the Seamen's Hospital. Visitable country houses are numerous, but an aristocratic town mansion like this one is rare of access.

The aristocratic streets roundabout tell a family story. One Hugh Audley bought the land in 1625. Hence Audley Street. It passed to a female descendant, Mary Davies (hence Davies Street), who married Sir Hugh Grosvenor. The Grosvenors became Dukes of Westminster, which gives you Duke Street.

Follow South Audley a few blocks below Grosvenor Square, and you come upon Mayfair's prettiest open space—an oddly shaped and surprisingly large garden without a name. Some attractive old houses are on it and a Jesuit church. Carry on down South Audley to Curzon Street, walk a block on Curzon, turn right, and you are in Shepherd Market. All along the way to this spot with its cluster of old streets and houses and passages you have a glimpse of the Mayfair that is passing: the eighteenth century of loo and love, the Firbank era of ladies in stained-glass attitudes, the Oscar Wilde period of quip and quibble, pun and paradox.

Stroll up Park Lane then, principally for the few handsome Regency houses that still remain, up to Marble Arch. It stands at a crossing so busy that a piece of Hyde Park, where the Sunday-morning orators held forth, has been lopped off to give the traffic more racecourse. Marble Arch was designed by John Nash for Buckingham Palace; proving too narrow for Victorian state processions it was then moved to the place near which the gallows, called the Tyburn Tree, entertained Londoners in the days of public executions.

North of Marble Arch and Oxford Street you enter the Borough of Marylebone. The name means either Mary the Good or, more likely, Mary the Bourne (stream, as in Tyburn, Holborn). Before London swallowed it, this was a village that developed into a town around eighteenth-century squares; it still retains its High Street and its curving Marylebone Lane. Portman Square, northwest of Selfridge's department store, is one of the many old residential squares whose fine buildings have become hoteled and officed. Baker Street begins here, a main thoroughfare running north to Regent's Park. That famous fictional address, 221B, where Mrs. Hudson looked after Holmes and Watson, where the Baker Street Irregulars came to report, and where the hansom cab deposited the veiled lady in distress, is engulfed by the unromantic Abbey National Building Society.

Marylebone has two tourist attractions. One is Hertford House on Manchester Square. The mansion of three art-collecting Marquesses of Hertford houses their Wallace Collection, named after their descendant Lady Wallace, who bequeathed it to the nation. This is one of London's most charming small museums. If time compels you to choose between the Wallace Collection and the Soane in Lincoln Fields, take this one. Its treasures are superb, and were chosen with a special eye for the colorful and gay, the rich and intimate. We particularly love the miniatures. The house itself is beautiful inside.

The second offering is Madame Tussaud's on Marylebone Road just east of Baker Street and the Underground station of that name. The waxworks attracts more visitors than any other admission-charging sight in London. It was founded by Madame Tussaud, the Swiss-French artist-in-wax who in 1802 took her Paris exhibit on a tour of England and never went back. She toured for thirty years, steadily enlarging her show. At seventy she decided she was getting a little old for road work, and settled down. The exhibit has kept growing both in size and popularity. The Chamber of Horrors, the best part, has some of her originals: death masks of Louis XVI, Marie Antoinette, and revolutionaries whose heads were brought to her fresh from the guillotine. (You may have read Sylvia's novel, *I, Madame Tussaud.*) The gallery of English kings and queens may help your history. There are some American presidents in wax, and sports and movie stars. The Planetarium adjoining is a science-entertainment offshoot.

Just north of Madame Tussaud's, Regent's Park begins; laid out by John Nash, it is named for his patron, who became Prince Regent during his father's prolonged insanity. (No, George III did not go crazy because he lost the American colonies. That only made him angry, not mad.) When Prinny (his son's nickname) had Carlton House in St. James's built, he decided he wanted a country mansion in what was then one of the royal hunting parks. But if he did make a country house there, how would he get to it? There was no through street. Nash made Regent Street and Regent's Park for him, but the mansion somehow never materialized.

Regent's Park covers 472 acres. In it is the Zoo (short for Gardens of the Zoological Society of London). It's not a pubicly owned zoo but the property of a private scientific-minded association founded in 1826. Hence, admission charge. Sunday, zoo-day for the family back home, is members' day here. Then the animals are yours only until 1 P.M. and at an increased charge.

This excellent zoo is the product of individual but not-for-profit initiative, and the exhibits always look superlatively groomed and smugly satisfied with their meals and lodgings. You feel like asking them to move over. The chimps are wonderful at their famous tea-party. (Hours not fixed; ask the BTA.)

One day we were having a leisurely chat with the curator, then Mr. Cansfield, and he was telling us that zoo lions, healthier than those snagged in the wilds, breed happily. One result: lions had become cheap, costing about three hundred dollars each. We twitted him about the declining value of this symbol of Britain. He turned his head and shouted, "Mike, how much did we pay for that last American bald eagle?" "Eight guineas!" Mike shouted back. "Ha!" cried Mr. Cansfield at us; "twelve and a half bald eagles equals one lion." "Which half?" we retorted, dodging the shame of it. The curator was kind. He introduced us to the most expensive animal, a rare African version of a jackass, symbol of (if anything) the human race.

Another beast of distinction is charming Chi-Chi, said to be the one and only Giant Panda in the Western world. He is an import from the People's Republic of China. Since such imports are barred from the U.S.A., here may be your only chance to see this engaging Oriental teddy-bear.

Queen Mary's Gardens in Regent's Park are among the loveliest of London's public grounds. They include a water-lily pond and an open-air theater. Snacks and refreshments are to be had in the summer, and just west is an extensive boating lagoon.

North of Regent's Park you find yourself in hilly Hampstead. Once a village, it is now the most prized of the residential suburbs, with interesting steep streets, houses, and unexpected corners. There are good restaurants. On the sightseeing side it's an outlying Chelsea with literary and artistic associations. Plaques on houses inform you that Keats, Constable, Romney, Du Maurier, Galsworthy, Dickens, Thackeray, Leigh Hunt, Washington Irving, all either lived or merely slept here. Open to visitors are the Keats House (weekdays 10–6); Fenton House, a late-seventeenth-century mansion maintained by the National Trust (weekdays 10–1, 2–5); and Kenwood House, an eighteenth-century Robert Adam mansion (weekdays 10–6).

Hampstead Heath is considered beautiful by Londoners because it is kept in its natural heathiness. A vast scraggly expanse of gorse and trees, high up and breezy, it gives long views over the metropolis.

Spaniard's Road goes on to Highgate, a sister suburb. Whittington Stone on Highgate Hill marks the spot where Dick Whittington is thought to have been sitting when he heard Bow Bells tell him, "Turn again, Whittington, thrice mayor of London." He turned, and became. Highgate has a beautiful park. In the cemetery the grave and bust of Karl Marx comrades that of Francis Bacon.

# WHAT TO DO
# ON SUNDAY

Sunday, among Latin peoples the liveliest of the week, is dead and dull in England. Shops and many restaurants are closed. Fewer trains and buses run; on some branch lines no trains at all. Theatrical performances are against the law unless run by "clubs," but movies may be shown after 4 P.M.

Among the things you may not do is make animal noises. The London County Council forbade Jimmy Elliott, the animal impersonator, to perform at a Sunday concert in Woolwich because animal noises are not permitted on the Sabbath—dogs and cats take notice. (We once heard a Sunday camel snort at the Zoo in Regent's Park, and he got away with it.)

If Authority tried to inflict the English Sunday on the French, the Italians, the Mexicans, it would face a revolt. Tommy guns and stink bombs would be needed. One never ceases to wonder about our English cousins—what makes them tick?

The Lord's Day Alliance is a powerful organization in a country where minds are so tradition-bound that it is difficult to change ways, no matter how irrational, once they have a start. (The U.S.A. has Connecticut without that excuse.)

What to do on Sunday?

In London and unweek-ended towns it is possible to walk along the streets and look at the houses at leisure. In the financial square-mile of the City, traffic is almost nil and you can dance a jig in front of Mansion House.

Many museums are open; LT's free "Museums and Art Galleries In or Near London" gives the run-down.

Many Stately Homes are open. BTA's free booklet, "Places of Interest In and Around London" tells you which.

How about a spot of worship?—as an Englishman we know used to say. The churches are open on Sunday. Attend morning service or vespers, in St. Paul's, Westminster Abbey, Southwark Cathedral, Westminstral Cathedral (Roman Catholic), or the cathedral or parish church wherever you happen to be. English cathedrals have singing and organ music of high quality. And churches should be seen at work as well as resting.

We were going to recommend visiting the vast crypt of St. Paul's but luckily checked back and discovered: No Crypt on Sunday. You'd think Sunday would be an ideal crypt day. We were going to recommend the Zoo in Regent's Park when we suddenly remembered that—as already noted—Sunday is Fellow's Day, the general public being allowed in only from 9 A.M. until 1 P.M., and for a higher price to boot.

It is a club; and so are the strip-tease joints. There are more than a dozen of these, most of them in Soho. They are evidently thought less harmful to public morality than is the theater, for they are open from late afternoon until far into the night. (In the weekly "What's On in London," in the midst of a page of nudity-revue ads is one for the London Association of the Blind!)

Ride the Thames steamer between Greenwich and Kew Gardens. It would be a better ride if they played Handel's "Water Music" on the way, but it's a wonderful-enough little voyage.

Kew Gardens is one of numerous lovely parks to be visited. There's always fun watching the water birds and land people in St. James's Park. Queen Mary's Gardens in Regent's Park are a dream. In other parts of that 472-acre green, cricket or football is going on, according to the season, and a large lagoon invites you to row. Battersea Park on the south bank of the Thames is a perpetual summer fun-fair in the Festival Gardens, from 1 to 10:30 P.M.

Without rucksack or compass you can take a three-mile walk right in the heart of London, from Horse Guard's Parade, across St. James's Park, Green Park, and Hyde Park, to Kensington Gardens and Palace, walking on grass all the way except at three road crossings. You can explore Hampstead and its Heath afoot, and go on to neighboring Highgate on its hilltop, from which there is a grand view of London. Take the Northern Underground to Hampstead, or the Bakerloo to Finchley Road or Swiss Cottage, and ask directions from the ticket-taker at destination. Be booked ahead for dinner in one of Hampstead's or Highgate's restaurants.

Sunday is a good day for moving from one place to another; but not, in the London or any big-city area, by road. To the traveler afoot in the open country, Sunday is like other days. Trees extend their shade, birds sing, brooks gurgle, just as if the Lord's Day Alliance didn't exist. In London and other towns look up the local Rambler's Club and join it for a walk in the country—but make arrangements a day or two ahead of time.

If you don't mind swarms of holiday-makers, join them at Windsor or farther up the Thames. In summer, river towns like Norwich, Chester, Oxford, Cambridge offer boating and steamer excursions and the waterfront is lively. If you're in London it's easy to take a train excursion to Cambridge, Oxford, Canterbury, or St. Albans for the day, or do Colchester and the Constable country (see East Anglia chapter).

Visit Madame Tussaud's or the Planetarium on Marylebone Road near Baker Street. Planetarium shows are from 3 P.M. until the evening and should be booked in advance.

If the Petticoat Lane flea market is still functioning as a Sunday-morning treat (Middlesex Street near Liverpool Street railway station), you may have fun in the melee and also pick up the right oddity for your Aunt Mabel or other problem relative. Keep your wallet tucked well away from the light-fingered.

A London Sunday abounds in concerts, recitals, and lectures, and in rallies for this cause or that. These are advertised in the *Sunday Times* and *Sunday Observer* and in the weekly *New Statesman*.

One special-interest tour we thought up—so far as we know it hasn't been organized or packaged—is to search out the tucked-away little gardens and courts that lurk in London's most unlikely places. This is an ideal Sunday hunt, for most of them are in the Sunday-deserted City. Living in London, in random walks about the streets one stumbles upon them by accident at the end of a narrow passage or under an arch that has teased one on. There must be scores of them; a few are mentioned in the description of Route Five. These should be self-discoveries, so we won't give any more locations. Some are gardens on the sites of ancient churchyards; others, occupying ground worth scads of pounds sterling per front foot, live on because of a sensible regulation that if an old graveyard is built upon, an open space of equal size must be left somewhere else nearby, so that the metropolitan lung area will not be shrunk.

An exciting joyride at a thousand feet is the helicopter tour of London from the Battersea Heliport. The flying windmill operates through the summer months and up to October 31. You can take the Standard Tour as far as Greenwich or the Alternative Tour as far as Tower Bridge. Reservations: Executive Travel, Ltd., 91 Jermyn Street, London S.W.1, WHItehall 4676. There is also a flight to Stratford-on-Avon.

This may sound silly, but it's been pre-tested: go visit a railway station: Victoria, Waterloo, Paddington, whichever is nearest your hotel. It's a hundred-to-one shot that every time you've been in a railway depot it was to catch a train or meet one. Go there for once unpreoccupied, an observer with no train to catch, no Aunt Hetty to meet, no goodbyes to say, no luggage or ticket or seat to worry about—and observe the worriers, the last-minute by-the-skin-of-their-teeth train catchers, the incoming stream from Torquay, Stratford, and Barton-le-Beans, Yorks.

A big London station is a cathedral of transport. Its bays and chapels and crypts are filled with kiosks, refreshment rooms, newspaper and book stalls, enquiry office, left-luggage, booking hall, porters, trainmen. The fagged couple following two porters bowed down under their luggage might have been you and yours. There's someone's sweetheart on the tiptoe of expectation, waiting for her Joe; a bevy of schoolgirls shepherded by a stringy-haired duenna; fifty Jamaicans off the boat looking about them in wonder; helpless old ladies who don't know what's the next move and Whitehall Foreign Office characters who do. Holmes and Watson were here before you, as was Graham Greene. Ah, and the London Airport is a three-ring circus, although harder to get to than the railway stations.

And there are the Sunday newspapers, superficially so different from the American. The weather forecast is different, with its "bright intervals" and "bright periods," and its amazing assumption that a temperature high of 73° for two days constitutes a heat wave. The popular Sunday papers run more to what journalists call "circus makeup" than American papers do, and are as

sensational in their handling of sex and crime as anything in the
U.S. The *News of the World*, the champ in this bracket, enjoys a
circulation of about seven million.

They carry more about nature, gardens, animals, birds, flowers.
In the height of the Blitz the magisterial *Times* found room on
its editorial page to devote to the duck-billed platypus. The head-
lines will amuse you, they are so unlike what you are used to:

A SCREAM—THEN PANIC

SPINSTER "SPOILED MY LIFE"

STRANGE INCIDENT AT BRAINTREE

are three examples. The American opposite number would be
more specific: BRAINTREE BABY SWALLOWS PIGGY BANK. The letters-
to-the-editor department sometimes have a shaggy-dog character:
"I would like to see big-screen television in the parks, it would
enable people to get together more in the open on fine evenings
instead of watching TV at home." "Britain wants more babies. We
shall not get them by Back to Nature methods." "The number of
persons bitten by bats must be so few, it has occurred to me that
a Bitten by Bat Society might be formed."

In the *Sunday Observer* almost the first thing we turn to is the
real-estate advertising, for the latest budget of gems from E. H.
Brook & Son, South Kensington, who deserve an Advertising Oscar
if there is such an award. Here are a few extracts:

Historic 16th century cottage nr. Henley, nrly ½ acre. Solid enough,
3 stone walls. Condition ghastly.

Doctor at sea must sell brand-new lux. house. . . Alleged garage
space (you have only to remove enormous tree, dump tons of earth. . .)

Home of Royalty. Delectable Q Anne house, glorious Bedfordshire
country. Huntin', shootin', fishin', & social climbin'. Superb maid might
stay: "Properly trained, she knows who to take into the dining room
& who to leave in the hall."

If you can bear the outside you will be entranced by spacious interior dec. in best Contemporary manner under aegis of aspiring actress.

. . . tiny bedroom (bunks for 2 dwarfs).

. . . Some of the decor has that well-bred slight shabbiness which
is so hard to imitate.

Decor new but hideous—plaster animals creeping over the walls, but
don't be put off, it's cheap. . .

Looks pretty grim but fabric believed sound.

More Town Houses Wanted. My sympathies to those who queued in blizzard outside office 8:30 Mon. (I lay in bed thinking of you.) But why not send telegram? To lady who wrote to "Mr. Sun, Chantry House": Sun. is short for Sunday & not namesake of Chinese revolutionary.—Roy Brooks.

The slick-paper illustrated society magazines like *Country Life*, *The Queen*, and *The Tatler* carry ambitious ads of estates and manor houses. (There should be back copies in your hotel lounge.) To read these is to enter a dream world. In Hampshire, "a lovely Jacobean manor house with a pleasing elevation of mellowed red brick, 7 bedrooms, 3 bathrooms, 3 reception rooms, central heating, garage, manageable garden, paddocks, etc., 15 acres with woodlands all about" is going a-begging for £17,500, only fifty minutes from London. That's only $49,000! Why sit we here idle?

One is torn between this and Elmhurst Farm, Slinfold, Sussex: "an agricultural-residential estate, a substantial house of character in own grounds [what other grounds could there be?] with 5 bedrooms, dressing room, 2–3 secondary bedrooms [for Brooks' dwarfs?]." Only one bathroom, but double garage, garden, squash court, 2 cottages, farm buildings—160 acres in all—going, going . . . $43,400, a give-away!

A harmless, pleasant Sunday game this, imagining yourself snapping up such properties and entering upon the lord-of-the-manor phase of your life.

No—Sunday need not be dismal. It's a challenge.

# PART III
# TEN SALLIES INTO ENGLAND

# 1. WINDSOR,

# OXFORD,

# AND THE THAMES

## § *WINDSOR*

Windsor and Eton are usually said in the same breath, like ham and eggs. You do them in one swoop. They even share the same railway station. The swoop can also take in Hampton Court on the way, and Stoke Poges beyond. That makes about nine solid hours of sightseeing. We wouldn't do it, but it's among the standard tours. We suggest you give Hampton Court a separate day, and if your time is short sacrifice Stoke Poges and skimp Eton.

Windsor is about an hour from London by road, a little more by rail. By train you go from Paddington or Waterloo (Waterloo is better). By road, if you haven't a car you can board a Green Line coach (bus) at Hyde Park Corner. You want to go at least one way by road because of Runnymede.

It's the castle that's Windsor's attraction. Arrange your itinerary to hie out there after seeing the Tower of London. These two great royal strong-points on the Thames give you a picture of medievally fortified England. You have to remember how important the river was, the No. 1 road.

The London fortress was there first. While William the Conqueror was having it built, he went up the Thames to Windsor, which was an old royal Saxon town complete with a Saxon palace. It was a low-lying town, but about two miles away the land rose. On the highest part of the rise, and protected on one side by a steep slope, stood an artificial mound. To William's eye for military scenery that mound must have been the prettiest thing in the landscape. It had been built up by some forgotten ancients who had also known a prime site when they saw one.

The mound and the land around it were part of a nobleman's estates—one of his own men, it must have been. William had been rewarding his boys rather too promptly and generously. But he wasn't one to give with one hand and take back with the other. He *rented* the precious mound. The rent, twelve shillings a year, was paid for the next five hundred years.

William threw up fortifications. One of his sons continued the work. But it was Henry II, a hundred years after William, who began to make the present Windsor Castle. He built in enduring heath-stone. His is the Round Tower which stands on the mound. He also raised walls and turrets, and tunneled secret sally ports. Henry II was the sad king who had so much trouble with Thomas à Becket. He had many other troubles too.

As the castle rose, merchants built houses and shops under its walls. What happened to that town on the river, the one with the Saxon palace? Well, in Windsor you keep seeing signs pointing to Old Windsor. That was it. Avoid it. It's an ugly village.

Windsor Castle grew little by little into the enormous and marvelously story-book affair you see today. It has held its own as a royal residence for more than eight hundred years. The present royal family, descendants of the Hanoverian Georges, adopted its good English name at the height of anti-German feeling during the first world war. They are now Windsors. Edward, who married for love and lost his throne, is Duke of Windsor, but he doesn't live there.

The most important event in all those centuries happened when the stones were still new. The central character is King John, son of the sad Henry. John was a nasty man and an exceptionally bad king. The barons—themselves no lilies—finally got together to curb the brute. They forced him to sign Magna Carta.

The scene is Runnymede.

Here you are on the flat, modernly dull road from London to Windsor. You're rolling along through the crowded town of Staines, where hurried new building is going on. Suddenly the town halts. It stops right on the verge of a green expanse that looks like the answer to a real-estate speculator's prayer. The long, bucolic meadow is Runnymede. It's preserved for the nation, and tourists, by the National Trust. But it won't mean a thing to you

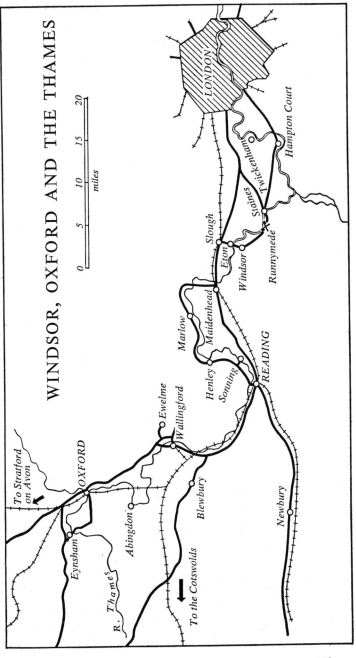

WINDSOR, OXFORD AND THE THAMES

unless you think of those barons camped on it under gaudy tents flying heraldic pennons.

Going on, pretty soon you're in Windsor town, and the castle rises before you, a grand bully. It was no good to John. The nobles knew better than to get themselves closed up with him in a castle like that. They were seven hundred years too soon to have read Scott's *Marmion*, but didn't need him to warn:

> And hopes thou hence unscathed to go?
> No, by St. Bride of Bothwell, no!
> Up drawbridge, grooms! What, warder, ho!
> Let the portcullis fall!

It was the barons who decided on the safe open meadow of Runnymede. Every day from June 15 to 23 (the year 1215) King John rode the four miles from Windsor Castle to Runnymede, where the barons hammered out the Great Charter. John, during the negotiations, nearly went mad with fury. He cursed, rolled his eyes, gnashed his teeth, gnawed twigs. The barons enjoyed the good June weather and ended with a splendid tournament.

John promptly broke all his Magna Carta pledges. Yet the document became the cornerstone of English liberties. It fired the imagination of later centuries. Freedom-fighters kept reading into it things that weren't there—and making them stick. So it's a Great Document, and the great grandfather of the American Bill of Rights—which sometimes also fails to guarantee what it guarantees.

If you're good at fanciful flights through space and time, you'll have no trouble linking Runnymede with Boston Common.

Time your Windsor jaunt to arrive for the Changing of the Guard, daily at 10:30 A.M. The same ceremony as at Buckingham Palace, it's more colorful at Windsor even though fewer men take part. You see a small contingent of bagpipes (or a band) followed by Redcoats, swing down High Street and into the castle, making an absurdly impressive parade under the massive walls and gateway. Falling in after them you watch the ceremony in the courtyard—no separation by iron fences, as at Buckingham.

*Redcoats.* This is where, with Magna Carta in mind, something else in history takes on life before your eyes. The American rebels knew these men, watched their stiffly disciplined maneuvers to the same howled and barked orders, saw the gracefully insolent officers strolling two by two. Here, in miniature, is the stylized military machine that did much to defeat itself in rough-and-tumble America.

Once it was formidable, terrible. Now it is toylike and archaic. But so perfect is the little pageant that even as you smile the years roll back, and on a stony parade ground an elite corps is under review for the last time before taking ship to Boston. . . .

The principal sights in the castle are the State Apartments, Queen's Doll House, Round Tower, Chapel, and Curfew Tower.

In the State Apartments we were struck by the general hideousness of formal royal grandeur (Herman Melville thought it "cheerlessly, damnatory fine"), and by the beauty and variety of the ceilings. Don't forget those ceilings as you go along.

The Queen's Doll House isn't a dear little thing that a queen played with. It's an ambitious affair designed by a sober, important architect and furnished by everyone in the country who could make miniatures for it. This engaging white elephant was presented as a gift to Queen Mary in 1923. She must have had quite a time deciding what to do with it. Tip: The official booklet on the Doll House is not worth buying.

There's no charge for walking up to the top of the Round Tower —the climb is punishment enough. When you get to the narrow stairs, think twice. This is the point of no return. Once you start up here, you can't turn back. But the view from the top, given a clear day, is splendid.

St. George's, the heraldic chapel of the Knights of the Garter, is, together with King's College Chapel in Cambridge, the most beautiful example extant of the ornate Perp. style. The lacy stone vaulting and the woodcarving are superb. Henry VIII is buried under a slab in the floor with Jane Seymour, a wife who kept her head.

The way to the Curfew Tower is through the Horseshoe Cloister, that court with the small Tudor houses. This tower is the one small part of the castle with that old, old look.

You can skip the Albert Memorial Chapel and the Dean's Cloister behind it. Go out and into the town and hire a carriage (if they're still available) for a ride up the Long Walk to Snow Hill. No cars allowed.

You can't see the castle when the royal family is in residence, which is usually during Easter and in mid-June at Ascot race time.

Windsor town is pleasant but unexciting. In 1961 its main streets had a thorough face-lifting, inspired by Norwich's example, to brighten its fine old houses. Part of the castle's outermost wall was taken down and green openness added to the upward curving sweep of the High Street.

RESTAURANTS  *  "Where do I eat?" you may want to know. Windsor does not shine in the restaurant field. The Old House is best, the Castle Hotel second.


§  ETON

The famous "public" (private) school is across the river from Windsor, at the top of its High Street, which is just about the only street in Eton. You can walk to it from Windsor, crossing the bridge; or take a bus.

Eton was the idea and the darling of Henry VI—a rare constructive project, for a king. He was only eighteen when he embarked upon it, a lank and solemn young man given to fits of melancholy. He had some reason for melancholy. This Henry's father, the hero of Agincourt, had died when he was a baby, and his lovely French mother had left him for a gay Welshman named Owen Tudor. Worse still, he had been born into the War of the Roses, and was to be its shuttlecock. But at this time, before his marriage to the battle-axe Margaret of Anjou, he had an unkingly passion to do Something Worth While, and was permitted to indulge it. Work began in 1441, and Henry was there to lay the cornerstone of the chapel.

This poor Henry had been born in Windsor Castle, and he spent as much time there as he could manage. Between battles and bouts of passive insanity, whenever he bumped into Eton students who sneaked into the castle to visit chums, Henry would give them a few coins and say, "Be good boys."

The little human gesture is touching. Henry stares while the boys bob, ready to run. An echo of something faraway reaches their Founder. "Be good." He himself had been a good boy, hadn't he? Dear God! But it doesn't bear thinking of.

Henry died in the Tower, "of pure displeasure and melancholy"

—or so it was given out. He was murdered. An unconvincing statue of him stands in the middle of Eton's school yard. Each year on the anniversary of his death, an Etonian lays a wreath of lilies in the cell where he died.

The college is a cluster of red-brick buildings with little towers and big twisted chimneys around courtyards. It's in the style called Tudor, which began well before the Tudor reign. Although somewhat messed up by later alterations and spottily brightened by modern repairs to bomb damage, it looks very old. The beautiful chapel has fifteenth-century wall paintings.

Opposite the chapel is the Lower School, the original schoolroom built by Henry and in use ever since. Beside it a passage goes by the dread doors labeled HEAD MASTER, and into the fields which brought from the Duke of Wellington his remark that Waterloo was won on the playing fields of Eton. Around the school yard the long lists of Etonians killed in wars are sadly to the point.

In the 1800's the young gentlemen's schools were notorious for brutality. School bullies tormented the smaller boys without mercy, and the headmasters taught on the principle that the buttocks were the seat of learning. Young Shelley at Eton, fagged and flogged, had no love for the dear old school. The headmaster in his time was Dr. Keate, who became famous for flogging eighty boys in one day—a record.

# § STOKE POGES

This is the churchyard of Thomas Gray's "Elegy in a Country Churchyard." We as schoolchildren had to memorize the poem— did you?—and vaguely remember it with nostalgia.

Why should anyone set out from Windsor on an hour's drive, made hazardous by the tentacled industrial town of Slough, just to see a country churchyard?

Because it is the loveliest churchyard in the world. It has old lych gates, a walk lined with tall rose bushes, tombs that are perfect little gardens, clipped yews, manicured greensward, a cozy old church (wear a sweater), and a Garden of Remembrance. Where but in England would you find such an endearing, and enduring, monument to a minor poet?

Well to one side you find the more usual kind of monument, an ugly pile, which says of the poet it honors: "He died July 30th, 1771, and lies unnoticed in the churchyard adjoining. . . ." If Thomas Gray was once lying there unnoticed, he certainly isn't now. Tourists by the busload come and go, destroying the peace the poet celebrated.

That's the trouble with Stoke Poges. The churchyard needs to be seen in solitude. A hundred trippers following a baying guide are ninety-nine-and-one guide too many.

# § *HAMPTON COURT*

Hampton Court is only thirteen miles from London, reckoning from Charing Cross, and easily accessible by London buses and by train from Waterloo. When it is part of a Windsor tour, with Stoke Poges thrown in, you return exhausted but feeling, "This time I got my money's worth!"

When we checked Hampton Court off our list, we found it wouldn't blank out. It remained unfinished business. We had to go back.

This is the palace that Cardinal Wolsey built in the enchanted days when he could do nothing wrong. It is a vast complex covering about eight acres and containing more than a thousand rooms. Yet it is so well ordered, balanced, and proportioned that it does not oppress or overwhelm. The red brick is warmer, somehow, than other red brick. The towers, gateways, and courtyards are just the right human size for affection. The decorative stonework and ornamental chimney clusters are gay. Sure taste, sober purpose, and an almost childlike delight went into the making of Hampton Court. More than any other man, Wolsey fixed the style called Tudor.

Thomas Wolsey was the butcher's boy who made good. He became a churchman because the Church was, for a commoner, the road to high office. As a young man he learned how to ingratiate himself with elderly noble patrons. Henry VII, at fifty a crochety ancient, made him his chaplain.

The sixteenth century had dawned, and bluff Prince Hal, Henry's heir, was the rising sun. Wolsey, while serving the narrow, grasping father, must have shown a different face to the son. To Prince Hal he revealed himself a man of mature years and wisdom, but not too old for sports, women, display, and lively foolery. Just the man, in short, for a young king who wanted majesty without tears.

Hal took the throne as Henry VIII in 1509. Within two years, Tom Wolsey became the most powerful man in the kingdom, and soon he was also the wealthiest. In London he built the mansion called York Place—Whitehall now stands on its site. Then on the Thames, within easy reach of London, he built a palace worthy of a chancellor and cardinal.

He was a busy man, governing both State and Church, yet he made time to supervise the building and furnishing of Hampton Court, from its water supply and drainage to coverlets and chamber pots. He installed five hundred retainers, a hundred sixty personal attendants, and an army of lesser servants, and kept two hundred eighty silken beds always ready for guests. He had gold plate in quantity, miles of velvet and satin hangings, acres of carpets and tapestries. His gardens were incomparable. Hampton Court then surpassed the present Buckingham Palace in size and splendor.

Ambassadors from Continental courts marveled at it. There was nothing like it in Europe, Rome aside. Henry was pleased. England had visibly become a Power.

And Henry took Hampton Court from Wolsey. It was for greedy Anne Boleyn that he took it, and York Place too, along with everything in them. Wolsey was lucky to die of an illness in time to escape the grosser ill of decapitation.

Fittingly, it was at Hampton Court in January 1536 that Anne Boleyn, Queen of England, surprised her husband with Jane Seymour on his knee. Four months later she laid her head on the block.

If you have seen Eton you will have, at Hampton Court, a feeling of familiarity. They are the same kind of architecture. Yet Eton is a century earlier, and was itself modeled on Winchester College, still another century earlier. And Winchester, speaking architecturally, is a castle crossed with a monastery. The slow line of development is clear.

What Wolsey did in Hampton Court was to make the castle

features entirely ornamental and playful. He concentrated on windows. He ran long galleries between the different parts of the palace so that he wouldn't have to cross open courtyards. He did away with the archaic Great Hall, making it instead a small entrance chamber. One of the first things Henry did was to tear down that chamber and make an old-fashioned Great Hall, complete with hearth in the middle and opening in the roof for the smoke to filter out. Henry was conservative. With this and other of his changes, nobody talked any more of the glories of Hampton Court.

But Wolsey's innovations lived on. There's scarcely a manor house in England that doesn't have a long gallery, Wolsey's suites of one room opening into the next, and Wolsey's basement kitchen. A few years after Wolsey's fall, Henry built St. James's palace in London—to prove that he could do it too? It's perfectly obvious that he couldn't.

There have been changes at Hampton Court since Wolsey's time and Henry's. You go through the State Apartments, about forty rooms (wear walking shoes). They are late seventeenth century, and were built to order for William and Mary. The tour takes in a little corner of Wolsey's palace and makes you want to see more. Unfortunately for sightseers, most of the old palace is lived in by royal pensioners.

You also see the gaudy chapel, and learn that Henry was there at mass when Catherine Howard, Wife No. 5, was arrested for adultery. Breaking away from her guards she ran to beg mercy of him, but was overtaken and carried off, screaming. She haunts the gallery beside the chapel.

Give yourself time to enjoy the gardens. They are unbelievably beautiful, and free.

RESTAURANTS  *  In summer, the cafeteria and tearooms near the car park are open. If you want a good meal, go across the road to the Mitre, which is expensive but worth it. If you'd like to lunch in a picturesque inn, walk or ride the mile to the Bell of East Moseley. Cross the Lutgens Bridge and turn up Creek Road opposite the railway station; you'll find it across the street from East Moseley's church. It is known locally as the

Crooked House, and you've never seen a crookeder. Its timbers are wracked with the rheumatism of five hundred years. The Hutters who run it make it a friendly informal place and set a good table at reasonable prices. The highwayman-dandy Claude Duval made it his rendezvous. He was eventually strung up for his crimes, and his epitaph in Covent Garden church pays him this tribute:

> Here lies Du Vall: Reader if male thou art
> Look to thy purse: if female to thy heart.

## § OXFORD

Oxford! City of dreaming spires! Egghead capital of the world!

Taxiing from the station we remembered a former visit. How, in the gardens of Magdalen, we watched the college deer gambol while we took turns reading aloud *Winnie the Pooh*, borrowed from the library of a maharaja's son whose rooms at Mrs. Pickering's we had while he was off on his Long Vac.

And how, in the chapel of All Souls, we stared with awe at the hundred stone figures under the carved canopies of the reredos, little knowing that fifty yards away, round the college dinner-table, its Fellows were creating the Tory policy of appeasement which paved the way for World War II.

And how——. But never mind. *Eheu! fugaces labuntur anni*, as the language still alive in Oxford puts it. Now we checked in at the Randolph Hotel and clamored for tea. The habit had us in its vicious grip. Dreaming spires could jolly well wait until we had fortified ourselves with several cuppas laced with milk and supported by toast and madeira cake.

Sipping and munching, we were startled to behold a new Oxford. Teatime was bringing strange creatures out of the woodwork. Into the staid Randolph's front lounge they crawled, male and female —it was not always easy to distinguish the sex—shaggy of hair, bearded, eye-shadowed, furtive, scowling, stunned-seeming, sloppy of garment, dungareed, leotarded, leather-jacketed, cowboy-booted, and pullovered in vomit-green. They sat; stared at us, at the wall, at their drinks, at one another, at nothing. They seemed to be waiting—for what? For Godot, for the revolution, for the nuclear war? Or only waiting to become men and women?

The head porter leaned over us to say, "Fair give you the creeps, don't they?"

Aye, porter, they did. Belatedly, but with a vengeance, Oxford had gone beatnik! Cambridge was never like this!

We wiped the butter from our chins, brushed the crumbs from our knees, and went off to see Oxford's changeless stones and gardens.

This time, we were really going to do Merton College. We had made a vow. Over the years we had several times started out for Merton and never got there. This time, bent on Merton and that alone, we veered left out of our hotel for a quick look at Worcester College. It would only take a minute. . . .

But let's start *you* off right.

Oxford is a university inside an industrial town of a hundred thousand population. It's the university you want to see. It consists of thirty colleges, each self-contained within its own walls. Each college consists of a series of buildings surrounding quads (quadrangles). Behind the quads are gardens. Figure an average of two quads per college, add gardens, add thirty chapels, dining halls and libraries (the sections usually, but not always, open to visitors)—and you begin to see what you're up against. Besides the colleges there are other notable buildings, and the famous High Street, and the Broad Walk, and the meadows. . . .

There are as many ways to see Oxford as there are to indite tribal lays. But not every blessed one of them is right. One expert has worked out an ingenious walk taking in everything of interest. It begins with a 145-foot climb to the top of Magdalen tower, followed by a one-mile perambulation of the Water Walks and of Magdalen's groves and gardens. Just for a start!

A nonsystem advanced by some veterans is to follow your own nose, saunter and meander where you list. But this is for the tourist with plenty of time.

Our own system, designed for a minimum of physical labor and a maximum of reward, is of course the best. It concentrates on the four most interesting colleges. It involves basic knowledge of the layout from advance mapwork.

Let your first act be to buy the local guidebook—at the hotel, the nearest bookstore, or the information office in the tower at Carfax, which is the center of town. The best is the forty-five-cent *Alden's Oxford Guide* (it has sold at this writing more than 368,000 copies). Less detailed, but sufficient for the hurried sightseer, is the twenty-cent *A Day in Oxford.*

Having done your homework, you will know that the part of Oxford that interests you is a half-mile square, bounded:

> on the west by Cornmarket and Magdalen streets, plus the nearer parts of St. Giles's and St. Aldate's;
> on the north by Broad and Holywell streets;
> on the east by Magdalen College;
> on the south by Christ Church College and the Broad Walk.

In this crowded area, the colleges most worth visiting are Magdalen (pronounced *Maudlin*), New College, Merton, and Christ Church.

Begin by walking on the Broad (you never say "street"; it's un-Oxonian) to that curious round-front building, the Sheldonian Theater. On the way, note on your left Balliol and Trinity, but do not let them divert you. That would be fatal.

The Sheldonian is behind the array of oversized stone heads whose features English weather has eroded. It was built in 1668 by Christopher Wren for University commemoration ceremonies. He was inspired by the Theater of Marcellus in Rome, but a very English cupola has got stuck up on top. Spend no time on the Sheldonian's interior but take the stairs (an easy climb) to the cupola for the eight-sided view of roofs, spires, pinnacles, towers, domes and, on the east, gas tanks. By recourse to your map, see if you can identify the buildings in view.

SPECIAL NOTE. We've brought you to the cupola not merely for the view but also to appreciate the fact that you needn't be concerned with architectural dates and periods. It's a relief to see that everything is hopelessly jumbled, and that a comparatively simple structure may combine Gothic, "classical," and an individuality that can only be called fantastic.

Coming down now, advance south with firm tread into the maze. It begins with Old Schools Quadrangle on which rise the Divinity School, the Tower of the Five Orders, and the Bodleian, one of the world's richest libraries. There is also the statue of the Earl of Pembroke, and over the ground-floor rooms ahead and on your left the names of the "faculties" of the Old Schools that moved out eighty years ago to give the Bodleian more space.

There are things worth exploring inside, such as the fine hall of Divinity, and those parts of the Bodleian the authorities will admit you to. If you are off-season or off-hours for the Bodleian, and if you have a good-looking young woman in your party, remember that even librarians are human. Let her run interference. But not now—later. We are bound for Magdalen.

If our tread has been firm enough, you and we suddenly erupt into an open space. Before us in the center grass plot is a freakish building: Radcliffe Camera, now a Bodleian reading room. Colleges cluster: on the east, Hertford and All Souls; on the west, Exeter and Brasenose, and over the roofs of Brasenose, Lincoln. Resist the impulse to call on them. (All about here is the locus of David Frome's *Mr. Pinkerton Finds a Body*, a whodunit that makes good Oxford bedside reading.)

On the south side of the square is venerable St. Mary's, the University church, with a long history we can't stop for. It fronts on the High, on which we walk eastward toward Magdalen's imposing tower. At the corner of Queen's Lane we stop for a backward look at the High. This is the best vantage point from which—the jam-up of traffic permitting—to see that fine street. But charge tourist propaganda with exaggeration when it speaks of the High's "streamlike meanderings." One slight curve doesn't make a meandering.

So we pass into Magdalen, conceded to be the wealthiest and loveliest of the colleges. It's the only one making use of Oxford's waterways. Magdalen has six quadrangles and some fifty acres of grounds. Wander through the quads, find the cloisters (by way of that passage through the Muniment Tower), then amble about the gardens and meadows. Watch the young men playing bowls on the greens with their girl friends. Look at the college deer in the enclosed park called the Grove; we hope that for you they'll be leaping and hurdling and not merely nibbling.

Magdalen's campus (a word never used at Oxford) is idyllic. In fact, its out-of-doors is more rewarding than the indoors. So when you have looked and walked your fill in the meadows where Joseph (*Spectator*) Addison, Edward (*Decline and Fall*) Gibbon, Prince Rupert, Charles (*Cloister and Hearth*) Reade walked before you, let us decamp by the exit on Long Wall Street and head for New College.

We go north, turn into Holywell, and after a hundred yards pass through a gate on our left and through the old city wall.

We are in a college six hundred years New, and here both outdoors and in are fascinating. Invade the Hall, a splendid room with oak ceiling and linenfold paneling. (Compare with your own college commons room if it had one, or your fraternity or sorority dining room.) Pass on to the lofty chapel, with its ornate reredos, the Joshua Reynolds window, the fourteenth-century window, and misericords (look under choir-stall seats). It has, besides, the great statue of Lazarus by Epstein, and a newly acquired El Greco. The Greco, easier for an enthusiast to walk off with than the Lazarus or the windows, has put an end to casual sightseeing. No wandering about alone any more. When the attendant leaves, you go. On the way out, promenade the wood-vaulted cloisters and the generous expanse of garden bordered by the old wall.

Last time we were there, we were about to issue forth into Holywell when we saw, across the street, four small rosy-cheeked boys who were scampering along suddenly stop and form into twos at the curb. In their school uniform of black shorts, blazers, and mortarboard hats they stood at attention until a larger boy, appearing from behind us, took charge and brought them into the college for practice in choir school. Wheels within wheels—the incident went off like a mechanical toy.

But don't leave New College by the way you came in. To save footwork, leave by the gate on New College Lane. As you follow this narrow alley into Queen's Lane, watch out for the traffic which can't make the turns without mounting the sidewalk.

Why not pop into Queen's—very briefly? After all, we've got half our chore done—two colleges down, two to go.

Queen's has eighteenth-century pseudo-classic façades and a colorful hall by Christopher Wren. But the inner essence of Queen's isn't something you can see. Possibly you can feel it. It is eccentric, and therefore typical of academic England. Members are summoned to dinner by trumpet instead of by bell. For Christmas dinner the main dish is boar's head, ushered in by carols, all to celebrate the escape of a scholar who, attacked by a wild boar in a nearby forest, had the presence of mind to thrust his copy of Aristotle down the beast's throat. Naturally the animal fell back and died. After the boar's head, a normal week is allowed to pass. Then, on New Year's day, the Bursar hands around needles and thread, saying, "Take this and be thrifty." Buried in this admonition is an atrocious pun in French on the name of the founder, de Eglesfield—*aiguille* plus *fil*. Got it?

One wonders if they're able to go through all this without feeling a little silly. But a titterer can always sober himself with the fact that Queen's has the largest collection of Slavonic books this side the Khrushchev Kurtain, and that anyone who wants to know what a certain medieval boyar said to a hostile hetman has to come here.

So on to Merton. But—

What is that sign across Queen's Lane? "The condition of this tower is dangerous. Please do not park or linger."

That's the church of St. Peter's-in-the-East. The tower is tired, having stood up for almost eight hundred years. Why not have a look around? But quickly—this time we *must* get to Merton.

Your local guidebook will tell you that the crypt is the oldest part and the most celebrated, but will fail to add that it is nearly always barred. You can look through the bars, however, and glimpse the old pillars and arches built about 1150. All the centuries from William the Conqueror's eleventh have left behind some reminder in stone in this small church. When last we were here we missed Merton because we peered at every stone in the churchyard looking for the grave of James Sadler, the first English spaceman. We never found it, but we did find the tablet in the west wall of the nave.

James was a dependable baker in the High until he read in the papers of the Montgolfiers' balloon ascents in France. He deserted his ovens and devoted his life to getting into orbit. Filling with hot air a homemade balloon sixty yards in circumference, he ascended, in 1784, to thirty-five hundred feet—the first Englishman to get so far off the ground. The next month he did it again. Twenty-seven years later he achieved his greatest triumph, getting blown from Birmingham to Boston (*their* Boston, not ours) in under four hours—for those days practically breaking the sound barrier. Sadler was the first human being to travel as fast as twenty-five miles an hour and live to be congratulated. Somewhere in the churchyard a space six feet by two and a half waited for him to crack up, but he never had an accident and died in bed at seventy-five.

Dropping in on St. Peter's makes a good change of scene. The peace and quiet here is like that at Gray's Stoke Poges.

But duty calls, and picking up our firm tread we advance upon Merton. There is a peril on the way—how to cross the High. The traffic is continuous and remorseless, and the only stop light is at Carfax, too far away. But we as guides have our limits; we have no formula for circumventing Oxford's traffic. We will assume that you have crossed, have found Logic Lane, have turned from it into Merton Street and have discovered on your left the college gate.

Approach Merton with deepest respect. It is the oldest Oxford foundation, dating from the thirteenth century. The buildings which house it compose the most interesting lot, architecturally, in the University.

See as much of it as you can, but certainly these: the thirteenth-century chapel, famous for its 650-year-old painted glass; the medieval library, with some old books still chained; the hall, rebuilt in Victorian times but retaining the antique atmosphere; the seventeenth-century Fellows' Quadrangle; and the Treasury or Muniment Room, the oldest college building in Oxford. Although talk about the weather—the oldest, most universal English preoccupation—did not originate here, it was here developed; the first consistent weather-recorder was a Merton sage.

In the Middle Ages, when to be controversial was dangerous, Merton was a hotbed of speculation. This college advanced the cause of free circulation of ideas—hats off to it. And an extra cheer for being the alma mater of Max Beerbohm—essayist, parodist, caricaturist, and author of the fantasy on Oxford university life, *Zuleika Dobson*. Admirers of the Incomparable Max should visit the new Beerbohm Room where his original drawings, books,

manuscript, and only dab at oil painting are on exhibit. Before
leaving Merton do the gardens, Dead Man's Walk, and the terrace
on the city wall (views).

Back on Merton Street, a walk west of some two hundred yards
brings you into the Canterbury gate of Christ Church. Largest of
the colleges, its five hundred undergraduates are several thousand
fewer than those of even a modest midwestern "cow college." (All
the colleges together have about 7200 undergraduates, of whom
about 1200 are women. Compare this with the 1961–62 enrollment
of the City University of New York's seven municipal colleges:
about 95,000 in round numbers.) Nevertheless "the House," as
Christ Church is called, has been educating youths into men for
about 440 years—among them Philip Sydney, John Locke, Ruskin,
Hakluyt, Wesley, William Penn ("sent down"—which means
kicked out—for nonconformity), "Lewis Carroll," Gladstone—and
so on down a long roster.

One of its several peculiarities is that the college chapel is also
the cathedral of Oxford. Another is that Great Tom, the 6¼-ton
bell in Tom Tower, bongs 101 times at 9:05 P.M. On the last stroke
all the porters shut the college gates.

From Canterbury quad bear right into Peckwater quad. It has
the library; you can skip this if your time is short or your feet hurt.
Skirting the Canons' Garden, go into Tom quad, the largest in
Oxford. It fails to be as impressive as the Great Court of Cambridge's Trinity or King's College, possibly because it is too large
for the height (or lowth) of its buildings. The gateway-with-tower
on the northeast corner is called Kill-Canon because of its drafti-
ness. If the quatrain that begins, "I do not like thee, Dr. Fell,"
means anything to you, look here for the statue of the victim.

Under the Tom Tower you find the grand staircase (elaborate
ceiling) leading to the hall, one of the glories of the house. It has
portraits by such masters as Reynolds, Gainsborough, Lawrence,
Millais, Kneller, and Lely. Your eye will be drawn to the famous
Henry VIII, ascribed to Holbein, which has typed that monarch
as conclusively as Gilbert Stuart's Washington has done for the
immortal George.

This noble medieval room has seen noble doings. Henry VIII,
Elizabeth I, James, and Charles I were here. Charles, doomed, his
head good for only five more years, assembled here those Members

of Parliament who were loyal. On leaving, take the right-hand stairway down to the kitchens, where an ox could still be roasted whole.

After all this, don't feel depressed by not getting excited over the chapel-cathedral. It is not one of England's great churches.

Now that we, with your help and our system, have at last managed to see Merton, we are going to leave you. As you went along you may have seen, here and there, new structures being built to add to the lively architectural confusion; for example, some dormitories that look like Florida hotels. Amid the ancient stonework the effect is startling—as if Granny had gone giddy, got herself a gamin hairdo, and had her aged eyelashes mascaraed. One of these is at Queen's College; another is at St. John's. Three new colleges are abuilding: Nuffield, endowed by the automobile tycoon, in a gabled style that attractively straddles Gothic and modern; St. Catherine's, and St. Anthony's. The last, designed by a modernist Danish architect should be, with its land- and waterscaping, a beauty.

If Magdalen's Water Walks did not give it away, you would hardly know that Oxford was on the Thames and the Cherwell. They call the Thames the Isis here, and you find it at Folly Bridge, south of Christ Church. From here to Iffley is the famous stretch of river where the college races are rowed. That other river, the Cherwell (*Charwell*) is for leisurely punting and canoeing. Boats can be hired at Folly Bridge and Magdalen Bridge. From Folly you can board a steamer for a river trip to Henley or Windsor. Given good weather—and when we did it, the weather was glorious —the two-day float to Windsor through locks and along idyllic shores is unforgettable.

WHAT TO DO AT NIGHT? * We went out one evening to meet the undergraduates in their favorite pubs: the Turf, the King's Arms, the White Horse (a few hoof-steps away in the Broad), the Bear Inn near Christ Church, and the bar of the Randolph. We found these solidly packed, with an overflow into corridors and out of doors. The Turf, up an extremely narrow alley off narrow New College Lane, is the oddest, having a "garden" populated by empty bottles, rejected lettuce, and primitive chairs and tables, some occupied by clusters of "beats" who were being alone with the universe. The expedition was a failure, for there wasn't room for even the skinniest tourist. And if there had been? The collegians form a club, a group of clubs. Nowhere do you feel so much the complete outsider as right in the thick of them.

On our train back to London we read in our *New Statesman* an extract from a letter published in the London *Evening Standard:*

> How can I get to meet one of those grubby, ill-looking girls who wear cotton trousers and their hair all over their faces? I feel she would help to make my life less humdrum while I am learning to be a char-tered accountant.

Man, go to Oxford, and at 4:30 P.M. stand on Magdalen Street near the Martyrs' Memorial, and take your choice.

SIGHTSEEING NOTE.    During the Long Vacation, mid-June to mid-October, the colleges are easier to see, but the students are gone, the tourists are there instead, and Oxford isn't the same. (This is also true of Cambridge.) The last ten days of May are wonderful, with the cricket matches, boat races, commemoration ceremonies and balls—but all the hotels are packed with parents, relatives, and sweethearts.

*HOTELS* * The Randolph (a Trust House) is a notable hotel, and biggest and best. In summer ask for a room in the older part; ceilings are higher, rooms more spacious. The W.C.s offer two kinds of toilet paper, Standard British and Approximate American—a boon. Breakfast is extra, and four kinds are offered: Continental, Plain, Short, and Full. The Plain is "Full breakfast without main dish"! Attentive porters, large lounges. . . . The Mitre has been bedding down people plain and fancy for centuries. When we went in to assess it, we were met by unfriendly porter, indifferent desk. . . . The King's Arms and Golden Cross are also old in service; tariffs much lower than at the other two.

*RESTAURANTS* * The Roebuck in Market Street is very good, the Regency in St. Giles's, good. These ratings are based on one meal in each. . . . The Mitre enjoys a reputation for good plain English cooking. On Oxford's rim are the Perch at Bonsey opposite Port Meadow; the Trout at Godstow Lock; and the White Hart at Witham. All three are in interesting country, historically and otherwise, and popular with university people. Ask directions in Oxford.

*ENVIRONS* * Iffley village is a mile and a half away, an enjoyable river walk or a short hop by bus. It has little more than a fine Norman church.

Eight miles north by the Worcester road is the pleasant village of Woodstock, with the Bear, good inn for eating or staying in. Behind it stands Blenheim Palace, amid considerable green real estate, a super-Stately Home presently valued at six million dollars. This vast ornate stone barrack, admired by architects, is the largest private residence in England. It was built "by the nation" for John Churchill, Duke of Marlborough, in gratitude for his victory at Blenheim (see Southey's famous poem, "It was a famous victory.") Open to the public (fee), it is hard to believe even when seen. Sir Winston was born here.

The guides, as in other Statelies, fill you in on family history, but some good bits don't get into the script. When we were part of the guided pack we were not told how the Duchess of Marlborough terrorized poor pale Queen Anne until the queen finally worked up the courage to sack the duchess from her boss-of-the-household post. In fact, Anne was so irked that for years she held back the money and the work on this outsize gift to the duke.

Recall that the Dukes of M. do not hold this property rent-free. They are obliged to pay the Crown a flag every year on the anniversary of Blenheim.

The trippers gather on the front porch. When about thirty have accumulated, the great doors are flung open. The wind being right, as it was when we were there, a draft the might of a half-gale blows the whole lot into a lobby the size of the Waldorf-Astoria's. You are inside a monument, not a home. To borrow from Randolph Churchill lines he attributes to one Dr. Abel Evans

> Thanks, Sir, cry'd I, 'tis very fine
> But where d'ye sleep, or where d'ye dine?
> I find by all you have been telling
> That 'tis a House but not a dwelling.

Blenheim is a form of palatial elephantiasis that deserves to be seen.

*TRAVEL FACTS* * Oxford is an easy run from London, fifty-four miles by express trains in sixty-five minutes; just under three hours by bus. Mid-May to mid-September, steamers ply between Kingston (near Hampton Court) and Folly Bridge, taking two and a half to three days with two overnight stops. Passengers may leave or board at any stopping place and take a later steamer, if space is available.

# § *THAMES PLEASURES & PLACES*

The best way to enjoy the Thames (pronounced *Tems*) is to know people who own a house on it somewhere between Windsor and Abingdon. Preferably with cabin cruiser.

It isn't easy to engineer this. We didn't—it just happened that English friends of ours moved from a commonplace suburb to a house near Bray. Their rose garden runs down to the river, their boat rocks beside their private pier, and Charley (a swan) calls daily. You may well envy our good luck, for the Thames is a holiday river.

If you don't have the right kind of friends, the second best way is the do-it-yourself. You can drive from one riverside village or town to another. Or be chugged in an excursion launch. Or go by rented boat—anything from a punt to a cruiser sleeping two to ten is available. You can spend hours—or weeks—on the river.

Anatomically speaking, a river begins at its head and ends at its mouth. The most famous of English rivers has the puniest of heads, the mightiest mouth. It begins as a dribble near Cirencester —so insignificantly that exactly where is a matter of debate—and travels some 210 miles to end as an imperial flood below London.

We are mainly concerned here with the segment of almost seventy miles between Windsor and Oxford. This is the pleasure Thames. From spring to late fall it is the gayest stream in the world. People swarm over it in everything that floats. Fishermen, picnickers, and lovers line its banks. The lawns of riverside inns bloom umbrellas and tables.

An old French guidebook to Guadeloupe, written by a Creole whose command of English matches ours of French, called a local park "the municipal lungs, where come the people to breathe."

This is not a bad description of the Thames. It is the Englishman's, and especially the Londoner's, playground and play-water. The census of river craft gives the total as 11,415: 7603 small boats, 3633 launches, 179 houseboats. The constant happy traffic moves through a landscape unblighted (except for a short stretch at Reading) by industry. Thanks to the century-old battle, still in progress, of the Thames Conservancy Board, the water is clean.

The pleasure Thames is full of variety. Meadows, groves, and gardens run down to the water. Mansions and bungalows, boathouses and locks, are sightly. Great willows droop over the stream. Islets float on it. Cliffs and wooded hills spring up and fall away. Swans sail up and down or waddle ashore imperiously begging.

*RIVERSIDE WINDSOR* * The castled royal town has always been an important river station. Crowds romp along the banks. There's a broad spread of public park on the river, stone quays, landing stages, two boatyards, marine engineers, supply shops.

TIP FOR WALKERS.   You can walk on the north bank from Windsor to Maidenhead by the footpath that used to be a towpath for barges. The path isn't well kept—every spring the first hikers have to tramp down the nettles. But it's a most pleasant walk. Bray is a better goal than Maidenhead; on the opposite bank, via ferry.

*BRAY* * The rambling brick and half-timbered village is a favorite with both river trippers and motorists. Its fine church has a Norman tower and a lych gate, and with the seventeenth-century Jesus Hospital (almshouse) is one of the sights hereabouts. Bray's lock is known for its prize-winning garden.

The Hind's Head at Bray is one of the famous Thames-side inns. So is Monkey Island Hotel, on an islet in the river joined to the mainland by its own bridge. Londoners drive out to dine at these two places. They used to come for the Hotel de Paris as well, but that is gone now. The ferry goes from Messum's Boatyard. No schedule; it's on hail.

You're just a little too late for olde-look Bray. Modern building is creeping in.

*MAIDENHEAD* * A busy town on a main line from London (Paddington station), it lacks distinction. But on the outskirts is Skindles Hotel, a de luxe resort with riverside gardens, bars, restaurants, dancing at night, good hotel rooms and lounges.

*CLIVEDEN* * From Maidenhead, one of the most beautiful reaches of the river lies ahead. The entrance to it is Boulter's Lock, half a mile upstream from Maidenhead bridge. Here ends the wide Thames plain, here begins the curving, luxuriant valley. Boulter's Inn, at the lock, used to be good; it had slipped last time we tried it.

Above the lock lies the spectacular Cliveden Reach—a soft green, idyllic, sweeping curve in the river bordered by high woods and cliffs. Cliveden, the Astor mansion, is on your right, most of it hidden from view by its wooded cliff-top. Now a National Trust property, it's open to the public Thursday afternoon. Cliveden has an American connection. Before she married Viscount Astor, Lady Astor was Nancy Witcher, daughter of a Virginia colonel.

*died May 1964*

COOKHAM * This riverside village has a woodsy setting, a lock, a narrow bridge, a stubby church tower, old inns, Tudor houses. The church is worth a visit in spite of its self-advertising signboards on trees: SEE A CHURCH MORE THAN 850 YEARS OLD.

The Bel and Dragon is a grand old inn, with garden. But our lunch there was only so-so. Then we discovered the Royal Exchange on High Street—a pub with snack meals run by the hearty, friendly Mr. McPherson, a man who loves his house and has made it a thing of beauty. The Exchange and the King's Arms across the street share a bit of Nell Gwyn history.

Nell Gwyn, and now Sir Stanley Spencer. Suddenly in 1962 Cookham gained international notice through the posthumous fame of a native son, a painter of decided individuality. A Victorian chapel houses the canvases celebrating trash cans, Bible stories, and homely local scenes. The Gallery, open in summer, also exhibits such touching Spenceriana as the rickety baby-carriage he used for wheeling about his paints and easel, his folding seat, his umbrella and his printed plea asking passersby not to distract him at work.

TIP TO MOTORISTS. From the village, search out the road marked Cookham Rise and Cookham Deane going to Marlow. Near the top of the Rise stands a trio of thatched cottages so perfect that you want to laugh in sheer delight. We call them the

Berkshire Beauties. You can park on the verge of the woods across the road to stare. Continuing, you drive through a midsummer night's dream of a woods to Marlow.

MARLOW  *  Above Cookham at Bourne End, the river curves between meadows and the Quarry Woods. Here lies a sail-boat reach where regattas are held. Bourne End reach is noted for its attractive riverside villas with beautiful gardens.

Marlow, farther on, is a pleasant small town and a good center for exploring the river and valley. Shelley's wife wrote *Franken-stein* in Marlow, little knowing what Hollywood monsters she was spawning. Earlier Izaak Walton wrote *Compleat Angler* here.

The Compleat Angler Hotel, on the site of the inn where he stayed, is elegantly Georgian and its groomed lawn spreads above the dramatic weir. It has a huge, fashionable restaurant and charm-ingly furnished rooms. At the Saturday-night dinner-dance, eve-ning dress is preferred. Prices run high—justifiably for a superior resort hotel thirty-one miles from London, twenty-one from Oxford, eight from Windsor. Among Marlow's old buildings, the Old Ship, an inn on the Henley road, is worth seeing; and in High Street, the Chequers. The Two Brewers, opposite the Com-pleat Angler, is just as old but has a roadhouse look.

CALLING ALL TOURISTS.   See Bekonscot in Beaconsfield (a few miles east of Marlow) while it's still there.

The most detailed guidebook we know says of Beaconsfield that it is 23 miles from London, and that from it visits can be made to Jordans (2 m.) and Chalfont St. Giles (4 m.)—"etc."

Lurking behind that *etc.*, we discovered for ourselves, was Bekonscot, on the Warwick road. This is a must if you have children or if the child survives in your own nature. Bekonscot is an enchanting miniature town spread over ten thousand square yards of miniature landscape, with churches, shops, hotels, a lake, bridges, an airport, two castles, Tudor, Georgian and modern houses, twelve hundred feet of lively toy railway, a race track, polo grounds. Doll-people sit on their lawns; a diver is about to take off; the pink-coated hunt is after the fox; at the race track the thoroughbreds are rounding the turn; and from the churches you can hear the choir singing. You walk about, and you are Gulliver in an English town. We were so spellbound that when we looked at each other to exclaim, our respective sizes gave us a shock. The scale, the gardening, the plan, the details, are perfect.

Bekonscot, in spite of the fact that it isn't allowed to advertise, has been visited since 1928 by more than three million people, including the royal family (confirmed repeaters), and makes some $28,000 a year, all of which goes to charities. The man who made it was a retired accountant named Callingham who was keen on gardening. It originated and grew in his vegetable patch. Growing it took a deal of trouble, but that was nothing compared to the trouble the Beaconsfield town council gave Mr. Callingham. They tried to close him down on the plea that Bekonscot brought so many people it was a nuisance! Callingham died in 1961 at the age of eighty-one. The Appeal Court has given the wonderful toy town until 1964 to move or obliterate itself.

You may go on to—

Jordans, one of the earliest Quaker meeting houses. Under the plain tombstones on its lawn William Penn, his two wives, and some of their children lie buried. Farther up the road is the Jordans Hostelry, where the Quakers first met, in the so-called Mayflower Barn, said to have been built with timbers from the *Mayflower*. The Meeting House and the Hostelry are places of serenity in lovely country.

Chalfont St. Giles, beyond Jordans, can be skipped.

*HURLEY*  *  Above Marlow the Thames twists south and west. Hurley is famed for its inn, Ye Olde Bell. It claims the founding date of 1135, making one raise an eyebrow—but why haggle? It specializes in good eating and good cheer. The service is not only impeccable, it is friendly, in a cheerfully antique dining room. Upstairs are hotel suites and bedrooms furnished in genuine period stuff (expensive, of course). A great house, much frequented by London escapists from Mayfair and Belgravia.

Islands apear in the river as it corkscrews past Medmenham Abbey, which for a time was notorious for the revels of the Hellfire Club, some black-mass romantics with twisted minds. The Thames, as if to get away from all that, suddenly decides to plunge south, and enters the Henley reach, 22 miles from Windsor.

*HENLEY*  *  The reach, more than a mile long, has been the mecca of oarsmen since 1829, when the first rowing regatta was held (Oxford won). The exciting contests for the Grand Challenge Cup for Eights, the Silver Goblets for Pairs, and the Diamond Challenge Sculls, take place first week in July.

Henley is a small market town with timbered houses on Market Street, Hart Street, and side streets and lanes. But modern building, including a "skyscraper," threatens. For a meal, and to see its incorporated fourteenth-century Chantry House, hie to the Red Lion.

WARGRAVE  *  About three miles south of Henley, this is a village favored by artists. The George and Dragon is the inn. Its sign was painted by two members of the Royal Academy. They painted on one side the traditional St. George on horseback with spear entering Dragon. On the other side, Dragon is defunct and George, dismounted and looking pleased, is defeating a tankard of beer.

SONNING  *  The reach of six miles from Henley to Sonning is one of the most beautiful. It passes Wargrave, where under the railway bridge the Thames is joined by the Lodden.

Sonning is among the loveliest of English villages. The old houses, exquisitely cared for, are either brick-and-timber or magpie, so that the village is all red, white, and black among its lawns and gardens. Sonning church has a famous peal of bells and some old brasses. Sonning Lock is one of the prettiest on the river, with a prize-winning garden. It's an old tradition that Sonning's lock-keepers must be "characters." One of them was a poet and bee-keeper.

Jerome K. Jerome called this village "the most fairy-like little nook on the river." A wealthy, highly touristed river resort, it is remarkable for the absence of cheap commercialism. Every inhabitant keeps his precious house and garden in perfect condition. When, recently, Sonning was ordered to adopt modern street lighting, the people refused flatly on the grounds it would spoil their village's appearance. They had to give in, but designed a modern approximation of coach lanterns, each so arranged as to cast artful patterns of light and shade on the houses.

There are no fewer than three famous inns. The French Horn, with a glorious willow tree on the river which is floodlit at night, is elegant and the most expensive. Its ground floor decor is Wedgwood, its bedrooms are Regency. The Bull, which was old in the first Elizabeth's day, is gracious and dignified in the early Tudor style. The half-timbered White Hart has its own personality and a famed rose garden.

READING  *  (Pronounced *Redding*) is the blight on the pleasure Thames. It's a 115,000-population factory town (Huntley and Palmer biscuits), but a progressive one, with a university, parks, a museum of Roman relics, an art gallery. It has a long pre-biscuit history but is not a tourist stop in spite of Oscar Wilde's having written here "The Ballad of Reading Gaol," and a monk the music for "Somer is icumen in, Lude sing cuckoo"—a medieval lyric which you may remember as the first item (unless Beowulf sneaked in) of your school Anthology of Eng. Lit.

STREATLEY, GORING  *  At Mapledurham Lock, above Reading, begins the third scenic reach of the Thames. The mill and weir at this lock have been painted and repainted by artists, amateur and pro. Then comes a broad stretch of a mile and a half where naval cadets are trained in boatmanship; the Nautical College is at Pangbourne village. Manor houses stand on the banks.

Streatley, an attractive village, is at the top of this scenic reach. Goring is across the river. The bridge between the two, with the lock and weir beside it, are as much painted as the Mapledurham scene. The Roman Icknield Way crossed the Thames here by ford. The good inn is the Swan at Streatley.

TIP TO MOTORISTS.  Go from Streatley five and a half miles up Riddle Hill to Blewbury. Brush by the outer or modern shell and get to the heart of this village. You find a maze of lanes among thatched, wattle-and-daub houses, and the Load of Mischief Inn— a medieval guffaw, its sign shows a man carrying his wife piggy-back. The little old church still rings the curfew, and has a chained Bible of 1613. Among the oddities are the walls topped with thatch —which is something like tying a bonnet on the kitchen stove. Blewbury was already venerable in 900 A.D., and Kenneth Grahame (*The Wind in the Willows*), who escaped here from his admirers, wrote to a friend: "It is only about 54 miles from London, but 5400 years remote from it in every other way." Author G. B. Stern was living in Blewbury when we came that way, but mindful of Grahame we spared her our adulation.

WALLINGFORD  *  It was a Roman settlement, had a borough charter in 1155, and in the Middle Ages boasted fifteen churches; three survive. The town today is only mildly interesting. The Lamb is a Tudor inn with Georgian complications.

TIP TO MOTORISTS.  See Ewelme near Wallingford but nearer (two miles east) riverside Benson.

EWELME  *  It makes no attempt to be a tourist sight. Please respect it.

This considerable village, bordered by watercress farms, has a church, almshouses, and school which form a fifteenth-century entity of strong, individual character.

On our first sight of the church, something about its checkerboard stone-and-flint façade made us tensely silent. The moment when a building talks, communicates, is almost unbearably suspenseful. Tentatively one tests, like an uncertain dog with all senses alert. The experience ends either in snarling disappointment or the gladness of wagging tail and ecstatic barks.

Ewelme's church is splendidly proportioned and very rich. There is much to see (buy the good church booklet), including heraldic stained glass. We were excited by the Chaucer monuments, which brought us to some history we'd known nothing of.

It seems that Geoffrey Chaucer (*Canterbury Tales*) had a son, Thomas, who became Lord of the Manor of Ewelme through his wife, Matilda Burghersh. Their daughter Alice married William de la Pole, Duke of Suffolk. Alice and William built the present church, almshouses, and school.

This Duke of Suffolk was horribly murdered. Shakespeare makes him a traitor with a fitting end, but our sympathies are with the duke. He was made the popular scapegoat for Henry VI's losses in wars with France. The King banished him, ostensibly to save his life. On an English ship off Calais, the duke found himself prisoner. A boat rowed out with a block and a masked executioner. The decapitation was badly bungled. Suffolk was hacked to death with a rusty sword in the little boat bobbing on the sea while the men in the tall ship leaned over the rails, watching and commenting.

Alice lies in the church in alabaster on her tomb, wearing the ducal coronet. The effigy is beautiful. The entire tomb is of alabaster, a highly elaborate affair. The church booklet advises you to lie on the floor if you want to see the frescoes painted on the roof of the tomb's lowest compartment. Her father, Thomas Chaucer, and her mother, the Lady Matilda, share a plainer tomb ornamented by medieval shields on which scholars have done some fascinating detective work.

At the back of the church is a heavy hanging. Go behind it, and you find a flight of stone steps deeply hollowed from long use. They lead to the cloister, which is a courtyard with the gabled almshouses around it. (Quiet! the houses are occupied.)

Leave the cloister by the north doorway. It opens into the churchyard. We found here the grave of Jerome K. Jerome, lover of the Thames, author of that minor classic, *Three Men in a Boat*, which you'll want to read when you do the river.

Ewelme once had a small royal palace. Nothing is left of it, but there's a village lane locally known as Queen Elizabeth's Walk. And somewhere among the watercress is the King's Pool, given that name because Anne Boleyn pushed Henry VIII into it one day when his pawing got on her nerves.

The fifteenth-century school buildings lie to the right of the church.

DORCHESTER  *  Between Wallingford and Dorchester you see the double hill of Sinodun, known to earthy locals as the Berkshire Bubs and Mother Dunch's Buttocks. At Shillingford bridge, the Bridge Hotel has a swimming pool and a reputation for good food.

Dorchester, where the Thame joins the Thames, was an important Saxon town. Its interesting abbey church was saved at the Dissolution by a local citizen who bought it from the Crown for £140 and presented it to the parish. The little town has cottages of thatched roofs growing moss and TV aerials. The inns are the George and the White Hart, fierce rivals in coaching days. The George preserves one of the old coaches. It was the abbey's hospice, and the raftered dining room was originally the monks' brewhouse.

There are photogenic villages hereabouts. Clifton Hampden, upstream and on Dorchester's side of the river, is dreamlike. Its inn is the Barley Mow, deserving the adjective *quaint*. Sutton Courtenay, across the river, is on a backwater in a lovely setting.

ABINGDON * You'll have noticed that the character of the Thames has changed. It is bucolic. The London holiday-makers are left behind. The fishing is better, the boating less traffic-ridden. Abingdon is the last town before Oxford. It was built thirteen hundred years ago around a monastic foundation. In the fourteenth century the people rose against the monks, helped by Oxford's mayor and undergraduates, and wreaked merry havoc. See the remains of the abbey, the Queen's Hotel (Georgian), St. Helen's church, the Guildhall. The town was called the Queen of the River, but is no longer beautiful.

Oxford is six miles away by water.

ABOVE OXFORD * The Upper River, from Oxford to Lechlade, floats only small craft. This is a Thames of birdsong, flowers, trees, meadows, and solitude. Among water lilies hide villages where the crash of a newspaper headline is unheard—Bablock Hythe, Cumnor where Amy Robsart died, Eynsham with its toll bridge, Stanton Harcourt, Radcot, Kelmscott where William Morris lived; his grave is in the churchyard. Finally, the small town of Lechlade.

The Thames is now a narrowing stream interlaced with brooks and shaded by willows and poplars. If you're troubled by a lack of occupation, you can try tracing it to a burble on the border of the Cotswold Hills and join the controversy about which burble and where. If you find the right one, don't drop a penny into it the way they do in Rome—you might stop it up. And then what would they say in London?

# § SWANS, LOCKS, BOATS

THE SWANS * You're bound to make their acquaintance. They cruise alongside the boats or waddle up to riverside inns demanding handouts. People who live on the Thames know them more intimately. When our friends were well settled into their riverside house, Charley introduced himself. He clambered up on their lawn, waded through their rose bushes, and probably would have knocked on their door with his beak if they hadn't come out with offerings. Thereafter, their land and piece of river was his territory and he chased other swans away from it. There was a little trouble with him about the rose bushes, but he soon learned to keep to the path. A swan on the water is the most graceful creature afloat; on land it's ridiculous. Charley, heaving his heavy body up on the bank and rolling up the path on big flat feet, looks like a drunken sailor. When we were last there, Charley brought us down to the river to present his wife and Junior, a ball of brown fluff riding on his mother's back, and almost ready to be "upped." One develops quite a feeling about swandom. The Thames birds are the mute breed—one-mate swans with a respectable home and family life.

There are about eight hundred of these snowy white creatures on the Thames. Three out of four are the property of the Crown, and severe is the penalty for harming or abducting one of the royal birds. The other two hundred are owned between the Worshipful Company of Dyers and the Worshipful Company of Vintners of the City; it happened that gifts of swans were made to them by a sovereign of the 1300s. Since 1363, swan-upping is done every summer on the Thames. Six skiffs flying standards, rowed by men in varicolored jerseys and jackets, the royal Swan Keeper in the first boat conspicuous in scarlet livery, go in procession up the Thames from London to Henley. Their job is to mark the cygnets (baby swans). Where grown swans have a mark on their beaks, their offspring have to be similarly marked. Unmarked swans belong to the Crown. Since the parents fiercely protect their cygnets, swan-upping is an exciting spectacle. It usually takes place in late July. The term comes from the cries of "All up!" when swans with cygnets are spotted.

The officer responsible for the welfare of the royal swans is none less than the Lord Chamberlain, but the subordinate in charge is the Queen's Swan Keeper.

*THE LOCKS* * There are twenty-four locks between Windsor and Oxford. They are admirably made water steps. Upriver boats swing into them to be raised to the next and higher reach of the Thames; downriver boats are lowered. The keepers who open and close the water gates live in lockside cottages. They all have gardens because (a) there's an annual lock-garden competition, and (b) it's the tradition. The gardens are judged by officials, nautical-looking gentlemen in white who go up and down the river in a beautiful launch with transparent casing over the shining engine. The winning lock-keeper receives a silver cup and a plaque for his cottage. In spring people go lock-visiting to see how the gardens are getting along.

The locks are meeting places and also points of eternal fascination. People gather beside them to watch the opening of the water gates and exchange badinage or news with the boatmen as the water lowers or rises and the boats sink down or bob up, until the second pair of gates is opened and the craft move out.

*THE BOATS*   *   Excursion steamers ply in season between Kingston (above London) and Oxford. You can get on or off not only at major stops such as Windsor, Henley, Marlow, Reading, but also at any lock. In London, at Waterloo or Paddington stations, you can buy combined rail-steamer tickets. British Railways–London Transport's Tour No. 7 is train from Paddington to Henley, steamer to Reading, return by train to London; tea on board. Fare, under two dollars.

A score of boatyards along the pleasure Thames sell, service, and rent boats. Most are in the Thames Hire Cruisers Association. If interested, write the Association's secretary, Boulter's Lock, Maidenhead Court Boatyard, Maidenhead, Berks., for the "Thames Cruising Guide," which costs about seventy-five cents. The booklet gives full details about the river, its traffic rules, how to manage a boat and negotiate locks, cruise cooking with suggested menu for a week, clothes, riverside towns, villages and inns, historical matter, fishing, maps.

European Yacht Cruises, Ltd., 36 Edgware Road, London W.2, is a tourist agency specializing in water holidays. It offers a week-long Thames cruise from Hampton Court to Wallingford, including a visit to Oxford.

# 2. SHAKESPEARE-
# ON-AVON

When you go to England for the first time, you will go to Strat-ford-upon-Avon. The statistics say so. For the American tourist it is the most visited place after London.

You will see a one-industry town in flower. Stratford is the fore-most of all literary shrines, and probably the greatest shrine in the Western world. The hordes, numbering annually half a million persons, testify that there's no business like show business. Here no monarch or martyr is honored, but a writer of plays.

The pilgrims come from everywhere. We stood by the book in Shakespeare's birthplace and watched them record their names: a notary from Rouen, a Sudanese tribal chief, a Peruvian diplomat, the Governor of Istanbul, a troupe of Finnish actors, a banker and his wife from Pittsburgh. Every country in the UN was represented in the book, plus Mao's China.

In the streets were American sailors on leave, and women's clubs on a day's jaunt, and—what was specially good to see—rough-handed Welsh miners and Lancashire mill-workers. In the sur-rounding meadows thousands were camping in tent and trailer.

Even if you hate crowds and the weather is bad and your feet hurt, you will love Stratford. There is magic in the air. There is excitement in the presence of so many drawn by an excellent cause from the far corners of the earth. And it is with careful pride that the Stratfordians have converted their market town into Shakespeare-on-Avon—Queen Elizabeth's Merrie England, with plumbing.

*SOME HELPFUL HISTORY* * Will Shakespeare
(let's have none of this Bacon-did-it nonsense) died here in 1616
at the age of fifty-two. It took Stratford 250 years to wake up to its
mission. In Will's own day his fellow citizens regarded him as a
dubious character. To their Puritanism the theater was a den of
vice. The return of the local boy who had made good, with a coat
of arms from the College of Heralds making him a Gentleman
and enough money to buy the biggest house in town, was to them
a slap in the face of Virtue. Somewhat as if a woman should return to Dubuque from New York with a fortune made as the
madam of the kind of house which is not a home. Six years after
Shakespeare's death, when his old London colleagues came to Stratford, they were paid by the town fathers *not* to play.

For a century and a half the only visitors interested in the great
Stratfordian were scholars and the literary. Their numbers grew.
In 1769 the landlord of an inn, smelling business, rallied the reluctant townsmen to a public celebration of Shakespeare's birthday.
The great Garrick organized the festival, which featured fireworks,
cannon salvos, processions, and a public breakfast—but no Shakespeare performance.

For the next hundred years the Garrick type of commemoration
prevailed. Stratford seemed destined to remain a backwater. From
this fate it was saved by beer and Americans.

The savior was Charles Edward Flower, a whiskered giant of a
brewer. Flower's Ales are still everywhere in Warwickshire (and
other counties) where men say "Cheers!" In 1870, when the burning local question was the erection of a monument to the Bard,
Flower spoke hotly against a granite shaft. "The monument we
want," he said, "is a theater."

A preposterous notion! Market towns did not support theaters.
Only London had theaters.

Flower barnstormed England to raise the money. The London
press ridiculed his project as an "elaborate burlesque of national
respect for a great memory." It made the mistake of calling the
Stratfordians "Nobodies."

The bearded brewer roared: "We've waited three hundred years
for the Somebodies. Now we'll show what the Nobodies can do!"

He gave two acres of ground on the river bank. In all England
only five thousand dollars could be raised for putting a theater on

it. But the theater was built, most of the money coming out of Flower's own pocket. And when he died he left a good part of his fortune to the Shakespeare Memorial Association, which he had founded to run the theater.

In April 1879 the first-night curtain rose on *Much Ado About Nothing*. Many seats were empty. Two weeks later a small audience gave generous applause to the end of the first Shakespeare season. There seemed no reason why there should ever be another—except for the existence of a theater and a brewer.

Every year in the spring, when Shakespeare's birthday rolled around, the theater opened for its brief season. In time the season was expanded from two weeks to three. Now the theater operates for eight months of the year. And here's an ironic twist: in 1960 the Stratford company invaded London. It established its own theater (the Aldwych) where it plays from December to March, carrying on the rest of the year with a second company. No more does London sneer at the Nobodies.

When Charles Flower died, his brother Edgar carried on, and then Edgar's ten sons. Outstanding in this bouquet was Archibald Dennis Flower. When in 1926 the theater burned down in the night, he said, "Just as well. It's time for a larger theater." Meanwhile he kept the performances going in a local movie house, which is where Lawrence saw them on his first visit to Stratford in 1929.

To raise the money, Archibald and his wife toured the U.S. and talked two thousand Americans out of nearly three million dollars. (Contributions from other parts of the world came to another million.) When you look at Stratford and go to its theater, be proud that America helped.

*SEEING   THINGS—THE   THEATER*   *   Plan to see a play—any play, whichever happens to be on. Here a great company performs in the most comfortable of auditoriums. There's an air of infectious excitement before the curtain goes up and during intermissions that is lacking in playgoing elsewhere. A Stratford performance will become a memory to be cherished. And this thought would probably come to you even if we weren't about to give it to you: since about four hundred thousand people yearly pack that theater, more playgoers see a Shakespearean play in a

single Stratford season than ever saw all of his plays in his life-
time.

And how much do they pay? Tickets cost from about three dollars down to fifty cents. You can book through a London ticket
agency, but will do better to get your seats direct from the theater
ahead of time by mail. To make your experience more complete,
book a before-show dinner or after-show supper in the theater restaurant which overlooks the river and the swans. Minimum is about
$1.50, the food good. (The snack bar takes pride in its hot dogs!)

Stratfordians are not averse to making money off tourists. But
they are in the picture because they have all become ardent Shakespeare fans. The time we stayed a few weeks gathering material for a
*Reader's Digest* article (meeting the mayor, the beadle, Sir Fordham
Flower, and other excellent persons), fierce debates raged on the
streets and in the shops. A talented young producer, Peter Brook,
had, it was charged, slandered Romeo and Juliet by reducing their
grand passion to puppy-love. In the pubs indignation waxed over
the bitter and rebuttal was hurled over the stout. A little old lady
of Back Lane shook her fist under the nose of the actor we were
chatting with, crying, "Don't you meddle with *our* Shakespeare!"

This last time it was a controversial Hamlet, and the headwaiter
at the Shakespeare Hotel stood by our table through our after-
theater cold turkey roundly denouncing the brilliant new actor's
interpretation. Between the acts the theater lobby had seethed with
the argument. We had the choking feeling that this was a first
night, a Shakespeare premiere.

In Stratford, Shakespeare is alive, however buried he may be
under that doggerel threat in the church.

*SEEING  THINGS—THE  TOWN*  *  When Flower
the First woke them up, Stratfordians began remaking their town.
They stripped from their homes, shops and inns the ugly plaster
fronts which later centuries had added, and revealed the fine timbered façades that had lined the streets in Shakespeare's day. Hidden fireplaces, cupboards, panels, beams, all the handsome Elizabethan details, have been restored. Every building and memory
connected with the poet and his time is lovingly preserved so that
the entire town is a monument shared by Stratford with the people
of the world.

But to be specific. The inclusive ticket to the places managed by the Birthplace Trust saves you forty-two cents over the piecemeal price. It admits you to Shakespeare's birthplace, with the garden said to contain every flower named in his plays; the New Place Estate; Anne Hathaway's Cottage; the house of Mary Arden, Shakespeare's mother; and Hall's Croft, the home of his son-in-law. Your ticket also includes Nash's house next door to New Place, and the Elizabeth Knott garden. In the New Place garden you will be right if you picture the poet sitting here on a pleasant day and writing like fury his last two plays, *The Winter's Tale* and *The Tempest*.

Walk the pleasant mile by footpath to Shottery, the way young Will used to take when he went courting Anne. As you come into the village, give a few minutes to the back gardens of the cottages named Thyme and Tapestry. They are beautiful, and they were there when Shakespeare was a lad. Then go round to the front, to the short street of four thatched cottages—a natural for the camera. (Alas, a modern bungalow has just been built alongside.)

These are cottages—the Hathaway place is a well-to-do yeoman farmer's house of some fourteen rooms, however picturesquely un-comfortable it looks to the couple from suburbia.

A hundred years ago there was a great scandal about that house, owned then by Alderman Thompson, one of the Birthplace trus-tees. An insider, he learned that the Trust wanted to buy it. He advertised the property for sale, and thus forced the Trust to pay nine thousand dollars for a house he had never bothered to keep in repair, and for which he was getting fifty-five dollars a year rent.

And do you think Shakespeare's ghost would have been indig-nant? After a hearty laugh, it would probably have admitted: "Verily, I was not averse to making a fast buck in real estate in mine own day. How else thinkst thou I purchased a coat of arms and New Place? On an actor's wages, forsooth, or a playwright's pittance? 'Swounds!"

The house of Shakespeare's mother is about two miles farther on. It can be combined with a visit to Charlecote Park, a typical manor house. Legend, that liar, has it that Will in the role of juvenile delinquent was caught poaching deer in its park.

Back to Stratford: a shilling admits you to Harvard House. Its connection with Harvard is that here lived the girl who married a man named Harvard whose son fathered the Ivy League. Since Harvard grads, students, and faculty get in free, Lawrence saved a shilling.

Collect the view of the town from Sir Hugh Clopton's bridge. (It was Sir Hugh, not Will Shakespeare, whom the town honored as its first citizen.) Regard the swans. Take a boat ride.

And visit the church. Here the Shakespeare family worshiped. Here the infant Will was baptized; here he is buried. There was probably some trouble about that burial. On Shakespeare's tombstone are carved the words:

> Good friend, for Jesus sake forbeare
> To digg the dust enclosed heare.
> Blest be ye man that spares these stones
> And curst be he that moves my bones.

In a row are others of the family, all in the place of honor in front of the altar. If this is their original position, it must have cost Shakespeare and his family a pretty penny. For the meaning of the epitaph was the fear of having his corpse disturbed, and it must have stemmed from an opposition to allowing an actor to be buried in hallowed ground.

Trinity Church is interesting in itself, Shakespeare or no. Raise the hinged seats of the choir stalls and examine the misericords. Note especially the one in the second stall from the altar, on the south. It portrays a fight between a man and a woman. He is pulling her hair and biting her thumb while she is pulling his beard, trying to gouge his eye, and kicking him in the groin. On the right is one in even more dubious ecclesiastical taste. A man is birching a naked woman's buttocks. He is sitting on her neck, she is upside down, and a dog is biting her leg. Did Shakespeare ever see this grotesque, and laugh?

MISCELLANEOUS. In Trinity Church's visitor's book the signature just before ours was of a man "from USSR." . . . At Anne Hathaway's cottage a waiting guide was reading the magazine, *Ideal Homes.* . . . The Judith Shakespeare tearoom and café boldly announces, "Wimpy Hamburger." . . . A Cozy Fish Saloon rears its ugly head. . . . Shakespeare souvenirs in gift shoppes: ashtrays, tiles, bookends, paper knives, mugs, etc., all bad. . . . Preedy's tobacco shop on the High Street sells American cigarettes;

also cigars. . . . The national temperance organization used to have a sign over its door, a quotation from *As You Like It:*

> For in my youth I never did apply
> Hot and rebellious liquors in my veins.

Telling publicity, especially as the Bard undoubtedly played the part of Adam, the old servant who speaks these lines. On this trip we failed to find the office.

*HOTELS*  *  The Falcon, White Swan, Shakespeare, Swan's Nest, are old Tudor structures doing duty as hotels, and worth including as tourist sights. Any of them is good. The Welcombe, a country mansion turned hotel, with lovely garden, is two miles out on the Warwick road (A46), its appeal confined to the motorist. The tightly budgeted should know that Stratford abounds in bed-and-breakfast places; we stayed in one once and were well served.

*RESTAURANTS, TEAROOMS*  *  The hotel dining rooms here are better than in most towns. There's also the Theater Restaurant, and the Mulberry Tree in Bridge Street. For teas, the Cobweb, in spite of its name, is best.

*TRAVEL FACTS*  *  British Railways offers a one-day (eleven-hour) conducted tour of the "Shakespeare Country" by rail and bus from London for under ten dollars. *By Water:* There's a five-day cruise on the Oxford and Grand Union canals to Stratford, including Leamington Spa, Warwick, and Washington's ancestral Sulgrave Manor. At Stratford it gives you a performance at the theater. Write British Travel Association, 680 Fifth Avenue, New York, for latest information.

You can go to Stratford by helicopter from Battersea Heliport on the Thames. For reservations: Executive Travel, Ltd., 91 Jermyn Street, London S.W.1, WHItehall 4676.

# § "*THE SHAKESPEARE COUNTRY*"

Most tours from London are packaged as "Shakespeare Country" tours. They usually include Warwick, Kenilworth, and Leamington Spa.

What's Shakespeare about Warwick, etc.? The poet probably visited Warwick and Kenilworth as a youth, knew the countryside around Stratford, and as a commuter between Stratford and London saw the England in between. But a good guess is that many a tourist has been over more "Shakespeare country" than Shakespeare ever saw. This "Country" is as mythical as Shakespeare's own "seacoast of Bohemia."

Well, it's a harmless gimmick. Let's go along with it.

Warwick is worth visiting on its own. Lord Leycester's Hospital is a fine example of half-timbered work. This complex of four-teenth–fifteenth century buildings was converted into an almshouse by Robert Dudley, Earl of Leicester and one of Queen Elizabeth's boy friends. It has so functioned for four centuries.

Warwick's pride is its child's dream of a castle, with shrilling white peacocks on green lawns, a stunning Great Hall, and magnificently furnished rooms. Not only a child's dream but Sir Walter Scott's, who called it "the finest monument of ancient and chivalrous splendor that yet remains to us uninjured by time." From castle gates to the Avon along Mill Street are old houses and an Oh-I-say! view of the castle. Oken's House harbors a collection of antique and period dolls and toys.

Kenilworth Castle, four miles away, is a picturesque ruin worth little more than two glances. It draws customers because it is near Warwick and because Scott made it romantic in a novel that twists history out of shape. Once when we walked out from Warwick to see it we had a good time largely because a piebald horse with pink eyes put his head over the fence to get it scratched and beg for sugar. He won't be there any more.

As for Leamington Spa—it isn't what you came to England for.

Of interest to motorists and hikers: Along the Avon north to Warwick and south to Evesham are many pleasant villages. Harvington, 9 miles southwest of Stratford, we remember with pleasure. Alcester, 6 miles north of it, on the streams Alne and Arrow, is a market town with memories of the Romans; tourists would bother it if it weren't off that beaten track. Two miles from it is Coughton Court, a sixteenth-century mansion with Jacobean trimmings.

At the Stratford tourist information office, where they sell the official guide, you can pick up a quantity of free printed matter about these and other nearby places of interest.

## § COVENTRY

From Warwick you might consider going about ten miles north for a complete change of scene: a progressive city of two hundred and sixty thousand. This is Coventry, which offers a sensational modern cathedral.

Coventry is new, and as old as sin. Here nine hundred years ago the virtuous Lady Godiva rode on horseback through the main street attired in her tresses. She wasn't risking much, for the tresses were long and police orders were out for everyone to stay indoors behind closed shutters. The interesting point is that she did it for the public good, to keep her husband from visiting his earlish anger on the town. Civic spirit is still a feature of this city, although exhibited in less romantic ways.

The lady is remembered by a fine modern statue and a handsome clock in the new town center. But Coventry makes no tourist festival of the legendary event. It is too busy manufacturing motorcars and -cycles. What spare energy it has it devotes to remaking itself. For its downtown was wiped out by the Nazi air raid of November 14, 1940. Here Hitler, who failed to destroy Canterbury Cathedral and London's St. Paul's, and only nicked Exeter's, scored a direct hit.

Nothing is left of Coventry's ancient cathedral but the walls. The new cathedral of ingenious modern design, so planned that the ruins of the old provide a grand approach, rears itself magnificently. It is a triumphant church. It puzzles us that publicity places emphasis on Forgive and Forget, for the scheme of preserving the ruins will forever stress Nazi barbarism. The ruins cry out Remember! And so it should be.

A few medieval houses still stand, but what the citizens are proud of and what you will want to see is The Precinct, the new downtown shopping complex. Here are fountains, statues, and murals in an effective composition with shops, a hotel, a circular café, a movie house, and a ballroom. The shops are arranged around esplanades and promenades from which wheeled traffic is excluded. An auto-manufacturing town which keeps the auto in its place! Parking is provided in multistory garages reached by elevated approaches.

Coventry has much to be proud of in its new city, but its drawback is lack of hotels. The Leofric is de luxe and always full. The Smithfield we emphatically do not recommend.

AFTER    THE    SHAKESPEARE    COUNTRY, WHAT?  *  The Cotswold Hills are just south of Stratford, and just west is the lovely Welsh border country. A traveler who hasn't made plans in advance may well stand paralyzed on Sheep Street in Shakespeare's town like the neurotic donkey who couldn't move because he was equidistant from two stacks of hay of equal size and appeal.

Our solution: see them both. We think so highly of them that we have devoted a section to each.

# 3. IN AND
# AROUND THE
# COTSWOLDS

As we pulled up beside the petrol pump, another car swerved alongside with a squeal of brakes, and a voice called to the attendant, "Say, could you tell me where's the Cotswolds?"

"You're in them," came the answer.

There was a moment of bewilderment. Then: "You mean, this is it?"

"No sir," said the attendant gravely. "These, sir, are them."

Our fellow American shot off, and we laughed and laughed—because we had been about to ask the same question.

It's easy enough to say what the Cotswolds are. They are hills forming a range that lollops, roughly, between the valleys of the Severn and the Thames.

But where exactly are they? There's nothing exact about them. The boundaries are flexible. *Cotswold* has such a pleasant connotation for the English that towns completely outside the area, like Evesham and Malmesbury, unobtrusively claim to belong. And when you head for the Cotswolds, you can't be sure you're really in them until you come to one of those lovely towns or villages that makes you exclaim, "This is it!" or "These are them!"

The area covers about three hundred square miles. The main gateways to it are: from the south, Cirencester; from the east, Oxford; from the north, Stratford and Evesham; from the west, Gloucester and Cheltenham.

The Cotswolds are a very English part of England. Their beauty is quiet. Their towns and villages, of gray or golden stone, are small, and distances are short. Clear little streams wind through them, cutting intimate valleys. There are no palatial mansions or cathedrals, and all the hotels are inns.

The best way to see this country—Lawrence says—is on foot with a rucksack on your back and a stick in your hand. That's the way he did it before Sylvia's woeful feet came into his life, and when given a chance he will tell you all about the marvelous time he had. One way you can't go is by rail. The railroads go round; only one secondary line penetrates.

You can do it by bicycle if you don't mind a lot of uphill pushing, with the bike become anchor rather than sail. You can do it by local bus from one village to another. And you can do it by car. That's the too-easy way we did it this last time, wrapping it up in three days, two nights, and calling ourselves idiots ever since.

Our itinerary, however—an almost-circular tour, in at Cirencester and out at Burford—was a good one. Here is our route, with asterisks to indicate interest:

Cirencester—**Bibury—Northleach—*Bourton-on-the-Water —*Lower and Upper Slaughter—the Swells—Stow-on-the-Wold—Bourton-on-the-Hill—**Chipping Campden— **Broadway and Broadway Tower—Stanton and Stanway— Shipton under Wychwood—**Burford.

If you come from the south, as we did, twelve miles before Cirencester you find yourself in the small market town of Malmesbury. It doesn't belong in the Cotswolds, nor does it belong handily anywhere else, but it can't be ignored.

Malmesbury was once a formidable place with frowning walls, a castle, and a Benedictine monastery. Only the ruined abbey church is left, truncated but restored. Norman, with Early English complications, it gives the impression of being a powerhouse of God. That big doorway to the south porch is worth a long gaze. Malmesbury also has a market cross which is one of England's finest. It looks like a giant's crown. A contemporary described it as "a right fair and costely peace of worke, made al of stone, and curiously voultid for poore market folkes to stand dry when rayne cummith." The folkes still use it, and so did we when the rayne soddenly came down, ecod! The Old Bell Inn, draped in a glorious wistaria vine, looked good to us, but we had decided to spend the night in Cirencester.

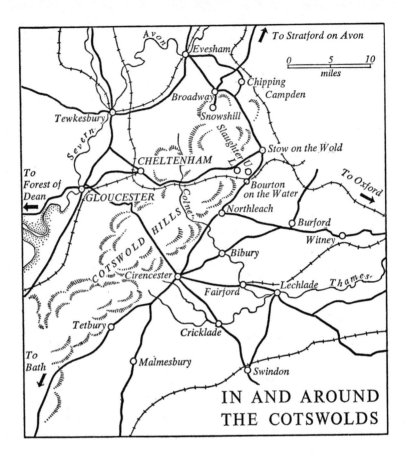

IN AND AROUND
THE COTSWOLDS

That proved to be our one wrong guess.

Weeks later, up in Derbyshire, we overheard a tourist remarking that Cirencester was one of the towns he liked best. We were dismayed. We searched our souls.

LAWRENCE (urgently): "Think! There must be *something!*"

SYLVIA: "There was that girl in the King's Arms—"

LAWRENCE (hastily): "No! That's not what I mean."

SYLVIA: "Well, there was that Elizabethan tomb in the church. . . ."

That is all we could come up with—a pretty girl and a tomb.

You leave Cirencester by A429, which is the Fosse Way—the Roman road which ran northeast all the way to Lincoln. It is the road the Roman Legions tramped; and later, the monks, pilgrims, merchants, mountebanks—all the motley throng of Jusserand's *English Wayfaring Life in the Middle Ages*. As you approach Coln St. Denis and Fossebridge on the way to Northleach, you are near the site of Roman villas and a temple. If you have time, turn off to see the remains of the villa on the River Coln between Chedworth and Yanworth. The natural setting is beautiful, and the National Trust is preserving both it and the wonderful mosaic floor partially uncovered.

Other Roman sites and slight remains dot the country along A429. The Romans probably built on a still older road or track, for one prehistoric camp and barrow succeeds another along Fosse Way. But only a trained eye can make them out.

On this last trip, however, we wanted to see Bibury, so we branched off on A433 and came in a matter of seven miles to what William Morris called "surely the most beautiful village in England."

Bibury is where we stopped to utter our first cries of "This is it!"

Bibury is one of the numerous Cotswold villages which has a river on its main street—in this case the Coln, burbling alongside the road. The eye is gladdened by a picturesque old mill, a handsome inn, and the almshouses called Arlington Row. It was Arlington Row which first made Bibury known as a beauty spot when, in 1898, a painting of it exhibited at the Royal Academy created a sensation.

At first glance the village seems a mere hamlet, but on exploration it meanders and spreads out. The beautiful church and churchyard, the village green with its spreading chestnut, the clustering, gabled stone houses in their gardens—everything takes its own good time to reveal itself, and all is perfect. There is not a wrong building anywhere. It's a long time since Bibury was "discovered," yet there is only one craft shop and not a touch of commercialism.

Between the mill and the inn are five acres of fishponds, constituting a famous trout hatchery. The Swan Hotel, formerly a coach house and now favored by fishermen, is as attractive inside as out, and its garden by the little river is a dream. This inn and this village will wring from you the tribute "Some day we must come back for a long stay."

The interest of Northleach, on the Roman road, lies mostly in its past. It had an important wool fair in the Middle Ages. You might guess this from the size of its market square and its church. Bourton-on-the-Water confused Lawrence; he scarcely recognized it. When he walked into it thirty years ago, it was a small, lovely village, wrapped in stillness. The entire population had gone off to market day somewhere else. He sat by the Windrush, which flows down the middle of the main street, and watched the only other living thing in evidence—a lone duck up-ending itself in search of whatever ducks are after in stream bottoms. For years he had spoken of Bourton as a village enchanted.

Time had wrought changes, and the population had returned from that market, bringing many others. Bourton is a large village now, extended by new building. It wears a touristed air. Some arty Chelsea types seemed to be at home. A lurid but interesting Witchcraft Exhibition advertised itself in loud letters. It is a pleasant place, if no longer enchanted.

We deviated from the Roman road to visit the Slaughters, Lower and Upper. They are hamlets, a half-mile or so apart, and the Windrush winds through both. Lower Slaughter is beautiful, Upper is pretty. We liked the human note in Upper's church that forty-four local men went out to fight in World War I, and all returned—"Hence there is no war memorial." And the tablet which reads: "The electric light in this church was installed to the glory of God and in loving memory of Arthur Shippen Wills of the Manor House."

With appetite whetted by the Slaughters, we made for the Swells, Lower and Upper. (There's also a Nether, which turned out to be only a manor house.) Upper Swell, though tiny, is the lovely one. But Lower Swell has the small, homelike Farm House Hotel, where we enjoyed a good home-cooked lunch. There are a few rooms; this is a pleasant place to stay.

Stow-on-the-Wold looks quite a town after these villages. It has a remarkably large market square, a fourteenth-century market cross, well-kept inns, gift shops, tearooms, and an air of dignified integrity. But having neglected to grow trees, it has a bare look. That's all we have against it. Certainly it's more attractive than Cirencester. You'll find good Cotswold pottery in the shops.

The Cotswold countryside is especially lovely as you approach

Bourton-on-the-Hill. The village ascends the long, long slope, and flowers spill over its garden walls. You are approaching the crest of the Cotswolds.

Running along the crest on "Five Mile Drive," nine hundred feet above sea level, turn right at B4081 for Chipping Campden.

The wholly delightful town of Chipping Campden is all honey-colored stone, and unmarred by the thousands who visit it. There's little more to it than the long, wide main street with grassy islands in the middle and stately buildings on each side. The old wool hall, fifteenth-century grammar school, Greville House (a wealthy merchant's home of 1380), and the handsome church of St. James are the specific sights. You go off the main street to see the church. Other than that, you just walk up one side and down the other, and find yourself happy to keep on doing this. Campden welcomes you but does not easily let you go.

There are four inns. We didn't investigate because we kept promenading. But from what we had already seen in the Cotswolds, we have no doubt that they're all good.

Three miles northeast lies Hidcote Manor with a garden—or rather, twenty-two gardens in one—a glorious complex of trees, flowers, hedges, pools, of intimate delights and wide panoramas. Maintained by the National Trust, the garden (but not the manor house) is open daily except Tuesdays and Fridays, April through October.

You now head for the trip's climax—Broadway and the Tower.

Broadway, a one-street village, is the most tourist-haunted of all places in the Cotswolds. On a summer week end you can hardly see it for the crowds, and everybody and his brother is having tea at the Lygon Arms. Like Chipping Campden, Broadway's houses are also of the golden stone—beautiful Tudor houses, mullion-windowed and gabled. The famous Lygon Arms, an expensive (but worth it) luxury hotel with spacious formal gardens, has skillfully incorporated a new modern wing.

From the village, go up 1024-foot-high Broadway Hill. A tower crowns it. For a small fee, you can climb its spiral stairs to the top. The view is said to take in thirteen counties, but since they're all colored the same, who can check? It is a breathtaking outlook on all sides, and provides an absorbing, if dizzying, lesson in Cotswold geography. You detect from here that you are at the northern tip. The hills stop abruptly, and far below lies the Vale of Evesham. The story about the tower is that the Countess of Coventry (the one current in 1800) one day said to her husband, "Dear, I wonder if we could see this hill from our house?" "Which of our houses, dear?" "Well, the one in Worcester." The earl gave orders to light a beacon fire on the hill the next night, and sure enough they could see it, twenty-six miles away. So the earl had the tower built in commemoration, and also just for fun.

Another story says he built it for a shooting box.

Toward the end of the century three romantics—the poets William Morris and Dante Gabriel Rossetti and the painter Burne-Jones—rented the tower. The poetry of the situation was marred— for Rossetti, because his housekeeping role was to carry provisions up from town, and for all three by the spiral drafts up that tower.

Just south of Broadway's hill is another of 920 feet—Snowshill, pronounced *Snawzle*. Two and a half miles east of that is Snows-hill Hill, almost as high, its name slurring to *Snawzl-ill*. You can see what the future holds. A coming generation of Snawzl-illians, noting that they are on a hill, will rename their place Snawzl-ill-ill. Who can say where this will end?

These are problems we can leave with the indigenes. Snowshill village has a pleasing personality and the fifteenth-century manor house with terraced gardens is open to the public. The house is a museum displaying an assortment of objects described as an "interesting and unusual collection," gathered by the last owner, a Mr. Wade, whose taste inclined toward the weird, the bizarre, and the hideous.

Three miles west of Snowshill by air, about three and a half on foot, and a very complicated way by car, is hidden away little old-cottage Stanton, embowered in gardens, with a church more than five hundred years old. Its sister village of Stanway is two miles south on a minor road which provides a lovely drive along a hill-side through the parkland of Stanway House. Stanway has an ancient tithe barn of massive timbers.

Going back to the main road, we deviated to look in on a curious inn, the Shaven Crown at Shipton under Wychwood. In Tudor times it was part of a monastery built in a lonely forest. The forest is mostly gone, the monastery too, but the stone-and-timber guest house still does business as a hospice. A fascinating relic, it deserves

a stop for lunch or tea, and a prowl through its rooms and courtyard. Its rates have lately been upped about 66 per cent—but you
may like to stay there anyway.

We had now seen the best of what the Cotswolds offer. There
was only one outstanding town still to be seen. That was Burford—
not properly in the Cotswolds but on the perimeter.      KHAKI - - WHERE ELSE?

Burford is more Cotswoldlike than Malmesbury on the other
side. It has, like Chipping Campden, a broad, long, and sloping
High Street with grassy banks and trees at the top. The Tudor
houses are of soft gray stone, like Bibury's, and there are more of
them on intersecting Sheep Street near the bottom.

Among the many assets of the little town are its inns—the Bull,
the Bay Tree, the Lamb, the Corner House, the Cotswold Arms,
the Golden Ball, the Highway. The Bay Tree and the Lamb are on
Sheep Street; the others on the High. Go inn-touring. These are
public houses, and your only opportunity to see what ancient
domestic living arrangements were like, since you can't poke about
in people's houses. Half the five-gabled Bay Tree, for example,
was the home of Sir Lawrence Tanfield, Lord Chief Baron of the
Exchequer in Good Queen Bess's time. The Lamb is even older.
For an overnight stay, these two inns are among the three best.

Before seeing them, however, we had fallen in love with the
Bull on High Street, and did not regret our choice. The Bull is
the rare kind of inn that has grown mellow naturally and unself-
consciously, and wears the air of knowing its business. Its radiators
were actually hot, and could be regulated. It had gay surprises,
such as a fine long gallery and an enormous lounge with furniture
of several centuries, from priceless antiques to the horribly new.

We came across the parish church and went in, having just the
day before read young Robert Louis Stevenson on the subject:
"I found my way to the church; for there is always something to
see about a church, whether living worshippers or dead men's
tombs; you find there the deadliest earnest, and the hollowest
deceit. . . ." It is handsome, venerable, and so was the sexton,
who told us he had been ringing and digging for forty-five years,
and that his father before him had been sexton for sixty years—
more than a century between the two of them! Thruppence admission to the garden, and not worth it.

Little Burford (pop. 1250) feeds and beds down thousands of

tourists, and remains unspoiled. The Gay Adventure Gift Shop, a few tearooms, some antique shops, and one studio with artist (he was still in bed at eleven, his bottle of milk waiting on the stone step), were the only signs of commercial enterprise. But big business once stemmed from this townlet. A schoolmaster named Huntley couldn't make ends meet, so his wife pitched in, baking and selling cakes and biscuits. Out of her oven came in the 1820's the great firm of Huntley & Palmer, the biscuit kings. The house the Huntleys lived and baked in is at the top of the High Street, opposite the Cotswold Gateway Hotel, an inn turned roadhouse.

*TRAVEL FACTS* * The British Railways sell a bargain booklet, "Rambles in the Cotswolds," with photos and sketch maps. If you are serious about hiking, join the Ramblers' Association, whose printed material is invaluable. From all the principal gateways to the Cotswolds, buses run, taking a minimum of luggage; and there are local services as well.

# § CHELTENHAM

On the western edge of the Cotswold Hills is a dowager of a spa— a veritable *grande dame* with a choker of pearls, a gold-mounted quizzing glass through which to stare down offensively low persons, and a stick to pound for liveried attendants who no longer come running.

Cheltenham is Regency, the architectural style of swank tempered by stateliness. The city was grandly planned, with generous public gardens, landscaped greens, and broad tree-lined streets. The rows of Regency houses are hung with canopied wrought-iron balconies, and such is their style that even in slight decay they reduce Rolls-Royces and Bentleys to tin toys. On the Promenade, we felt shabby. The Promenade calls for wide-skirted ladies taking the air under tiny, gay parasols, and top-hatted gentlemen in carriages drawn by glossy bays. It is a Georgette Heyer setting. The last modern period in not actual disharmony with it was the Edwardian.

If you want a complete change of atmosphere and pace, try Cheltenham. You may like its spaciousness, its look of a period piece, and its pervasive gentility.

Cheltenham was little more than a benighted village until the eighteenth century. Its new history began in 1738 when Captain Henry Skillicorne married Mr. Mason's daughter. On ground owned by Mr. Mason a spring bubbled. Skillicorne, a student of nature, observed that pigeons gathered there to feed on the saline particles, and that they were fat and saucy. The spa of Bath being then in boom, the two men conceived a wild hope. The water, tested, proved to have "medicinal properties." Mason raised a thatched shed over it, to the dismay of the pigeons, and announced his find.

Captain Skillicorne, retired from the briny deep, now founded a new career on these salty inland springs. He built a Pump Room and a Temple of Health, laid out grounds and gardens. Hotels rose. The curious came. Someone lauded it to George III. In 1788 he paid a royal visit, accompanied by Queen Charlotte and the princesses. Gossipy Fanny Burney was along, and scribbled in her diary: "I scarce ever passed so prodigious a crowd as was assembled. The people of the whole county seemed gathered together to see Their Majesties; and so quiet, so decent. . . ."

Incredibly decent the place still is—so decent that we were mildly shocked at that naked Apollo in the Ladies College.

We were irresistibly sucked towards the Ladies College by its enormous Victorian-Moorish ugliness. The porter caught us staring, and insisted on taking us through the complicated establishment from Abigail to Zelda. "In attendance," he declaimed, "are more than eight hundred ladies, aged eleven to twenty, from all over the world." When Lawrence asked at what age they became ladies, he took it for a reasonable question and was for hauling us before the Principal (pronounced in capitals). "She can tell you," he assured us. "She Knows All." We pleaded a pressing engagement.

At the bottom of the Imperial Gardens is the Town Hall, which isn't what we thought and you think. It has nothing to do with dog licenses and council meetings, but is the social center, with mineral waters on the side. It is the post-Skillicorne version of a Pump Room, and something cultural is always going on in its halls. On our night out it was jive, to the din of the Mike Cotton Jazzmen and the Delta Jazzmen. It didn't seem possible, but there it was. The youthful gymnasts were utterly un-Regency.

Around the corner of the Queen's Hotel is a shopping area named Montpellier Walk. It has pretensions.

The next afternoon, walking along a street, we read a notice: BLIND PERSONS USE THIS PASSAGE—KEEP CLEAR. Curiosity took us up the narrow passage and deposited us before a church that seemed buried in its own graveyard. It was of considerable size and in the center of town, yet so hidden that not even its spire was visible from the streets. Going in we made the acquaintance of one of the most likeable of old parish churches.

It was the seamed almost toothless verger who helped make it so. The verger is the church housekeeper. This one was in love with his house and put off his supper to tell us about his aged sweetheart. "My dears, this is the church of St. Mary the Virgin, built by the Augustinians early in the twelfth century. It has more beautiful stained glass, my dears, than any other church of its size. . . ."

It has indeed. Turning out the lights, the fond old verger showed his two dears the effect the twilight made. A half-light, at once eerie and warm, suffused the church as if the stained glass gave out a glow of its own.

When he snapped the lights on again it was to show us the tablet put up to the memory of Skillicorne—the longest, wordiest carved obit in any church. Among its crabbed remarks is a puzzler stating that the Captain had been "a Strict Valetudinarian" toward the end of his days.

Then he had to show us the great treasure locked away in the vestry—church registers on vellum, the earliest volume going back to 1558. "That's eight years before Shakespeare was born, my dears, in Stratford not far away," he said, peering at us over the top of his spectacles. His arithmetic was exact, and he let us touch the wonderful books. The rector, he said, had still older registers, going back two centuries farther, to the time Chaucer was born.

Then he locked the vestry, and the church, and gave us a tour of the churchyard, where he pointed out curious punning epitaphs, and a preaching cross. And, in the pavement, brass markers, local standard measures, where shady merchants once had to prove their probity by measuring out their woolens in public—in utmost public, under the very eye of God.

Then it suddenly dawned on our little old verger that we were

Americans, and back into the church we had to go, wondering about supper meanwhile. We had to see the Stars and Stripes given by American General Lee at the end of World War II, and be informed that scores of our boys married English girls here. It may happen that this page will fall under the eye of an American veteran and his Cheltenham wife who know and love St. Mary's even more than we do.

In Cheltenham we had gone from the purest Regency, to the Victorian, to jive, and back to the only thing left of pre-Skillicorne days—the beautiful church. There remained one more un-Regency experience.

From the church, we fell into the one restaurant open late. It was Ah Chow's on Clarence Street. The man Chow had done his ingenious best to pretty it up Orientally. The phone booth alone, with its half-door of bamboo, its tiles and sunburst decoration, was as much worth a look as any medieval piscina. Ah Chow had been English-corrupted to the extent of offering chips (French fries) as an alternative to rice, and his green tea was jasmined— a Chinese custom in England. But the food was palatable.

Cheltenham has a famous music festival in July, horse shows in summer, steeplechases in winter, a cricket festival, two nearby golf courses, and swimming indoors and out.

HOTEL  *  The Queen's Hotel, a Trust House, is the grand hotel of *grande-dame* Cheltenham, built on a generous scale and not merely in harmony with Regency but serving as the architectural climax of the city.

# § TEWKESBURY

The bus from Cheltenham does the nine miles to Tewkesbury in a leisurely forty-five minutes. From the top deck we surveyed the spring-bedecked countryside. It was soft and flower-strewn, and dotted with neat villages, each around its church (one with the oddest wooden belfry). A sudden brief black storm ended with a triple rainbow. One end came out of a barn, and the arc was so low and near we felt sure we could run out and touch it.

Tewkesbury hasn't the remotest resemblance to Cheltenham,

but Cheltenham may have looked like it before it went Regency. This is a town of medieval half-timbered buildings, some bearing strange names—the House of the Nodding Gables, the Ancient Grudge, the Hop Pole, Ye Olde Hatte Shoppe (which isn't one). Among them we counted seven old inns; and among *them*, the Black Bear, built in 1309 and looking every long year of being the oldest hospice still alive in Gloucester county, although now only a pub. The Black Bear stands above King John's bridge over the Avon. The bridge, built seven hundred years ago, was being widened—not supplanted, only widened—when we were there.

The town has a spectacular abbey church, all that is left of an important monastery. Begun in 1087, its basic fabric is Norman. The fourteen powerful Norman columns in the nave put one in awe. The grand effect is somewhat spoiled by the fourteenth-century vault—stone needle-embroidery too fancy to stem from those masculine columns. Moreover, the roof is like a cap that drops down over the ears. It is fitted under, instead of over, the clerestory windows. It's interesting to see, here in this church, how later centuries did not know their business. Elsewhere in England they did; but not in Tewkesbury.

Across the road is the abbey mill, its wheel still turning, thanks to the Town Council. The mill and the row of half-timbered cottages beside it are as picturesque as anyone could wish. While we were admiring, another sudden gale blew up out of nowhere and drove us into the mill in a fury of dust and pebbles. Here, in a spacious tearoom we were served one of the poorest, don't-give-a-damn teas in England. It was laid out for expected excursion busloads which we hope, for their sakes, were teaing elsewhere.

Only four miles from Tewkesbury (less than three by footpath) is Deerhurst with its rarity of a large Saxon (pre-Norman) church, and Odda's Chapel. In Saxon times Tewkesbury knew two ecclesiastical brothers, Odda and Dodda, by some called Oddo and Doddo or perhaps even Tweedledum and Tweedledee.

*HOTELS* * One of those picturesque buildings by the mill is the triple-gabled Bell Hotel, once the monastery's guest house. It looks like the best of the inns. Among the others is the Royal Hop Pole, which is popular; it owns a long garden running down to the Avon. Dickens, who knew this inn, had the Pickwick Club stop there to dine. In this Pickwickian haunt, now owned by a Welshman, we were served our Danish lager by a Ukrainian bartender. Structurally the most interesting of the inns is the Tudor House Hotel, which was new when Henry VIII was throwing his weight and dinner bones about. Mr. Bigland, a thoughtful and intelligent host, will be glad to show you around. Have lunch in its paneled courtlike dining room.

# § GLOUCESTER

Gloucester is not in our opinion worth a stay. It lacks appeal. But as a junction point and gateway to pleasant places it may be a necessary overnight stop. If so, a visit to the cathedral is worth while.

County capital, Gloucester is busy enough for twice its seventy thousand population. Downtown it stumbles over itself in its hurry, and over you. Its liabilities and assets are summed up in the New Inn, one of England's oldest hotels, with galleried court where in Shakespeare's time plays were acted, three bars, a good restaurant, and a rich patina of history.

The cathedral is the main object of interest. It has fifteenth-century Perp. additions on a strong Norman base. This powerful church was in fact the first face-lifting job in the last of the Gothic styles. The surgical success set a new fashion in church architecture.

When you look at the great tower and the soaring pinnacles, what you behold is the ironic result of one of the shoddiest and most unnecessary royal murders in the crime calendar of English history. When Edward II was assassinated in 1327 in nearby Beverley Castle, probably at the instigation of his beautiful French queen, Isabella, and her paramour Mortimer, both Bristol and Malmesbury monasteries refused burial. They feared Isabella. Not so Abbot Thokey of Gloucester. The abbey church (as the cathedral was then) lacked a saint or martyr as pilgrim attraction. The ambitious abbot, smelling a valuable corpse, risked royal displeasure by conveying the body to Gloucester—in his own coach— and entombing it in the presbytery.

Immediately it began to work miracles. Pilgrims crowded in with their offerings. The abbey grew rich. The murdered king's son, Edward III, beat his breast and provided the wherewithal for a shrine. Pause before it in the north ambulatory, noting the shelf or bracket on which pilgrims deposited their gifts.

The monastery boomed. The abbot sent to London for the best Court mason-architect to refashion the Norman church in the newly developed Perpendicular style. For years the work went on around and over the pilgrim files.

Another famous tomb here is that of a murdered prince. In the center of the presbytery lies the wooden effigy of Robert Curthose (Shortlegs), Duke of Normandy, son and heir of the Conqueror. He was done to death 193 years before Edward II. It is an odd coincidence that both Edward and Robert were men of low I.Q. Edward was in fact feeble-minded, and would have gladly lived a quiet life in a country cottage. The stupidity of Shortlegs was that of a Butch the Warrior, who swung an efficient battle-axe in a crusade to the Holy Land but couldn't play the game of high political trickery. It was his brother Henry who had the cunning, and Curthose came home to die a mysterious hushed-up death. As was decent, Henry paid the funeral bills and the cost of the tomb.

But the cathedral has wonders less bloody. The cloister with its fan-tracery ceiling is almost decadent in its beauty. In contrast, the centuries-older crypt and the unique triforium of the apse are awesome in their simplicity and strength. Lift up a few of the choir-stall seats. Among the misericords are some of the finest grotesques and caricatures ever carved in wood.

Gloucester was old when the Romans came and, pushing the Britons out, called it Glevum. A great deal of history happened here, and knowing it lends interest to the place. An example is the memorial to Bishop Hooper at the West Gate (the city had walls), where he was murdered in 1555, but not before he had taken the first Gallup Poll and issued the first Hooper rating. Surveying the 249 clergy of his diocese, he discovered to his episcopal dismay that:

171 couldn't recite the Ten Commandments.
 33 didn't know in what book they appeared.
 10 were unable to repeat the Lord's prayer.
 30 had no idea where it could be found.
 27 didn't know the name of its author.

Here and there in the city are old churches and houses. But Gloucester is a one-treasure town, and that treasure is the cathedral. Of it Francis Bond, sound authority, says: "Internally it abounds above all others in ever varying vistas and perspectives and dramatic contrasts of light and shadow. . . . It is one of the greatest glories of England and the English race."

HOTELS  *  The New Inn was accommodating pilgrims and travelers at the time of Edward II's murder. Local legend says the unfortunate Lady Jane Grey was proclaimed queen in its yard in 1553. All the same, we modern pilgrims report that we had a poor room and were generally poorly served, and next time will try the Bell, which some locals say is better.

RESTAURANTS  *  Dining rooms of the Bell and New Inn.

ENVIRONS  *  The Forest of Dean (staying at Speech House is a treat) is nineteen miles away by local bus. Beyond the Forest are Ross and Hereford; Chepstow, twenty-seven miles away, is an hour by train.

Medieval-keeped and moated Beverley Castle is a Stately Home worth viewing and only sixteen miles and forty railway minutes away; accessible also by bus. It was here Edward II was tortured and done away with. It has been lived in by the same family since about 1150. It should be said that the Lord Beverley of the day was not "in residence" at crime-time. Its great days long over, the little town dozes under its castle, its naps interrupted only by tourists in charabancs.

Stratford-on-Avon is on the direct railway line by way of Cheltenham. Another line runs into the heart of the Cotswolds.

# 4. CANTERBURY
# AND THE
# CATHEDRAL PROBLEM

Not until our fourth trip to England did we go to Canterbury. In all that time nobody said to us, "How could you be so stupid?" With a last lingering look at England's most magnificent cathedral from the hilltop in Dane John park we are saying it to ourselves, and notifying you that it should be the object of one of your first sallies out of London. You needn't be an architect, a poet, or a pilgrim to become passionate about it. True greatness has a speaking quality. It declares itself.

We arrived in Canterbury in a pouring rain, and the train pulled out with our umbrella in it. Something always happens with umbrellas. They are the special concern of poltergeists who snatch them away when you aren't looking. Our poltergeist was especially attentive—he had also seen to it that the shops were sold out of umbrellas. Soaked to the skin, we went into the cathedral to get out of the rain.

A service was in progress. Signs asked us to sit down and be quiet for the duration. The nave that rose up and around us looked plain. Electric lights were doubtful ornaments in the vault high above, but their hard stare didn't reach far. They left us mites in semi-gloom. Our eyes were forced to concentrate on a central picture far ahead.

There seemed to be a broad platform raised on steps. A wide pointed arch on its near side framed a narrower arch on the far side through which one tall slim candle shone; and around these arches lay a quiet wealth of pierced stone. An organ played, invisible boys sang, and now and again a robed figure passed the opening. It was tantalizing, as if we shared a double peephole on remote mysteries.

Sitting on small hard chairs in damp discomfort, we communicated by notebook:

"Did they do it deliberately, to be different?"

"They didn't tell me. I wasn't there."

"Nave a masterpiece of understatement in stone?"

"Rot!"

"*Ou est la parapluie de ma tante?*"

"*Avec ton* blasted *oncle.*"

The question about the nave is interesting. That's Sylvia, who likes to know what she's *supposed* to be feeling in order to take off from there, usually contrarily. In fact, the nave is the poorer part of this great church. The window problem wasn't solved, hence the modern electric lights.

The first question is the good one and calls for a better answer.

A cathedral nave was originally a big bare hall intended for the public, the laity. They were shut off from the rest of the church, where the priests and monks worshiped, by a tall screen of wood or stone.

Nowhere is this plan and purpose clearer than at Canterbury. Here the separation is sharp, dramatic. Christ's Church (the cathedral's proper name) was the chapel of an important Benedictine monastery. The usual screen was not enough for the devout monks. They had the entire eastern body of the church, screen and all, raised clear above the level of the nave.

A venerable verger told us that the people, standing in the nave —no chairs then—followed the mass by the tinkle of little bells, knowing by this system just what part of the service was going on. But they often came into the nave as we had, to get out of the weather; the market was just outside. Devotionally, they were closer to God in the crypt.

When you're in the nave, before going up, go down. The crypt entrance is in the right-hand (south) aisle.

Canterbury's crypt is a marvel. It's a great church in itself, vaulted, pillared, and as rugged as the soaring pile above is graceful. When you go straight down into it after coming into the nave, you are doing what the early pilgrims did.

Because in those days the important shrines, goal of pilgrimages, were in the crypt. As the worship of saints and relics grew, pilgrims began coming in thousands. Aisles had to be built around and between the shrines to ease traffic jams. In its size and its maze of pillared "avenues," Canterbury's crypt is bewildering.

Imagine yourself one of an endless, hysterical pilgrim stream and you can see how pressure from behind would hurry you along, around, and out. If you had come to spend some time at the holiest of England's holy shrines—that of St. Thomas—you'd be furious at being forced through so fast. For remember, you had come, probably on foot, fifty or two hundred miles for this moment, and your purpose was deadly serious. To pray at this shrine, to touch it, kiss it, and leave your propitiating gift, was to cure yourself or some loved one of a disease, or to rid yourself of a load of mortal sin. Little wonder that the traffic jams sometimes led to riots in which pilgrims were trampled.

In 1220 the relics of St. Thomas were moved from the crypt up into the church behind the high altar, where they were more accessible.

The move, usually dismissed in a line or two when it is mentioned at all, was tremendously important to thirteenth-century Christendom. For years before the event, news of it circulated through Europe, and everywhere people prepared to attend. "*Mi alma*," said the lady in Toledo to her spouse, "the Estrugos are going to Canterbury for the Translation. If they can afford it, so can we." "*Mijneer*," said the merchant's wife of Antwerp, "five new gowns are *not* too much. It's a long way to Canterbury." "*Per bacco*," swore the Venetian courtesan to her princely protector, "if you don't take me to Canterbury, all is over between us!"

The poor went too, begging bowls in hand, stopping at pilgrims' hostels, each with his gift for the saint.

The Translation of St. Thomas was performed with such pomp and splendor that it took four successive archbishops (after the officiating Stephen Langton) fifty years to pay the bill. But it was a good investment. Now the pilgrims came in the tens of thousands, enriching the monastery. They soon wore hollows into the stone steps you mount into the choir, called after them the Pilgrims' Steps.

The man responsible, in death, for the glories of Canterbury and of many another cathedral, had been the right hand of

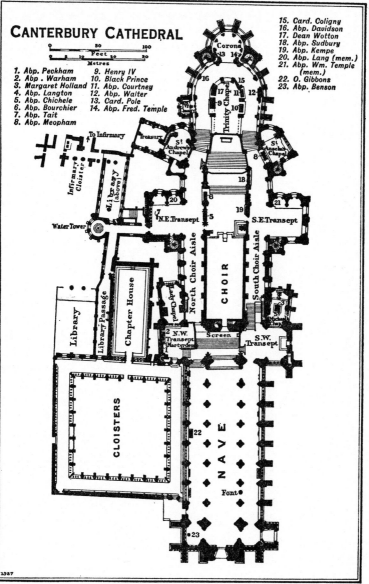

# CANTERBURY CATHEDRAL

Feet
Metres

1. Abp. Peckham
2. Abp. Warham
3. Margaret Holland
4. Abp. Langton
5. Abp. Chichele
6. Abp. Bourchier
7. Abp. Tait
8. Abp. Meopham
9. Henry IV
10. Black Prince
11. Abp. Courtney
12. Abp. Walter
13. Card. Pole
14. Abp. Fred. Temple

15. Card. Coligny
16. Abp. Davidson
17. Dean Wotton
18. Abp. Sudbury
19. Abp. Kempe
20. Abp. Lang (mem.)
21. Abp. Wm. Temple (mem.)
22. O. Gibbons
23. Abp. Benson

Corona
Trinity Chapel
To Infirmary
Treasury
St Andrew's Chapel
St Anselm's Chapel
Infirmary Cloister
Library (above)
Water Tower
N.E. Transept
S.E. Transept
North Choir Aisle
CHOIR
South Choir Aisle
Library
Library Passage
Chapter House
N.W. Transept (Martyrdom)
Screen
S.W. Transept
St Michael's Chapel
CLOISTERS
NAVE
Font

John Bartholomew & Son, Ltd. Edinburgh

239

Henry II, a more conscientious king than most. Thomas à Becket was a gay, brilliant, and forceful character, fond of personal splendor. When sent by his king on an embassy to France, he traveled with——. But let Charles Dickens describe it:

When he entered a French town, his procession was headed by 250 singing boys; then came his hounds in couples; then 8 wagons, each drawn by 5 horses driven by 5 drivers; two of the wagons filled with strong ale to be given away to the people; four with his gold and silver plate and stately clothes; two with the dresses of his numerous servants. Then came 12 horses, each with a monkey on his back; then a train of people bearing shields and leading fine war horses splendidly equipped; then, falconers with hawks upon their wrists; then, a host of knights, and gentlemen and priests.

*INACCURATE!*

And, comments Dickens in his underrated *Child's History of England*, "The King was well pleased with all this, thinking that it only made him the more magnificent to have so magnificent a favorite."

It happened that seven years after Henry's coronation, the then archbishop of Canterbury died. Henry was tackling the problem of Church reform. He wanted to make clerical criminals responsible to the lay courts. For this job he needed the ablest man in the kingdom, one he could trust absolutely, the Church being a powerful adversary. He chose the magnificent, unpriestly Becket.

Incredibly, Becket as archbishop became a completely different man. Here's Dickens again:

So of a sudden he completely altered the whole manner of his life. He turned off all his brilliant followers, ate coarse food, drank bitter water, wore next his skin sackcloth covered with dirt and vermin (for it was then thought very religious to be dirty), flogged his back to punish himself, lived chiefly in a little cell, washed the feet of 13 poor people every day, and looked as miserable as he possibly could.

Becket became Henry's bitterest enemy. He fought to make the Crown entirely subject to the Church, and himself in consequence more powerful than the king. His personality must have been split so classically that a psychiatrist—if there had been any— would have been enchanted with him.

Henry, of course, was not enchanted. He couldn't help loving

Thomas anyway, and was himself split between grief and rage. His courtiers suffered with him. There came a day when Henry cried out in despair for delivery from "this low-born priest." Four knights quietly slipped out, traveled to Canterbury, and killed Becket in the cathedral.

It was a sensational murder, as cool and principled as that of Julius Caesar, and the results were far-reaching. Becket, who as archbishop had been violently disliked, at once became a martyred saint of universal appeal. To win pardon from the Church the king, barefoot and stripped down to his shirt, had to walk through Canterbury town to submit to a flogging in the crypt. At the last minute they let him throw on a coarse woolen cloak because—on that solemn day back in the Middle Ages—it was pouring.

While the king, reduced to the humblest pilgrim in Christendom, is splashing through the Westgate toward the cathedral that looms ahead, mistily compelling in the rain, we're smuggling you in before he gets there for an unavoidable lesson in layout. All cathedrals and large churches have the same basic features. When you don't know them you feel lost. It is possible you are more knowledgeable than we were—if so, skip this.

To begin with, a *cathedral* is the seat of a bishop, who governs an ecclesiastical province as a governor rules a political province. The archbishop is the overlord of bishops. England has two archbishops—the primate at Canterbury and the other at York. Canterbury Cathedral, as the seat of the primate, is the mother church of England.

The cathedral is built in the form of a cross. If you weren't born with a built-in compass you have to get your bearings. The long end runs west-to-east. As you stand with your back to the great western doors with the whole length of the church before you, the main parts are, in order: the *nave*; the *choir* with its *stalls* and the *high altar* (or *chancel*); the *processional aisle* or *ambulatory* sweeping around; and finally, the most important chapel. Usually it's the Lady Chapel, dedicated to the Virgin. But in Canterbury it's Trinity Chapel, and something else was added beyond that— Becket's Corona.

The *aisles* are wide corridors on each side (north and south) of the nave between the *bays* of pillars and arches, and the walls.

The *screen* between nave and choir does not cross or shut them off; they are for processional purposes and for access to the various shrines, tombs, chapels, and minor altars along the aisles and in the *transepts*.

The transepts? These are the arms of the cross. They extend at right angles from the nave and/or the choir. Thus there is a south transept and a north. Some cathedrals (Canterbury is one) have two sets, in which case they are referred to as southeast and southwest, northeast and northwest. The transepts contain chapels and may lead to auxiliary church structures, such as the cloister, chapter house, library, etc. The *reredos* (pron. rear-dose) is the decorated screen behind and above the altar.

So much for the church considered horizontally. Looking up, you see the *triforium*, an ornamented stone gallery that runs around just above the pillars; and above that is the *clerestory* (pronounced *clear-story*), which is windowed.

(The clerestory was developed to deal with the light problem. The gloom of churches was no more mystically inspired than the gloom of castles. People never did love darkness. They just had to put up with it until the architects learned how to support and pierce thick stone walls for an ever greater expanse of glass without danger to the whole massive *fabric*—the structural shell. When they got far enough along in that direction, king, duke, and prelate could build palaces to live in instead of uncomfortable castles, and ordinary people could have many-windowed houses.)

The intersection formed by the transepts is the architectural focus of strength. It must carry the *central tower*, called a *lantern* if it has windows. Sometimes it has a *spire*. The medieval architect-engineer had a hard time with the tower problem. Towers kept falling down, catastrophically.

The *vault* is the ceiling or roof—in Norman very plain, in Gothic elaborately ribbed or fan-traceried. If it is ribbed, the crossings of the ribs may be studded with painted or carved *bosses*—decorative buttons (there may be hundreds) on the church's upper vestment. It's a good idea to carry binoculars (we had a pair of opera glasses) because the details, some eighty feet up, are invisible to the naked eye.

From high to low: the cathedral may have a basement, and a picturesque one, usually its oldest part. The *crypt* is not a burial place but an architectural survival from early Christian times when often a church was built underground and came to enshrine the rescued remains of a martyr.

But now we've got to get out—fast! King Henry II in his shirt and cloak is turning into Mercery Lane—we are warned by the sudden hush that falls on the crowd massed in the Buttermarket. We slip out the way we came in, which is not by the great western doors of the nave—these are for processionals only—but by a small door (when roofed, it's a *porch*) at one side. Down in the crypt, before the brand-new shrine of St. Thomas, the candles shine on brawny priests and monks who stand ready with whips. The Crown lies low, the Church towers over all. And so it will be until the reign of another Henry—the Eighth.

Canterbury was a leader and innovator in English cathedral-building. What went into the creation of the great church you see today can be divided into two periods: Before Becket and After Becket.

BEFORE BECKET

1. Lanfranc, William the Conqueror's archbishop, puts up a cathedral on the site of an older one, and also builds a Benedictine monastery—all in only seven years. (Dates, for those who like them, 1070–77.)

A hurried affair, Lanfranc's church was small, dark, inconvenient. The choir was so short the monks had to use part of the nave. There were no aisles, and there was a crying need for chapels. Each monk in the hundred-monk monastery had to say an individual mass every day. The monks were falling behind in their devotions. Pilgrims were already packing the crypt, drawn by the shrine of St. Dunstan.

2. So, in less than twenty years, remodeling begins. Main problem: no one can bear to tear down the two lovely towers at the western end. Solution: don't touch the western part at all but pull down everything beyond the transepts and rebuild, extending to the east.

But won't that make the east part stretch dangerously far from the lateral strength of the transepts?

Yes; but this can be cured by a second pair of transepts.

What? Two sets of transepts!

Well, why not? More room for chapels.

Because of Lanfranc's towers a new structural style was born at the very beginning of the great English church-building boom. English cathedrals, thrusting eastward, became longer than those on the Continent; the length called for a second set of transepts; the extra transepts gave architect, stonemason, carver, painter, gilder, broader scope for enriching the interior.

But it was because of Conrad's choir that the new style caught on. Conrad was a prior, and the remarkably spacious new choir was done under his direction. It was a sensation, known far and wide as "Conrad's glorious choir."

(Dates of the new work: 1096–1115.)

### AFTER BECKET

1. Four years after Becket's murder in 1170, with pilgrims pouring in, a terrible fire destroyed Conrad's choir. People went mad with grief, "cursing God and His saints for the destruction of their church." What to do? Build—by God! More cathedral is needed, anyway, for St. Thomas.

The monks send to France for the great architect William of Sens, who arrives full of newly fashionable Gothic plans. But the monks won't let him tear down anything of Conrad's that can be saved. He has to use all his ingenuity to build his Gothic cathedral into, around, and over the Norman-English one, and no matter what he does some lines will not run straight. After four anxious years he falls off a high scaffold. The monastery engages another William—William the Englishman—who carries on happily. The cathedral marches—to the east. The choir is now even longer and grander than Conrad's. Beyond it, raised on a third level, the final chapel goes up; and beyond that, lovingly, delightfully, an odd round chamber: the Corona, or Becket's Crown. Under the floor the Norman crypt too has been extended with Gothic arches and vaulting, and stone-carvers begin to ornament the plain Norman columns.

The cathedral of the two Williams won all England over to Gothic. It was a style which would reign for four centuries, evolving natively from this Transitional to Decorated, and culminating in a burst of stone and glass elaboration, higher and higher lines, ever greater window space and complicated roof ornament in the Perpendicular style of Tudor times.

2. The old Norman nave and transepts come down at last. The new nave is early and experimental Perpendicular; other cathedrals do it better. Lanfranc's famous old towers remain, but later they too are replaced. (The new nave and transepts are 1379–1400.)

3. A building spurt (1495–1503) heightens the central tower and makes minor improvements. The monks keep working away at that tower, unsatisfied, until Prior Goldstone gets at it. The result, what you see today, has been pronounced by experts the most beautiful tower in the world. One look and you don't need those experts. Bell Harry, named affectionately after a Prior Henry who gave it its bell, is the crowning masterpiece of Gothic in England. It's—it's—why, look at it! Why sit there reading this when you could be there? Go!

Apart from the umbrella situation and the cathedral, what is Canterbury like?

Most ancient towns seem to be either open or shut in. Canterbury has the feeling of openness. We wouldn't call it beautiful, but there is sky and space, and the city is bright even in the rain.

In part, Canterbury's openness results from the terrible beating it had to take from Hitler's bombers. That evil man had a diabolic hatred of cathedrals. Luckily he missed more than he hit. The gaping holes are filled up now, and on them stand shop and office buildings in a modern style that is not aggressive. Love and care have gone into the rebuilding.

As you look up the main street, the visual knockout is the old Westgate with its two imposing towers. It is a doorway in one of the greatest highways in history—the coast-to-London road. Up and down this road came invaders, traders, processionals, pilgrimages. Romans, Saxons, Danes, Normans passed this way.

Give yourself time for a tribute of awe. To do this without getting run down by a car, stand near St. Dunstan's church above the Westgate. You are on a slight rise. The road, sweeping into the town, drops just enough to show you, through the gate, the bulk and towers of the cathedral. This last two hundred yards of the Pilgrim's Way was once crowded with inns, taverns, pothouses, and all the world on foot or horse. Travelers arriving after the town gates were shut stayed in places like the two surviving inns, the Falstaff and the House of Agnes.

WHAT TO SEE * 1. The cathedral. You come to it by way of medieval Mercery Lane, off the High Street, pass under a beautiful gate, and find yourself in the Buttermarket smack by the cathedral. As a pilgrim you'd have been one of the hordes fighting their way through hawkers of food, candles, souvenirs, rosaries, medallions—ordering and paying for a mass at a special counter— shuffling downstairs to crypt, upstairs to shrines in chapels. If finical, you'd be carrying a bunch of lavender to sniff. At the site of the Martyrdom you'd force a place among pilgrims on their knees, swaying, chanting, droning, working up to a state of ecstasy. Today you're not so close to heaven and hell.

NOTE 1. Its stained-glass windows are among this cathedral's glories. And look for the tomb of the Black Prince (played up as a romantic hero, played down as wholesale murderer of civilians), and for St. Augustine's Chair in the Corona.

NOTE 2. Many tours time their arrival for the climb to the top of Bell Harry. If the tour is hurried, we suggest you wander about by yourself while the others climb. It's better to come unpackaged and stay in Canterbury a couple of days; but if you can't, you can't.

2. Cathedral precincts. There are wonderful things here—the cloister, the Norman Staircase, the Water Tower, and some beautiful nooks with bomb-damaged walls, grass and trees framed in their empty arched windows, pieces of carved pillars about. We loved the low-beamed passageway to King's College.

Son et Lumière was introduced in August, 1962. This is a night-time spectacle in sound (voices, music) and dramatic illumination reconstructing the pilgrimages and Becket's murder. Son et Lumière is a new art form developed in France, and spreading. The Canterbury production will make your spine tingle. It should not be missed. It is given nightly in summer, Sundays excepted.

3. Ruins of St. Augustine's Abbey. The abbey predates William the Conqueror's cathedral. St. Augustine, a reluctant missionary sent over by the Pope, is given far too much credit for Christianizing England. The Saxon King Ethelbert was a Christian before he came and made his job easy by ordering wholesale conversion of his Kentish men. Augustine then went to Rochester, but returned

to Canterbury in a hurry and a huff. The Rochestrians had thought him haughty, impossible, and had hung fishtails on his rear.

The abbey ruins are a surprise, revealing that post-Roman, pre-Norman England—usually pictured as culturally bleak, black, and bare—could build on a big scale. Workmen are digging, groping, tenderly handling crumbs of stone, trying to put Humpty-Dumpty together again. Bits of wall, gates, guest hall, and chapels survive, a pagan pillar stands, and the extensive site has been carefully cleaned to show the whole ground plan.

4. Main Street. It stretches southeast–northwest and keeps changing its name. Starting from the northwest, it reads: St. Dunstan's Street, St. Peter's Street, High Street, Parade, St. George's Street. The Westgate is northwest, and beyond it, once outside the gates, is *St. Dunstan's church.* King Henry stopped here and changed his clothes to begin his penitential walk.

A simple church, it looks its age outside but is poorly restored within. Under a marble slab, Sir Thomas More is buried—just his head, that is. Sir Thomas was executed in London in 1535 and his head displayed on Tower Bridge. His loving daughter, Margaret Roper, stole the head and carried it to her home in Canterbury. She willed it to this church when she died. (Brave Margaret Roper! But what was housekeeping like with father's head around, and how could Mr. Roper and the children stand it?)

Move along, past the two old inns, following King Henry's ghost. At the gate, the Westgate Gardens stretch along the river Stour. A little farther along is Queen Elizabeth's Guest House; where she slept is now a tea shop. St. Peter's Street becomes High Street where, unexpectedly, a narrow branch of the Stour rushes under the street. Let Henry wait here while you go into the *Pilgrim's Hospital,* once a hostel for the poorer pilgrims. It has a twelfth-century undercroft, a refectory with small painted gallery and the faded fragment of a fresco; and chapel with a basket ceiling.

Short river tours start from a landing across the street, by the row of timbered cottages called The Weavers because Huguenot weavers used to live there.

On High Street by Mercery Lane, note the startling wooden gargoyles over the doorway of Boots the Chemist. A street-cleaner pointed them out to us, saying proudly, "You won't find *them,* not their like, anywhere!" He pursued us to show, by the next building, a stone in the sidewalk bearing the worn letters CHEQUERS, and with his broom brushed off a bit of the building by the walk to bring out old stonework carved with miniature arches. So here, where a tobacconist keeps shop, used to be the famous inn, the Chequers of the Hope. (It's depressing when you find only a tiny piece of some fabled "used to be.")

If you're still with Henry, turn into Mercery Lane for the cathedral.

5. Miscellaneous. The city is still ringed in part by Norman walls but there's little left of them. You see Tower House in the Westgate Gardens, and at the other end of town the remains of the castle keep incorporated into a pretty war-memorial garden. . . . Dane John Park is a pleasant green area where schoolboys and clerks eat their lunch. From its high point you have a fine view of the cathedral. . . . The modest remains of the Black Friars and Grey Friars can be skipped.

HOTELS  *  The Chaucer (a Trust House) is the best, with cheery rooms (we had one with bath) and friendly management, and is just enough out of town to give relief from the crowds. It's within a two-minute walk of St. George's Street, which is the lower end of the main stem, and a five-minute walk to the cathedral. Our second choice: Cathedral Gate Hotel. About six hundred years old, it has fifteen rooms, three baths, and a chintzy lounge on the Buttermarket. Plain but pleasant; you can lean out of your window and snap photos of the cathedral. Five of its rooms are singles, and it's a particularly good place for the single woman. Third: the Falstaff, an old inn run with pride. Owners weren't around when we explored. The maid who showed us through tsk'd that everything was "old-fashioned," having no notion that this older-than-old-fashioned is the tourist's delight. The Agnes, across the street, we rank below the Falstaff. The big County Hotel on High St. is commercial.

RESTAURANTS, TEAROOMS  *  The Burgate, near the cathedral, has tearoom downstairs, restaurant upstairs. The Weavers' Restaurant has lunches and teas, which we did not enjoy. We liked the Cathedral Tea Rooms (front part of Cathedral Gate Hotel). Slatter's is a big restaurant with big menu near end of St. Margaret's Street. Of the hotel restaurants, the Chaucer is best.

*TRAVEL NOTE* * The bargain one-day tour to Canterbury is by British Railways–London Transport, Tour No. 4. The cost, with lunch, tea, and guide, is well under ten dollars. If driving: the BTA's free "Seeing Britain by Road" has an itinerary (No. 2) for southeast England which takes you to Canterbury via Rochester, Maidstone, Tonbridge, Tunbridge Wells, Sissinghurst, and Ashford, and then does the coast as far west as Southampton.

*CANTERBURY ENVIRONS* * 1. Fordwich, two miles and a half from Canterbury, used to be its port when the strait that made Thanet an island was wet. The little Town Hall on the river Stour is marvelously ancient, unique, worth every effort to see. In addition there's Fordwich church—small, very old, and one of the few that still have box pews—and a charming little High Street with a couple of round oast-houses.

2. Chilham, about four miles from Canterbury, is a lovely village even though touristically prettied up. It perches beautifully on a hill, the flat top of which is the spacious square with black-and-white houses on each side. Chilham "Castle" is a mansion sometimes open to visitors. There's a sixteenth-century church. The White Horse Inn is popular with tourists and the gentry.

Best way to do both, if you haven't your own car, is to hire one. Two hours should do it, unless you lunch at Chilham.

3. The Cinque Port, Sandwich, is on the sea directly east of Canterbury about twelve miles by road. On the sea? That's an exaggeration; it was once a brave port, but the sea silted it up, and Sandwich on the Stour is now two miles inland. Here are remains of the walls, and old buildings on tortuous cramped streets. A footpath by the Stour brings you, in a mile and a quarter, to what is left of Richborough Castle, from 40 A.D. for a thousand years an important coastal strong-point. If you're going to see Rye you could (skip) Sandwich, but not if you love these ancient relics of small towns, each of which has its own quality. Not everything about Sandwich is old. Two golf courses are nearby and another about five miles away near Deal. In fact this entire south coast is noted for its links. Other sports available are bathing, sea-fishing, and wild-fowling. Good hotel, the Bell, a Trust House.

in Mayor's office, see wooden nutcracker for fingers' stalling witnesses

# 5. WYE TO DEE, AND THE LAKE DISTRICT

The two names that look like an exercise in spelling out letters of the alphabet are rivers. The Wye is at the bottom and the Dee at the top of what is called the Border Country—a strip of 110 miles, as the *bran* (Welsh crow) flies, bordering on Wales. The highlights, winging from south to north, are the Wye Valley, Ludlow, Shrewsbury, and Chester.

## § *THE WYE VALLEY*

The river Wye winds in from the west, from Wales. Dipping south at Hereford, it passes Ross and Monmouth, then Tintern and Chepstow, and slips into the Severn estuary, which flows into the Bristol Channel, which debouches into the sea. All the way it has carved out a valley of varied loveliness.

At the bottom of it is *Chepstow*, a pleasant old town with one of the Border's great castles built by the Normans to keep back the wild Welsh. Chepstow's castle, on its rock shelf high above the river, is a spectacular ruin. A sixteenth-century gate straddles the town's main street, and from it extend remains of the old old walls.

If you make Chepstow (four hours by train from London) your Wye headquarters, you are within walking distance of Tintern, Windcliff, and General Wintour's Leap—scenic beauties. And only twelve miles away (bus) is the dramatic ruin of Raglan Castle. (It was owned by William Randolph Hearst when we first saw it many years ago. That was on a Fourth of July, and Hearst's local

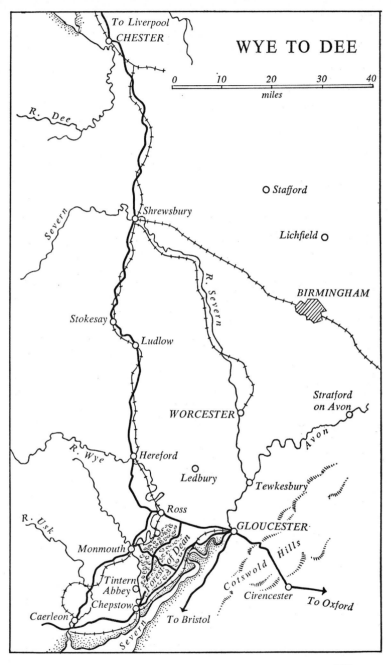

WYE TO DEE

To Liverpool
CHESTER

0  10  20  30  40
miles

R. Dee

Severn

Shrewsbury

Stafford

Lichfield

BIRMINGHAM

R. Severn

Stokesay

Ludlow

WORCESTER

Stratford
on Avon

Avon

R. Wye

Hereford

Ledbury

Tewkesbury

Ross

R. Usk

GLOUCESTER

Monmouth

Forest of Dean

Cotswold Hills

Tintern
Abbey

Cirencester

To Oxford

Caerleon

Chepstow

Severn

To Bristol

agent had armed the kiddies with little American flags and was parading them through the village, almost creating an international incident.)

*Tintern Abbey*, five and a half miles north of Chepstow, celebrated by Wordsworth, is a twelfth–thirteenth-century Cistercian church in ruin; a splendid ruin, thanks in part to its natural setting. In an amphitheater of upholstered hills the roofless walls and windowless arches stand eloquently mute on velvety greensward in ineffable grace by the most tranquil of rivers. Architecturally, the ruins are exquisite. They arouse in everyone much the same feelings. John Aubrey in the seventeenth century said it better than we can, for all his rickety spelling:

And as in Prospects, wee are there pleased most Where something keepes the Eie from beeing lost and leaves us roome to guess; So here the Eie and mind is no lesse affected with these stately Ruines, than they would have been when standing and entire. They breed in generous Minds a Kind of Pittie: and sett the Thoughts a-worke to make out their Magnifice as they were when in Perfection.

*Monmouth* and *Ross* are Wyeside resort towns, with golf, boating and fishing. Monmouth is the county town of Monmouthshire. Henry V of Agincourt fame was born there; so was the chronicler Geoffrey of Monmouth, from whom Shakespeare cribbed. It has a thirteenth-century gatehouse on a bridge. Ross is hilly and stands at a great horseshoe bend of the river. Either of these two serves as well as Chepstow as a good center for exploring the Wye Valley.

*Symond's* (pronounced *Simmons*) Yat lies between them. Here some rather overpowering scenery is crowded into a small space— rapids, cliffs, and a hill with grand views of the meandering river and the high green groves and meadows it waters.

Our own way of doing the Valley was pleasant but out-of-the-wayish, costing us something in car-hire. We chose the Forest of Dean for headquarters. The reason: spang in the middle of the Forest is a handsome stone palace called Speech House. Built as a hunting lodge for Charles II (1676), it is now a hotel. Here the Free Miners of the Forest gathered to argue and settle claims. They had held this folk court around a stone on the site long before Charles II was imported from France to dandle cuties on his throne. The great hall, with paneled walls and carved tribune on a dais, is now the hotel dining room, but the Verderer's Court is still held there.

A verderer—you were about to ask?—is an officer of the forest. At Speech House the King's Verderers sentenced poachers to flaying alive or some other horrible end for letting fly an arrow at the king's deer. The Forest of Dean was one of many royal hunting preserves. Monarchs were psychopathic about their deer. That there are no longer any left in this forest is not surprising. The Free Miners had it better than Robin Hood in Sherwood. Having worked the mines under the woods since Phoenician times, they knew their way about in the subterranean network of tunnels. Today the verderer presides over the ancient folk court of the Free Miners.

We stayed three weeks at Speech House, partly because of special attachment to our enormous four-poster bed. Every day, once we worked our way out of eight feet of bed, we had a world to explore at every point of the compass—Gloucester and the Cotswolds to the east, Wales to the west, and the Wye Valley to north and south. There was good company at Speech House, and when we weren't exploring we argued in the politely tolerant British fashion the great problems of the day. In between, Lawrence won the (unofficial) table-tennis championship of the Forest of Dean.

*HOTELS*  *  Speech House, our favorite, is isolated. Chepstow has the George, with garden flanked by a piece of the old wall and a ruined tower; also the Beaufort. In Ross, the Royal Hotel is considered the best. Ross also has the venerable King's Head, the Swan, and the Valley. All four are Trust Houses (so are Speech House and the George in Chepstow). The Symond's Yat hotels didn't look promising to us.

We're now bound for Ludlow, our next full stop. But moving north along the Wye, we come to *Hereford*, a cathedraled county town. (It is under four hours from London's Paddington station.)

Sometimes it may seem to you, as it has to us, that there are too many cathedrals in England. There have been occasions when one or the other of us has exclaimed petulantly, "Oh no! Not another!" This happened in Hereford, but once inside our mood changed. Those Norman piers that march down the nave—petulance (or crankiness, ill-humor, irritability, querulosity, crabbed-ness, protervity [rare], peevishness) dies in their presence. Thanks to the mixture of styles, Hereford Cathedral fascinates. Among its treasures is the Mappa Mundi of 1313, a medieval map on vellum that includes Paradise (now called Outer Space) and shows Jerusalem as the center of the universe. Extra-interesting because it reminds you how the builders and worshipers of this noble church saw their world.

If you're making this journey by car from Hereford north, visit thirteen miles away, on your way to Ludlow, one of England's lovely villages. *Eardisland* we'd like to claim as our personal dis-covery, since it's in no guidebook we have seen. It stands by the slow-flowing River Arrow's dreamiest spread, a village of half-timbered houses, trim gardens, idyllic peace. To reach it, scorn the direct road, A49, and take instead the more scenic A4110 out of Hereford. You'll be traveling most of the way over the old Wroxeter–Kenchester Roman road. If your map doesn't show Eardisland, ask at Stretford, eleven miles out of Hereford, for directions.

NOTES FOR A FUTURE VISIT—1:    If you enjoyed the Wye Valley, consider for next time the equally lovely but less peopled vale of the River Usk, in Wales. Start from Caerleon, a King Arthur claimant, and *walk* to Brecon (wonderful horses there) and if you're still fit, on to Penpont and the Black Mountains. As this is a Welsh invasion, we can't say more about it since for lack of space we've had to rule out Wales and Scotland. Of course you can make this trip less intimately by car; but you shouldn't. Wilfrid Goatman, who knows the country, says (to our applause): "From Newport to Penpont is about 45 miles. A good driver might cover it in under two hours. But he would be a fool to do so."

FUTURE VISIT 2:    A wonderfully silly thing to do is to follow Offa's Dyke, using your feet, a car, a bicycle, or a horse. (This route would be perfect for the pony-trekkers.) Offa was a Saxon king who pushed the Britons into Wales, found they wouldn't stay pushed, and dug a 140-mile ditch, backing it up with an earth-work, from Chepstow all the way north to Prestatyn where the Dee enters the Irish Sea at Uffern, which means "hell" in Welsh. It's a fairly direct line from Wye to Dee. Here and there you'll lose it, to pick it up farther on, for farmers have plowed up sections.

Aside from its hoary age—more than eleven hundred years—the Clawd Offa, as the Welsh call it, has nothing in itself to recommend it. But along it lie remote villages, castles, mansions, rugged hills, mousy streams, and staggering scenery. You will come into hamlets that haven't seen an American since six Eisteddfods ago, for you will be Offa the beaten track.

Offa used the Wye and the Dee as nature-made defenses. Above the Wye, you find the Dyke at a bulge in the river near Bridge Sollers at Mansel, west of Hereford. Then it runs north, passing through or near Presteigne–Knighton–Clun–Mainstone–Montgomery–Welshpool–Oswestry–Chirk–Llangollen–Prestatyn. The best part begins at Presteigne, and you can get there by train. If you do it all by car, you'll have a good time playing tag with the Clawd as you try keeping to the lanes and minor roads on the one-inch-to-the-mile Bartholomew's map you had better have with you. Afoot, at horse or awheel, you'll be traveling far away from any rumor of UNO, SEATO, NATO, and cold war. Let Them send men and monkeys to the moon; Offa's Rut on earth is less daft, more fun.

# § LUDLOW

The train had loped past cows pathetically islanded on tufts in a watery landscape. The rumor had got about that this was the wettest and coldest autumn since 1772. Everybody asked everybody else if he had heard, and felt better. So chillily fell the rain that Ludlow's supply of shillings gave out.

Stopping for tobacco supplies in a shop on King Street, we asked for shillings in change. Alas, there was not a shilling in the till. There would be no tillings in the shill—tut, shillings—until Friday (this was Wednesday). Why? Because on Friday the collectors would make the rounds, unlock the little tin drawers of the gas and electric heaters in the hotels, and put the shillings back into circulation.

Lawrence's cough shook the little seventeenth-century shop. The tobacconist's lady looked at us worriedly. She took Sylvia aside for a whispered conference. She hallooed, and a buxom woman appeared and joined them in committee. Sylvia in due time ex-

plained: "They're shocked that we're going without winter undies
—woolies. They're taking us to some shops."

So we went shopping. Aie, what the English wear in October!

But our friends were right. In the out-of-doors our noses continued blue but our wool-swathed torsos were snug. Every time
we passed the tobacconist's one or the other of the ladies would
hail us or dart out to ask how things went. If we came in they
would introduce us to customers in the shop as "our Americans,"
and everyone seemed inordinately pleased with us. The doctor,
called once, kept coming, leaving his card if we were out—probably
interested in the psychosomatic effect upon his patient of both
flannel and human warmth.

Ludlow *is* friendly. So pleasant is it that bad weather here matters less than in any other place we know (London excepted).
It's not only the people. The buildings, the very streets, the far
horizon, wear a friendly look. And when the sun did come out
for us, it only gilded the lily; for this is one of the most sightly
towns in England.

It covers a rounded hill—rounded except for the sheared-off
bluff where the ruins of its great castle defy a guileless landscape.
The town center occupies the summit, and the streets fall away,
revealing cycloramas of alluring rural peace roundabout the rivers
Corve and Teme.

Downtown is crammed with colorful houses, odd corners, mysterious alleyways, innyards into which Pickwickian coaches used to
roll. There are more than a score of old magpies (black-and-white
timbered buildings) that stop you in your tracks. You are bound
to believe the official guidebook when it says, "Almost every building in the older part of Ludlow has been scheduled by the Minister
of Housing as 'of special architectural or historical interest.'"

The queen of them all is the Feathers on Corve Street. Dating
from 1521, this inn is so resplendently gabled, timber-patterned,
and carved it is nearly absurd.

Across the street, the Bull looks ordinary. But walk into its yard
and you see its long flank, handsomely timbered, crookedly bulging
with age, and highly photogenic.

At the bottom of the yard, cramped stone steps mount. Follow.
You come out upon the garden of the rose-stone church of St.
Laurence. Happening to glance back, you stand and stare. The

Bull's steps had led up the side of a narrow building which, now seen from the front, is a perfect gem—the oh-so-quaintly ancient Reader's House, thought to have been Ludlow's earliest grammar school. Carefully restored, it is open to the public.

The church garden (with benches, thank the Lord and St. Laurence) look far out over the open country to the north. The church itself, mostly fifteenth-century, is beautiful. We liked the misericords in the choir stalls—not hard to find; the seats are kept raised so you can admire those carvings in high relief that look like illustrated medieval gossip, vivid and intimate.

Now go on. From the south flank of the church, the narrowest of lanes (tuck your elbows in) takes you to the town square, with such buildings all around, every one playing a character part, that you don't know where to look first.

By your side is the Butter Cross, a baroque ornament; nothing Butter or Cross about it, but let that pass. On your immediate left is a pantile (arcade) stretch of spectacular magpies, the Angel Inn one of them, De Grey's tearoom another. To the right are four crowded parallel lanes that make up what should have been a single, wide high street; they lead to the castle. And dead ahead is Broad Street with a medieval gate that draws you to explore what's through and beyond.

Broad Street is lined with low cottages on one side and dignified Georgians and Regencies on the other. Downhill all the way, the street curves just a trifle, and that trifle delights the eye, as does the way the sidewalk and houses gradually sink below the street level on the downward sweep.

Stopping at every other house, crossing the street for a near view of a fine door, a glimpse into a long garden, a visit to the attractive antique shop, you come down to Ludford Bridge above the teeming Teme. An old stone packhorse bridge, during World War II it supported rolling convoys carrying crated American bombers—and survived.

Ludford, on the other side, is a suburb-hamlet. After you cross the bridge, you will see on your left a narrow lane curving sharply as it climbs. Take it, and—

It's a pity to be telling you all this, for part of the fun of travel is stumbling on things. Well, you will probably make your own discoveries elsewhere, as we made ours here.

We followed the lane, and discovered the tiny, wonderful church of St. Giles, entirely hidden from below by trees and shrubbery, with the magpie deanery beside it and a cat asleep on a compost heap. (You can't count on the cat, but put that little thirteenth-century church on your list of musts.

Coming down the lane, we crossed the road and, impelled by urgent curiosity, mounted some steps and found ourselves on the sloping edge of Whitcliffe Common. A scraggly expanse opened before us. What to do—go on, or back to town? Lawrence looked peaked, but, "Go on, of course," he said heroically.

There were rough tracks. They mounted gradually, higher and higher above the river, and suddenly, on the other side, Ludlow Castle showed its river face. In town, only a hundred yards from the Butter Cross, the castle gave no hint of its size and dramatic stance. But from this western height we saw its fighting side on the craggy cliff. Very little imagination is needed to hear armor clanking and horns blowing, and see pennons fluttering in the wind. But what we best remember in the castle's long history is an unromantic incident.

In the time of King Stephen, about 1150, the rebel border barons captured Ludlow Castle. The king himself came to direct the siege. He brought with him Prince Henry of Scotland, who was his hostage. One day the king and his precious prisoner were taking a stroll under the castle walls. The rebels on the ramparts quietly lowered a grapnel, hooked Prince Henry, and began to haul him up. The king grabbed him by the legs and yanked. The prince almost came apart, but the king managed to get him down in one piece.

We were still walking on Whitcliffe Common. In the nick of time a tavern appeared on the left—the Ludlow Arms, bowlers' bivouac. The bowling green was a large square of the most verdant velvet. It had taken eight centuries of rain and rolling, our host guessed, to produce that turf. Anyway, said he, it was second in age only to Plymouth's. No Drake bowled here, but generations of earls, barons, sirrahs, and their varlets. The green is only a century younger than the castle, and there has always been a tavern beside it.

We set down our tankards. Lawrence wiped his mustache, Sylvia renewed her lips. We fared forth, winding down a pretty road that returned us to Ludlow by way of Dinham Bridge and the new swimming pool, entering the town almost under the castle ramparts. The cowardly sun scuttled behind dark clouds. The rain resumed. Lawrence coughed.

"Dear, you're not well—remember? Don't you think you'd better rest a bit on the parapet?"

"Rest? No! Let's see what's up this Pepper Lane."

Ludlow exerts a powerful effect. Where the eye is led on and on from one prospect to another, the senses purr, the soul expands, the lungs fill (cough! cough!). The result is an adventure-explorer feeling that makes even a bronchitic tireless. In the town you feel the countryside's pull. You give in. Out in the meadows, hills, and country lanes, the town with its strong silhouette dominated by castle and church towers draws you back. Lawrence invented a term for Ludlow's rare quality: "hypnotic ambivalence."

*HOTELS* ∗ About the Feathers—our hearts sank when we were conducted upstairs to the attic. Needlessly. Our room was smart, our private bath smarter, and we had an excellent electric heater of modern design; we could drape our laundry on it. But some rooms we glanced into looked a little grim, particularly the singles. . . . The Angel has less atmosphere but friendlier management; large rooms, including a few handsome ones with private bath. . . . The Bull, a local hangout, needs perking up. . . . Castle Lodge will be open for guests at this reading. A fine old building of stone and timber by the castle gates, it looked promising to us. . . . The Ludlow Arms beyond the river has rooms for a few in season, but functions chiefly as a bowlers' and hikers' tavern. It's friendly, clubby, but plans to become an olde motel!

*RESTAURANTS, TEA SHOPS* ∗ De Grey's serves lunch and tea behind its Tudor bakery, and on summer week ends people queue up to get in. Pikelets, the local version of crumpets, are good. Everything is home-made. The locals rate the food higher than we do, but it's an institution in Ludlow. Ask for its folder, which is humorous. . . . A modern little café with booths is beside Castle Lodge; same old food. . . . The Angel has a snack bar, friendly, eager to please, but alas, s.o.f. . . . . For dinner, the restaurants of the Feathers or the Angel.

ENVIRONS  *  You are among the Shropshire hills, and rugged Wales looms up in the west. No matter in which direction you wander, you can hardly go wrong. The countryside ranges from merely pretty to entrancing. Pleasant villages abound, and hills (the Clees to east and northeast) with grand views. The village church is often a surprise.

Don't miss Stokesay Castle, only seven miles north of Ludlow just off the Shrewsbury road. This is an ancient fortified manor house with an Elizabethan gate and a baronial hall. It sits on a dreamy (except for the railway tracks) plain that is farmed to its very gates. Even the moat produces. It grew water lilies once, now it grows baronial vegetables. Stokesay is almost the last fortified farmhouse to be spared by the centuries, and it saddened us to see a collapsed corner shielded by tarpaper.

# § SHREWSBURY

Would you know a dingle if you saw one?

Shrewsbury has a twenty-five-acre park called the Quarry, and this park has a dingle. The dingle is a dimple in the park, a cupped depression, every inch cunningly landscaped. It has a fountain, a pond with ducks, a winding stream with tiny islands. It has terraces, flowers, trees, bright birds, benches. In it ladies knit, old gentlemen doze, a lawyer lingers to read his newspaper, lovers bill, and tourists coo.

You don't go all the way to the Welsh border to see a dingle. But when you find one there you're glad.

Shrewsbury is Shropshire's big county town (pop. 50,000). Its tourist attraction is its flocks of timbered black-and-white houses. Narrow passages among them lead to tiny squares, flights of street steps, or someone's never-come-sun front door.

The city stands on a knobby finger of land thrust into the wide, looping Severn, across which it flings two principal bridges, the English and the Welsh. The Normans ringed the finger with a dark red castle, and built a dark red abbey below the English bridge. Today, what remains of the castle offers a view over the railway yards, and the abbey church sits dustily on an island in the traffic.

Before we left Ludlow, the manager of the Feathers phoned to book us a room at the Raven, for some centuries Shrewsbury's leading hostel. She set down the telephone looking stunned. "It's gone!" she said.

"Gone?"

"They—they've torn it down!"

Shrewsbury is only twenty-eight miles from Ludlow. Yet so swiftly had it razed its famous inn that Ludlow hadn't heard the news. It was a shock. Almost you could feel the age-old timbers of the Feathers shivering with apprehension. With the Raven wiped out, was anything safe?

No; for the Crown was going too.

Arrived in Shrewsbury, we stared at the gaping space where the Raven had been and where an office building was to rise. Moving on with funereal tread, we stopped at the Crown a block away opposite St. Mary's Church of the two-hundred-foot octagonal spire. That old inn was an empty shell, a House of Usher waiting for its fall. The trouble with progress (as Mr. Polly said) is that it keeps going on.

For a hundred years Shrewsbury has been destroying its treasures. Castle Street, the main business artery (where the Raven stood), and its extension Pride Hill, have become line-ups of the standardized, too-familiar chain stores you find from end to end of Britain—Woolworth's, Burton the Tailor, Boots the Chemist, Smith the bookdealer, Achilles Serre the dry-cleaner, Cadena, Marks and Spencer, and so on. (To balance these there is one original—Pelican Snelson, tobacconist.)

Yet, so generously did the past endow this border capital that it remains one of England's most richly half-timbered cities, surpassed only by Chester. It is hard to decide where to put the emphasis—on indignation, or on thankfulness that much still remains.

Your main occupation will be exploring the streets and lanes south of Pride Hill and the Market Hall. Down past St. Mary's (a church worth some minutes) is Dogpole Street, with a passage taking you into St. Alkmund's Square. Here's the crooked old house of E. Lightfoot, Bookseller. The opening beside it brings

you down Bear Steps and into Fish Street, Grope Lane, Butcher
Row—narrow winding streets with leaning houses and unexpected
passages—the medieval heart of the city.

This area of greatest interest is only about 350 yards (one-fifth
of a mile) square. It is bounded by Shoplatch and Pride Hill on
the north; St. Mary's, Dogpole, and Wyle Cop on the east; Milk
Street on the south; and Princess Street on the west. Revisit this
complex of crooked, hilly lanes, and you'll always find something
you missed—like the Three Fishes on Fish Street, an old tavern,
and next to it the neat little old house announcing in its window
that Mr. and Mrs. Baines offer bed and breakfast.

Look at, and in, the Golden Cross Hotel, built in 1428 (but
not well kept). At the bottom of Princess Street you find Old
Chad's Church in dark-rose stone, now demoted to cemetery
chapel and robbed by St. Mary's of its fourteenth-century stained
glass. The Old Market Hall, on The Square, is Elizabethan, and
the two magpie houses opposite date from the same time (late
1500s).

Shrewsbury is noted for its cakes and ale, and for its public
school, founded 1551, where Darwin, Judge "Bloody" Jeffreys,
Sir Philip Sidney, and Samuel Butler of *Erewhon* and *The Way
of All Flesh* were educated. An odd foursome of Old Boys!

Beyond the Welsh Bridge, the suburb of Frankwell is older than
it looks. Here's where strangers and Welshmen were allowed to
settle. The "Frank" of Frankwell was something like the Liberties
of Shakespeare's London where playhouses and bawdy-houses fled
to be outside the city's judisdiction.

In a sixteenth-century chronicle, we found a hint of what
Shrewsbury was like when its magpies were young:

This yeare 1533 uppon twelfft daye in Shrewsbury the dyvyll ap-
pearyd in Sainct Alkmonds churche there when the preest was at highe
masse with greate tempest and darkness. . . . He passyd through the
churche terynge the wyer of the sayde clocke and put the prynt of hys
clawes uppon the iijth bell and toocke one of the pynnacles awaye with
hym and for the tyme stayed all the bells in the churches within the
sayde towne that they could neyther toll nor rynge.

These cosmic catastrophes used to happen when both heaven
and hell were close to one's hearthfire. Today the dyvyll wears a

Burberry over his tail and a bowler on his horns, and he doesn't bother with clocks or pinnacles but bulldozes away an entire building before you can say "wattle-and-daub."

*HOTELS*  *  It's the Lion (a Trust House); comfortable, but on the dull side. Dickens stayed there. In the Georgian ballroom Paganini played and Jenny Lind sang. . . . On Fish Street in the old quarter, we investigated the house of Mr. and Mrs. Baines offering bed and breakfast. It's a charming place. Mrs. B is a collector of antiques with an eye for both beauty and comfort. Five bedrooms, shining modern kitchen, cozy (if cluttered) parlor, modest rates.

*RESTAURANT*  *  Sidoli's, the one on Castle Hill, serves good Italian food. While waiting for your *cotolette Bolognese* and *zabaglione*, surreptitiously watch the English family having dinner out, and the young man giving his girl a treat. They're having fish and chips or roast beef! As our dear little waitress Rosella remarked, with southern passion: "These people!"

*BY RAIL*  *  Expresses go from Paddington station to Shrewsbury in three and a half hours.

# § *CHESTER*

Chester is a knockout. It is the most strikingly "medievalish" of English cities—all black-and-white, gabled, carved, orioled, casement-windowed.

As you come in along the main street the effect is as gay as a masquerade ball. The clincher is the clock on top of the Eastgate. It stands high on four legs of fancy ironwork with a face of red and blue and gold under a peaked green cupola like a daring hat. This delightful trinket commemorates Victoria's Jubilee, her sixtieth year as Queen, in 1897. Like a wink it betrays the real tone of this city—Romantick.

From one end of England to the other are towns with lingering medieval buildings. What's unique about Chester is that it has not only preserved the old but, for a century at least, maintained the style in modern construction. Some of the modern, like the Gothic town hall, is painfully pseudo. But much of it is artfully enough done to take you in until you see, high up under a gable, the date 1867, or 1902. This dating, by the way, is proof that Chester was frank in its imitating and not trying to pass off a modern structure as antique.

So, while you can't take Chester seriously as a medieval city, you can enjoy it as a spectacle, and admire a civic unity absent in such towns as Shrewsbury. And if by this time touring has got you down, you have only to look at the Jubilee clock to revive.

Shrewsbury had a dingle. Chester has the Rows. It also has the Walls. After you have checked in at your hotel your first problem will be—which to do first, Rows or Walls? Our advice: be guided by the weather. In rain, do the Rows. In bright periods, do the Walls.

What are the Rows?

They are second-story arcades extending for the depths of a block or two along the four arms of the city's main crossing. But this isn't saying enough.

Picture a street frontage of tall half-timbered houses with ground-floor shops. Instead of the usual second story, the entire line shares a kind of broadwalk which is roofed by the medievally projecting upper stories. These broadwalks, arcades, or galleries are the Rows. They have balconies on the street side and shops on the inner side. With the street-level stores, the Rows form a two-story shopping center. They inevitably bring out the camera and, just as inevitably the query, *Why?* What is the reason for this strange construction?

Chester's official guidebook suggests the Rows may have been built in front of and on top of remains of Roman buildings lining the Roman-made main streets. (Chester was the camp of the Twentieth Legion, the *Valeria Victrix*.) But they remain puzzling, and the theory doesn't explain the crypts.

Walk along the Row on Eastgate Street at the lower level, and you will see that Brown's department store has its ground-floor china department in a large vaulted crypt. Then, fully a block farther along on Watergate Street, go down into the premises of Quellyn Roberts, Wine Merchants—another crypt.

We had discovered Brown's first. It sent Sylvia straight to the city's museum (notable for Roman relics, by the way) to ask what a crypt was doing in a store. She was disappointed to be told: "It's only a thirteenth-century cellar." If a cellar, why wasn't it dug deeper? And why was it in front instead of in back where strong Roman walls—if they did exist—would have served as support? And why—?

There were no answers.

At Quellyn Roberts a Mr. Perry, a crypt-enthusiast, was a strong partisan of Roberts' as against Brown's crypt. Brown's, he said, has been over-restored, scraped down, washed, and modernly lighted. Roberts' crypt is in its original state. What's more, it's a double crypt, more extensive and impressive.

Mr. Perry received the museum's verdict with indignation. "Cellar!" Under the massive stone vaulting, he and Sylvia laughed together at the very idea, while Lawrence wandered among the wine bottles. Mr. Perry believed the crypt had been built as a monk's chapel.

Sylvia wanted to know—had the chapel run along two blocks and got covered by the Rows, leaving pieces of itself to be discovered by Brown, Quellyn Roberts, and Leche House next door (which also, it was rumored, had some crypt)? But wouldn't that make the supposed chapel as big as a cathedral? And why had the Rows got built over those crypts? And why—?

No answers.

So we went to Leche House, which is entered from above, on the Row. Named for the family whose mansion it had been, it was now occupied by Kenyon's antique shop. Mr. Kenyon himself, a quiet, fragile old gentleman, welcomed us. Crypt? Yes, there was one below, but no entrance to it from his shop. He dismissed the crypt question and showed us around.

Leche House has an enormous two-story Elizabethan stone fireplace with a hidey-hole in it. It has some decorative plasterwork which Mr. Kenyon discovered after removing six layers of plaster-and-lathe plus forty layers of paint. It has a musician's gallery and two queer chambers in back, one called "The Ladies' Bower," the other, "Katherine of Aragon's Powder Room." And it has another small chamber with a squint hole looking down into the main hall with fireplace.

"I doubt very much," said Mr. Kenyon about his squint hole,

"that it was used, as common theory insists about these devices, by the ladies to spy on the gentlemen." He forestalled a *Why?* by adding with gentle dignity, "We are not that kind of people."

Mr. Kenyon was an endearing antiquarian. We were not entirely certain what century he was living in—or rather, how many centuries at one and the same time. Sylvia kept bombarding him with *Whys*—about the Powder Room, the Bower, and especially about crypts and Rows. How kind and patient he was! But at last he said, musingly, his soft blue eyes holding a wide wonder at the queer ways of women: "Why do people always have to know *Why?*"

There was no answer.

So we leave the Rows problem to you, and with it Chester's crypt controversy. But don't miss Leche House, the best of this city's authentic old magpies.

Now to the Walls.

Chester is the only city in England still entirely walled. The circuit is two miles. The Walls run—like the Elevated in Chicago's Loop—right around the heart of town, giving views on both sides.

Clamber up the narrow stone stairs where the wall bridges the Eastgate and displays the Jubilee clock, and start walking counterclockwise; that is, north. Your first view will be the cathedral and its grounds. As you go along you see the various broken towers, the Roodee racecourse, the backs and fronts of houses, church spires, the River Dee, parks, Roman remains.

The river should remind you that Chester was once a port town trading from Scotland to Spain. In the fifteenth century the harbor began to silt up, and Chester had to watch a contemptible village named Liverpool take its place as a great port. But the mayor of Chester still holds the title of Admiral of the Dee!

When you come to the Dee Bridge, you may recall that

There was a jolly miller once, lived on the River Dee,
He worked and sang from morn till night, no man as blithe as he,
And this the burden of his song forever used to be,
"I care for nobody, no not I, and nobody cares for me."

The mills used to be at the south side of the bridge. The miller held a town monopoly. So the old verses are not pro-miller; they celebrate a misanthrope who overcharged and didn't mind being hated. We were enchanted to discover this, having learned the song as tots and wondered how anybody unloved and unloving could be jolly. *That* question, at any rate, was at long last answered.

If you have a moonlight night, do the Walls then. The best walk is on a bright warm summer night, when the towers look formidable, the Dee glimmers silver below, and even the chimney pots are beautiful. When we did it, all along the way shadows stirred and whispered. Suddenly we heard a giggle, and "Oh, you mustn't!" So we discovered the modern use of the Walls. They were serving two miles of loving couples engaged in a better sport than shooting arrows or tipping buckets of boiling oil on people.

Chester has a cathedral of warm red stone, originally an abbey church. Its nave is stubby, its south transept too large and its north too small, and parts seem to have been tacked on as afterthoughts. We like it. We like its many styles and details, its unexpected passages and vaulted chambers—rectory, St. Anselm's chapel, parlor, chapter house, consistory court, cloisters.

A tablet on a pillar advised us to

Stand for a few moments in this North Choir aisle and look at the wall opposite. Let your eye rest to begin with on the beautiful stone sedilia in the Sanctuary, and, when you have taken in some of their beauty, carry your eye deliberately up one of the pillars as far as the capitals; stay there for a moment and then. . . .

We followed the directions to the letter, and found them exact and rewarding. But the final one—"As you walk around the Cathedral say to yourself now and then, 'Eight hundred years of English history is looking at me from these walls . . . ,' and so on for a long lyric paragraph—we couldn't go through with it, so we put a contribution into the box instead.

TIP: The booklet "Chester Cathedral," by Frank Bennett, is excellent. You can buy it in the church.

We were astonished to read that this church, centuries before, had once combined sacred services with a ball game. An old document records that a ball rolled in through the open door, was seized by a canon, and tossed about from hand to hand while dean, canons, and choristers "sang the antiphon."

As the canon seized the ball, so we seized an idea: is such behavior a key to the riddle presented by gargoyles on towers, imps and synthetic beasts on triforiums of nave and transepts, and the sardonic or merely humorous carvings on misericords? We did library work, and came upon medieval episcopal complaints of the Peck's Bad Boy conduct of the clergy. During services, it seems, it was not uncommon for canons, monks, and choirboys to talk and joke loudly, make derisory animal noises, pelt one another with walnuts and fruit, and from the clerestory gallery drop hot tallow from candles on the pates of those below. And there was the inevitable, eternal "card" who played for laughs by mocking the officiating priest.

Mocking the priest performing his holy office? To modern minds such behavior, barely tolerable in schoolboys or soldiers sick of routine, is sacrilegious. Yet the stonemasons and wood carvers also mocked. Can you imagine in a parish magazine today a cartoon showing the minister as part devil? What a scandal! But there are carvings portraying churchmen with fox or donkey heads, or with devil's tail and hooves peeping below the cassock.

There in Chester we learned something new about the past. Stone and wood record the old truth that man swings from Dr. Jekyll to Mr. Hyde and back again. He founds an almshouse for the poor on Sunday, and on Monday swindles them. He goes on a holy Crusade, hot for booty. Out of religious exaltation he builds a great church—and only exalted men could build so sublimely— and then, to enrich it, steals the bones of another church's saint. He covers the portals, reredos, windows with saints and Biblical scenes rich in spiritual feeling—and inserts imps, gargoyles, and carved ribaldries that stick out their tongues at the mood of holiness.

Modern man has lost heaven—it has become outer space beeping signals from galaxies of other universes. And he has lost hell too—it is no longer judgment but the casually accepted threat of nuclear destruction. His religion has become decorous and sedate. He is as incapable of misbehaving in church as he is of being caught in the grip of a heavenly vision.

In Chester Cathedral we had our little moment of truth, and thereafter churches were no longer "sights." For we realized, as we hadn't before, that a church is more than one kind of Gothic overlaying another—that it is a place where men worshiped, and slipped; rose above themselves, and fell below. One can't reach back eight hundred years and understand all. Yet when he reads of outrageous behavior during divine service, or is startled by the irreverence of a wood-carving under the hinged seat of an archdeacon ten steps from the high altar, he can feel that he is meeting someone not entirely unlike himself, a man with an irresistible desire to be a maverick and say *No!* to the boss.

But away from those eloquent stones! Take a boat ride on the Dee. Stroll through Grosvenor Park. A wonderful thing is here— a scented garden for the blind. It is one of several in England that somehow resulted from the coronation of Elizabeth II. (Brooklyn has one too, in its botanical garden.)

And there's Chester's Zoo.

This friendly animal village is in the suburb of Upton, ten minutes by bus from the Odeon Cinema near Town Hall. Stamina is not required. Not only is it easy to perambulate, but there are wheelchairs for the elderly or tired, and a canal system with a tour of the animals by motorboat, through lavish rose gardens. The beasts, uncaged, are confined to home by pits, moats, fences.

The impression is of a home-made zoo, a labor of love in which chimps, elephants, baby hippo, penguins (two sizes), and sea-lions all lent a hand, paw, trunk, or flipper. A feature is the Nocturnal House, lit by artificial moonlight. The genets, bushbabies, and other night creatures are up and about, and you can look into their great baby eyes. They seem to be saying, as they stare at you, "Never in my born days have I seen such a creature!" (On returning to New York we read in the newspaper that some American curator had thought up a wonderful new thing—an artificially illuminated house for nocturnal animals. Well, well. . . . Someone will be inventing the sundial next!)

*HOTELS* ✳ The eighteenth-century Grosvenor has style, elegance. We found it one of the best hotels in England outside London. The Blossoms, built in 1896 on the site of a famous inn and sporting a half-timbered façade, is a close second. Both are on the main street hard by the Eastgate. The Queen (a Trust House) is by the railroad station, too far from the center of things for the tourist.

*RESTAURANTS* * Chester's drawback is its eating places. Bolland's and Quaintways have bakeries in connection, but the breads and pastries were not available to lunch and tea patrons. As for the meal we had at Clemence's—well, we'd prefer to forget it. Stick to the Grosvenor (expensive) and Blossoms hotel dining rooms.

*LOCAL TRIPS* * In summer you can rent a rowboat, canoes, or self-drive motorboat on the Dee. Excursion launches go to Eccleston Ferry and back in under an hour. Two big motor-coach companies run frequent excursions in summer, mostly into North Wales.

*EVENTS* * On the river: North-of-England rowboat races in March; sailing regattas in spring and autumn; sculling championship in October. Early in May come the important Chester horse races, which have been held since 1540. In May and in March, when the Grand National is run in nearby Liverpool, the Chester hotels are crowded.

*TRAVEL FACTS* * Population about 59,000. Chester is 180 miles from London; by the fast train four and a quarter hours. It's 24 miles by road from the Liverpool airport.

*ON THE WELSH BORDER AS A WHOLE* * Regional bus services connect the towns, and local buses visit the neighboring villages of each of them. Travel agencies offer Wye Valley and Welsh Border tours. Excursion steamers ply the Wye and Severn as well as the Dee.

North of Chester lie Liverpool and Manchester and their Black Country hinterland, as interesting to the tourist as Gary, Indiana, and the West Virginia coal mines. But endure, and you come out at the far end into a region celebrated by great poets and fellow tourists for its beauty—the Lake District.

# § *THE LAKE DISTRICT*

In 1770 a Mr. and Mrs. John Wordsworth of Cockermouth, an unremarkable little town in northwest England, produced an infant son. Twenty-nine years later this son, now a struggling poet, returned to the region of his birth and settled with his sister in a cottage in Grasmere village. Poet William's friend Sam Coleridge took a house in nearby Keswick and persuaded another junior poet, Robert Southey, to come too. The lovely and dripping countryside became poet-infested. Charles Lamb, poet as well as essayist, was wooed but declined on the grounds that he hated mountains and found more natural beauty in London's Strand than around the Lakes. But De Quincy, Ruskin, and Rossetti came.

Wordsworth, celebrating daffodils and simple people like the girl of low I.Q. who insisted "We are seven," launched the romantic movement, a revolution against the brittle neoclassicism of the eighteenth century. It led on to Keats, Shelley, and the Brownings. Literary and nature tourists made pilgrimages to Wordsworth's remote corner of England. It became a resort area. Now Lakeland, comprising some twelve hundred acres, roughly thirty-five by thirty-five miles, is England's first national park.

It is Rocky Mountain landscape in miniature, with sixteen lakes and numerous meres, lakelets, rivers, and rivulets. The gentle valleys carpeted with wildflowers are offset by sudden explosions of crag and cleft, of gorge, waterfall, and jagged peak. Windermere, the largest lake, is only ten and a half miles long. Scafell Pike, the tallest mountain, strains up to a height of 3210 feet. Tranquility dwells side by side with savage grandeur. Turn a corner and you may find yourself in what looks like a valley on the moon. Stand beside Wastwater; it does you no good to say, "Pooh! you're only three miles long and half a mile wide!" The dark stillness of that super-pond of formidable depths and menacing mountains is intimidating.

The appeals of the Lake District are scenery, literary association, and its own ingrown personality. The last strikes you primarily in the names of towns, villages, scenic points: Buttermere, Cat Bells, Skiddaw, Thirlmere, Sour Milk Gill, Naddle Beck, the Drunken Duck (an inn), Dollywaggon Pike, Aira Force,

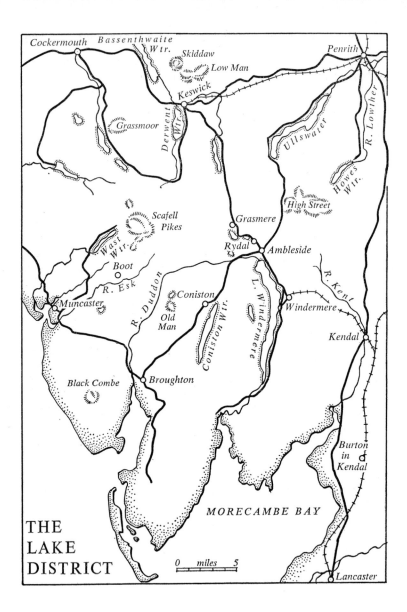

Cockermouth
*Bassenthwaite Wtr.*
Skiddaw
Low Man
Penrith
Keswick
*Grassmoor*
*Derwent Wtr.*
*Ullswater*
*Howes Wtr.*
*R. Lowther*
*Scafell Pikes*
High Street
*Grasmere*
*Wast Wtr.*
Rydal
Ambleside
Boot
*R. Kent*
*R. Esk*
*R. Duddon*
Coniston
Old Man
*Coniston Wtr.*
*L. Windermere*
Windermere
Muncaster
Kendal
Black Combe
Broughton
Burton
in
Kendal

*MORECAMBE BAY*

THE
LAKE
DISTRICT

0    miles    5

Lancaster

Floutern Tarn. It is sheep country, thinly populated and with Scottish complications, being just below the Scottish border. It is great angling country, a center of breakneck rock-climbing, and a hiker's paradise. The motorist can see much of it, but the ramblers and climbers see all.

The Grasmere Sports—crag races, local-style wrestling, hound-trailing—are held in Grasmere village on the Thursday nearest August 20. On the day before, sheepdog trials take place in the dales. This is an entertainment that should not be missed. Rydal Park is the best place to see them.

Ambleside is a pony-trekking center. Regattas are held on Lake Windermere. Golf and tennis are played.

The main drawback to a Lakeland visit is rain. If you spend a week and get three days of bright periods, you've had a dry time. In a field by the road to Keswick a sign boasts: "Here is the wettest place in England!"

Secondary drawback: apart from Wordsworthiana the district has no historic interest. Architecturally too it is empty. Natural scenery is the be-all and end-all, and this you can find in the national parks of the U.S.A. from Maine to Oregon. With sun on it.

Good centers for exploring the area are Keswick, Grasmere, Ambleside, and Windermere. Keswick has Greta Hall, where the Coleridges and Southeys lived, and is handy to Derwentwater, the most beautiful of the lakes. A rewarding tour by road is from Keswick around Derwentwater, visiting Borrowdale, the loveliest valley. Grasmere offers Dove Cottage, where Wordsworth lived, and the churchyard where he, his sister, and his wife are buried. (If you're on Wordsworth's trail, you will visit Glenbarrow Park where he saw those daffodils—750 rugged acres, in which is Aira Force, a waterfall. You'll also go to Cockermouth to see the house where he was born.) Windermere is the most popular center, and a steamer plies the lake. Ambleside, an attractively situated little town, has a church with a Wordsworth memorial chapel.

SHOPPING * This is one of the few places in England where rural crafts of quality still flourish. You find woodwork, wrought iron, stone- and metalware, jewelry, rushwork, pottery, embroidery, and etchings. The work is not amateur or primitive but skillfully designed and executed by master craftsmen. You can visit studios and workrooms at Ambleside, Keswick, Kendal, Clifton, Borrowdale, and elsewhere. The annual exhibition of the Guild of Lakeland Craftsmen is held in Ambleside during late July–early August.

CAUTIONS:    *Climbers:* wear nail-studded shoes, carry a compass and the handbooks issued by the local Fell and Rock-Climbing Club describing each step of the way. *Motorists:* have your brakes checked for those steep grades. *Cyclists:* have your heads examined. *Everybody:* take umbrella and rainwear.

*HOTELS*  *  Old England and the Belsfield at Windermere; the Keswick (at the railway station) and Queen's at Keswick; the Prince of Wales at Grasmere; the Salutation at Ambleside. There are scores of resort hotels and boardinghouses. Many offer reduced rates for stays of a week or longer. Don't expect to be charmed by your quarters.

*TRAVEL FACTS*  *  Local buses reach every available populated place; excursion-bus circular tours are arranged in each of the centers.

From Chester to Windermere is about 90 miles by rail or road; to Keswick, 110. In summer, express trains run from London into Lakeland, and many travel agencies feature motor-coach tours. The BTA booklet, "Seeing Britain by Road," deals with the District in Itinerary No. 8. BR offers combination rail–motor coach–motor yacht tours.

# 6. AROUND
# SALISBURY
# PLAIN

## § "WINCHESTER, I LOVE YOU"

One of the hopes you carry to England is for the sudden vision, the window overlooking time. Winchester may provide you with that rare experience. It's an evocative city, and beautiful in a way that grows on you with deepening surprise.

From the diamond-paned windows of our room in the Manor of God-begot, I have a view of the decorative market cross, and a jutting half-timbered building crowded so close to it that I wonder why. And wondering, slide into a kind of trance, a vision of the past as it was right here from this angle. I see uneven streets that widen and narrow without plan—gables and overhangs and abrupt, narrow passages—and Elizabethans going about their work between the cross and the gibbet. Here we are in a house on their High Street, an inconceivable couple intruding into their lives from an impossible "apartment" in the New World. The year is 1558. The house is new. In London Bloody Mary is in her grave, and red-haired Elizabeth has just mounted the throne. . . .

So Sylvia, seeking to penetrate the unseeable, and confiding to her notebook while the other half of the expedition lies in bed with a fever from a virus unknown to Tudors.

But about God-begot, whose age-blackened beams fostered her vision: the Manor is simply an old inn. It sports the puzzling inscription: A.D. 1052–1558.

In Saxon times there lived in Winchester one Aelfric. Our room, instead of bearing a number, was named for him. We were curious,

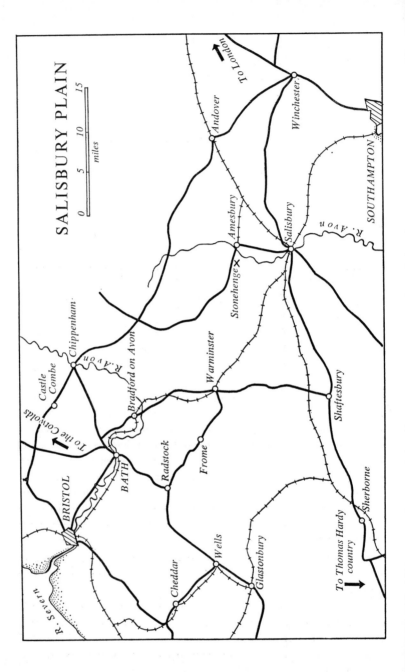

SALISBURY PLAIN

To London
Andover
Winchester
SOUTHAMPTON
Amesbury
Salisbury
R. Avon
Stonehenge ✕
Chippenham
Bradford on Avon
R. Avon
Warminster
Shaftesbury
Castle Combe
To the Cotswolds
BATH
Radstock
Frome
Sherborne
BRISTOL
Wells
Glastonbury
Cheddar
To Thomas Hardy country
R. Severn

0   5   10   15
miles

and found out that Aelfric had been dubbed the God-begot; that is, Goods Getter, purveyor; in short, wholesaler. Aelfric converted his gains into land. Queen Emma (she became a neighboring bedroom) acquired the land and bequeathed it to St. Swithun's monastery. She died in 1052, which accounts for the first date. The monastery probably built a pilgrim hostel on it, which perpetuated Aelfric's nickname. The present inn was put together five hundred years later.

There you have it.

St. Swithun (he turned out to be the private lounge) was a ninth-century Bishop of Winchester who built a bridge over the Itchen and had an affinity with water. He asked to be buried where rain would drip on his grave. This was done. But when he was sainted, his body was moved to a shrine inside the church. On that moving day it began to rain. It rained for forty days, beginning the tradition that a wet St. Swithun's day means forty days of rain.

Thanks to Lawrence's virus we settled into the cramped, creaking, bulging, sagging old inn. Every day Sylvia went out to explore Winchester, returning to Aelfric with her notebook full of finds:

FIRST DAY  *  Hard by Buttercross saw a passage, Little Minster, and popped into it; can't resist a passage. It opened into long, pleasant Symond's Street. On one side ran the high cathedral wall. On my side, a long building identified itself as "Christes Hospital. Founded 1607. Endowments of this house are applied to the maintenance of 6 old men, 1 matron, 4 boys." A square sort of man stood on lawn with his square tabby, taking in the air, and me. I complimented cat. Man replied for cat, identifying self as in charge with present matron, his wife. "Isn't it a lot of building for 6 old men, 1 matron, 4 boys?" "No more boys," he said. "They're five hundred now and have big school elsewhere. Sorry, no visitors allowed." Upon which he took me in to admire six carved wooden chairs, all that's left of original furniture. Chairs were fine. Thanking him, I went my way, thinking—But it's a big building for 6 old men, 1 matron, 1 matron's husband, 1 cat.

Cathedral wall made a sweeping turn on St. Swithun's Street. Fine old houses, bright, shining. At street end was great stone cathedral gateway with wistaria dripping down, gateway and vine framing half-timbered buildings. Across the way Kingsgate, with triple arch, framed a broader scene of curved streets. Squeezed right up against Kingsgate was an odd half-house with steeply slanting red roof—more roof than house. For a long time I just stood and stared. This must be the most beautiful corner in Winchester—maybe in all England. . . .

Finally went up to funny half-house, discovering small sign, "St. Swithun's Church." A church? Door opened on a steep stairway, and at the top—yes, a church, the rain-saint's very own; small, cozy, incredibly old. In gratitude, dropped a shilling in the box. Wonder how much money we've dropped into how many boxes by this time.

Coming out, walked through cathedral gateway. Weathered half-timbered houses formed Cheyney Court. Broad green lawns spread from it to stone ecclesiastical buildings, the cathedral towering over all. Again that uncanny feeling of having dropped back into the heart of a medieval day—utter quiet, timeless blue sky, the world of stone and grass at a standstill. A ghostly experience. The squatness of the cathedral towers broke through, bringing me back to here and now, and my unplugged ears heard a bus rumbling somewhere.

The interior of this church overwhelms, with its wealth and wilderness of white stone, carved wood, stained glass. Lost in it, I suddenly noticed a tweedy woman dusting the choir stalls which engulfed her like a bay and rose clifflike above her. I had to laugh. She looked up at me, smiled. "Quite!" she said. "Isn't it absurd—dusting a cathedral?"

SECOND DAY * Up High Street to Westgate, bearing left for the Great Hall, only remnant of William the Conq's castle. The Hall, at far end of Victorian-Gothic county offices, makes them look ashamed because it's real and they're fake. Inside cluttered with makeshift Assizes court, but magnificently proportioned.

Hanging on one wall was King Arthur's Round Table—spotlighted! Didn't look like a table—more like an enormous wheel of fortune, one of those contraptions prosperous medieval guilds set up to St. Catherine. Winchester, the first English capital, likes to think itself Arthur's authentic Camelot. But Arthur never sat at a thirteenth-century Catherine Wheel! Oh well—who cares?

Whatever it is, it's a Phenomenon, and fun to puzzle over. . . .

Out and to Westgate. Neat museum up in gatehouse (where debtors were jailed), with interesting city relics. Guard removed carpet covering a floorboard to show me clear inscription carved by a prisoner. Pretty, flowing script, and the unknown also carved his hands and feet, and a heart in one hand. He must have been in love. I liked him, long ago gone but leaving a sweetness.

Wandered back to my favorite corner, this time going through Kingsgate. Here's another part of town, the school part, with streets of well-kept old houses boarding boys and masters. Its main stem is College Street. Here Jane Austen died in her doctor's house (plaque). And here, farther along, is great Winchester College. Porter, round and pink, gave me conducted tour (usual fee). Chapel is beautiful! But how grimly the students are living; medievally! "Why?" I asked. "If founder Wykham had known about plumbing and central heating, wouldn't he have installed them?" Porter (kindlily): "Ah, yes, but he didn't know." "But you know about them now." "Yes." "So—?" He gave me his pale pink smile.

*THIRD DAY* &#42; Discovered another passage by Buttercross, with a church in it—St. Lawrence, mostly fifteenth century. Had looked for it before but couldn't find it. Worth seeing.

This was Great Minster passage, opening into The Square and Great Minster Street; more old houses, beautifully cared-for. Street brought me to cathedral again for another look. This awesome church isn't something to barge into and out of, and consider done. Outside again, found the tomb of that Grenadier who died "of a violent Fever contracted by drinking Small Beer when hot." Then the remains of the chapter house—a small, lovely ruin. Finally the deanery, its porch a marvel of low thirteenth-century vaulting and pillars.

Ambling on, suddenly was at my dear Cheyney Court. Out through my gateway-with-vine, through Kingsgate, down College Street, and this time kept on past college into a parklike road leading to the deep-flowing Itchin river. Turning left on an inviting path, discovered river promenade—the Weirs. This brought me to High Street's lower part, here called Broadway and in care of a big stone statue of King Alfred holding his sword aloft as a cross. From stone bridge behind Alfred I admired the old City Mill, so fragile and beautiful; hoped it would survive a few hundred years more. Just now it's a youth hostel.

FOURTH DAY    * After scanning skies, decided to walk the two miles to St. Cross Hospital. Trotted down now-familiar College Street, and instead of turning to Weirs, crossed a little bridge, turned right, and beside a fenced house found a lane down to river. Along the river was a path that might be the one I was looking for. To make sure, asked a long, sad man who was behind the fence doing something to a racing shell. He said this was the college boathouse. He confided Wintonians were "sticky." Said they'd dug up some Roman bits and pieces a while back and from the way they carried on you'd think nobody else had any Romans. "Now in London—" He was a Londoner, and homesick. Said, Yes, this was my path.

So off I went. After a hundred yards, found path blocked by a settled party of swans—no way round except into river. Outlying swan stood up, stretched neck, hissed. I stopped dead. A swan on water is part of scenery; a swan on land, with neck thrust out and wings open for battle, is a fearful monster. We stood for some seconds almost nose to beak, and I knew I was frightened. He knew it too. Suddenly an episode in a P. G. Wodehouse story, about Bertie Wooster being marooned on an island with an angry swan, flashed into my mind, and the Wooster's comment that it was funny about swans, how their eyebrows sort of met in the middle. I began to laugh uncontrollably, and the swan retreated a few feet in surprise. But as soon as I had pulled myself together and stopped laughing he advanced on me. I backed, and yelled to my racing-shell friend. He routed the enemy with a boat-hook.

Path was narrow, the vista broad—over the Itchen's "water meadows." Watery sun above, cindery mud underfoot, not a soul about. St. Catherine's hill rose on left—compelling mound with a mystic grove on top. Some say Druids; others, Nonsense, grove is only 200-odd years old. I like to think Druids.

And so into St. Cross, guided by its tower. At gate, a beaming porter leaning out for the entrance fee said, "You'll be wanting the Wayfarer's Dole. When you come out, ask me for it. You can only have it by asking, y'know." He seemed so happy, in anticipation, that I couldn't ask him what it was and why I should be wanting it. St. Cross has a great church. Founded 1136, it gave me my first grasp of what "time-honored" means. Church must have been all glowing with warm colors, welcoming the pilgrims. Lantern tower a beauty.

On my way out, porter beamed at me very hard and meaningfully. I thought for a second, then remembered. "Please, may I have the Wayfarer's Dole?" Delighted, he gave me a little square of bread and a wee horn-cup of ale, explaining that by ancient custom St. Cross gave the Dole to pilgrims but it was then a whole loaf and a deep horn of wine.

The main road was only a block away. Returned to town by bus in five minutes and hurried to walk the Weirs once more. But it began to rain. Stood under a tree that wouldn't let a drop touch me. Found myself patting its trunk, feeling happy and sad at same time. Lawrence much better, tomorrow we leave. We must come back someday, very soon. Winchester, I love you. . . .

*WHAT TO SEE* ✻ If pressed for time, concentrate on the cathedral and close, Winchester College, and St. Cross Hospital.

1. Cathedral. Begun in 1079, it is one of the greats. Note the exceptionally long nave, the mortuary chests of Saxon kings, the chantries of Bishops Fox and Wykeham. In the grounds, don't miss Deanery Porch and Cheyney Court.

Above and beyond all, do not fail to attend the cathedral's *Son et Lumière,* which rivals that of Canterbury. Its premiere took place July 19, 1962, on the 1100th anniversary of the death of St. Swithun. It is scheduled nightly in summer, Sundays excepted, but check with the BTA or your Winchester hotel.

2. Winchester College and College Street. The college, first of the "public schools" (contrast it with your high school or junior college back home), was founded in 1382 by William of Wykeham. Winchester grads are called Wykehamists. On this same College Street are the house where Jane Austen died, the ruins of Wolvesey Castle, and the Weirs (river promenade). To or from college you go through Kingsgate; see St. Swithun's Church there. See also Kingsgate Street, one of the most attractive on the college side of town.

3. Westgate with its museum, and nearby, on Castle Hill, the Great Hall (closed to sightseers if Assizes are in session).

4. High Street from Westgate to the City Bridge. Keep eyes

open right and left for: Georgian building of the *Hampshire Chronicle*; the former Guildhall; Buttercross; Manor of God-begot; the Pentice; Abbey House and grounds (park); St. John's Hospital (almshouse); statue of King Alfred; City Mill (seen from bridge); and Chesil Rectory (in Chesil, or Cheese Hill) beyond the bridge. The passage beside God-begot inn is Royal Oak Alley, with the old Royal Oak pub in it. The passage runs through to St. George Street, from which the back of the inn is worth seeing. Across the street are ancient stones in the wall of the *Southern Echo*'s building.

5.  St. Lawrence Church in the passage to Great Minster Street; the Square and its museum; Great Minster Street for itself.

6.  Outskirts. St. Cross Hospital (almshouse and a great church). St. Catherine's Hill and St. Giles's Hill for long views; a famous fair used to be held atop St. Giles's.

TO BEAR IN MIND.   When you look King Alfred's statue in the eye, remember that Winchester was England's capital in his time, and even earlier. Egbert, first king of Angle-land, made it the capital in 827, 665 years before Columbus sighted America. Brian Vesey-Fitzgerald's *Winchester*, on sale in local bookstores, gives history and is also an appreciation of the city.

*HOTELS*  *  The Royal is the best—cheerful, immaculate, well run, good location. . . . For the more quaint and picturesque, try the Manor of God-begot. The Winchester and the Southgate are good but they're on the busy main highway to Southampton.

*RESTAURANTS*  *  The well-known Elizabethan (formerly the Criterion) on Jewry Street in a Tudor building, has risen in quality of food and service under Mrs. Hill. Good for lunch; dinner prices are far too high. The Minster, handy on The Square, and the Chesil Rectory, are cafés.

*SHOPPING*  *  If you're looking for an antique clock, drop in on G. H. Bell's shop in The Square. . . . For antique furniture, Viney, on Cheesehill Street across the bridge, is an attractive place.

*TRAVEL FACTS*  *  Winchester (pop. 26,000) is less than three hours from London by train or road. It is twelve miles from Southampton, and for tourists wanting an alternative to an immediate descent on London it is an excellent entrance to provincial and rural England.

ENVIRONS * Chawton, seventeen miles from Winchester. Jane Austen lived here; three rooms of her house are shown. . . . Romsey, 10 miles; small market town with ancient abbey, a museum in the thirteenth-century "King John's Hunting-box," the River Test with view from bridge of Broadlands, Georgian mansion where Queen Elizabeth II honeymooned.

# § SALISBURY

"Peaceful," said the books of Salisbury. "Uneventful, serene." Hah!

Our taxi inched through the traffic to the Red Lion. The fourteenth-century coachyard was a chaos of cars backing and filling to get in or swerve out. Registered and duly introduced by Landlord Thomas to his famed skeleton clock, we made for the dining room. There wasn't a table to be had. Too impatient to wait, we strolled out to look at Salisbury.

Brisk shoppers filled the streets. The market square was solidly massed. Around the old market cross housewives were buying glassware that a Red Indian would have rejected with an Ugh! (some tribes say Pfui!). Weaving and dodging, we tangled with tots and baby carriages. The city seemed to have been invaded by ten thousand women who had made the sidewalk in front of Woolworth's an unofficial pram-park. Mothers were flying from shops to babies and back again, giving comfort to both.

We sought haven in the cathedral close. Even that was unserene. From the cathedral streamed an astonishing congregation leading every make of dog and carrying some protesting cats. A special service for animals had just been concluded.

We had arrived on a Tuesday. The next day—Wednesday—no booths, no babies. Nothing. We were accustomed by now to the buttoned-up look of an English town on Early Closing, the day shops close at noon. But in Salisbury the quiet seemed deafening.

On Thursday, however, things began to perk up. On Friday they were humming. And Saturday was Tuesday all over again.

If you stay as long as a week in an English town you begin to feel its rhythm. Salisbury is the best place we know to experience it in a zoom-fft sort of way. This is because it's a boom town, military headquarters of the Southern Command, which has converted the Salisbury Plain—once favored by the solitary hiker—into a vast training ground. Out there in the permanent camps, young couples are busily producing pink-cheeked babies. Apart from that activity life would be bleak for them were it not for the nearby Big City.

It was here on Salisbury Plain that William the Conqueror assembled his victorious army after the Conquest. And twenty years later, in 1086, after he had established his power, he called together his great barons and prelates and their subalterns in an assembly of sixty thousand, and had every man-jack of them swear personal fealty to him. This was a wrinkle new to feudalism, for in the feudal hierarchy every man's allegiance was primarily to the man above him. William's was a step toward the national state. The assembly must have been a wonderful mass of color and movement: of colored tents and striped awnings and pennons flying and knights in armor. Not easy to imagine in a world of barracks and khaki in the flat disappointing country around Stonehenge.

Salisbury was founded to get *away* from the military. In the days when the big brass wore armor, they were in supreme command of the fort town of Old Sarum. In 1220 the town, fed up, moved out on them. The prime mover was a bishop Poore, who negotiated successfully with the Pope and the king to make a new city down by the river. He laid out New Sarum—now Salisbury—neatly and efficiently, and started the cathedral, which was finished in thirty-eight years. It is one of the great English churches.

Pass under the High Street gate, and Bishop Poore's cathedral bursts full upon you in open, unobstructed view. It rises from a plain of grass and soars up and up, piercing the sky with its pointed spire. It is theatrical, a *coup d'oeil*. And that's the trouble —further acquaintance is bound to be anticlimax. What's more, a cathedral built all in one style lacks the interest and excitement of one that got pulled down here and built up there, incorporating fresh ideas. So we must report that Salisbury is not our favorite cathedral. Experts call it "the perfect norm." That may be what's wrong with it—perfection.

More than the cathedral we enjoyed the close—the far-spreading green with a variety of houses around it, one dating from the fifteenth century. Take a leisurely stroll all the way round. Each house is distinctive, a lived-in period piece. There are at least a dozen we wish we could move into right away. But the beauty is eighteenth-century Mompesson House, built for a wealthy merchant and adorned inside with rich paneling and plaster work. It is open to visitors May through September, Tuesdays and Saturdays, from 2:30 P.M.

Wandering about the close, you come to orient yourself by its three gates—Harnham, Queen Anne's, and High Street. They bring you out into different parts of the city.

From Harnham gate, by a zig here and a zag there, cross the bridge spanning the Avon into East Harnham. Take the street on your right to the Rose and Crown. Go there—don't fail. In the inn's bar order a long drink, take it out to the garden that runs down to the water's edge, and admire the finest view of the cathedral, the view that Constable painted from about where you sit. On your right is the old bridge and a handsome old house; and there will be busy ducks on the water and swans being graceful and disdainful; and in the long, wide middle distance the cathedral spire rises from the trees.

For a pleasant walk, continue on the Harnham Road when you leave the Rose and Crown, and bear right into Lower Street, at the end of which is the river and the Old Mill. This ancient building is now a sixteen-room hotel with restaurant, on the mill race. The water, meadow, and cathedral views are uplifting. You cut back to town across the mill bridge and meadows to Long Bridge and Mill Road. Better ask directions before leaving the Old Mill Hotel.

If you have a car, you could combine a visit to the Rose and Crown and the Old Mill (part of the way to the Mill can only be done on foot; park the car), with the pretty village of Coombe Bisset, two miles from West Harnham.

Since Salisbury was planned geometrically, with wide streets cut into checkerboard blocks, it lacks the fascination of a city like Winchester, which just grew. But even at first glance certain buildings stand out from the too-uniform blocks—notably the Haunch of Venison (a well-known restaurant) and Beach's bookstore on High Street, which leans and undulates in a most satisfying way.

Then there is Watson's on Queen's Street. It's a china-and-glass shop with cluttered windows. We passed it many times, window-shopped, passed on. But one day something about the building itself called out to us. We stood for some time trying to peer inside and listening with the third ear. We walked in, warily.

To us there came a tall, mildly melancholy man who fixed us with a keen blue eye. "We are," he announced, "an Ancient Monument."

Watson's is "Ye House of John a'Port," built in the fifteenth century for a wealthy wool merchant; and Mr. Skelton, its manager, was in love with it. He pointed out beams and timbers, and the wattle-and-daub understructure. He urged us up a Georgian staircase to show us the Jacobean room, which was the one he loved best.

There he told us how Watson's, upon taking this house in 1930, had in redecorating accidentally broken a bit of wall and discovered the oak paneling. The Ancient Monuments man came. Paint and plaster were chipped away under his guidance, and slowly there was revealed not only the paneling but a stone fireplace with a carved overmantle.

"We're an Ancient Monument," Mr. Skelton repeated. "It is a grave responsibility. And costly." He stared out the window, far-seeing. "There is scarcely a house in this city which does not hide something."

That evening we strolled through Salisbury's duller streets. We found the old Joiners' Hall on St. Anne's in a sad state of dilapidation. But across the way was a beautiful half-timbered house, showing the Joiners how it might look if it only tried.

"That one," Sylvia decided in a delighted leap of fancy, "is the house of the Ancient Monuments man!"

The orange street lamps came on. Garish blooms, they made everything look eerie. The shapes and forms of houses, doors, roofs, stood out, various and homely. Nothing was uniform and ordinary any more as in daylight.

Here, row upon row, was the everyday Englishman's home—a small house, old but sturdy, faced outside according to the fashion of an era when a family was in the money; the rooms inside, plain boxes, thickened by centuries of redecorating. Somewhere, deeply buried, was the original structure with its prideful details and craftsmanship. And that Ancient Monuments man had his eye on it, and was waiting.

The Ancient Monuments man is lean and long, with a face all hollows and ridges. He has a thin, twitching nose, and his eyes are cavernous. From his half-timbered lair he emerges daily, rain or shine, and he bicycles about, leisurely.

Suddenly he raises his head, and the long nose twitches. In the concealed city that is his, and his alone, the innocently boisterous Smith family have brought down a piece of their parlor, revealing a corner of an undoubted Tudor fireplace. There he goes, the Ancient Monuments man! He goes like the wind, and everybody knows the sound of his gnarled knuckles on the door where, inside, the Smiths are frantically trying to sweep the telltale rubble under the rug.

*WHAT TO SEE* * 1. The cathedral (1220–58), considered a classic in Early English.

2. The cathedral close.

3. Church of St. Thomas (fifteenth century). The city meanly crowds this gem which has richly decorated beams and paneling, and a magnificent Doom fresco.

4. Domestic architecture: the inns, John a' Port's house, Ye Halle of John Halle (lobby of Gaumont Theater), and Church House.

*HOTELS* * The Red Lion claims to be "one of the finest examples of an old coaching inn remaining in the country." It is. Excellently hosted by William Thomas, it is a center of Salisbury life. . . . We also liked the Rose and Crown across the river, the inn with Constable's view. It is bossed by a mother cat who sees to it that visiting dogs keep their place and beat the floor with their tails when she passes. . . . The White Hart, a Trust House, is on the dull side. . . . The King's Arms, once run down, has lately come up, but the TV set in the lounge is a mistake.

*EATING PLACES* * Have one meal at the Haunch of Venison—"Ye Olde Established Chop House," it calls itself. . . . Among a good number of good tearooms, the Chelsea Room of the Red Lion is best. Get there early. The fresh-baked doughnuts and crumpets go fast.

*SHOPS*  *  Watson's for bone china and hand-cut crystal. They have an enormous stock and experience in tourist-selling, packaging, shipping. . . . "Krene of Vienna" is a good beauty parlor. For cut, shampoo and set, Sylvia was charged seventy-five cents.

*TRAVEL FACTS*  *  By rail from London the journey takes a hundred minutes. Winchester is twenty-seven miles east. Salisbury is a busy bus and motor-coach center connecting with Winchester, Southampton, North and South Devon and Cornwall, Bath, South Wales, Cheltenham.

# § *OLD SARUM*

The old town is only ten minutes from Salisbury by bus. The bus station is on Endless Street, and you get off, seemingly, at nowhere. You walk up a slope, and there you are, on top of a broad circular hill, undulating toward a saucerlike dip in the center, entirely carpeted with groomed grass. All around are heaps, mounds, circles, faced with small stones embedded in mortar. Each of these shaped piles of rubble has a big neat number on it, so that the first impression is rather of a miniature golf course. You locate the numbers on a plan you bought on coming in, and find out what each thing is (or was, rather) if you've a mind to—Gatehouse, Well, Great Tower, Chapel, etc.

In spite of the minigolf aspect, you get the feel of the place almost at once. It's not that of a medieval ghost town but of a natural, ancient site—a dry-moated hill standing high and remote on top of the world. The wind blows hard from any or all quarters, mysteriously. There are long views over long low hills.

The remains are those of the great Norman castle and fortified town which were carried down little by little, stone by stone, to make Salisbury. But there were fort-towns here much earlier, far beyond memory.

Old Sarum was a prehistoric hilltop settlement—like St. Catherine's hill at Winchester, in a direct line with it and, like it, situated on a treeless chalk down. Neolithic and Bronze-Age men chose such sites to live on, high and dry above the dank forests and the river valleys up which invaders came. From one to another ran primitive high roads over grasslands. It took thousands of years, and the development of agriculture, for people to begin to move down.

You feel those thousands of years on Old Sarum. We know of no other place that brings you, in a giant stride, so close to the crack between the night and light of civilization.

# § STONEHENGE

"Laying down my stick and bundle and taking off my hat I advanced slowly, and cast myself—it was folly perhaps, but I could not help what I did—cast myself with my face on the dewy earth, in the middle of the portal of giants, beneath the transverse stone; the spirit of Stonehenge was strong upon me."

So George Borrow 150 years ago, as told in *Lavengro,* and we don't doubt he did just that. He wouldn't do it today. He'd feel silly. There's a parking lot, an admissions hut, and tourists of all nations. Military planes zoom overhead. Barbed wire spoils the view on one side and a busy road does the same for the other.

Stonehenge is a circle of monolithic stones, the remains of an important temple. How did the stones get here, and when? Who built the temple, who worshiped in it? Archeologists are still debating these matters.

The earliest theory is that Merlin the magician transported the temple bodily from Ireland by means of spells. He was the greatest magician that ever semi-existed and had been around working wonders for several eons before turning up and casually lending a hand to King Arthur. The theory is, of course, unscientific, but it is a record of the awe in which this place was held long after its life had departed. It is also a record of special regard for Merlin.

It is now thought that Stonehenge dates from between 1700 and 1500 B.C., give or take a couple of centuries. That it was the work of Bronze-Age men. And that they were sun-worshipers whose Merlins here performed gory rites. When it was flourishing, the temple may have seemed to the Britons bigger and grander than Westminster Abbey looks today. There isn't much to it now. Six tourists in the ruins make a crowd.

Stonehenge is only some ten miles from Salisbury, but it is one place in England you can't easily get to by public transport. We took a bus to Amesbury and another to Larkshill. It wasn't a jolly ride. The Plain is dotted with military camps. From Larkshill we walked through one of the biggest of them, feeling conspicuously civilian, and on along a rutted country road. We had our small reward in seeing the stones rear up as we approached.

To return to Salisbury, we begged a lift from two fellow Americans. They were grimmer than Stonehenge. The conversation was brief and went something like this:

*They:* "Up in Scotland they told us that the English jack up all the prices for Americans."

*Us:* "That's not true!"

*They:* "Antique shops, they're the ones."

*We:* "Do you buy antiques?"

*They:* "No."

Morals: 1. Don't trust a Scot on the subject of the English. 2. Keep up your spirits when touring, no matter what. You're in Merrie England—be merrie! 3. The best way to get to Stonehenge is in your own or a hired car.


# § *MRS. CHUBB'S SHERBORNE*

Away back when we were a-courtin', a project that drew us together was collecting American town songs. One that delighted us we plucked from Illinois. The tune and a few lines survive in the memory:

> I wandered the whole world o'er
> And then I found Desplaines. . . .

> *Chorus:*  Happy town, happy town!
> Never can be beat.
> The streets are paved, conditions best—
> You will like Desplaines!

Years later, wandering the whole world o'er, we came to Sherborne, a place we had never heard of. Its soft-colored stone and the grace of the curving, ascending main street caused us to break into, "Happy town, happy town!" It was a tribute.

Hotels were beyond our means. We found in a side street a house named the Brambles with a hand-lettered card in the window: "Bed and Breakfast. Mrs. Chubb."

Mrs. Chubb's parlor could have served for the set of a Victorian play. Plush-framed photographs, "God Bless Our Home" in needlework, and a penmanship diploma decorated the floral wallpaper. Wax flowers bloomed on tables under glass bells. Whatnots were thickly populated with knickknacks, among them Mrs. Chubb's two most prized possessions—a rose of Jericho and a stuffed owl.

Mrs. Chubb was a small, skipsy woman with big blue eyes, a country girl's complexion, and a way of mounting the stairs to the bedrooms like a ballerina in effortless, airy flight, talking all the while. She was at once genteel and larky. There was a teen-age daughter Chubb, speechlessly shy and floating ribbons from hair and dress. Our praise of her breakfast ham and eggs with butter-fried potatoes brought a blush of deep Dorset red. At the upright piano in the parlor we tried to teach Chubb Junior the real Dixie swing of jazz, but it was Mrs. Chubb who caught the rhythm. For three days we were part of the family.

Before leaving we contributed our laudatory inscription to the guest book and read the comments of preceding guests: "Short visit but sweet," "Comfortable digs," "*Joli ménage.*" A week before, a multitude had descended upon the Brambles: "Noble & Harris, Furniture Removers. 4 men, 1 lady, 2 children, 1 dog, Plymouth to London." After them came: "Three maids from Lady Rugge-Price. Miss Hinks, Miss Bolan, Miss Wall." They had put their heads together and composed this:

> If from home you have to wander,
>     Never fear.
> There's a welcome and good cheer
> At the Brambles in Sherborne dear
>     With Mrs. Chubb.

It is perilous to return, after long absence, to a place where one was vividly happy. But on this last trip we had to see Sherborne again to check dutifully on whether it was worth urging on other travelers. And perhaps we could pay our respects to Mrs. Chubb who was so alive then, we did not doubt she was still so.

At the railway station we inquired after her and the Brambles. Neither was known.

This time we put up in style at the Digby Hotel, former town mansion of the Digbys, from ancient days the great family of these parts. We walked out and admired the slow curve of Low Cheap and High Cheap, the bright shops, the ageless houses of russet stone, the timbered inns, and the long green hill smiling down on all of it. Our relief was enormous. Sherborne is blessed with that indefinable quality called Presence.

The small town has an abbey of which we had only the dimmest recollection. This was odd because there is so much to it. We went through it now, and it was all new to us.

A complex of buildings, mostly fifteenth-century, it takes in a city block. They were once monastic. Most of what is not church houses one of the oldest of English public schools, founded in 1550. The boys dine in a paneled great hall, watched from a niche by a childlike statue, blue, white, red, and gold, of the boy King Edward VI, their Founder. At one end of the complex are medieval almshouses of antique stateliness.

The abbey church has a Norman core. Some Saxon work survives. Within, it is beautifully ornamented and its fan-vaulting is superb. But what held us for some time was a plain cracked slab, erected (it said in carved script) "in Remembrance of a Great Hailfstorme," May 16, 1709—"which ftopping the courfe of a fmall river weft of this Church cauf'd" a flood in the abbey garden, "running with fo rapid a ftream" that it forced open the north door and was "2 foot 10 inches high as if paff'd out at this South Door."

Now, if we had seen the abbey and church during our Chubb visit, surely we would have remembered this. Sylvia had always a passion for the old English ſ-like s. That seemed to prove we had not seen the abbey. Yet here it was, the biggest, grandest thing in Sherborne. How could we have missed it? We *must* have seen it, after all. Had something happened to our minds in the interval, blanking out the abbey church, the Tudor public school, the almshouses?

We had the uncanny feeling that we were two entirely different people from the couple that had stayed at Mrs. Chubb's.

But never mind that. Sherborne, as we were saying, has Presence.

It has wealth and breeding. It's a famous hunt center, known as the Melton Mowbray of the south, and its golf course is panoramic. MGs and Jaguars park in the streets. The people are well dressed, unlike the citizens of big-town Yeovil only five miles away. The shops wouldn't let Knightsbridge down if translated to that quarter of London.

On the other side of the River Yeo at the edge of Sherborne, a long hill (fine views) bears the ruins of the bishop's castle. It overlooks the wide parklike acres of the Walter Raleigh-initiated Sherborne Castle of the Digby family. Nearby stands the picturesque Walter Raleigh Lodge, serving as a dower house, and across the road is the small family church.

Digby is a famous name. In the seventeenth century Sir Kenelm Digby, the handsomest man of his day, married Venetia Stanley, the most beautiful woman. According to a contemporary gossip, when Sir Kenelm's mother objected to Venetia as a notorious courtesan, he replied "that a wise man, and lusty, could make an honest woman out of a Brothell-house." And so he did, to the extent that a portrait of Venetia hangs in the State Apartments of Windsor Castle.

We were still questing after Mrs. Chubb. Taking tea at the Spindleberry, we sounded out Mrs. Spicer, who served us her homemade cakes. Mrs. Spicer, new to Sherborne, thought the provision merchants across the Cheap might know. They knew of a Miss Chubb, we learned, selling dresses in a shop down the street.

We popped in, and there was our Miss Chubb, no longer beribboned, still shy, but slightly less speechless. She took us home to her Mum, saying only that Mum was getting on, her memory wasn't what it used to be.

The Chubbs now lived on Hound Street in a house that was not the Brambles—they were no longer taking paying guests—but looked the same. So did Mrs. Chubb, except for snowy white hair that made her eyes look larger and bluer, like those of an unwinking doll. Her skin was as fair, and flawless. She was as light on her feet and as larky as ever.

"Eighty-three!" she said of herself. "And not a spot on me! Doctor says he's never seen anything like it!" She chattered away, going back and forth in time with skipping ease. "I used to bathe Mr. Churchill. 'Twas back in 1898, or '99. I'd run away from home

to London and found work in a bath-massage house. . . ." Sylvia
had the sniffles, and Mrs. Chubb prescribed: "Salt and soda, a
handful of each in a hot bath, and right to bed with four lumps
of sugar. Three you take before sleep, and one in the morning.
Feeds the heart." She knew!

"The stuffed owl, Mrs. Chubb?"

She took us into the parlor—and there everything was, just as
we remembered—the whatnots, the flowers under glass, the photographs and penmanship diploma, and—. The piano was gone. We
were almost afraid to ask, but we needn't have been; nothing hor-
rid had happened. Chubb Junior had grown up to marry and give
his Mum grandchildren. He lived in Yeovil. The piano had gone
to grandchild number one.

"And there," said Mrs. Chubb, "is Owl, sitting in the window.
The night constable likes Owl. When he passes he blinks his light
at him. 'I like to see him blink back at me,' he says." She laughed
like a girl.

"And your rose of Jericho?"

She was delighted that we remembered it, and pointed out its
bowl. "It's still blooming."

Lawrence, suddenly a Victorian gallant, said with a little bow:
"Just like you, Mrs. Chubb."

And Mrs. Chubb blushed, and dropped a curtsey.

She brought out a pile of yellowed old guest books, blew the
dust from each as she took it up, shook her head, put it down. She
stopped at one she said was the right year—our year.

We opened it, lightly arguing with her—but she was right. Here
was the page, here the faded inscriptions: "Noble & Harris . . . ,"
"Three maids from Lady Rugge-Price . . . ," and the verse,

> If from home you have to wander,
> Never fear . . . ,

and under that, our own contribution: "We loved every minute.
When Hitler's gone, we'll be back." That was 1939.

We marveled over Mrs. Chubb's memory. And we cried triumphantly, "We said we'd be back, and here we are!"

But Mrs. Chubb was looking at the message with a slight frown.
"Yes," she said, "they all come back. Every one." Still she stared.

"But who," she asked, "is this Hitler? A queer name. I don't re-member *him* staying here."

*HOTELS* * The Digby is by far the best; pleasantly fur-nished rooms, extensive grounds. The Half Moon is so-so. Among the inns, we took a fancy to Capt. Pyman's George Hotel, 1404 or even older, once a pilgrim hostel.

*RESTAURANTS* * The Digby's dining room was the for-mer ballroom, almost as immense and high of ceiling as the nave of the church. It could feed a regiment, and with only six diners chomping their beef-and-two-veg it looked lonesome and resounded hollowly. But we were told there is a smaller dining room, some-times used. Not that this matters—the food was the same. This may change, however. The cuisine at the Half Moon was better. The Spindleberry Café on Cheap Street had more eatable lunches and teas than either.

*TRAVEL FACTS* * Sherborne is thirty-four miles west of Salisbury; nineteen miles north of Dorchester, county town of Dorset (not worth your time); nineteen miles south of Glaston-bury (via Yeovil), and so on the way to Wells and Bath. From Bath via Bristol you can go on to the Wye Valley and the Border Country, or to Malmesbury and the Cotswolds. Sherborne is also on the way to Devon and Cornwall via Exeter (for South Devon and Dartmoor); and to Taunton, Somerset, for North Devon.

It is served by the British Railways and by long-distance bus lines; and of course by regional bus lines.

# § *BATH*

Our train was rolling through a countryside of neat and rounded hills. Suddenly, on and among those hills and as if between heaven and earth, there popped up curving, solid ranks of houses, English by their chimney pots but otherwise improbable, like a settlement on Saturn. "What's that?" we asked each other.

So we came to Bath.

Some time later, we found ourselves hanging over the wall of the promenade called the North Parade, entranced by a bridge. It was an airy affair with little shops on it, playfully Florentine. Oval tunnels were set like medallions into its lower façade—at any moment Lohengrin might come floating through in a swan boat. The river was so still that the confection was doubled by its perfect reflection in the water.

Pulteney Bridge (1771) was designed by Robert Adam, the architect who created so much of Georgian England that his name is almost synonymous with it. Yet by the time he came to make his bridge, the city was already a full-blown Georgian triumph. So he tried something different—a Romantic fantasy, a captivating make-believe. His bridge is an expression of his delight with this city.

Well. . . . Here you stand on the North Parade. For a small fee the pretty gardens just below are yours. There you can stroll, or laze in a canvas chair (fee), and listen idly to band music. The formal flower beds carry out the mixture of playfulness and sober craftsmanship. We liked the Humpty Dumpty formed of clipped hedges and posies. And alongside is the river, broadening to the weir—and that bridge.

Is there anywhere a piece of river which has been made so ornamental as this Avon of Bath?

But now you turn your back on it and walk—ignoring the abbey and the Pump Room. Regulation sights, they can come later.

Bath rises, curls upward in stately fashion, the rows of Georgian houses turning with the hills they stand on, slowly and evenly. Someone there was who didn't love a straight line. Or a bump. Or a jog. The streets are gradient arcs, and unexpected greens may glorify a single, gratifying tree spreading a wide circle of shade. Up you go to the great wheel called the Circus, and then to the even more daring Royal Crescent. These are tests of architectural showmanship on a grand scale. Do they come off? You have to go, see, and decide for yourself.

It's an odd city, like nothing else anywhere. It is built entirely of stone. This famous Bath stone is curiously sand-toned and flat. It takes a little getting used to. At first the buildings look alike —precise files, ceremonial, like a regiment marched out for review. Gradually the details emerge in windows, doors, columns, and ironwork. Next you begin to grasp the artfulness of gardens and squares, and observe how they glow against the backdrop of stone. And finally, as you amble and poke about, the scope and the scale, the whole gracious and elegant order, unfolds.

Bath is a charmer.

It began as a spa in (they say) 863 B.C. when a Prince Bladud, heir to the throne of some little British kingdom, contracted leprosy. Wandering about, a miserable outcast, he found work caring for the pigs of a remote village. One day he discovered he had contaminated the pigs. Afraid to tell their owner, he got permission to drive them across the river on the plea that the pig-pastures were better there. The pigs, once across, made a dash for a bubbling muddy wallow, and they came out cured. Bladud plunged in and returned to health and a jubilant kingdom.

A happy ending! Bath has the happy-ending feel.

From Bladud to Beau Nash is twenty-five hundred years. You cross that space by using the Romans. They built (54 A.D.) splendid baths at the springs, with steam rooms and central heating, all pillared and roofed. Through the four hundred years of occupation every Roman soldier posted in Britain must have tried to wangle leave for Aquae Sulis, as they named it. But when the Romans left, their bathing establishment fell into ruins and was covered over. Chaucer's lively Wife of Bath came from a cloth-making town— nothing said about baths.

It was eighteenth-century man who rediscovered bathing, and very daring he was too. We find in our favorite Eleventh Edition of the *Encyclopaedia Britannica* the weighty warning: "Baths often produce injurious effects when used injudiciously." The date is 1910. So the people who were steeping themselves in Bath's mineral waters two hundred years earlier must have been a devil-may-care lot. Of course they didn't come for cleanliness but for health.

They came by way of terrible roads infested by highwaymen, to a small medieval town crammed into the river valley and notorious for its stench and filth. They paid exorbitantly for scarce lodgings. They were the prey of card-sharks and quacks. They brawled and were quick to use their swords. In the open pools, they bathed in ballooning yellow canvas, surrounded by floating bowls of soaps and scents, while from the houses around the householders flung unspeakable things down on them. Still they came.

A new day was dawning. The eighteenth century was preparing

to become the Age of Reason. Bath, as you see it now, is the creation and showpiece of that age.

The easiest way for an American to define the Age of Reason is to think of Benjamin Franklin, its great American embodiment. He was a man of tidy mind, concerned with good housekeeping on earth, where men of previous centuries had been more concerned with heaven. He had good-housekeeper counterparts in Bath—Ralph Allen, who owned the quarries; the architects Wood, father and son; the enlightened Dr. Oliver, who wanted a hospital but is best known as the inventor of the Oliver biscuit (still made in Bath). These men are known, but there were others unknown. They began to tear down the old town and make an entirely new one dedicated to beauty, health, and civilized entertainment.

Into this Operation Bootstraps came Beau Nash.

The Beau was a man of about thirty, baggy under the eyes and jowled around the chin. He was penniless and friendless. Yet within a few years he was cleaning up the city, regulating manners and dress, providing entertainment and presiding over it, making streets and roads passable, collecting money for Oliver's dream hospital, enforcing a rent law.

He outlawed dueling and the wearing of swords.

He transformed arrogant lords and ladies into persons the plain folk could approach without being spat at or spitted. He changed those medieval plain folk into almost-moderns.

He created a social revolution that spread from the little spa through England, and was even felt abroad. He was a founder of modern civilities, and of the modern resort.

Beau Nash was not a handsome man, or even very bright. His title *Beau* came from his passion for tidiness and his personal elegance. How did he make himself the benevolent despot? No one knows, not even Edith Sitwell who wrote the Nash-Bath success story in a book.

For some forty years Beau Nash ruled Bath. All the Somebodies paid him deference. Yet, for all his historicity, he wears the same aura of remote and solemn myth as Bladud.

In Bath, you become uncannily aware of a single personality behind everything you see—civilized, orderly, and exquisitely mannered. Bladud and his pigs are no more, but Beau Nash still walks his streets.

*WHAT TO SEE* ✳ 1. The city as a whole, of which a historian says: "Bath is a sort of Pompeii of eighteenth-century architecture." Note the trimly picturesque old shop fronts. Note also how from a height such as Camden Crescent the effect is hurt by one unfortunate modern object—Bath's skyscraper apartment building, put up in spite of public-spirited protest.

Bath has a literary past. Authors found its air congenial. Among those who produced here are Henry Fielding (*Tom Jones*), Swinburne ("Ballad of Bath"), Sheridan (*School for Scandal*), Oliver Goldsmith (*Life of Nash*), and Dickens, Smollett, Fanny Burney, and Jane Austen. Sheridan met his future wife here and eloped with her.

2. The abbey. Dating from 1499, it is mostly late-Perpendicular, rich and handsome.

3. Pump Room. It's that late-Georgian building standing in what was abbey property. It incorporates the excavated Roman baths which were discovered when the old priory was razed during the Georgian building boom. The Pump Room takes its name from the pump (now a fountain) at which you drink the mineral waters—a once-fashionable rite. The name is confusing because it isn't a room but a building of many rooms. Take a conducted tour (there's one every half-hour) through the Roman remains, the most important and impressive in Britain. Concerts, sundry entertainments, and Saturday-night dances (formal dress still required) are held in the Pump Room.

SIGHTSEEING NOTE. There are intensive, exhaustive city bus tours. Inquire at your hotel or at the Information Bureau in the abbey plaza. The Bureau can also arrange for one of the city's honorary guides to escort you on foot or in your car. No tipping, says the Bureau firmly.

*HOTELS* ✳ We liked best the Lansdowne Grove, on a height with views; bright, resortlike, friendly, and an easy bus ride to the North Parade. . . . The Francis, on Queen Square, would be our second choice, sharing place with the Pratt on the South Parade. . . . We found the Royal York on George Street depressing. Its bar, however, is popular on Saturday night. An oddity is the small Gay Hotel with a tiny garden on the river, of which it is immensely proud; Sheridan fell in love with Eliza Linley in its grotto.

The guests seem to run to "characters." This place may be fun. . . . There are many small hotels and guest houses (bed-and-breakfast) for limited-budget tourists. Like the Gay, the small hotels prefer to take you on for at least a week on a full-pension deal. If you're staying a while, investigate.

RESTAURANTS, TEAROOMS  *  The Hole in the Wall on George Street is run by an ex-schoolmaster who concocts strange dishes from old Continental cookbooks. Chez Robert, farther up, was excellent when it had a Dutch cook; it no longer has. For tea, the best is Fortt's on Milson Street; try a Bath bun and Oliver biscuits. Tea in the Pump Room's gallery has long been a sad experience; this may change.

BATHS  *  Some people come to Bath for the baths, hydrotherapeutic and physiotherapeutic. An inquiry to the Municipal Information Bureau will bring you complete information.

BATH FESTIVAL  *  The Bath season opens in spring with ten days of great music and a variety of cultural and social events. In the autumn there is a Bach festival. If you plan to be in Bath on either of these occasions, arrange your hotel booking well in advance. Dates and details of the festivals and of any other important scheduled events are available from the Spa Director, The Pump Room, Bath.

TRAVEL FACTS  *  You are in a major touring center. Local buses go to outlying towns and villages. In spring and summer, excursion buses make circular trips to farther-off places such as Salisbury and the Wye Valley (Tintern Abbey).

Bath is 2 to 2½ hours (105 miles) from London by train or road. If driving, get the BTA's free booklet, *Seeing Britain by Road*, for its itinerary with map under "Main Route No. 3."

ENVIRONS  *  For miles all around Bath spreads the green, wooded, gently hilly country that Compton McKenzie called the very essence of England. In this eighteenth-century landscape lies Castle Combe, one of the loveliest villages in England; and Longleat, seat of the Marquess of Bath, one of the finest Stately

Homes. Unfortunately, they are in opposite directions. Having done more than a baker's dozen of Statelies, and being hurried, we hired a taxi in Bath to go to Castle Combe, stopping at Bradford-on-Avon and Lacock. The trip, plus tip, cost us seven dollars.

*Bradford-on-Avon.* We liked the small Saxon church of St. Lawrence, dating from 700; and the tithe-barn at Barton Farm. The tithe-barn, fourteenth-century and the best-preserved in England although on a private farm, is a great stone structure, steep-roofed and grandly proportioned. It has too much character to be passed off as a "barn." Bradford also has the Swan Inn; its dining room in medieval times served as a courtroom.

*Lacock.* A handsome village of old stone houses, it is carefully protected by the National Trust. Its thirteenth-century abbey is now a residence, but you can walk in its park. The church of St. Cyreac has a fine "barrel roof."

*Castle Combe.* Drop the "Castle" and call it *Coom.* This village too is National Trust. It is beautiful, knows it, and works at it with a fine pride. It nestles in a dell by a gurgling stream. It has a great market cross and delightful houses with smiling gardens. Where once was a castle is now the Manor House Hotel (approached by its mews, which stable horses) sporting its own gardens adorned with classical balustrades and pergolas. (We took note of this attractive but high-priced hotel for some future stay.) Down the street is the Sign of the Angel, a tiny inn with seven rooms to let, bulging walls, great beams, a dining room gleaming with silver and white napery. There are other inns, but this one is extraordinary in its perfection. You can lunch here only if you book ahead.

We were admiring the market cross, which is a stunner, when a creature from outer space roared up on a full-sized motorcycle. It wore heavy boots, a sou'wester, and a black hood, having come through heavy weather. Peeling off its outer garments it revealed a snub-nosed young woman with dancing eyes—a London stenographer with three weeks' freedom, charging about the country solo and at that moment hungry. We hated parting company with her, but our man James had to get back to Bath for a wedding.

*Claverton Manor.* Colonial arts and crafts came to America by way of England. They have been collected and brought back to England by two Americans supported by a foundation, and are housed in a Georgian mansion about three miles from Bath. One room is a New England country store where you can buy reproductions of early American china. Another is "Conkey's Tavern 1776," which sometimes offers gingerbread fresh from the oven, served by English girls in American costumes. The garden has been replanted as a reproduction of Washington's at Mount Vernon. Tea is served on the terrace.

# § WELLS

Between Bath and Wells lie twenty-one miles of Mendip Hills which the gossipy bus does with frequent stops in just over an hour. Wells (pop. 6000) is small but a "city" with a cathedral that is one of England's joys. As soon as you see the curiously squat bulk holding up that massive central tower, and the west front which is like a fanfare of trumpets, you know with a thrill that you are in for something fresh, original.

Dating from 1184, this is one of the smaller cathedrals but looks one of the grandest. In the 1200s Jocelyn, a building bishop, finished the west front with a great stone screen wider than the nave, elaborately carved with niches and figures. Whence came Jocelyn's inspiration that he could put a fancy mask on a plain face with happy effect? Theoretically the whole idea is wrong. But it comes off. The west front gives size and grandeur to the exterior. It probably didn't look as if it belonged, however, before the central tower rose to complement it.

Medieval men built by guess and by God. A hundred years after the west front was consecrated, Dean John de Godelee heightened the central tower, which had been too short. Less than fifty years later the tower was on the verge of collapse from its own weight. If it fell it would wreck the whole church. In an emergency meeting an unknown genius proposed inverted stone arches inside the church at the three points of greatest stress. A makeshift born of panic and despair, these gigantic stone frames of hourglass shape are the most spectacular feature of Wells Cathedral.

The north transept has a joyous fourteenth-century clock with jousting knights who ride around every hour and get banged. This transept leads to the superb chapter-house stairway. Medievally folksy stone carvings cover the capitals of the pillars. It's on the capitals of the south transept that you must look for the stone people in the agony of various toothaches. Thanks to Bishop Bitton II, Wells was the tooth-tortured pilgrims' mecca. Dying in 1274, he became a saint who began working dental miracles. For the stone work on the bosses of the vault you need binoculars.

TIP. Be on your best behavior. The vergers tend to be officious.

Across the road from the cathedral and through the Chain Gate you find the Vicars' Close: two facing rows of fourteenth-century houses with tall chimneys and diminutive gardens. Wells was a secular cathedral served by nonresident canons who, being often absent, appointed vicars as substitutes. Until these houses were built, the poor vicars had to find lodgings in the town. Each house had originally only two rooms. Many are now combined, and they are still occupied, if not by vicars at least by theology students.

On the other side of the cathedral you go through the gate called the Bishop's Eye to the moated courtyard of the thirteenth-century Bishop's Palace and wait to see the swans of the moat ring the gatehouse bell to demand food. (People say the ducks do it too when the swans let them.) We never had luck, but you may.

Wells is a quiet and dignified old town. If you care for cathedrals more than for spas, you may prefer to stay here rather than in Bath. Among the many inns on Wells' main street, the Ancient Gate House is worth visiting. It incorporates pieces of the old city wall and has odd passages and stairways.

*HOTELS* * The Crown, the White Hart, the Star, the Swan. The Ancient Gate House is structurally the most interesting, but as a hotel needs smartening up.

*ENVIRONS* * Wookey Hole, four miles west, is a very wookeyish cave with interior decor of grottoes, stalactites, underground river, and other standard cave fixtures. The Cheddar Gorge and Caves, some eleven miles west, are the usual in caves and a scenic gorge. Both Wookey and the Cheddar are heavily touristed. For once it is true that you have bigger and better back home— leave them to the British trippers who have no hopes of ever seeing Mammoth Cave or the Grand Canyon.

Longleat House is about twelve miles east—from Bath it is twenty-three miles. This sixteenth-century Stately Home, seat of the Marquess of Bath, is worth seeing. If you go from Wells, on the way is Frome (*Froom*), a sizable town with old buildings, big market place, steep and narrow streets. The pretty village of Mells, three miles west of Frome, has the manor house of the Horner family to which belonged Mother Goose's Little Jack Horner who sat in a corner, pulled out a plum and boasted of his intelligence. The plums were deeds to the Horner estates, and were hidden in the pie from government raiders.

Driving from Wells or Cheddar to Bristol, look in at Chew Stoke—a village of no great shucks but with an oddity in its past. It had the main shrine of an all-England Saxon saint named Wigefort but popularly called St. Uncumber. *Uncumber* is an obsolete word meaning "to shed a load." This saint was resorted to by wives who wanted to be rid of their husbands. Oats had to be offered at the altar.

Just how a wife went about it is a puzzle. Old Scrooge sees his wife packing. "Where ye off to?"

"Goin' to visit Mother. Be gone a week or two."

"What're ye packin' the bag of oats fer? Be Mother a horse?"


# § GLASTONBURY

In Wells our host at the old inn finished his story about medieval dust-ups between the canons of Wells and the monks of Glastonbury. "Now *there's* a place you ought to visit," he said. "Every American should pay his respects to Glastonbury."

"Why Americans?"

"Because it's the ruins of Big Business—the biggest business, the Crown aside, of medieval and Tudor England. More interesting, though, if you read up on it a little." And he handed us two pamphlets: "Did Christ Come to Somerset?" and "Glastonbury: Its Story from Celtic Days to the Twentieth Century."

Dipping into these, we were persuaded.

Glastonbury is only six miles from Wells, and so might easily be dismissed as Wells Environs with the judgment, "Scant remains of an abbey." Although strictly correct, this wouldn't do, because to Glastonbury come people from all over, strangely drawn.

Glastonbury is a small town, the size of Wells. At first and last view, its most striking object is Tor Hill on the outskirts, 525 feet high and crowned by an old church tower. From its summit, given a clear day, one can see the Bristol Channel. More: for miles in every direction—south past Beltonsbury, east to Filton, west beyond Meare, north as far as Cleves—where extended of old the domain of the Black Monks, the richest, lordliest religious foundation England ever knew.

These Benedictines of Glastonbury ruled thousands of acres comprising, at the time of Domesday Book, one-tenth of Somerset's population. They owned manor houses where abbots and their seconds in command could rest from their labors. And they had labors! The monastic fief was a vast estate with serfs and tenant farmers, vineyards, beehives, cheese factories (Cheddar), wine cellars, fish-curing establishments, storage houses, salmon fisheries, eel ponds, piggeries, canals and waterways, a system of postal couriers, and its own police to pounce on poachers of abbey fish or game. The abbot was a feudal lord, a power in the land.

The heart of the domain was the abbey at Glastonbury, the earliest Christian foundation in England. Of this abbey, what is now visible to the eye is easily told; but the real thing is what the seen implies.

Not what is, but what *was*, counts here. This is the champion has-been of all England. No place has claimed so much and been left with so little.

Glastonbury claimed:

*Item:* Joseph of Arimathea. He was said to have arrived in New Testament times with eleven disciples, carrying the chalice of the Last Supper (the Holy Grail), which for reasons unknown he buried in Tor Hill. A variant is that the boy Jesus came with him to nearby Priddy and taught the natives how to extract tin. Another has St. Joseph bringing phials of the Savior's blood from the Crucifixion. More stoutly affirmed is the tale that as St. Joseph sat down on Weary-All (*Wyrral*) Hill, his staff took root and became a thorn bush which then blossomed every Christmastide.

*Item:* a holy spring known to have effected many a cure in olden times because it ran blood. (Modern man knows it as a chalybeate spring, one whose water is rust-colored by its iron content. Hence the miracle fails to work on him.)

*Item:* the Isle of Avalon, to which King Arthur was rowed to die.

Glastonbury was in ancient times a place of marshlands and shallow lakes. In 1191 the monks dug up from sixteen feet underground an oak coffin with (they said) the remains of King Arthur and his errant Queen Guinevere. They reburied it in the abbey church behind the high altar.

*Item:* St. Patrick. He came to organize the first monastic foundation, and returned to die in 463. St. Bridget also paid a call.

*Item:* St. George. Somewhere hereabouts he slew the Dragon.

Believe or reject—but if the latter, curb your skepticism. One is happier going along with the local climate of opinion—at least on holiday. The ground under your feet was trodden for thousands of years by men whose religion was magic. Christianity, in this first Christian outpost in England, is a matter of only yesterday, as time goes. Tarry in these parts and you will find many a "Zomerzet" elder believing in things that walk at night. An abbot is supposed to haunt an inn. An ancient dame assured us that she had several times seen Arthur and his knights riding with pennoned lances.

Superstition only in Somerset? England is dotted with hotels and inns which have a Room 12A instead of 13. In London, some streets skip No. 13—Fleet, Oxford, Praed, St. James's, Haymarket, Park Lane. We once lived in New York on the fourteenth floor of a hotel that had no thirteenth.

The more you know about Glastonbury, legendary or real, the more fascinating it becomes. Because there's so little to see, ignorance here is not bliss, but boredom. Times past make up 90 per cent of the show.

A lively past it was. When Bishop Savaric bypassed Wells in favor of Glastonbury, the canons of Wells made two surprise raids on the abbey. In the second, on January 25, 1200, they carried off five monks as hostages.

The major scandal of the Middle Ages was the battle between Canterbury Cathedral and Glastonbury Abbey which went on for three hundred years. Canterbury was Glastonbury's main pilgrimage rival, and it had the remains of St. Dunstan, who had been a Glastonbury boy and an abbot. Glastonbury was bitter about that. After Thomas à Becket was murdered in Canterbury, his shrine began to draw the greatest pilgrim crowds ever. This was too much for Glastonbury. Twelve years after Becket became St. Thomas, the Glastonbury monks unveiled a shrine to St. Dunstan, the "true remains." A pilgrim tide began to set in toward Glastonbury. The rival Benedictines of Canterbury raised all kinds of a row. But they got nowhere. The dispute was closed only when Henry VIII dissolved monasteries and put an end to all shrines.

With the Dissolution, what happened in Glastonbury was tragic.

The sixtieth abbot, Whiting, was executed "for treason" on Tor Hill, his body quartered and his head stuck up on the abbey gate. A royal commission looted the abbey's enormous treasures. Then the people descended upon the abbey and tore it down, using the stones to build houses and barns and pave that wet place by the pigsty. There was a vindictiveness, a wholeheartedness, about the destruction that leaves one wondering how well the Black Monks were liked.

All this hits only the high spots of the Glastonbury epic, but if it isn't drama we'll eat our copy of "Did Christ Come to Somerset?" Speaking of eating, one last word about the Black Monks. They did many a good deed. Our history booklet says of the accomplishments of thirteenth-century abbot William Vigor: "In the first place, he improved the beer."

England needs that man again.

Now from the sublime to the matter-of-fact. Glastonbury today is a solid and not attractive town. The abbey ruins are in the center, surrounded by a high iron fence. You enter by a turnstile after paying the usual fee. Most of the enclosed space is lawn. There are bits and pieces of walls and pillars, and marked sites where this or that once stood. The most substantial ruins are of St. Joseph's Chapel and the Abbot's Kitchen.

In the town, salute the George and Pilgrims' Inn, with a decorated façade behind which it has been lodging pilgrims, religious and tourist, for almost five hundred years. Besides this, you can look up two Perpendicular churches; a fourteenth-century tithebarn; a row of sixteenth-century almshouses; and miscellaneous venerable buildings of no distinction. The Blood Spring is at the base of the Tor, in a garden called Chalice Well.

HOTEL  *  Our sensational discovery in Glastonbury was something entirely modern—the Copper Beech Hotel, named for the magnificent copper beech tree in the garden. This hotel has comfort, taste, and the best home cooking we have ever devoured in a hotel. We stopped there for tea, and after sampling home-made cakes and jams and examining the bedrooms, changed our plans and stayed the night. Here is a Queen Anne house built up to modern taste, every item well-chosen—the bed linen, the towels, the soap, the wallpaper. We grabbed Room 6 with the huge bath-room three steps down; ask to see it even if you don't get it. Rates are high at the Copper Beech, but worth it.

# 7. THE FAR WEST:

# DEVON

# AND CORNWALL

Devon and Cornwall are rural counties. They form England's southwest peninsula, and their southern shores are favored by its warmest winters. Nature has upholstered them lavishly and supplied each with a bleak moor for contrast. Their seacoasts, much indented and estuaried, are inevitably acclaimed as Rivieras, and it's a marvel the sheer weight of the holiday-makers who pour into them doesn't sink them.

In all this peninsula, with a history as long as Father Time's scythe, there is no Norwich, no Cambridge, no Ludlow or Sherborne, no major populated place of outstanding interest. Here and there are villages and fishing towns that might be enchanting if they weren't so packed with trippers, alternately cooing and slapping their children.

As it is, the attractions are mainly scenic. Here is what you will find on a car or bus tour, starting with Exeter, turning up through Cornwall, and coming back toward London by way of North Devon and Somerset.

## § EXETER

The mildly pleasant county town of Devon lost many of its medieval attractions to the bombs of World War II. It still has its cathedral, which can be thoroughly shopped in short order. We like its bright fifteenth-century clock.

The close is small too, and not closed. This semicircular green yields its verge to a car park. Among old houses on its town side is Mol's Coffee House, where sea dogs Drake, Gilbert, Frobisher, and Raleigh hobnobbed. It's now part-occupied by an art dealer.

The Guildhall is Exeter's second pride. Part of it was built in 1593–95. But the eye-catching timbered roof with wooden gargoyles was done in 1466. In fact, the Guildhall was rebuilt in 1330; it boasts of being the oldest town hall in England.

Exeter has held a city charter since about 1200. It was an important seaport on the tidal river Exe until a Countess of Devon built a weir across the river below it and cut off navigation. The town sued, and the case went on at a smart pace for three hundred years. Exeter won; the weir was ordered removed. By that time the river was no longer navigable.

Other attractions are the priory of St. Nicholas, the church of St. Mary Steps, the medieval street of Stepcote Hill, Parliament Street, and Watty's delicatessen. We tried to buy a put-up lunch at Watty's in Martin's Lane because a sign in the window said Box Lunches Put Up and we thought it would be fun to picnic at a place on the map called Guzzle Down. But Mr. Watty cried, "Put up a lunch? Such things we don't do!" We took him by the arm, conducted him out of doors, and pressed his nose signward. He was astonished. "Why don't you take it down?" we asked. He admitted it might be a good idea. As we left two days later the sign was there still. Oh, Watty, Watty!

Exeter contains people of such engaging human weaknesses. A café lists "spaghetti on toast" and "baked beans on toast" among "American Dishes." And here's a news story about a local murder:

George Jeffries, 19, a bootmaker's assistant, who called at the shop a few minutes past six, told the police that he was startled to see the legs and body of a man, whom he now knew to be Mr. Oliver, behind the counter, and he saw a little blood. He left the shop, stood undecided and agitated outside, and then hurried home and had tea.

The Information Bureau is on Queen Street.

*HOTELS*  *  We stayed at the Royal Clarence by the cathedral and liked it. The White Hart in South Street is oak-beamy-old and looks pleasant. Two good houses stand in parklike grounds:

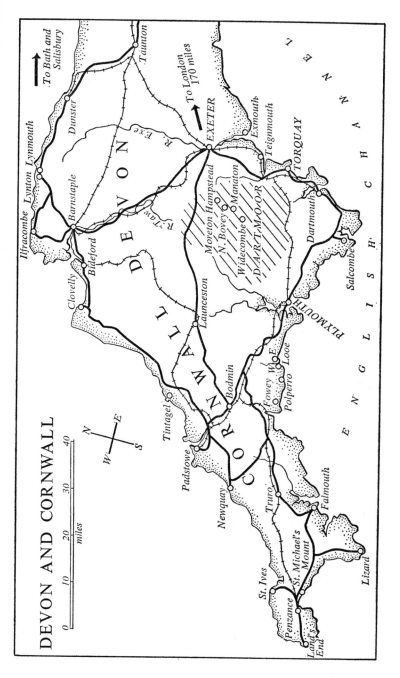

# DEVON AND CORNWALL

N

W — E

S

miles

0   10   20   30   40

To Bath and
Salisbury

To London
170 miles

Taunton

Dunster

Ilfracombe Lynton Lynmouth

Barnstaple

E X M O O R

R. Exe

EXETER

Exmouth

Teignmouth

TORQUAY

Bideford

Clovelly

D E V O N

R. Taw

Moreton Hampstead

Manaton

N. Bovey

Widecombe

D·A·R·T·M·O·O·R

Dartmouth

Salcombe

Launceston

PLYMOUTH

C O R N W A L L

Tintagel

Bodmin

Fowey W.
Looe
Polperro

Padstowe

Newquay

Truro

Falmouth

St. Ives

St. Michael's
Mount

Penzance

Land's
End

Lizard

E N G L I S H   C H A N N E L

311

the Beech Hill and the Imperial. The Devon is a motel on the Exeter bypass.

RESTAURANTS  *  The Chevalier wears an air of distinction. The Royal Clarence's grill room is good.

TRAVEL FACTS  *  Exeter is a railway junction of east–west and north lines, ten miles from the sea, 170 from London.

ENVIRONS  *  We had been told that Topsham, four miles away, was picturesque and untouristed. We found it untouristed. Topsham once built mighty ships. Doing business with the Dutch, some of its houses took on a Dutch look. But its Strand is untidy. The little town as a whole wears a listless air. A few miles out the Old Bridge Inn, a tavern bowed down with age, stands on the Clyst.

We bypassed Exmouth, knowing it for a standard British seaside resort, and came to Budleigh Salterton, an old village which has become a beach resort. Crowded in summer, it is quiet in spring and fall. It was so quiet when we were there (spring) that when Lawrence stalked a seagull along a wall and the silly bird tottered into a hole left by a missing brick, it counted as an Event. However, the lunch at the cliff-top Rosemullion Hotel was good.

The thatched village of East Budleigh, some three miles north, has a church with the Raleigh pew and fine carved bench ends. Hayes Barton, the large farmhouse where Raleigh was born, is a mile west in pretty country crisscrossed by winding lanes. It is lived in, but you're supposed to be able to see inside if you ask nicely. As we drew up the rain came down in torrents, we were trapped in the car and couldn't test this. We liked the country, and East Budleigh.

Fingle Bridge lies fifteen miles west of Exeter and can be taken in on a slight detour on your way to deeper Devon. It's a cul-de-sac, a natural beauty spot hemmed in by woods and high hills along the river Teign. First-rate walking and fishing country.

South and west of Exeter the road rolls over low hills, and above hedges you see white or pink farmhouses with thatched roofs. The high bluish line on the sky isn't a cloud—it's Dartmoor.

*Moretonhampstead.* A gateway to the moor that is a plain small town in lovely country. The White Hart is a popular lunch stop.

*North Bovey.* This hamlet is one's dream of Devon, what you hope to find all over but don't. It's a scatter of thatched white-washed houses, the largest the Ring of Bells inn. A ragged green is shaded by the grandfather of all trees and grayly ornamented by a stone cross. That's all. But everything is casually perfect. We were the only non-Boveyites present, and the natives paid us no heed. The inn's dog and cat sauntered out together to be petted and scratched, and then, having done their part, went back.

*Manaton.* Another version of North Bovey: a long village green with venerable trees around it, a church on one side, a long low farmhouse of stone and thatch at the top. A bench on the green was sprouting lichen. We wondered who filled the church on the Sabbath. Walks up various paths and lanes uncover houses hidden behind trees and hedges.

*Widecombe-in-the-Moor.* Thirty years ago Widecombe was one of Devon's lovelies. The tourist trade has corrupted it. Just about every other house in the gray stone village which reclines in a hollow of the moor is in the curio-souvenir business. The important citizen is Will Young, "the famous Cottage Potter," as his signs proclaim, in Ye Olde Glebe House. Ye Glebe inside is a clutter of crafted horrors. In the aisle a traffic sign says Keep Left to keep ye trippers shuffling along in order while a youth planted copwise watches to see that there's no shoppe-lifting. What was a meadow is a rutted parking lot, and every other minute (and this off season) an excursion bus snorts in to discharge yet another load. Unless you're studying crowd psychology, avoid the place.

*Totnes.* An ancient town on the river Dart, the most important market town between Exeter and Plymouth, it has, according to our guidebook, "unique charm." Yes, in its way. Down the passageways you see rough, bulging stone walls that speak of dignified age. But the façades have been slapped on over ancient fronts—stuccoed, plastered, painted, or given an ugly concrete face. Each building is an individual idiot in this daft town. The new civic center in startling modern has nothing to do with the rest of the town. The promenade along the old walls is itself walled in so you can't see the lovely unbuilt-on countryside. The town displays a genius for painstaking self-uglification.

# § *TORQUAY*

This queen of the seaside resorts is an Englished Riviera. (Our hotel advertised itself as "the English hotel in the Mediterranean manner.") Torquay is the Old Established. If you were English, you'd spend your holiday here to acquire or maintain status. In the winter Torquay is less chilly than almost anywhere in England, and come spring, the sea does at times try for a Mediterranean blue. The curve of the land rises to hills and cliffs with terraced houses (seven hundred of them are hotels and boarding houses) in quite a Monte Carlo way. The town authorities are alert and know their business. They have built walks, flower beds, gardens, a marine spa, golf courses (six); they father festivals, illuminations, concerts, dancing, beach and water sports—everything to keep the boredom of away-from-home-and-business at bay. If this middle-class Xanadu palls, there is still the fresh countryside to visit. A grand walk can be had along coastal footpaths.

If you want a taste of an English seaside resort, this is the best there is.

We stayed at the Imperial, the premier hotel, and it did well by us. The dining room is impressive, the food excellent. Evening dress is required for dancing. The Imperial comes high, but if you want Torquay you want the Imperial.

*ENVIRONS* * *Cockington* village, a short walk, shorter ride, west of Torquay, is very pretty, thanks to those authorities who keep it in protective custody. It consists of thatched cottages, a church, a mill wheel, Ye Olde Wishing Wells, Ye Olde Forge, winding lanes, and lagoons, and is served well garnished with gardens.

*Marldon,* three miles farther on, is noteworthy for its old church that has monuments to the Gilberts. Humphrey Gilbert, Walter Raleigh's stepbrother, colonized Newfoundland.

*Compton Castle,* a mile beyond, is the country seat of the Gilberts. It shows its best side as you come into the forecourt on the driveway—rose-tinted old stone walls. Inside, most of it is rebuilt, and so recently it seems new. Walter Raleigh Gilbert, R.N. (Ret.), showed us through and said that his name has been in the family since the great Elizabethan Gilberts and Raleighs, as has been the tradition of going into the Navy. Compton is open to the public Monday, Wednesday, and Thursday.

*Brixham* is a fishing town at the southern end of Tor Bay. If it's to be seen at all it should be by boat excursion from Torquay. The water approach brings out its best: the square harbor, the shipping, the land rising on three sides in terraces of flat-faced color-washed houses with stairway-streets mounting and twisting off to right and left. Fishing still goes on in spite of the annual tourist catch. Ferries between Brixham and Torquay run every forty-five minutes; the trip takes half an hour.


# § *DARTMOUTH*

The old and famous town at the mouth of the Dart has character. The streets are steep, and are just a little short of picturesque. The colorful bit of the Butterwalk makes you sigh for more. The church is worth visiting. The almost-landlocked harbor with its ancient fortresses at the mouth wears a genuine seagoing air.

Dartmouth has played a brave role in England's naval history from the Middle Ages to the June 1944 Normandy invasion. This was a town of privateers, brawlers, and honest merchantmen that waved goodbye to the Crusaders. When Chaucer included a Shipman among his pilgrims, he made him a Dartmouth man. Seamen have long been trained here. On the excursion boat up the Dart we beheld women sailors smiting the waters with oars from their longboat to the barks of a female coxswain.

*HOTELS* ✳ Three good ones here, all on the waterfront's fine promenade: Queen's, the Raleigh, and the Royal Castle. We stayed at Queen's in a pleasant, immaculate room, with windows on the waterfront. The Raleigh is next door; its owner and his Swiss wife hold diplomas and awards in the hotel and cuisine lines. The Royal Castle has oak beams, some four-poster beds, and a Georgian dining room.

*RESTAURANTS* ✳ The Raleigh's is the best. The Dartmouth Arms, a tiny old pub in Bayard's Cove, looks exactly the place for burly nautical types. We found it filled with young men wearing artistic beards and pullovers, and young women heavily eye-painted. The barmaid was a lady of sophistication. The food was good, particularly the soup; the hot dogs a pleasant surprise.

*ENVIRONS* * Take that short, delightful boat excursion to Dittisham (half-hour); in summer it goes to Totnes in three hours, and is still more delightful. The original Dittisham is a clutch of houses on the water. We later visited it by car, plunging down into it on a narrow, crooked road, almost tumbling into the Dart. Miracles had to be worked to get the car turned round on a piece of concrete the size of a game of hopscotch. It's a dangerous descent. Up at the top are fine modern houses of the well-heeled in retirement. They have selected one of the most beautiful spots in England.

*Salcombe.* This is another Dartmouth, but smaller, resting on a complicated, scenic, landlocked bay, its main street on the waterfront. It is neat and trim, and, save for the Pixie's Forge, which harbors a wilderness of gimcrackery, it is uncheapened by its popularity. The parking lot is where the U.S. Navy removed some houses for its tense take-off for Normandy. That American sojourn has left a reservoir of local good will that a tourist can draw on, and that speaks well of the Navy. In the late spring and summer Salcombe and its region are beautiful.

The hotel is the Salcombe; excellently run. Here in Room 12 Lawrence met, or rather felt, his first ghost.

# § *PLYMOUTH*

The once-great port, still a major naval base, has come upon evil days. Badly blitzed, it is being rebuilt in charmless concrete. Unhurt, however, is the famous Hoe, an extensive windy green 120 feet above the sea, wonderfully shaped by nature as a lookout broad enough for nearly the whole population.

Drake is Plymouth's great man. Gone off to singe the king of Spain's beard, he had been given up for lost. But one day he came sailing in on the *Golden Hind* with a fortune in gold and jewels. That was a great day for Plymouth, Elizabeth, and England, and the Hoe is the place from which to try to imagine it. Later, in 1588, Drake was bowling on the Hoe when the Spanish Armada was sighted. He insisted on finishing the game. The story may be apocryphal, but what of it?

When the *Mayflower* put in for repairs, the Pilgrims took shelter in the wine cellars of the firm of James Hawker, which still does business in the same building and obligingly shows Americans over the premises. Hawker's believes they took aboard a cask of Pedlar sloe gin to fortify themselves on the rugged voyage. Not far from the Hoe on the Barbican is the stone and tablet showing where the Pilgrims landed and took off for that place in the New World they named Plymouth in gratitude to this one.

For a hotel, we say the Grand, on the Hoe, a huge place with an air of faded grandeur and gentility. It gave us the best coffee we had in England.

TRAVEL NOTE 1:   Plymouth is at the mouth of two rivers, the Plym and the Tamar. The Tamar is the boundary between Devon and Cornwall. If you're driving, go into Cornwall by bridge; the ferry may mean a long wait. Inquire at the hotel.

TRAVEL NOTE 2:   Boat excursions in summer leave from Phoenix Wharf and go twenty miles up the Tamar. From there smaller boats ride to the upper reaches. The Tamar is highly scenic.

*TRAVEL FACTS:*  *  Plymouth is 251 miles from London by rail, a journey the express train (with restaurant car) makes in five and a half hours. Expresses run to the North, the Midlands, North Wales and the Border Country, and into Cornwall.

When you cross the river at Plymouth you're in gray-stone Cornwall, which the guidebooks still insist is "unspoiled." Someone should tell them.

Cornwall is populated by ancient Celtic Britons who for centuries cut themselves off from the rest of England as a deliberate act of the spirit, enjoying superstition, saints, ceremonies, rituals all their own. It was a happy hunting ground of folklorists. They would come out with tidbits like these:

When a Cornishman sees a ghost he says *Numny dumny* and it goes away. He may not know what the words mean but the ghost does.

Yellow is bad for rheumatism. A Cornishman walking from Newquay to Bodmin in a yellow necktie died of rheumatic fever.

Today superstitions and legends are commercialized in post cards and souvenirs. All those garden dwarfs may once have been the stunted Saint Neot who spent his life standing up to his neck in water in his holy well, living on a never-failing supply of three fish. But today they're pure, unhallowed Disney. A Cornishman who wants to mind his old ways has a problem, with the local inn and pub run by Chelsea-style escapists, his beach littered with bathing huts, his streets haunted by artists and himself by tourists looking for a real honest-to-saint Cornishman.

LOOE * We came from Plymouth by way of Crafthole Village and its Finnygook Inn, which we mention only because we like odd names. The entrance to Looe is somewhat marred by railroad tracks and a gas tank, but don't mind. Looe is a tourist and fishing town that deserves to be called quaint. It lies tilted between high cliffs on the sea and its low-lying river, and the narrow streets of little old houses wind and climb.

You will be drawn by Ye Olde Cottage (1555) and the Smugglers Hotel (fifteenth-century, it claims) with restaurant in "Smugglers Dungeon," and the old abandoned Guildhall and the charming courtyard of the beauty shop, and many another oddity. On the debit side is a little too much stucco and the painful outsize souvenir shop called the Pixie's Halt.

The Golden Guinea, where we had lunch, is a many-roomed restaurant occupying several old houses, modernized with booths, electric-lighted skulls, piped-in music, and effective wall paintings by Pioggio, an artist from Gibraltar who has ornamented much of the "Cornish Riviera." Such of the walls as aren't Pioggioed are scripted with interesting quotations, such as:

EXTRACT FROM THE RULES OF COURTESY, ANON., 1685.

'Tis not good manners, as soon as you are sit at the table, to bawl out, I eat none of this, I eat none of that, I care for no rabbit, I love nothing that tastes of pepper, nutmeg, onions, etc. If you happen to burn your mouth you must endure it, if possible, if not, you must convey what you have in your mouth privately upon your plate and give it away to the footman; for tho' civility obliges you to be neat, there is no necessity you should burn out your guts. In conference with a person of quality, it would be sawcy and ridiculous to pull him by the buttons, the sleeve, or the hand, and most of all to punch him on the stomach.

The Golden Guinea was the labor of a young man from Birmingham who confided that most of Looe's enterprises are run by "foreigners" like himself. The Cornish don't care for them, he said, but here they are and here they mean to stay out of love and good business.

What is a Cornish gaffer like? On a previous visit we were rowed from Downderry to Looe by an old fisherman who asked if we knew his nephew. "Where does he live?" we inquired. "In Australy." He couldn't understand that Australia and America weren't in the same place and that they were farther apart than America and Cornwall. We had a momentary glimpse into a primitive mind, illiterate, to whom, for instance, there are only two places: here and not-here, and all the not-heres are naturally over there together.

*POLPERRO* ∗ This fishing town is even more quaint, picturesque, and touristed than Looe. Warned by the contours of Looe we parked at the top of the road and walked down, between villas offering bed and breakfast. Almost at once we came up against the dreadful whimsy of "piskies," along with a Smuggler's Museum, Buccaneer shops and cafés, and a Piggy-Wiggy restaurant. It isn't Cornishmen that do this, and those who do it are not trying to tempt the locals. The extraordinary thing is that Polperro triumphs over all. That street where the Pol river tumbles between the houses, and all about, down to the tiny harbor with its businesslike fishing smacks and spectacular rocks, is wonderful. The shape of the place, even the houses under their prettified whitewash and color-wash, with shouting signs and gimcracks, sends out the powerful feeling of being real and misused. Polperro defies and makes ridiculous this commercialized cuteness. Especially when a half-gale is blowing, and the angry sea invades the narrow harbor and throws wave after wave at the rocks, nature takes a hand and reduces the gimmickry to paltriness.

You must see Polperro. (You should have seen it three decades ago when only artists had discovered it.) The question is, How? We were there off season, and yet there were plenty of sightseers. In summer it must be like Saturday night on Main Street.

WALKER'S NOTE:   From Looe to Polperro and from Polperro to Fowey runs a lovely over-the-heather cliffside walk. For all we know, it runs farther along the coast, but that part we did afoot years ago. It is the only way left to see Cornwall, really.

FOWEY  *   There are two Foweys divided by a river; a car-ferry connects. Fowey (*Foy*), with winding streets but wider ones is larger and more resortish than Polperro, but neat, brightly painted, with a considerable harbor and a fifteenth-century church. Fowey is the Dartmouth of Cornwall, with a sea-adventure tradi-tion. It was also the home of Sir Arthur Quiller-Couch, in whose adventure novels it figures as Troy Town. *Hotels.* The Old Ferry Inn is best. The huge Fowey is the typical English resort hotel.

TRAVEL NOTE.   Although these three are the best known, being more accessible, the Looe–Polperro–Fowey pattern of small town or village on indented coast occurs again and again with slight variations in Mevagissey, St. Mawes, Falmouth (biggest but dull), Mullion, Mousehole (very quaint; pronounced *Moozle*), St. Michael's Mount (inferior copy of Mont St. Michel across the channel in Brittany), St. Ives (artist-haunted), and Newquay.

We decided to cut across the peninsula, going Wadebridge–Camelford–Tintagel. Wadebridge, where we stayed the night (not stopping for the very pleasant scenery around Bodmin) has noth-ing for the tourist. It was our gain, for we managed to get a bed at the Molesworth Arms, an old-fashioned country-town hotel, with very characteristic locals playing darts in the public bar and talking dialect. The house is a good four hundred years old. We half-expected pitcher-and-basin treatment, but there was plumbing.

Penzance (no pirates) and Land's End (nothing there but rocks signifying end of the land) are not worth time and mileage.

# § *TINTAGEL*

This is Cornwall's scenic spectacular. But first you must go through a nondescript village of stuccoed houses, gift shoppes, the hotel with "Equestrian Knights Stable and Lounge," King Arthur's car park, King Arthur's Hall (souvenirs), King Arthur's Café, etc. Then you are free to make the walk on the road labeled "To King Arthur's Castle and Beach" (imagine Uther Pendragon's son in a bathing suit), with a fine view of REFECTORY all the way—the ugly shack has its name painted in giant letters on its roof. You turn left at the Refectory, climb some stone steps—and oh!

A curved, natural bridge of rock connects the mainland with an outthrust, towering rocky pile over which the castle ruins are scattered. It's a thrilling, fearful climb in wet weather with a strong wind tearing at you and the sea furious below. And away up there, after paying your entrance fee for the strange, scanty ruins, you can climb on. There's a sense of great heights, rocky grandeur, elemental forces, and a vanished epic race. What matter whose ruins they are? Tintagel is glorious.

*BOSCASTLE* * A lobster-fishermen's village flanked by great cliffs which are being protected from disfigurement by the National Trust. The village is guilty of harboring a pottery which turns out pixies, mugs, and the like. The spacious Wellington Hotel above the village is a good place to lunch or spend the night. Let's hope the Australian owner is still there; he was threatening to go to the U.S. Look into the gentlemen's lavatory for the huge porcelain washbasin, a work of art worthy of museum space.

*CLOVELLY* * Now you're in Devon again—North Devon. Clovelly is a fishing village on a long steep street, its houses one on top of another. A child or a sprightly adult can manage the climb; the municipal transportation is by donkey. It's an oh-my! picturesque eyeful and then you are free to go on to

*BARNSTAPLE* * On the way you go through Bideford, not worth a pause, and if you have plenty of time, visit the coast at Westward Ho for the view. Barnstaple is a good busy town, once a seaport, mildly interesting, with an excellent hotel, the Imperial, which should be your overnight stay.

*LYNTON–LYNMOUTH* * These twin places on the Bristol Channel are also scenic spectaculars. Lynmouth is the village at the mouth of the two rivers Lyn; Lynton is the bigger resort high on the cliff-top. This entire north coast with the far views over the sea, and south over rolling country is magnificent. You are on the homeward stretch now, and may, like us, stop every now and then to park the car and climb out for still another panorama. Some steep hills along this way, and then you roll into two prize villages:

*SELWORTHY* * About five miles east of Minehead on the Porlock road in scenic woodland country lies thatched Selworthy, a village permanently among the loveliest ten of England. A few miles farther on and you enter another of the top ten—

*DUNSTER* * You are now out of Devon and in Somerset. Exeter is far to the south, and in between are Exmoor (Lorna Doone country) and Dartmoor. Dunster's prides are a Yarn Market, a castle, a priory church, a famous inn, and many fine old houses. This is another treat like Burford on the edge of the Cotswolds, a place of substance, dignity, and grace. Almost every structure is well placed and pleasing. You feel that here no "foreigners" could take over; they would become Dunsterized. The Luttrells have been the important family since the fourteenth century and still live in the castle, which is open to visitors at certain hours of certain days—the complicated schedule is posted at the gates and in the inn. *Hotel*: The Luttrell Arms dates from the fifteenth century. Its core is Gothic and it has decorative Jacobean details.

This is a fitting end to the Devon–Cornwall ride. You are pointed east, toward London, but you can easily go from here east and then north to Glastonbury, Wells, Bath, and the Cotswolds or across to the Welsh Border country.

# 8. THE SOUTH:

# KENT

# AND SUSSEX

On a map of England, draw a line north from Southampton to Reading, then east from Reading to Canterbury and the coast. Everything in the pocket formed by your lines is the South of England. While it is not a definite region either geographically or politically (by counties), it does have a historic identity.

The South of England is that part of the island through which callers, friendly and hostile, came and still come, from the B.C. days of Julius Caesar and his legions down to today's tourists who pour through the Channel ports and Southampton. William of Normandy came this way; so did Hitler's sky-fleet of flying bombs. It was this stretch of coast on your penciled map, so near the Continent and so invitingly indented with landfalls, that made England, in self-protection, a seagoing nation just in time to welcome Spain's Invincible Armada and prove it vincible.

Touristically speaking, the biggest thing in these parts is Canterbury. Canterbury has had its own chapter, including a lecture on Gothic architecture into the bargain—the architecture that came the same way, from the Continent to the South of England, spreading thence all through the land.

England's southern exposure contains much to see. But no clean-cut organized tour can cover the sight-worthy places. It takes zigging and zagging to get everything in. And you wouldn't want to concentrate on the Kent–Sussex country, soft and pretty though it is, to the exclusion of everything else.

We have ourselves done parts of the South at different times and in various ways: by going out from Chichester; by taking up headquarters in a Sussex country hotel; by staying with friends in a Sussex village and being taken around by them; by dropping down to this place or that from London.

So from out of our experience comes this advice on what to do:

Keep this chapter dog-eared or otherwise marked so you can easily turn to it. Check the places that most appeal to you. Then, either get them into your itinerary deliberately. Or

> when you find yourself near,
> 
> or want to hie out to a definite someplace from London on an off day,
> 
> or decide to go for a drive through pleasant country dotted with Sights,

refer to this chapter. Everything here, as your map will show at a glance, is within easy reach of London by car, bus, or train. The purple and other prose following the names will indicate what we think of them. (None of that short-cut asterisk business.) We will be moving along the map from east to west. But first—

*A SMALL DOSE OF HISTORY* ∗ There exists in the U.S.A. (at least it did twenty years ago, and we haven't heard of its demise) an organization called the Society for the Restoration of the Dukedom of Normandy.

"What in the world have Americans got to do with that?" you ask sharply. "And restoration to whom?"

"Restoration to England," we reply glibly. "When William the Conqueror took England he retained his Normandy dukedom. His successors finally lost it to the French, and spent the lives of thousands of ordinary medieval Joes to get it back, and never did."

"So what concern is it of ours?" you ask, and rightly. "That would play hell with NATO, giving Normandy back to England. How do the Normans and the French feel about it?"

"The Society has never asked them. Actually, its main concern is genealogical. Each member traces his lineage back to some Norman knight who helped William beat Harold and the English in 1066."

This fictitious dialogue breaks open a fact not known to many Americans who visit England—that for the greater part of English history the main enemy was France. You know the names of Poictiers and Agincourt, of Joan of Arc, of Napoleon, and the

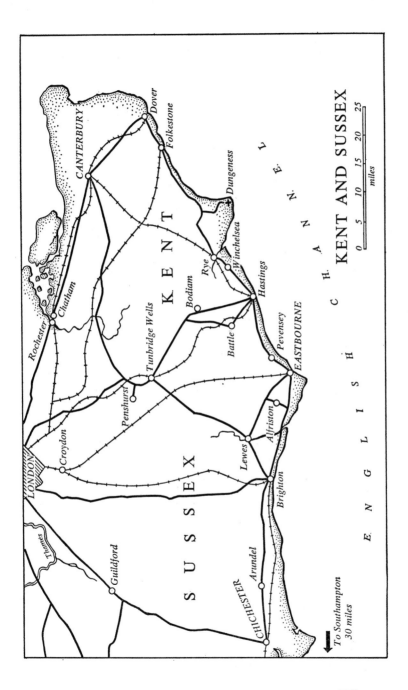

KENT AND SUSSEX

0   5   10   15   20   25
miles

Black Prince, and Laurence Olivier as Henry V. They're to the point. The French kept making quick strikes at the English Channel ports. The English did the same on the French side. This went on even between wars. Raiding and counterpiracy were endemic.

That is why, in Winchelsea, you may see a man go up to the top of the old fortification known as the Strand Gate to gaze out at sea in the direction of France. What looks he for? He looks for the sails or steam of a French invasion fleet. He and his predecessors have been staring out to sea from the Strand Gate for some seven hundred years. You may feel like shouting, "The danger is thataway!" pointing to the east. Forbear. It isn't done. The watchman is still looking for an invasion fleet such as the one of 1357 that all but did for Winchelsea, and the other, twenty years later, which burned everything combustible in neighboring Rye.

# § RYE AND WINCHELSEA

We agree that both should be awarded the adjective *enchanting*, although there is a slight family disagreement as to which of the two is more so. Sister towns, each has its own vivid personality. If you see one you're bound to see the other as well, for the distance between them is almost exactly the length of New York's Central Park from 59th to 110th streets—less than three miles.

Both are officially towns, but Rye has eight times Winchelsea's population. Rye is hilly and black-and-white (half-timbered). Winchelsea is level and of stone. Both used to be ports, and were added to the Cinque (pronounced *Sink*) ports by, it is thought, William the Conqueror. Channel waves and currents have removed them from the sea.

Rye has a people inured to trudging up and down steep cobbled streets, keeping house in ancient dwellings, amusing tourists, and getting scraped by trucks in its narrow main street. At the top of its hill are the parish church, the town hall, and on the cliffside the Ypres (pronounced *Wipers*) tower and museum, from which there is a glorious ("Oh, I say!") view upon Winchelsea and the Channel. The church clock is one of the oldest still in working condition, with two eighteenth-century quarter-boys who strike the quarter hours, but not the hour itself. Tourists like ourselves gather to watch them do it. Alas, all we get for our pains is a couple of bongs, and the cherubs go dead for another fifteen minutes.

Inside you see the eighteen-foot-long pendulum swinging back and forth. The climb to the clock works and the belfry chamber for another view is worth making if you're fit.

Rye is a busy place, tourist-jammed, and with more traffic than is good for it. High Street is lined with souvenir shops but there are better shops above, near the church. Rye pottery is the buy here. Mermaid Street is a steep line of some of the most picturesque houses in any English street. Just off it, on West Street, is the house where Henry James lived and wrote.

The Rye golf links, about a mile and a half out on Rye Harbor (buses) are famous and draw golfing tourists.

*HOTELS* ✳ The Mermaid, the Flushing, the George. They are old inns. On one visit when we walked in to have a look at the Mermaid, a surly landlord shooed us out—he wasn't having anyone darken his door who might not spend money. He isn't there any more. . . . On our last trip we lunched at the Flushing, a fifteenth-century house with a sixteenth-century mural in its dining room. We not only had a capital meal but poked about the medieval cellar which once had a private door on the sea side for smugglers. The Flushing was being run by a young couple eager to please, and it looked to us like a good place to stay. . . . We did not investigate the George.

*Winchelsea*, with a population of 580 and an area of about a dozen city blocks, prides itself on being "England's smallest town." It is a delightful, open, sunlit place. Sunlit? Yes, even under dark skies, even in the rain, it has a smiling aspect. The few streets are wide and grass-verged, the lovely houses well kept. Nothing cramped here, and no hurry. Why ever did Henry James choose to live in Rye with this serene and gracious little town next door?

French raiders ruined the beautiful abbey church, but what remains is still in use and there is enough to please mightily. Within are the tombs of the Alards, fine work beautifully lighted. You lift your eyes to the delicate windows and the contrasting heavy crossbeams of the roof, and your heart lifts too. The tombs in the graveyard grow flowers.

The museum, in the medieval Court Hall, is a treat. Look for the primitive painting on wood of St. Leonard, puzzlingly dated 1300–1400. The sweet gentlewoman in charge demonstrated for us the horrible man-trap. "Now stand well away," she warned. She kicked an iron gadget and the great teeth came together with a crash. "Snappo!" she cried. "It has probably torn many a poacher's leg off, that!" See the Armoury, a handsome stone mansion, one of many fine old houses.

We kept our eye on the Strand Gate, wanting to see the keeper perform the ancient rite of scanning the horizon for the French invasion fleet. Not seeing him, we pursued him through the town. But it would have taken a man-trap to catch him. He's the local odd-job man, and we were always one job behind him. Keeping the Gate is one of his odd jobs, and his pay for it is £1 2s ($3.10) a year.

Winchelsea has had a continuous line of mayors and keepers of the Gate from time unremembered. The inductions, on Easter Monday, take place in the Court Hall and faithfully follow the medieval ceremonies. *died 1327*

When Winchelsea was thriving, Edward I came to confirm Magna Carta, and Edward II set out from here for the battle of *1346* Crecy. The French paid sudden and bloody visits. In 1357 they practically did for the town. Then the sea took a hand, first drowning it, then silting up the harbor, and it was reborn where it now *should be Edward III* stands, two miles inland. That is why you find it with broad streets in a grid or checkerboard pattern—a medieval planned town.

The hotel is the New Inn. It occupies a beautiful building.

# § DOVER

Between Rye–Winchelsea and Canterbury, Dover is one of the original Cinque Ports which, in return for certain rights and freedoms, were pledged to provide on demand ships for the royal fleets. It has been important since Roman times, had a major role during the first and second world wars, and is both a military base and a seaside resort.

It is said that two million travelers pass through Dover in a year, making it the greatest passenger port in the world. But who stays? It's the rare tourist who even dreams that Dover may have something more than customs and docks. There are of course those poetic White Cliffs; and there is Dover sole, which tastes even better here than elsewhere.

For more than seven hundred years it has been Dover's fate to be a door without a parlor, for even in the Middle Ages it was the premier passenger port. Then the tourist crowd was composed of flocks of pilgrims—English ones off to Rome, Jerusalem, St. James of Compostela, and European ones bound for such English holy places as Becket's shrine in Canterbury, the Thorn of Glastonbury, and Our Lady of Walsingham in Norfolk. The purpose was not to bring back snapshots and so many dollars' worth of purchases, but a soul shriven clean of sin, and holy relics without dollar or customs limit. The Lion-Hearted Richard embarked here on his Third Crusade (1190); Woodrow Wilson disembarked on his Peace Crusade (1918).

You may find Dover worth some hours of your time. The grand Norman castle, on a cliff four hundred feet above the town, is still militarily occupied. Among the parts you can visit are the underground passages and the donjon keep of 1181 with walls twenty feet thick.

But Dover Castle is a youngster compared with the *pharos* or lighthouse the Romans built about A.D. 50; its bottom half is the oldest structure in England, if we refuse to accept Cleopatra's Needle in London as a structure. At the opposite end of the time scale are the modern car-ferry terminal and the ultramodern "coach-hotel." The latter, designed for the accommodation of cross-Channel excursion-bus trippers, is Florida egg-crate architecture borne aloft on stilts.

Other things to see: churches; Maison de Dieu, a thirteenth-century pilgrim hostel; and the fine seventeenth-century mansion beside it. And the streets, the Regency terraces above the beach, the people, the harbor activity. The tourist who takes in Dover will be one up on his friends who have done only the regular treadmill. "Dover?" they will exclaim. "Well, now, I never thought of that!"

*HOTELS* * That egg-crate affair on stilts is the Dover Stage Hotel. Unless you plan to cross the Channel the next morning, you'll be happier at the White Cliffs on Waterloo Crescent.

## § *THE R.H.&D.*

Down the coast about twelve miles is Hythe. If you have children in tow, stop there and buy a round-trip ticket on the miniature railroad. The Romney, Hythe & Dymchurch is an honest-to-goodness commercial line, running fourteen miles to Dungeness on a track of fifteen-inch gauge, with real if pint-size locomotives and cars. Every trip is a festival. Crowds come to ride, and as avid as the children are the locomotive engineers who visit on their day off from their own main-line jobs to polish the engines and beg for a chance in the cab. During the war the tiny railway did a man-size job hauling pipe for Operation Pluto, armed with ack-ack guns in this hot corner of the Blitz.

You're on the Kent–Sussex border, and at the right place to take note of a foreign element which slipped over from across the Atlantic while Winchelsea's watchman was gazing the wrong way. A Minnesota entrepreneur has opened on the Farnborough bypass England's first drive-in roadhouse and threatens to add thirty-nine more. This one has a thirty-five-car parking lot and serves sandwiches called fishwich, oxburger, hamdinger, and shrimpboat, to be consumed by "two-fisted appetites." Would you care to risk the "broasted chicken cooked by magic ray"? The food is out of cans and deep-freeze. As the *Observer's* reporter noted at the grand opening, the fishwichery is between Elmer's End and Pratt's Bottom—gastronomically as well as geographically.

## § *TENTERDEN*

This pleasant town is between Hythe and Rye, ten miles from each. Just outside is Smallhythe Place with the fifteenth-century house which was the home of the great actress Ellen Terry. Preserved by the National Trust as a memorial to her, it is devoted to her costumes, photographs, and mementos. No musty museum, it provides a moving experience even for those who never knew the thrill of Dame Ellen's acting. The house itself is worth seeing.

*DOSE OF HISTORY NO. 2.*  *  In Dose One, we wrote of the troubles between England and France. Here we come to their roots. We go back to the Dark Ages, when a Scandinavian pirate named Rolf the Ganger established himself and his Northmen in a part of northern France which was called after them—Normandy.

William the Bastard was the sixth Duke of Normandy in the line of descent from Rolf. He is the William who won for himself the name of Conqueror. That he was earlier "the Bastard," by the way, is nothing against him. The Normans were not a marrying folk. Marriage by the Book was not then so general in the Western world as it became.

Why did William of Normandy cock an eye at England? What business was it of his?

Well, it all began with Emma, a Norman beauty and daughter of a previous duke, who was sent to England to marry King Ethelred the Unready. Because of the disturbed (to put it mildly) conditions in England, two of Emma's sons were brought up in Normandy. One of them, Edward the Confessor, became king of England. Emma was William's great aunt; Edward was a second cousin. So England was in William's family.

Edward promised William the throne if he should die childless. He did die childless. But the throne was then claimed by Harold, a powerful English earl. On a visit to Normandy, Harold had sworn (said the Normans) to support William, and now, with Edward's death, was breaking his sacred oath. As for the English people, while they preferred the English Harold, they were fairly used to foreigners. Between Ethelred the Unready and Edward the Confessor they had had the Danish Canute, and they were being threatened by another Harold, from Norway.

(The complicated story of eleventh-century England is repellent, powerful, dramatic, fascinating. There is now, at last, a good book on it—*William the Conqueror*, by George Slocombe.)

In September 1066, William the Bastard, leaving Normandy

in the hands of his capable wife, set sail for England with all the men he could muster in about a thousand ships of the long, slim, curved-prow Viking type. They beached at Pevensey. Earl Harold had been patrolling the Channel, waiting for them, but had had to dash up north because Harold of Norway had chosen this inconvenient time to attack. William was incredibly lucky—Earl Harold was a great warrior, probably even greater than William himself, who was no mean slasher, having spent his youth licking all his murderous Norman barons.

On the other hand, the English too were lucky. For William, who took England, was a remarkable administrator and a great man. From that faraway and long-ago time, when he lived and loved his Matilda, and when he fought his barons at home and then brought them together to fall on England, he towers above ordinary men—a huge, black-browed, epic figure, a civilized (for that age) and enlightened Viking.

At Pevensey, William flung up a makeshift castle within the walls of a Roman fort, and then sailed down the coast a little way to Hastings, which provided a better haven. Earl Harold, having defeated the Scandinavian Harold in a terrible battle, had no time to rest. He came south as fast as he could to meet the Normans. The great encounter—the battle of giants—engraved the date 1066 on the minds of English schoolboys thereafter.

The Battle of Hastings was not fought at Hastings but seven miles to the northwest, at a place the Conqueror called Battle and where he had an abbey built to make good a vow to the Almighty. After 1066, Norman overlords mingled with Anglo-Saxons to create the British nation and the English language.

*Hastings*, once an important Cinque Port, is now a seaside resort. Little of the old survives—some narrow streets, fishermen's houses, a fishing museum, a smuggler's cave, and the ruins of William's castle.

*Battle* is more tourist-worthy. An attractive small town with a broad, countrylike main street, its chief point of interest is that abbey, even though it now houses a school. The ruins and grounds cost a shilling to see. The grand battlemented Gatehouse frowns down on High Street, and at one side the Pilgrim's Rest is a colorful companion to it. This fine half-timbered house was a

Maison Dieu, a pilgrim's hostel. It is a good port for tea (home-made cakes) and worth examining within and without. There are many fine old buildings in and just off High Street.

Nearby is the village of Seddlescombe, with an odd church. All along the roads hereabouts you see aged thatched cottages sporting TV aerials. The rolling countryside of the Downs and the Weald has few spectacular moments, but is deep green pastoral country, very satisfying any way you wander.

*Pevensey* has the remains of William's castle, the one that replaced the hasty wooden structure he put up on landing. The Roman wall surrounds it.

# § *KENT–SUSSEX COUNTRYSIDE*

In a succession of lovely spring days such as we were lucky to have, the cherry trees were in blossom, the ewes were looking after their newborn lambs, and the Kentish oast houses looked rakish sitting on the landscape with caps askew. The country runs to long views. On the horizon, tufts of white cloud over the Channel were doing sentry duty. Kent is called the Garden of England. We could not see that it was any more gardened than Sussex. Forsythia, daffodils, tulips, primroses, cowslips, magnolia were rioting in front yards and orchards, and carpeting the slopes, ignoring county borders just as we were.

We went through pretty villages. Dallington was one, with a church high-perched, and the eighteenth-century Folly of John Fuller of Brightling Park. Brightling village has a very old Norman-Early English church (the rectors go back to 1070) and the tomb of "Mad" Fuller in the form of a large pyramid.

*WADHURST* \* Wada's Wood, anciently, Wadhurst is interesting principally because here in 1863 Tom King the Englishman trounced the American Keenan on Sparrow's Green, where the schoolhouse stands now, for a thousand pounds a side in the last of the bare-fist, knock-down fights. It was held "in secret," being against the law, and was attended not only by the whole countryside but by hot-for-blood fans from London who came in a special thirty-car train. Wadhurst was mining iron as far back as 500 B.C. The iron railings around St. Paul's churchyard in London were cast here (this is disputed by neighboring Lamberhurst). The parish church has a unique collection of cast-iron floor slabs, thirty of them, monuments to dead ironmasters and their kin.

*BODIAM* ✳ Between Wadhurst and Battle stands romantic Bodiam Castle, complete outside, a ruin within. You won't want to miss it. Surrounded by a broad moat filled with water lilies, Bodiam is a castle disarmed by beauty as well as by Cromwell.

*TUNBRIDGE WELLS* ✳ Above Wadhurst, is a big-town spa with parks and one notable feature—the promenade called the Pantiles.

*PENSHURST* ✳ is seven miles north of Tunbridge Wells and five and a half west of the market town of Tonbridge (bus), and if you're anywhere near, go to see it. The Stately Home of Penshurst is usually open Wednesday, Thursday, and Saturday, but check before you go. The uniqueness of Penshurst Place among noble mansions is that it is a late medieval (fourteenth-century) house only slightly tampered with by Elizabethan additions, thanks to the fact that the Sidneys were not wealthy. It was the home of Sir Philip Sidney, the *chevalier sans reproche* and all-round Elizabethan whose death in battle brought an extraordinary outpouring of more than two hundred elegies, none of which remembered that he had faults.

Among other features, the house has a great hall unaltered from the time it was built in 1340, and Sidney relics in the armory. An odd and beautiful corner of old houses by the church will excite your camera eye. The whole set-up of great house, church, and village tells plainly of a time when the lord of the manor owned the houses, the peasants, and the house of God and its pastor, who was his dependent and servant.

*BRIGHTON* ✳ Seaside resorts are scattered all along the coast from Margate west of Canterbury to Falmouth in Cornwall. They are crowded havens of the Englishman on holiday. Unless you're a social psychologist on a Fulbright, avoid them; they have no charms.

Brighton, however, has a Sight to be respected as an amusing, Kubla-Khanish creation—the Royal Pavilion, built by the Prince Regent (later George IV) in 1784, and described by some wit of the day: "It is as if St. Paul's had gone down to the sea and pupped." Its creator was the Regent of Regency, which term sums up the style and period he embodied just as Victorian does for the era of another royal figure. Brighton, as the largest of the southern seaside resorts, is called "London by the Sea." This, we feel, is a libel on London. We'd call it England's Atlantic City.

Brighton is fifty miles from London, one hour by electric train.

Inland, the South Downs are soft, sweeping, treeless hills of lovely lines. Alfriston is the largest Downland village, and the great favorite.

ALFRISTON  *  In spite of its popularity with motorists out for a drive, Alfriston is still a must. It lies in the narrow valley of the Cuckmere River, and used to be a smugglers' stronghold. Blank out from your mind and eye (if you can) the ugly modern extension at one end, and also the gift shoppes—and the village stands as a hoary, "be-damned-to-ye" character of immense age and strength.

The Star Inn, which was being built when Henry V was fighting at Agincourt, is the joy of inn-collectors with its roof of heavy slabs of Horsham stone, its odd carvings, its Tudor door and oak rafters. The queer wooden lion outside is the figurehead of a ship wrecked on the coast a mere three hundred years ago. There are many fine old houses. Alfriston's church, for its size and local importance, is called "the cathedral of the South Downs." The fourteenth-century parsonage beside it is being preserved by the National Trust.

Within walking distance in this gap of the South Downs are the hamlets of Alciston and Lullington (Lullington claims the smallest church in England), and between Lewes and Newhaven, a little farther on, dreamy Telscombe in a hollow.

BERWICK  *  On the way to big-town Lewes, Berwick is a flint stone village in a cul-de-sac. Its church is worth seeing. Its bomb-damaged walls have been restored with modern murals which make the interior warm and gay with color. The entire restoration job in this small Saxon and Early English church is original, controversial and, in our opinion, highly successful. We were interested to see, in the guest book, visitors from all over the world, including a party from the USSR.

Firle Beacon, beyond, is a flat-topped hill more than seven hundred feet high with a grand view over the Downs and larks twittering overhead. (Don't look for a beacon; there isn't any.)

GLYNDEBOURNE * Continuing in the direction of Lewes, you come to Glynde, a small, nothing-much village in pretty country, notable not for itself but for outlying Glyndebourne. In 1933 John and Aubrey Christie settled in the Tudor manor house called Glyndebourne and built in its extensive garden what has become a great little opera house, seating eight hundred and always packed. If in London on a summer afternoon you see people in full evening dress carrying picnic hampers, you'll know they're on their way to Victoria station for the train to Lewes which connects with the special buses for Glyndebourne. There's a restaurant of sorts out there but most operagoers prefer to picnic-sup in the lovely gardens during the long intermission.

If you want a Glyndebourne evening, book well in advance through your travel agent, have evening dress, decide whether you'll picnic or dare the restaurant, and go no matter what the weather. The performance will be first-rate, and a Glyndebourne outing is something to remember. The Opera Festival season usually begins at the end of May and sometimes carries on into October.

LEWES * An ancient town spread around its ruined hilltop castle. We couldn't get into the castle, since it was an off-season Sunday and we had forgotten our battering ram—the castle was noted for impregnability. Stuck in Lewes for half a day, we found it lacking interest. But it does have two good inn-hotels, the White Hart and the Shelleys.

ARUNDEL * Between Lewes and Chichester but nearer Chichester, Arundel is touristically important for the great castle of the Duke of Norfolk. Best viewed from the bridge over the Arun, this is a magnificent heap of building. There's a tiltyard in one of the baileys, and the real thing in barbicans, complete with portcullis and drawbridge. The great park is always open to the public (cars excluded). Before you go, check for dates and times of admission to the castle; His Grace has a complicated schedule.

When we were going through we overheard a fellow American say to his wife: "Did you hear that? Nine hundred years they've been living in one house! Sort of puts you in mind of Eddie Guest, doesn't it?"

"How's that, Joe?"

"Isn't he the guy wrote, 'Takes a heap of livin' to make a house a home?'"

There's good walking on the banks of the Arun.

CHICHESTER  *  This marks the Far West of Sussex. Beyond is Southampton, and southwest Hampshire, and Dorset, and the southwest counties of Devon and Cornwall. Chichester is a small-cathedral town that we took to at once in spite of everything being against it.

First, it was raining. We had just got off the *Queen Elizabeth* at Southampton, and we set off to Chichester in a hired car through a solid downpour. Two months before we had been rained and flooded out of England, and we seemed to be back in the same sopping rut.

"Into each life some rain must fall," said our driver unctuously.

"Yes, but why so much?" we asked, and determined on the minimum tip.

Our first care, after checking in at the Dolphin and Anchor, was to find a pair of rubbers for Lawrence. Chichester has four shoe stores. In the first, the clerks climbed up ladders, searched the high shelves and balcony, and came down with a pair for a midget. Sorry, but rubbers were out of stock. At the second store they had sold out and forgotten to reorder, but brought out fishermen's hip boots; wouldn't they do? At the third, the owner jimmied open a trapdoor and disappeared down a ladder. From below came bumps and crashes. He finally appeared in the opening with cobwebs in his hair but no rubbers. At the fourth place they offered stout ploughman's shoes, and finally in desperation introduced us to a formal row of Wellington boots standing without legs or feet in them, from little boy's size to a great pair made to the measure of someone like Richard the Lion-Limbed. "Could you use these?"

Canterbury had been for us the town sold out of umbrellas. In Chichester, where we had an umbrella, the famine was in rubbers.

In our hotel, we had been given a bleak room in the attic. The lounge looked pitifully shabby. The upholstery badly needed cleaning and repairing—but this is generally true of hotels all over England. It's fresh off the ship or plane that you notice it. Later you take it in stride. The receptionist, however, refused to help us to make a somewhat complicated long-distance phone call. A man standing by, regarding us with bored detachment, was, we later learned, the manager.

So it was in personal pique and a pouring rain that we saw Chichester—and even in these adverse circumstances it was likable.

This town of nineteen thousand, has a fine old market cross, a homey cathedral, a promenade along the remains of the ancient walls, and charming squares and eighteenth-century streets. In the Pallant, that most curious stage-set part of town, are Georgian houses of character. You'll be brought up short by one of them, the Dodo House, with two idiotic stone birds on its gateposts which, when erected, were supposed to be dignified ostriches. Chichester at once hailed them gleefully as dodos.

On North Street, almost every house takes the eye. It's a pleasure to walk along any of the four main streets that center on the market cross; or St. Martin's and its tiny square, and the little curving lanes and odd corners. Priory Park is lovely. We enjoyed a snack in the attractive lounge of Ye Olde Punch Bowle on East Street, and got giddy on its famous punch-liqueur.

The main sight is the cathedral. It is one of the second-division cathedrals, an engagingly lopsided affair with a detached bell tower. We enjoyed every bit of it, from the strong Norman columns to the piggy-bank gargoyle at the door. The choir stalls have some good misericords, but hard to get at. There's a wonderful twelfth-century Lazarus carved on a stone slab, some beautiful windows, traces of wall paintings, and the tomb of Richard Fitzalan, Earl of Arundel, who threw a lot of weight in his day and of whom our guidebook said: "Beheaded 1397; restored." The cloisters and close are pleasant, but we never solved the problem of getting into the Bishop's Palace. A sign on its door said not to ring *there*, which was only negatively helpful.

Chichester's summer Theater Festival was triumphantly launched in 1962 under the direction of Sir Laurence Olivier with two Elizabethan plays and Chekhov's *Uncle Vanya*. The playhouse seats 1,360, and has a restaurant and a large car-park. Players include many of Britain's leading actors. The program changes each season. For schedule, ask the BTA.

The Goodwood racecourse is about five miles out of town. The horse races, run in the week of the last Tuesday of July, are among England's fashionable events. The manor house of Goodwood (the racecourse is in its park) is the seat of the Duke of Richmond and open to visitors on Thursday afternoons in the summer.

Close by Chichester on the Channel is the largish village of Bosham (pronounced *Bozz'm*). Disregard the suburban part and concentrate on the fishing-boating part. It's a beautiful village and has the church where Earl Harold worshiped before visiting William in Normandy and taking that oath to help William to England. Bosham is also the place where King Canute ordered the ocean tide to keep away, but it advanced as usual and wet the royal feet (no rubbers then, either).

*H O T E L S * Chichester's Dolphin and Anchor is notable as two old inns thrown into one. They used to be fierce rivals, the Dolphin being a Whig house and the Anchor a Tory. Structurally, the Dolphin and Anchor is interesting, but it needs a management more interested in its guests. We liked the look and friendliness of the Ship Hotel, a stately Georgian building with superb Adam staircase.

*T R A V E L   F A C T S * BTA's *Seeing Britain by Road*, Itinerary No. 2, takes in Surrey, Sussex, and Kent. This is free, as is British Railway's timetable folder, "Conducted Rambles in Sussex, Kent, Surrey, and Hampshire," issued quarterly. Chichester is seventy miles from London, under two hours by train (change at Havant).

# 9. EAST ANGLIA
# AND CAMBRIDGE

Teatime in the Edwardian lobby of St. Ermin's Hotel in London. While waiting for the lugubrious servitor to bring our toast we found in a pile of old *Tatlers, Fields,* and *Queens* some guest's abandoned map of Norwich.

We knew something of East Anglia but had never visited Norwich. Its anatomy absorbed us. Maps are exciting, they tease the imagination. This one looked dizzyingly complicated. We made out a blue snake that wriggled from top left, changed its mind halfway, dived lower right and off. The snake was the river Wensum. A black spot on it was "Pull's Ferry (abandoned)." A bulky cross in pale green grounds was a cathedral.

Here the long-lost waiter arrived with the toast from lower left. At the same time the head porter converged upon us from upper right, his pink face grave, his formal body stiff with embarrassment. "Sir—and Modom—Reception, er, hum, regrets. . . ."

Reception, manned by remote young ladies who must certainly be daughters of needy peers striving to save their Stately Homes— Reception (bother its ancestry!) was unable to extend our booking. Tomorrow, Sir, the Motor Show opens; followed next week, Modom, by the Dairy Show. Then the Queen opens Parliament, after which——

We ceased to listen, his meaning having penetrated. Tomorrow at noon we would be out in the streets of a city solidly booked from cellars to attics.

Sylvia took in hot tea and the cold fact of eviction. Lawrence, a map-happy man, remarked, "Norwich has a Tombland."

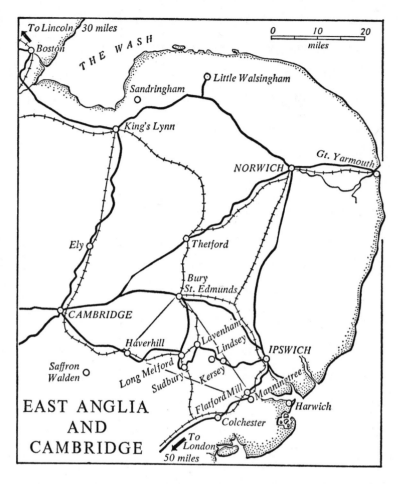

EAST ANGLIA
AND
CAMBRIDGE

"Cemetery? Are we as desperate as all that?"

"Look." He pointed. Under the blue snake's pause before its change of mind lay an oddly shaped white space lettered TOMB-LAND. It wasn't a cemetery. It had a hotel on it.

Somerset Maugham would have noted the look that passed between us. Next day, leaving London to motorcars, cows, and the Queen, we were on the fast train to the metropolis of East Anglia.

East Anglia is the eastern bulge of England, extending on its north to the deep basin called the Wash and including northern Essex, Suffolk, Norfolk, and eastern Cambridgeshire.

Before being carved into counties it was an Anglo-Saxon king-dom, more Anglican than Saxon, and its notables were of the kind you find in saga. There was Wuffa, after whom the people were for some time called Wuffingas. There was Eorpwald, who was slain by Ricberht. And Ecgric, followed by King Anna, both slain by Penda of Mercia. All the kings seem to have died with their sandals on. They lived slaying until slain.

It is from the Angles that East Anglia—and England (Angle-land)—got its name. At the time of the Domesday Book, that eleventh-century census of taxable properties, East Anglia was the wealthiest and most populous part of the Conqueror's new realm. Its wealth came from the back of sheep. The great era ended in the eighteenth century when steam-powered looms took the weav-ing to the Black Country in the north, where the coal was. So most of East Anglia remains as Constable painted it two hundred years ago.

It is an off-side part of England, consequently less touristed than other regions. An asset. It is mainly flat and fenny. The marshes, called fens, are drained now but scrubbily keep their identity. The wide horizons and cloudscapes draw claustrophobic artists; it is the country of Constable, Gainsborough, John Crome, and the Cot-mans. But the fens still look primeval. One expects them to ooze.

## § *NORWICH*

When you don't have what most other cities have, you become proud of not having it—the not-ness gives distinction. Norwich (rhymes with *porridge*) is proud to have no main street or central square. Almost as irregular as London, and further complicated by a hilliness unexpected in East Anglia, it claims to be one of the most interesting cities in Britain for anyone to get lost in.

It is.

For the tourist, however, it does have a focal point—Tombland. The romance of the name did not collapse when we found out it derives from the Saxon *toom*, meaning an open space. It's a broad, irregular oblong. On one side runs the wall of the cathedral, pierced by two flint-and-stone gates, Ethelbert and Erpingham.

Tombland was the center of the Anglo-Saxon town. When the

Normans moved in and built their monastery and cathedral, the square became a battleground of town and gown. The monks, mounting the wall, would hurl insults and more solid objects down on the Anglians in market assembled, who would respond with interest. These pleasantries erupted (1272) in a major battle. The victorious townsmen set fire to the cathedral. While both sides were burying their dead the Pope laid the city under an interdict. It had to win grace by seeing many executions, paying a heavy fine to the Pope, and building Ethelbert. The Erpingham gate was put up a hundred years later by "the knight grown grey with age and honor" (Shakespeare), Sir Thomas Erpingham, leader of Henry V's archers at Agincourt.

Before you tear off in all directions (Norwich has an inspiriting effect) we advise you to find Tombland Alley. It's at the lower end of the square beside the leaning Steward House, which is beside the Samson and Hercules House. Stand inside the narrow passage and look out. The Alley's opening, in itself photogenic, encloses a view that leaps across the square, goes right through Erpingham gate, and is closed by the west door of the cathedral. The details and spatial relationships of this triple-doorway view make it a coveted camera shot. If you don't own a camera, you'll be just as happy standing there looking. The passage runs around the churchyard of St. George's and comes out on Princes Street.

The Samson and Hercules House, now a dance hall, is named after the two amusing old figures in front. The Steward House on the Alley keeps the name of the man whose home it was during Kett's peasant rebellion (1549). When the rebels kidnaped the mayor of Norwich, Augustine Steward carried on, and his house was the headquarters of the royal armies sent to put down the revolt. Robert Kett was finally captured and hanged. Steward was considered a hero for about four hundred years, when it was decided it had all been a mistake and Kett was the hero. The city then put up a tablet to him on the castle walls where it had hanged him. Moral judgments on historic events, however overdue, are meaningful to the living, and Norwich is a city with a deep sense of responsibility to its citizens past, present, and future.

You are still in Tombland. What to do next? Tombland is not the best place to stop and think, since it's one of the city's main traffic hubs. It persists in looking medieval in spite of Georgian façades, Purdy's Restaurant, the car park, subterranean public conveniences, and double-decker buses that come charging up to devour queues of unmedieval Norvincians.

The cathedral calls. But wait. There is another outstandingly photogenic place nearby.

A little beyond the Alley, at the Maid's Head Hotel, Tombland narrows into Wensum Street. Look to the left for Elm Hill. Narrow, curving, cobbled, mounting a hill, this lane ranks with the Shambles of York as one of England's most picturesque streets of old houses. You'll want color film; the houses are painted pink, pale green, coral. One of them is an attractive craft shop where you may find a piece of East Anglian pottery to take home. The little church at the top, St. Peter Hungate (entrance on Princes Street) is maintained as a museum of Norfolk church art. Visit when you've time.

You'll keep coming back to Elm Hill. So leave it now for the cathedral, which we rank as one of the five greatest in England.

When you enter the precinct by Erpingham gate, on your left is the chantry chapel (1316) which for four hundred years housed the Grammar School. Elizabeth I's great lawyer, Edward Coke, got his early schooling there. So did a boy named George Borrow, who was mercilessly flogged by the vicious master Dr. Valpy. The most famous of the boys who managed to survive was a spindly little chap who went off to sea when he was twelve, Horatio Nelson. The school has been transferred to other buildings in the close, but this one is still in use as its chapel and is open to visitors.

Before you rises the cathedral's west front.

One extraordinary thing about Norwich Cathedral is a negative —it never had an important saint attracting the pilgrim revenues which swept other churches into the medieval rebuilding frenzies. The result is an exciting positive—it remains one of the most Norman of cathedrals.

Before going in, take a good look at the central tower. Ignore the soaring spire it holds aloft; even at its best it was merely spectacular, and now it is suffering from stone decay. But the square Norman tower all by itself, massive, pinnacled, and elegantly ornamented, is superb. Now walk around to the east end to see the apse with the flying buttresses. Beautiful; and, in England, unique.

Apse and tower form the most famous, the most photographed, prospect.

Here too is Life's Green with the grave of Edith Cavell, executed as a spy by the Germans in World War I. The tablet omits her eloquent last words: "Patriotism is not enough."

We didn't speak of apses in the cathedral lesson (Canterbury chapter) because the only English example is at Norwich. This semicircular east end was the tradition in early Christian churches, based on the architecture of the Roman law court (basilica). Since Norwich never extended itself eastward to accommodate shrines and pilgrims, it alone keeps the ancient apse, which here dates from 1096, when the first bishop, Herbert de Losinga, laid the foundation stone. Within, you find a thrillingly Norman ambulatory, or processional aisle round the apse, two chapels radiating like ears, and the bishop's throne raised in the middle of the apse exactly where, in the Roman basilica, the judge used to sit behind the pagan altar, which became the Christian high altar. Only a few Romanesque cathedrals in Europe have this early-Christian arrangement, and Norwich is Romanesque.

You probably won't be prepared for its patrician air. We weren't. Norman, we assumed, must always be crude in its power, and dark. The power is there, right enough, but carried with grace and ease by clustered columns. White stone, clean lines, regular ranks of rounded arches in three stories, rich uncluttered decoration, generous light, all make for elegance and urbanity. Norwich in its great old age looks more modern than many younger churches.

This cathedral displays a remarkable collection of misericords and bosses. The vividly carved misericords are under the seats of the choir stalls, which themselves are noteworthy for their rich fifteenth-century carving. For the 328 bosses—those colored stonework buttons punctuating the beautiful vaulting of nave and transepts—you should have binoculars or opera glasses. A tilted enlarging mirror in the nave helps you make out the details of a few. "Noah's Ark" and "The Temptation" are the most delightful of these stonework primitives.

The Monk's Door and the Prior's Door lead to the cloister, the largest in England. The bosses in the low-roofed cloister walks are easier to see than those in the high-vaulted church. Look for the startling faces-with-leaves, one in the east walk and one in the west.

TIP. Among the booklets sold in the cathedral the one by Thurlow is excellent, the one by Le Grice has more photos of bosses and misericords. Why not get both? "The Children's Guide to Norwich Cathedral" is good for adults as well.

Walk through the close to Pull's Ferry on the river, once the cathedral's water gate. There's no longer a ferry (the old boat was rotting away on the bank when we were there), but the medieval gateway remains with its long low arch for wagons and its smaller one for people. It is the delight of tourists and painters. An architect lives in the ferryman's house adjoining the gate. From Pull's Ferry the view of the cathedral across the green expanse of playing fields is breathtaking.

Many Jacobean buildings in the close are rented out to solicitors, accountants, and surveyors.

We invaded the close late one moonlight night. The spire looked glorious with a silvered cloud impaled upon it. Near the Ethelbert gate, on the green, a row of Queen Anne houses slept. A lone window threw a bar of raw light across the dark. Within, a young woman was typing like mad while two men conferred across a desk. It was an estate-agent's office. J. B. Priestley, wandering about the close on a night before ours, had the fancy that in such offices you could "buy or rent nothing but remote crazy manors." In this one the late-working agent's minion must have got onto something weird and wild, for he suddenly lunged out the door, jumped into a small car hiding in the blacker shadows, and was off in a series of explosions that shattered the stillness like machine-gun fire. Gradually the Middle Ages seeped back into the close and settled in under the ancient moon.

Above Tombland in the higher part of town, the market place provides a second focal point. Lively, colorful, and expansive as a Brueghel canvas with its striped awnings over booths, grand city hall on the Stockholm model, chequered stone-and-flint guildhall, St. Peter Mancroft church, rows of varitinted shop buildings, and the massive castle's keep looming in the middle distance, this square of a thousand awnings is highly dramatic.

The market was animated with buyers. We ambled from flowers

to crockery to fish. At a corner stall four men were lined up devouring oysters with the feverish intensity of a contest, while the stallkeeper hopped from one to another removing empty shells and supplying more of the succulent bivalves. The four were coupled by the necessity of sharing two towels which hung from stanchions. The sequence was: grab oyster, dip into sauce, gulp, grope for towel and give it a wipe-twist—which endowed it with a new red-brown stain; repeat. Legs were planted firmly apart, hands flew, towels agitated and darkened, empty shells clattered into a bucket.

A mite of a girl with braids down her back ran up and tugged at an oyster-cannibal's coat. "Papa! Mum says quit that and come along!" Papa reached behind to brush her away, growled "Ur!" and stayed in the race. The little girl gave him another tug. Papa's eyes rolled as he gulped and wiped. A fresh bowl of oysters came his way. The child now took a new line; she began jumping up and down, screaming, "Papa! Papa! Papa!" The gorger was shamed; he turned and shouted, "Be off with yer!" The three paid no heed; they had gained half a plate on him. We tore ourselves away from this strange tragicomedy, this oyster-passion, this new twist to the old melodrama of "Father, dear father, come home with me now."

The fifteenth-century guildhall includes a crypt and dungeons. A prize exhibit in its Elizabethan council chamber is a Spanish admiral's sword sent home to his city by Lord Nelson. St. Peter Mancroft's immense church is noted for its stained glass, its bells, its grave of Sir Thomas Browne (*Urn Burial*) inside and his statue outside.

Between market place and castle, the open space that formerly was the cattle fair now does duty as car park—the cattle now meet on the outskirts of town. Here George Borrow met his first gypsies, followed them up Mousehold Heath and began to haunt their camp. The result years later was *Lavengro* and *Romany Rye*. An object here transports you suddenly to Paris: a sheet-iron *pissoir*, owing its existence to the needs of cattlemen, and still in business.

The castle consists of a great keep or donjon on a mound. Only a part of it remains castlelike; the rest is museum, with an art gallery of the Norwich School of landscapists: Crome, the Cotmans, and their followers.

It is easy to get happily lost in Norwich's maze of streets and lanes. Before you do, look for these places:

1. Curat House, near the market place on Haymarket Street. Conspicuous is the handsome old wineshop. Visit its medieval wine room. Next go into the courtyard beside the shop, open the oak door, and walk upstairs into the restaurant. You don't have to lunch or dine, but the food is good. Both the shop and the restaurant (of many rooms) were built in 1460 as the mansion of merchant-sheriff John Curat, an important citizen who lived in style. Curat's arms are carved here and there: a Q and a rat. (In the cathedral, Bishop Lyhart's arms are carved in stonework [ask the verger to point them out to you]—a hart lying down. Our verger laid these pictographs [called *rebuses*] to punning, but we think their use, in illiterate days, was more practical than humorous.)

2. Strangers' Hall at Charing Cross: a medieval mansion with architectural features of the fourteenth through the eighteenth centuries, it is a museum of domestic life, with furnished period rooms and a lovely little courtyard.

3. Maddermarket Theater behind it. The Maddermarket sold the red dye for Norwich cloth. In Shakespeare's day the popular actor Will Kemp, in a publicity stunt, jigged the Morris dance from London to Norwich in nine days, ending at the Maddermarket, where with graceful ease he concluded by jumping the church wall. The church is still there, right up against the theater which, in a way, commemorates the feat. The theater is an old building made over into an Elizabethan-style playhouse. Here since 1921 the Nugent Monck company of Norwich players have been putting on Shakespeare and experimental plays. This strictly amateur band is famous. Get tickets for whatever is on the boards. If you're here between seasons, knock on the door. Whoever is inside, sewing or hammering toward the next production, will take you around. They are proud of their theater.

Norwich was for us a discovery. We felt thankful to the peers' daughters who had pushed us out of the sheltered life of St. Ermin's Hotel. It is old and quaint and full of surprises. It is modern, proud of many achievements, and civic-spirited. Its baby-food, cereal, mustard (Colman's), shoe and other industries are without curse of belching chimneys. The hobby and sideline of Norvincians is raising canaries—they have been adept at it since Flemish weavers brought their birds over with them centuries ago.

We haven't had room here to do more than scratch the surface of Norwich. We haven't even mentioned what you may well find the most interesting busy-spot of all: St. Andrew's Plain. (These curious little squares and open spaces called plains probably get the word from Dutch *plein*, a reminder of the fact that for hundreds of years Norfolk and Holland have had close trade and other relations.) St. Andrew's Plain is bordered by St. Andrew's Hall, once the nave, and Blackfriars Hall, the chancel, of a church set apart in Elizabethan times for Flemish refugees from religious persecution. Up a narrow passage is the Bridewall, which was once a jail, but before that (1360) the home of a rich merchant. It is now a museum, and a very interesting one, of Norwich history, works, and ways. Nearby is the great hall of the house of John Suckling, the poet, and St. Andrew's Church, one of Norfolk's richest, and on the other side of the Plain on Princes Street, the St. Peter Hungate church museum, with hoary and rare ecclesiastical remains.

And all those lanes, alleyways, passages, and dead ends: Golden Ball, Elephant Yard, Unthank Road, Rampant Horse Street, Three Kings Alley, Lower Goat Lane, Back of the Inns, Ten Bell Lane, St. Laurence Little Steps, Apple-Tommy Mews, Don't-Go-Farther Alley. Even the standard double-decker bus is taking a load to—if you can believe the sign in front—Heartsease Est! Another bus will take you out of town up to Mousehold Heath, where Kett's rebels and Borrow's gypsies camped, and the view over Norwich is magnificent, and you more than agree with the touchingly modest motto: "A fine city, Norwich."

*HOTELS*  *  The Maid's Head in Tombland may have a false Tudor front, but it has a heart of gold and is truly ancient. It has been steeped in history since the time it was the brew-house of the medieval monastery. If you're lucky or persuasive you may be able to tease a copy of its forty-two-page illustrated booklet from Reception. We rank this hotel-inn first. The Royal on Bank Plain is large brick Victorian, unbeautiful but comfortable. Royal and Maid's Head have the highest rates. The Castle Hotel and the Bell (Trust House) face each other at the foot of the Norman castle, and are adequate. Slim budgets will like the Oxford House Hotel at 3 Princes Street, a good Georgian building, homely-messy inside, clean, run family style. One of the family, a fine-looking old gentleman, is cook and works at a lump of dough as if he were Rodin.

RESTAURANTS \* Purdy's in Tombland and Curat House in the Haymarket serve good food with style and in an old-world atmosphere. The Boar's Head in Surrey Street and the Trowel and Hammer in St. Stephens' Road were recommended to us but we didn't try them. We did try Princes Café Restaurant on recommendation and didn't go again.

INFORMATION BUREAU \* A friendly, helpful staff at 24 Exchange Street, just off the market place. Buy the official guide (twenty cents).

# § "THE WEDGE"

On our last trip we went straight to Norwich on the fast train from London. If you'd like to make *going there* part of your tour, driving, and visiting tranquil rural parts unspoiled by modern industry, route yourself to take in:

COLCHESTER \* An ancient place with city walls, castle, old houses, it is at the same time a hustling town of sixty thousand on the main London–Norwich line by rail and road. What is it they hustle over? Well, oysters, for example. They were at it as far back as October 1661, when Samuel Pepys told his diary: "After office done, went and eat some Colchester oysters with Sir W. Batten in his house." Not just any oysters, mark you. If you can be here on the Thursday nearest Trafalgar Day (October 21) you will find yourself participating in Colchester's annual binge, the Oyster Feast. Our inn's porter told us, "We talks oysters, we sells oysters, we eats oysters." At the bar we caught a snatch of talk to bear him out: "It is true the oyster has enemies. Who hasn't?"

Colchester also grows roses in extensive nurseries. The Red Lion, a fine inn, has a piece of Roman pavement, fourteenth-century cellars, fifteenth-century wattle-and-daub, and bits of every subsequent century. The Cups is a little less venerable, merely four hundred years old; you eat your dinner there in a beautiful Adam-like

Assembly Room. The Red Lion is medieval in atmosphere, the Cups Georgian. The handsome old buildings are many.

"*THE WEDGE*" * This term, uncopyrighted, is our own. Nine miles north of Colchester, at Manningtree, you enter the Essex–Suffolk border country which extends up the valley of the Stour and its tributaries as far as Haverhill to the east, and north to Bury St. Edmunds. Join the three: Manningtree, Haverhill, Bury—by lines, and you have a wedge thirty by sixteen by twenty-eight miles about sixty-five crow's-flight miles from Charing Cross.

Why go there? The attractions are sleepy villages, slow-moving towns with noble parish churches, timbered and pargeted houses, excellent inns, in the most peaceful and little-changed part of England. Wool and weaving made fortunes here. The golden tide, receding, left beauty unmarred behind it.

At Manningtree on the Stour estuary, abandon your car and give your feet a chance. Take the river path to Flatford Mill, where John Constable lived. Strolling this untroubled valley, you see what the budding young artist saw when he mooned along here during the years the American colonies were fighting for independence. Carry on to Dedham and Stratford St. Mary through pastoral country of river and woods under the wide Constable sky. The sky is streaked now by military jets, but little else has changed. You don't have to be a landscape painter to love the Constable country—but it probably helps. Neatly enough, when we returned to Colchester from Stour Valley we read in the press that Christie's in London had just sold a Constable canvas for $240,520.

Thomas Gainsborough, generally ranked higher than Constable, was born in Sudbury, twelve miles from Colchester and slightly less from Dedham and Stratford. Sudbury's three old churches and many timbered houses make it worth visiting. There's a Yankee connection, too. John Winthrop, Connecticut's first colonial governor, was born in nearby Groton, which gave its name to the American rival of Eton. Winthrop's father, first governor of Massachusetts, was born six miles away in Edwardstone.

Many other places in the Wedge are worth a call.

*Long Melford*, a few miles beyond Sudbury, is Long because it lines two miles of main street. It boasts two Tudor mansions, Kentwell Hall (with moat) and Melford Hall. Elizabeth I was entertained at Melford Hall; she and her numerous train all but bank-rupted their host. The beautiful "wool" church has tombs of the Cloptons, the great wool family. The Bull is a famous inn.

*Lavenham*, five miles on, once the wealthiest of wool towns, is now a living museum of stately timbered houses. Here we once vegetated happily for ten days, and Sylvia encountered a ghost —a hair-stirring experience. In more ways than one Lavenham is a marvelous ghost town. It is nearly all black-and-white. The half-timbered houses built by wealthy merchants still look opulent, more dreaming than moldering. In one of them, on Shilling Street, a lady named Jane Taylor wrote little verses a hundred years ago; among them one that begins, "Twinkle, twinkle, little star. . . ." To the great flintstone church bell-ringers come from afar for the privilege of ringing the changes. The Swan is the most innish of the old inns we have enjoyed in England.

*Kersey*, five miles from Lavenham, gave its name to a coarse woolen cloth. A stream flows through it. Kersey too is rich in Tudor houses, and is probably the prettiest village in the Wedge, while Lavenham is the prettiest town. *Lindsey*, a mile and a half on, gave its name to the linsey-woolsey which clothed so many American colonials.

*Bury St. Edmunds*, eleven miles from Lavenham, once great and important, is a brick town of twenty thousand inhabitants with the sad remains of an eleventh-century abbey. Its odd name de-rives from the abbey's popular shrine of an East Anglian saint. Its town hall is Jacobean, and most of the houses are of the seven-teenth and eighteenth centuries. The Angel, across the street from the abbey ruins, is an inn Dickens knew.

*IPSWICH* * We are definitely out of the Wedge now. You can go on to Norwich from Bury St. Edmunds by way of Thetford (the Bell is the inn), the ancient town in which Thomas Paine was born. If you are in Colchester and aiming at Norwich, con-sider stopping over for a day or two hours at Ipswich, the largest (pop. 105,000) East Anglian town after Norwich. Dickens was fond of the Great White Horse at Ipswich, and placed Pickwick there to have his famous contretemps with the lady in yellow curl-papers. This splendid inn is so well kept that you may well expect to hear the halloo and rattle of the Pickwick coach.

Ipswich's thriving business goes on among some handsome old buildings. The great one, the pride and joy of pargeting, is Sparrowe's, otherwise the Ancient House, in the Butter Market. It is quite possible that this black-and-white house with the wonderful decorative, molded plasterwork (pargeting) is the most splendid timbered house in all England. The Ancient House, built for a merchant, is occupied by an excellent bookshop whose owner is proud to show Americans around, upstairs as well as down.

We carry on to Norwich, and return to London by way of King's Lynn, Ely, and Cambridge, with an illogical side trip to Boston.

*TRAVEL FACTS*  *  If driving, have the BTA free booklet, "Seeing Britain by Road," which contains an itinerary (with map) of an East Anglian circle tour more ambitious than the one we outline here, and perhaps more so than is called for.

Although the automobile is the handiest vehicle for seeing the small places, in these days of rail and motor-bus travel no one need be immobilized. The combined British Railways–London Transport Tour No. 5 does the Constable-Gainsborough country in one day, by rail to Colchester, thence by motor coach, for the beguiling rate of $2.25—packed lunch included.

A traveler with ample time can do it on his own, by rail and motor coach. By American standards, distances are short. Local buses fan out from all the main towns to all the villages.

*THE BROADS*  *  This book being devoid of the low and vulgar, the name "Broads" refers only to a complex of indefinite, wandering waters lying northeast of Norwich near the sea. They are infested by boatmen, who sometimes refer to them recklessly as lagoons. We were never able to like them. When we heard that Cap'n Birch, our sailor-host of River-Breeze-on-Thames, intended to explore them, we asked him to report. Here is his judgment.

Countryside: unkempt; scenery: monotonous; villages: undistinguished; churches: thatched; water: dirty; industry: catering for boaters; boaters: moronic; food: scarce; birches: surprisingly cheerful.

There are windmills, but they don't make up for the rest.

## § KING'S LYNN

"Why," queries its official guidebook, "has King's Lynn failed to receive the attention that it deserves?"

It proceeds to answer itself in a musing way: "Certainly the situation of Lynn, on the banks of the Great Ouse, two miles from the southern shore of the Wash, does not *look* attractive to the average inquiring visitor. Probably his mental image is one of a dreary expanse of flat monotonous fen stretching away in every direction. . . ."

"Never mind the mental image," we said to it crossly after exploring. "It's the real image that counts, and here it is right before our eyes—a dreary expanse of flat, monotonous, etc. . . ."

This city of twenty-six thousand on the watery edge of the fen (marshland) with a sluggish river which at low tide displays a collection of mudbanks far out into the broad silting-up bay called the Wash, likes to think of itself as an English Bruges. It is not. It is only itself—a minor seaport and a town with a vacant stare.

Like smaller Topsham near Exeter, Lynn (one is permitted to drop the "King's") is supposed to be colorfully Flemish from ancient trade with the Netherlands. But its touted Dutchness is diluted. There is only enough to bring to mind one of Simenon's Maigret stories of gray atmosphere and mild puzzlement, along with the conviction that everything will come out in the Wash. But tourists with special tastes love it.

Lynn has many things to see. We rather liked Red Mount Chapel, in the middle of the park called The Walks. It's an odd red-brick octagon which pilgrims bound for Our Lady of Walsingham visited to pay their advance respects to the Virgin. It was ingeniously designed to hurry those visitors along in single file, taking them in one door, up a narrow stairway, past the little shrine, and out through another door. As purely functional architecture, it has the interest of Frank Lloyd Wright's Guggenheim art museum in New York—in a tiny way.

In the Saturday Market Place, St. Margaret's is a handsome church. Its beauty lies in the Early English chancel; its rarest treasures are two large fourteenth-century brasses. The Robert Braunche brass is amusing. The wealthy merchant was obviously a status-seeker. He is shown with his two wives (he had one at a time), and at the bottom is a lively scene of the feast he gave Edward III, in which the *pièce de résistance* was roast peacock. Six hundred years after his demise in 1364, Braunche here still brags of his great moment.

He had a right. In the Middle Ages the peacock was the proper dish to set before a king. To prepare, cook, and serve it required great skill. The bird was skinned and redressed, the tail fanned out and the crested head wrapped in linen which had to be kept moistened during the roasting. When done, the feet and beak were gilded, and the beak further prepared to sprout brandied flames. Not to have a serving for every guest was the worst of *faux pas*. Braunche had six, brought in as fully dressed as warships in a royal review, to the sound of horns. The correct carving of royal peacock was by itself an art. At a peacock feast knights took and renewed oaths, swearing "I vow to God, the Holy Virgin, the Ladies, and the Peacock" to do this or that great deed.

The father of Fanny Burney was St. Margaret's organist, and Fanny—that eighteenth-century gossip and author of *Evelina*—was born in Lynn. So was George Vancouver, baptized at the font, who grew up to become Captain, R.N., and to have named for him places geographical many thousand miles away.

And in the churchyard you'll find the pitiful epitaph:

"Here lies Poor Sparkes / James Sparks, Brewer and Victualler / His friends were many and constant / His enemies few but bitter / His heart once sincere and brave / But borne down with more than man could bear, / Died Oct. 12, 1752, aged 50 years. (*Erected by the Friendly Society of Free Men.*)"

The Guild Hall (Tudor) is opposite the church, and has a fine checkered front. It is still in use. When the magistrates gather they are in the presence of seventeenth-century mayors frowning down from the walls along with a forbidding-looking medieval king. On show are the old mace and other regalia of office, and the prize item, King John's Cup.

Of High Street, between the two market places, the local guidebook says: "A few of its buildings are good and others are not so good." True. (We became fond of that booklet. Buy one in Lynn.)

On the vast Tuesday Market Place, the main square, we thought well of St. Nicholas Chapel—its ornate porch and its great windows. Miscellaneous old buildings are to be found in various narrow streets off the two squares.

We tried to walk out to the Fisher Fleet and the Wash, but the roads were dug up for repaving, the rain came down, and after following the detour for a few hundred yards we decided to let the Wash go hang and took shelter in a customs shed. The customs man told us that the little Dutch freighters in the basins brought lumber from Finland and Russia.

But we couldn't work up enthusiasm for King's Lynn. The sights are all minor.

If you plan on visiting Lynn, go in summer and pray for sunshine. We were told that the low-tide mudbanks have a beautiful sheen when the sun comes out, and that the lampposts are hung with baskets of flowers imported from more blooming towns.

Odd notes: the town gave its name to the Massachusetts shoe city. Here it manufactures merry-go-rounds.

*H O T E L S* ✻ The Duke's Head and the Globe are rivals on Tuesday Market Place. You won't go wrong in either. Both houses set a good table. The Duke's Head (a Trust House) occupies a handsome building put up in 1685. The tilt of its grand staircase is such that a walk up or down it is as good as one gin-and-bitters.

*T R A V E L   F A C T S* ✻ A crack train, the *Fenman*, makes Lynn from London in a little more than two and a half hours. You can also come by train from Cambridge.

*E N V I R O N S* ✻ Fifteen miles away at Castle Acre are the ruins of a Norman priory and the remains of some considerable ancient earthworks.

But an expedition of more interest is to Castle Rising and Sandringham. Castle Rising—wonderful when-knighthood-was-in-flower name!—is only five miles northeast of Lynn in good walking country. See the massive remains of the Norman castle, and the village under it. There's bus service between Lynn and Castle Rising.

Sandringham, an off-duty residence of the royal family, is about three miles farther on in the lavender country. In summer the fields are purplish with lavender, which is grown on the royal estates. Harvest time is usually August to mid-September. Lavender was brought by the Romans from the Mediterranean and took kindly to the English climate, developing new virtues and fragrances. On Wednesday and Thursday in summer, if the royal family are not in residence, you can see the beautiful gardens.

If driving, you can return to Lynn via Hillington, turning right when you come to road A148. Total round trip, eighteen to twenty miles.


# § BOSTON

Across the Wash from King's Lynn and on the river Witham, Boston, in the southeast corner of Lincolnshire, belongs geographically to East Anglia. It is little touristed, but we don't see how a Yankee can resist going there, if only to send a card home for the shock of the postmark. In this original Boston an American learns history he never knew or has forgotten. When he retails it to the home folks it should draw a fascinated "Waal, dew tell!"

Boston was 950 years old when the Pilgrim Fathers made their first attempt to escape. It grew up as Botolph's Town around the monks of St. Botolph, patron saint of seamen, and was for a while a port second only to London. The Hansa merchants had wharves and warehouses here, as in Lynn and London.

Business was so good that the town could afford a grand church. St. Botolph's church was begun early in the fourteenth century and finished two hundred years later. The outstanding object in the town is the Stump—an understatement for a church tower that rears 288 feet above the plain and is visible for thirty miles. For four centuries the Stump by day and its lantern by night have been a boon to seafarers.

The Stump with its beautiful octagonal lantern is more impressive than the church interior, where many a Puritan worshiped. Still, it gives one a thrill, and it does have good misericords in the choir stalls.

John Cotton, grandfather of New England's Cotton Mather, was vicar of this church for twenty-one years before he emigrated. The chapel to his memory was restored by New England Bostonians. Among the books John Cotton authored is one with the interesting title: *Milk for Babes, Drawn out of the Breasts of Both Testaments, Chiefly for the Spiritual Nourishment of Boston Babes in either England.* . . . Ambrose Bierce would have called it Puritannic Acid.

St. Mary's Guildhall, dating from the fifteenth century, is a second worthy place of pilgrimage for Americans. Here in the courtyard the Puritans tried, sentenced, and jailed the Pilgrim Fathers.

"What!" we exclaimed. "Puritans imprisoning our Pilgrims! And this in a town that bequeathed its name and the spirit of liberty to the capital of Massachusetts? the Athens of America? the Hub of the Universe?"

Aye. And they did it with enthusiasm.

We had a dim feeling that our college history had mentioned in passing that the Pilgrims were separatists from the Anglican Church (Reds), while the Puritans were merely reformers (Liberals). In England they hated each other with the hatred that often arises between liberals and radicals, exceeding their detestation of the common enemy, reaction.

The Pilgrims, in the guise of merchant adventurers led by Brewster, chartered a ship in Boston and came to town from Scrooby and other parts as quietly and unobtrusively as they could. They were refugees from religious persecution bound for more tolerant Holland. But just before sailing they were betrayed by the ship's captain. Boston authorities took them off the boat. Crowds jeered and jostled them through the streets. In the guildhall they were sentenced to thirty days in jail—their leaders for longer. Their possessions were confiscated. The cells are on view.

That was in 1607. Later they did manage to get away to Holland. It was from Leyden that the *Mayflower* and the *Speedwell* set sail for the New World in 1620. They had to put in at Southampton for repairs, and there John Alden ("Speak for yourself") joined them. The *Speedwell* was leaking so badly they had to put in at Plymouth—with trepidation, one may believe, for might it not prove another Boston? Luckily they fell in with friends and were hidden in a wine cellar. In gratitude they named their American landfall after the town. In Plymouth the vintager Hawkins has since returned the compliment by naming his establishment Mayflower House. In Plymouth the *Speedwell* was abandoned and everybody crowded aboard the *Mayflower*.

Ten years later—1630—the Puritans under John Winthrop left England with a respectable charter from the king empowering them to establish a colony. *Their* gratitude took the rather sycophantic form of calling the harbor they entered Charlestown, after their un-Puritan king. Their next settlement they named Boston after the town that had been home to most of them, including an ex-mayor and an ex-alderman.

To the Pilgrim Father in the New World, the name Boston must have had an ill sound.

That guildhall with the cells was, in a much earlier time, the Guild of the Blessed Virgin, an enterprising association. It sent a delegation to buy or cajole from Pope Julius II, a hard bargainer, the power to grant pardons in remission of sins. In medieval times this was a privilege worth much in coin of the realm. The chief of the mission, one Thomas Cromwell, concocted a brilliant plan. Learning that His Holiness had two weaknesses—a sweet tooth and a fondness for songs—he took along "various gelly confections." In Rome he waited until the Pope returned one day hot and hungry from hunting, and at the psychological moment introduced his "gellies" to the tune of a three-part song rendered by himself and his two companions. The pontiff was so pleased that after devouring the confections (a cardinal had to sample them first to make sure they weren't poisoned), he traded the pardoning power for the recipes.

We regret to report that Boston makes none of those wonderful "gellies" today. Nor does Rome.

Boston has much the same watered-down Hollandish air as King's Lynn. In the environs are windmills and red-brick cottages. There is even a tulip-land in toward Spalding. You keep expecting to hear a foreign tongue. The ruddy-cheeked, sturdy Bostonians talk in singularly high-pitched voices. The town (pop. 25,000) is capital of a prosperous farming region. Best time to be around is market day when the farmers are in with their cattle and produce, closing bargains in the pubs with huge gulps of beer.

As a pilgrim-in-reverse, you may go on to Scrooby in Notting-hamshire to see Pilgrim Father Brewster's manor house and the pew he occupied in church.

HOTELS   *   The Peacock and Royal is strategically situated on Boston's market place. The White Hart has good accommodations. There is also the Red Lion.

TRAVEL FACTS   *   Boston is 117 railway miles from London, 35 from Lincoln, about 30 from King's Lynn.


§  ELY

A backwater drenched with history, most of it dramatic and some of it unintentionally comic, Ely is inhabited by ten thousand un-dramatic souls and dominated by its strangely lovely cathedral.

Two travel guides we know separately liken this church to a great ship under full sail. It may be we were low on ecstasy the three times we encountered it, but it looked no more like a ship than a windjammer ever looked like a cathedral. The notion stems from the way you see it, on approaching from miles away, appar-ently rising all alone from the flats.

Close at hand it is, at first, less impressive because harder to take in. Walk toward it slowly, and it begins to awe you anew. That castellated west tower is a wonder almost eight centuries old. The whole medley, composed of four hundred years of dif-ferent varieties of Gothic fitted together, is a gigantic stone museum of every architectural style from Norman to Perpendicular.

The most remarkable feature of the long interior is the octagonal central tower and lantern. When one thinks of medieval crafts-men, one inclines to think small—of crafty carving, ingenious jigsaw work with colored glass, elaborate or fantastic details. In England we were constantly being surprised by the inadequacy of the persistent conception. The cathedral makers thought big. Ely's central tower was an engineering victory on a grand scale. It is held up by corner posts of oak sixty-five feet long. But the technical feats, though they wring a salute, do not prolong wonder. Does it matter how the posts were searched for all over England, how they were jockeyed into position, and what weight they have supported for six hundred years? What does matter is the combined effect of bold strength and airy beauty.

There is a profusion of extraordinary things: the richly decorated Monks' and Priors' doors, the undercroft, the roof bosses, the carved misericords, the imaginative and capricious stone carving on the capitals and above the choir stalls (those Imps of Ely), and the fifteenth-century carved and painted transept ceilings. A gloomy day doesn't bring out the extravagant details. But on a sunlit day what you see may bring suddenly to mind that line from Shakespeare's *Henry* V: "The singing masons building roofs of gold."

Coming out of the cathedral, whether the sky be bright or dark, the military jets you can't see make themselves heard. They too are part of Christendom as we Christendumkopfs have made it.

There's little more for you in this lowly, stony town except St. Mary's Church, dating from 1215, and King's School, part of the cathedral precincts. We stood in grounds muddy from much rain and watched the rubber-booted schoolboys slosh to what looked like a reconditioned Elizabethan tithe-barn. We talked with a bright youngster who asked to look through the "Pictorial History of Ely Cathedral" we had bought in the church. He read about his school: "What better setting could one hope to find for a school? And who would exchange the lovely old buildings in which the boys live and work and play for any of our modern erections? Most of them date from the Middle Ages."

Our boy said he had been visiting a friend during the holidays. "He goes to that big new technological school near Hatfield House—you know it?" We did. "Well——" Yearning and envy were in that one word. Then the thin shoulders straightened and the clear young eyes accepted fate. "It's not the same thing at all, is it?" "No, not at all," we said gently. With gloomy pride he sloshed on to the Middle Ages.

Ely's history is weird. It was an island in the fens and on a muddy river populated by eels—an unlikely site for human habitation. Yet it was already hoary by the time William the Conqueror came up against Hereward the Wake. It had a double monastery of monks and nuns when the Venerable Bede was young. (He must have been a boy once.)

Long long ago, in Saxon times, the daughter of an East Anglian king was married to Tonbert, a lord of Mercia. She was Etheldreda, but her name was either *pronounced* Awdrey, or *was* Awdrey. It is sometimes hard to get Angle-and-Saxon affairs straight.

This lady refused to accord her husband the expected privileges. The story, pre-D. H. Lawrence, omits painful scenes and does not give Tonbert's reactions. What you next know is that he died. Etheldreda-Awdrey then did a most uncalled-for thing. She took another husband, this time King Egfrid of Northumberland. She gave him the same "Don't touch me!" treatment. Egfrid, either shorter-tempered or healthier than Tonbert, insisted. Etheldreda fled. Egfrid pursued. His hairy Northumbrian hands were stretched out to seize his reluctant bride when suddenly some waters (the chronicler neglected to warn us there were waters about) rose to foil him. Etheldreda was saved. Egfrid went back to Northumbria, pondering, and is heard from no more.

One assumes the chase took place over the marshes, and that the waters which rose to the rescue were of the eely river Ouse, because in honor of the miracle a nunnery rose on the Isle of Ely. Etheldreda was its founder and first abbess. She died there of a quinsy, or inflammation of the throat, contracted from kneeling from midnight to daybreak on cold, damp stone floors. But she laid her fatal illness to divine punishment for having fondly worn a necklace.

Ten years passed, and her sister, Sexburga (a name fraught with possibilities) discovered Etheldreda's body to be perfectly preserved; looked around; and by another miracle found a beautiful white shrine all ready for it. Sexburga became the second abbess. From the beginning, whoever touched the coffin was immediately healed of whatever ailed him. Pilgrims came in greater numbers than patients today to the Mayo Clinic.

When Sexburga died, her niece Ermenilda succeeded her, and she too died a devout virgin. These two were buried near Etheldreda—who by now was being definitely called St. Awdrey—and Ely had a peculiarly holy triple shrine of female saints. But in 870 the marauding Danes descended, sacked the place, half-destroyed the abbey church, and slaughtered the nuns.

Many decades later Dunstan gave Ely a new start as a Benedictine monastery. He built a church around the remains of the three saints. A fourth saint was soon added—Wihtburga, another sister of Etheldreda.

Wihtburga was an acquisition of Ely's abbot, Brihtnoth, a vigorous, Teddy-Roosevelt type. Seeking to increase Ely's sanctity potential, he took encoffined Wihtburga "not very reputably from its resting place at Dereham," says the "Pictorial History."

"Not very reputably" shyly conceals an epic of tenth-century body-snatching, the kind of enterprise that helped make the pilgrimage era lively.

Brihtnoth saw no reason why the minor-league monastery of Dereham should own the remains of Ely's great saint's sainted sister. He lost sleep. Finally he hatched an elaborate plot.

He and his monks made a festive trip to Dereham, inviting its monks and townsmen to "a feast of brotherly love." Not all the monks of Ely made the full trip; some waited in a boat on the Ouse.

Brihtnoth and his stalwarts wined and dined the Derehamites into a stupor, and in the stilly night lifted Wihtburga's coffin out of its shrine and made off with it. Twenty miles overland they had carried it, to the banks of the Ouse, when they heard the Derehamites panting in pursuit. They tumbled the saint and themselves into the waiting boat and began to row and pray frantically.

The men of Dereham intercepted the boat at a bend. Running along both banks they pelted the monks with clods of earth and stones. Some of the heroes suffered bruises and contusions, but they won the great race and Wihtburga. She was safe with them because Ely was well fortified.

A century later William the Conqueror, triumphant through most of England, stood among his men on land dry and firm enough to hold them and stared over the quaking, wetter land to the fortified, holy Isle of Ely. He faced no small problem. Ely would not surrender and could not be taken. Its Robin Hood—Hereward the Wake—from a camp in the miasmic marshes had long been waging successful guerrilla warfare against the Normans. Hereward had won the reputation of being a sorcerer.

The whole look and feel of the place, the ancient sanctity of the Isle, and the uncanny appearances and disappearances of Hereward and his band, filled the Normans with superstitious terror. William himself felt the dark enchantment, but he was experienced in taking impregnable strong-points. He settled his men to starve Ely out, and meanwhile busied them with building a three-mile road over the marshlands.

In due time an emaciated delegation from Ely came out ready to give up and to betray Hereward by showing the Normans the way to his camp. To prove their good will they brought along a sorceress who offered to work her powers against those of Hereward. William built a wooden tower in which he imprisoned the enchantress and had her pushed well ahead of his advance. Hereward couldn't resist setting fire to the tower. The Normans charged, and fought in the light of flames that revealed Hereward's position. The sorceress, forgotten, was left to burn. So ended the last organized resistance to the Conqueror.

William caused the present great church to be built around the hallowed Awdry-Etheldreda, Sexburga, Ermenilda and the stolen Wihtburga. Early in the twelfth century it was ready for the sainted four. Hordes of pilgrims were attracted, especially by the great fairs in June and October. As at Canterbury, there wasn't enough shrine-room for them. The apse had to be pulled down and the cathedral extended eastward with a six-bay presbytery in which a new shine was erected. In 1252 Awdrey-E. was "translated," Henry III coming to the dedication of the new shrine. If you ask, a verger will point out where it stood.

Around the octagon eight sculptured corbels (projections for supporting timbers and arches) portray scenes from the life of this Etheldreda the Unready. The illustrators did not choose the most interesting episodes.

Awdrey-Etheldreda has her reward on high. But on low, the English language has immortalized her in its own way. It has appropriated her name for the word *tawdry*.

Ely's great markets were called St. Awdrey's Fairs. In time this was elided to S'tawdry. Like all fairs they were crowded with stalls selling gimcrackery, fripperies, trinkets. *Tawdry* crept into the language as a designation for the kind of trash you get stuck with at a fair. So at long last the story comes full circle with the strange irony that a religiously virtuous woman who believed her death was punishment for wearing a necklace should have her name thus enshrined in the language.

You might call it an inverse miracle.

*TRAVEL FACTS* * Ely is forty-one miles from King's Lynn by rail, forty-five by road—a mere commuter's hop. Seventeen miles south is Cambridge. To Norwich is about eighty miles by rail.

There are frequent trains to Cambridge and London, so that if you arrive in Ely before noon you can give the cathedral two hours or so and catch the next train south—or north, or east.

## § *SUDDENLY, CAMBRIDGE*

In traveling, a change of scene and pace is just as welcome as it is in the routine of home and office. Such a change is yours if you go from Ely to Cambridge, a distance of seventeen miles.

Ely is heavy with old, unhappy, or hard-to-believe things, with impossible Brihtnoths and Wihtburgas, with faceless Angles and Saxons. The land is so flat as to be almost concave, more sky than landscape. Everything is so quiet you can hear the past tick.

And suddenly, Cambridge. Suddenly, because you don't merely arrive, you erupt into it. Cambridge is dynamic. It is movement, activity, youth, a living drama played against a marvelous backdrop that began building in the thirteenth century and faces not yesterday but tomorrow. "Many shall run about, and knowledge be increased," saith the Bible somewhere. And here are the many running about, mostly on bicycles—some dons breasting the wind with streaming beards—and knowledge is being increased like everything.

Milton and Pepys went to school here. So did Tennyson, Byron, Newton and Bacon, Wordsworth and Macaulay. In the Cavendish Laboratories behind Corpus Christi College, Thomson and Rutherford did their revolutionary work in physics, and the Russian Peter Kaptiza nursed along the idea that became the first sputnik. As the many run about, you can almost hear the final countdown, beginning with Erasmus and marking off the centuries to C. P. Snow of Christ's College.

Of course, if you come in the "long vac," the summer vacation, the effect is not the same. Then you erupt into fellow tourists who are running about on their own feet. Then Cambridge is merely beautiful.

"Oxford and Cambridge," people say—seldom, "Cambridge and Oxford." For not a few, however, Cambridge comes first as a tourist experience. The colleges are not as chaotically jumbled as at Oxford. Each displays itself more fully, and you feel less intrusive and more welcome among them. The town is pleasanter, Oxford having become industrialized. The river in summer is both a public way and an integral part of the university; you can go boating among the colleges. But—

Caparisons are odorous, as Mrs. Malaprop, without benefit of college education, said. If you ask us: "Which one should I visit, Oxford or Cambridge?" we must answer, "It would be a pity to miss either of them." If you then say: "But I haven't time for both. So which should it be?" we can only tell you that in our family the vote is a one-to-one tie.

We had a time taking you and ourselves around Oxford, if you remember. Oxford, in growing, had to compress itself within medieval walls. Cambridge, never walled, spread out gracefully and naturally. It is therefore easier to see. You can walk over much of it in a day, if your metatarsals are as sturdy as Gothic arches. Your program could run like this:

1. For orientation and preliminary survey, go up one side and down the other of the seven-eighths of a mile of main drag—a continuous thoroughfare changing name from south to north: Trumpington, King's Parade, Trinity Street, and St. John's Street.

The parade of colleges on this stretch, from Trumpington north, reads: Peterhouse, St. Catharine's (with Queen's behind it), King's (with Clare behind it), Caius, Trinity, St. John's. Across from St. Catharine's are Pembroke and Corpus Christi.

The oldest, structurally, is the part of Old Schools called Regent House. Old Schools (lecture halls) is between King's and Caius and behind the classical Senate House which serves for end-term ceremonies. (The oldest structure in Cambridge, actually, is the tower of St. Benet's Church in the street of that name, parts of which are absolutely Saxon.)

2. Go to King's College and, letting nothing else distract you, visit its chapel, which is on the north side of the Great Court, the one with the fountain in the middle. (By the way, where Oxford has quads, Cambridge has courts.)

King's College Chapel is a late stone-and-glass flowering of Renaissance (Perpendicular) Gothic. It is one of the most ornately beautiful structures of the Western world. The walls are mostly stained-glass window reaching from the floor almost to the intricately fan-vaulted roof eighty feet above. The sixteenth-century screen is a glorious wall of woodcarving. In every detail this chapel is a marvel. A church without aisles or pillars, it is daringly original.

King's College was founded by Henry VI in 1440 as the link of higher education to his Eton. You may remember poor Henry, half-crazed by his troubles (War of the Roses), rising above them just far enough to say to his Etonians, "Be good boys." As a young man he directed the planning of King's College Chapel and laid the first stone in 1446. Sixty years later Henry VII, the first Tudor king, visited Cambridge and was so excited by the half-built church that he not only took it in hand but left money for the work to go on after his death. Henry VIII finished it—on the screen are carved the arms and monogram of Anne Boleyn.

It gives one pause to think about that sixth Henry. Was an architect lost to the world because he had to be a king?

It gives one to think about the seventh Henry too. His reputation for miserliness had made him look small-souled.

Buy at a table the pamphlet, "King's College Chapel: Comments and Opinions"—pro and con from noted appraisers since 1564, Queen Elizabeth I being the first. It's hard to believe anyone could ever say a word against it. Yet here is one William Gilpin in 1769: "Its disproportion disgusts." And Sir Anthony Carlisle, 1804: "Its ornaments are in bad taste." Theirs was an age that misprized both Gothic and Shakespeare. At the other extreme is Wordsworth with three sonnets.

This superb church should be experienced in action as well as in repose. Don't miss the candlelit evensong at five-thirty. (Check on the time with the college porter.)

3. Concentrating on the west side of the main street, walk in the courts and go through to the Backs. Since you are at King's College, begin there. When you pass through the archway of the building at the west end of the Great Court, you find yourself on a dream of a lawn going down to the river Cam. This is King's piece of the Backs.

*The Backs* is the name given to the river frontage—the lawns, gardens, and meadows behind this row of college buildings. Here, where weeping willows bow down to the water and birches stand tall and little bridges curve above the shining river, may well be the loveliest man-made landscape in all England.

You can't walk along the full length of the Backs because there is no connection between one college and another. You keep going in and out. The colleges are beautiful and various enough to make this a pleasing exercise. You can float along the Backs on the river. If foolhardy, rent a punt—a clumsy boat which must be poled along. The unskilled finds his pole stuck in the mud, himself frantically hanging on it, the punt floating away. To be safer, rent a canoe. (Boat hire at Magdalene Bridge and at Mill Lane; summer.)

4. The main street runs into Bridge Street at St. John's. At this point you'll be tempted by the Round Church. Succumb. Go in and rest your weary feet. This is the Church of the Holy Sepulchre (one of four round churches in England), dating from 1130 and looking much older. While resting, buy and read the threepenny leaflet about the church.

But don't pass by St. John's College, the one with the heraldic gateway. It has a Bridge of Sighs over the Cam, and its courts are wonderful.

5. Walking west on Bridge Street, visit Magdalene (*Maudlin*) College. If you can be there during term between 2:30 and 3:30 P.M. you can see the Biblioteca Pepysiana, the library left to his alma mater by that excellent public servant, avid diarist, and confirmed flirt, Samuel Pepys. The original *Diary* in his original shorthand is there. The two courts of this college and the broad gardens beyond are delightful.

6. Visit Emmanuel College if you want to pay your respects to the memory of John Harvard, founder of the first American college. It's off St. Andrews Street. Christ's College is nearby.

*MISCELLANEA* * The Fitzwilliam Museum is that too-assertively classical building on Trumpington Street beyond Peterhouse College. As with the artist who hated the Eiffel tower in Paris and sat under it so that he wouldn't have to see it, so with the Fitzwilliam—the best way not to see it is to go inside and look at its treasures. It has a great collection of portraits, miniatures, paintings, period furniture, armor. . . . In Peterhouse College poet Thomas Gray ("Elegy in a Country Churchyard") had rooms in the building on the right in the first court. Having a phobia about fire, he set iron bars into the window on the court and kept a rope ladder handy to attach to the bars for easy exit. One night his fellow undergrads placed a tub of icy water below his window and raised a false alarm. It was a highly successful practical joke, but Gray, unamused, promptly moved to Pembroke College. The bars still mark the window. . . . Trinity, darling of Henry VIII, the largest and most famous of the colleges, has a magnificent court with fountain. . . . Clare College owns one of the prettiest gardens. . . . Hobson Street is named for the "Hobson's choice" man, who used to hire out his horses in a system of strict rotation. . . . In the neighborhood of Magdalene College are several picturesque old houses. There are others in the side streets and lanes, and around the market place. . . . The bookshops are tempting. When Mr. Sam Pepys revisited the scenes of his youth three hundred years ago—October 14-15, 1662—with a friend, they looked in on the Bear Inn, where a member of the University "told us how the room we were in was the room where Cromwell and his associated officers did begin to plot and act their mischiefs." Delightful to see that even back then people were curious in this tourist fashion. (Cambridge was two nights by horse from London.)

NOTABLE SHOP * Bacon's, tobacconist, here since 1810, is an institution. Among its customers were the brothers Tennyson, Edward VII, and the humorous poet Calverly—who penned verses to it. Ask within for Mr. Balham. He's a mine of information, is as friendly as you could possibly wish, and has a remarkable collection of pipes.

EVENTS * On Poppy Day, first or second Saturday in November, the town is taken over by the students, who stage every kind of stunt their nimble minds can devise in collecting for a civic fund. It's a day-long, town-wide rag of carnival hilarity which reveals that intellectual Cambridge can be as young-silly as any midwestern cow-college. Be sure to carry plenty of small change.

May Week is not a week but ten days, and slops over into June. Madrigals are sung from punts on the river near King's College. The Bumps take place—an exhausting game of boat collisions. Then come the Footlights Review and the May balls. Be warned that for this period every bed in town and outskirts is booked well in advance.

ENVIRONS * A pleasant walk of two and a half miles, about a mile of it along footpaths by the river Cam, brings you to Grantchester, the village loved by Rupert Brooke. You can pole or paddle out to it. Your destination should be the Orchard Tea Garden. If you'd like to do another mile, go on to the village of Trumpington for one of England's oldest inns, the Green Man (1340).

HOTELS * We stayed at and liked the Blue Boar (Trust House), an old inn which has the merit of being in the thick of things on that main street of many names. Students like it too and gather in its lounges. . . . The University Arms, grander, looked dull to us. So did the Royal (not grand) on Trumpington Street. . . . The Lion in Petty Curry, off the market, is a small inn with pride. . . . If you prefer something rural and yet in town, the garden-embowered Garden House may suit you.

When Lawrence tramped England on next to nothing, years ago, he stayed in a boardinghouse near the market, and found himself among student boarders from Wales, Kenya, Burma, and Italy. At mealtimes lively talk tumbled about, drawing him in. He had a wonderful, stimulating time. Recalling it, he demanded angrily of Sylvia in the Blue Boar's quiet dining room, "What in blazes are we doing in this place?" The answer, which Sylvia didn't bother to give, was, "We have more money now and less spirit of adventure."

If you can stay three days or more, try a boardinghouse or guest house for a rewarding Cambridge experience. They advertise and are listed in Cambridge's official guidebook.

RESTAURANTS, TEAROOMS * Another way of drawing within earshot of vibrant youth is to eat in restaurants favored by the students. One we liked for its exotic food as for its *brouhaha* was the Shahí, a bit of Pakistan in All Saints Passage near the Blue Boar. Here eat and argue all the colors the human race comes in, and not just the pink-gray mixture miscalled white. A pretty blonde is sitting at table with ebony Africans—and the world doesn't collapse! . . . The continued popularity of the Scotch Hoose on Market Hill speaks well for it. . . . The Dorothy is the best of the cafés. . . . For tea, try the Copper Kettle on King's Parade. For high tea on Saturday or Sunday, it's the Friar House on Benet Street. . . . There are sandwich-snack lunch and tea places.

TRAVEL FACTS  *  By the fast train London and Cambridge are only forty-five minutes apart. British Railways in combination with London Transport offers an inexpensive whole-day tour of Cambridge and Ely, and one of Cambridge alone. From Cambridge, long-distance buses go to the Midlands and the East Coast, and excursion buses in summer go everywhere on a variety of tours.

# 10. DERBYSHIRE,
# LINCOLN,
# AND NORTH
# TO THE ROMAN WALL

In northeastern England are things you wouldn't want to miss: York, Fountains Abbey, Derbyshire dales, and Yorkshire moors; dramatic dour Durham; and the lonesome Maginot line that the Emperor Hadrian's legions built.

Lincoln and Bakewell, the southern limits of the country dealt with in this section, are approximately halfway between the Channel and the Roman Wall.

For the carless, a circle tour would run like this: by train, London–Lincoln–York–Durham–Newcastle; then the Wall by bus; then train by way of Manchester or Sheffield to Buxton and Bakewell for the Derbyshire dales on your way back to London.

Alternatives: At the Wall you can carry on to a little short of its western end and start your return trip from Carlisle, northern gateway to the Lake District.

Of course it isn't necessary to begin this excursion from London. It's better to take off from some point farther north where you happen to be: Chester, Warwick, Ely.

## § DERBYSHIRE

Derbyshire is a midland county off by itself—not on the way or handy to any other place. Its attractions are Haddon Hall, Chatsworth, and the dales.

One of us wanted to go there for those two Stately Homes;

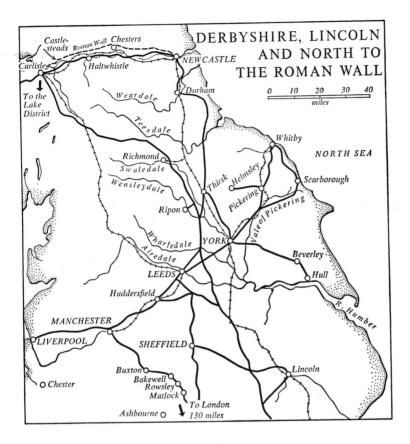

DERBYSHIRE, LINCOLN
AND NORTH TO
THE ROMAN WALL

Castle-steads  Roman Wall  Chesters
Carlisle
Haltwhistle
NEWCASTLE
To the Lake District
Weardale
Durham
Teesdale
0  10  20  30  40
miles

Whitby
NORTH SEA
Richmond
Swaledale
Wensleydale
Thirsk  Helmsley
Ripon
Pickering
Scarborough
Vale of Pickering
Wharfedale
Airedale
YORK
LEEDS
Beverley
Hull
Huddersfield
MANCHESTER
R. Humber
LIVERPOOL
SHEFFIELD
Buxton
Bakewell
Rowsley
Matlock
Lincoln
Chester
Ashbourne
To London
130 miles

the other, to walk in the dales. For both purposes Rowsley and
Bakewell are the centers.

Derby (*Darby*), the county seat, is of interest only if you want
to see how Rolls-Royce motors are made. The scenery begins a
few miles up the line at Amergate and Whatstandwell. At Matlock
it becomes dramatic. The railway (the road too) runs between
cliffs and tall hills clothed to the top in greenery—introduction to
the dale country.

The dale of the Wye (no relation to the Welsh one) all the
way to Buxton is fouled by the railway, its yard, and its black
soft-coal smoke. A local joke refers to the blot on the landscape
as National Rust Property. Luckily the trees grow tall and full.

Matlock is a spa in two distinct parts—Matlock and Matlock

373

Bath. The first is high and open, the second in a ravine. Once they were beautiful and unspoiled; you're thirty years too late for them. Pass on.

*ROWSLEY* * This scattered village found at the top of Darley Dale sounds Dickensian but isn't. Here the rivers Derwent and Wye come together. The fishing is esteemed. The village is important because of the good Peacock Inn with its garden and outstanding cuisine. Peacock guests have fishing rights to the piece of river belonging to Haddon Hall Estates.

Rowsley (*Rosely*) is a center for walks. We set out on one after tea. We went south of the village up into the hills around Stanton-in-Peak. Laburnum, masses of rhododendrons, and lowlier buttercups and daisies bloomed everywhere. A sunset rioted, twilight set in with a slim crescent moon, and we got back to the Peacock in time to devour an excellent dinner.

This walk had so much beauty in it that next morning we repeated it, with extras—Stanton Lees, Stanton Woodhouse, and down past the quarry by a footpath through open fields; some four miles in all.

In the afternoon we were about to set off, reluctantly, on the three-mile walk to Haddon Hall when a bus came along and took us there in five minutes.

*HADDON HALL* * Medieval mansion of the Dukes of Rutland, it ceased long ago to be lived in but, restored, is well kept up for sightseers. Its situation and gardens are superb. What brings the tourists here (the women, who bring their men) is the story of Dorothy Vernon and her elopement with Sir John Manners four hundred years ago. You can read all about it in a sentimental best-seller of many years ago—*Dorothy Vernon of Haddon Hall.* It didn't really happen, but it might just as well have. That novel has made Haddon Hall a romantic place. Almost everybody goes swoony here.

*BAKEWELL* * This town, four miles from Rowsley, is a major center for rucksacked ramblers and bus-trippers. About 150 years ago a Duke of Rutland tore down the old buildings and made a new town. It is all of dull gray stone and dark slate roofs.

The only buildings of interest are the parish church, Maurice Goldstone's antique shop, and the Rutland Arms Hotel.

Goldstone, a big, red-headed, splendidly bearded man, is a passionate antiquarian specializing in the medieval. He has been digging into and restoring his complicated house, which somehow escaped the building boom. Its oldest parts date back to 1280. He welcomes visitors and will be glad to show you round.

The church has a unique collection of Saxon gravestones, and the Vernon and Manners tombs. Note the tomb of Sir Thomas Wendesley in the Vernon Chapel—a full-size alabaster effigy of a knight who died in 1403. But above all, find the modest monument in the wall at the east end of the nave, south side, of Sir Godfrey Foljambe and his wife, 1377. There's something so intimate about it that in one moment it bridges the gap of centuries.

The Rutland Arms is a Regency structure on the site of an older inn, the White Horse. Jane Austen stayed here in 1811, seven years after the doors opened, and there's a Jane Austen bedroom. The hotel could be more attractive, but it does have an air. During redecorating, Regency red was discovered under some layers of paint, and reduplicated. It's a notable red.

As you travel about England, collecting local guidebooks, you find yourself in possession of some odd accounts of odd happenings. Bakewell's booklet is a prize item. In it, the high points of Bakewell's history run something like this:

Late 13th century: house now occupied by antique dealer built.
Late 18th century: Duke of Rutland tears down old town, rebuilds.
1796: the Great Riot.
Late 19th century: Bakewell Pudding invented.

The last two events are the most interesting.

Bakewell Pudding, well known in England, was contrived by accident in the Rutland Arms. Mrs. Greaves, the landlady, was giving her cook final directions for making strawberry tart: "Stir the egg mixture into the pastry shell, spread strawberry jam, and then—" At this moment her important guests arrived and claimed her attention. The cook poured the egg mixture *over the jam* and popped the thing into the oven. When it was served, Mrs. Greaves was horrified—but, my dear, the guests adored it and begged for the recipe. Ever since then Bakewell means *pudding* to the English. Sylvia asked our English friend Beryl Birch if the technical part of the tale made sense. Beryl said: "But of course. If the jam is on the bottom it's a pudding, and if it's on the top it's a tart. Everybody knows that!"

We were going to buy a Bakewell pudding in the local bakery, but it looked discouraging.

Now, about that riot of 1796. The local guidebook reports:

> In that year the Militia were being balloted for, and the inhabitants of the neighboring villages, believing that the county of Derby either raised more men or paid more money than other counties, assembled about 40 in number. raw-boned men with clubs, clot spades, miners' spades, etc., and marching up to the Town Hall made a speech signifying their intention of coming on the day the Magistrates met to oppose "the business."

If this isn't clear, never mind. The best follows:

> It was market day and the farmers and others were dining at the White Horse. The waitress, Sally Stevenson, came running in, exclaiming, "The mob is coming, the mob," upon which it was thought proper that no one should notice them. The mob asked to lend them a frying pan, which Mrs. Smith did. They then drank each a gill of ale, for which they paid, and marching down the town went away, no one in the town joining them in any way, but laughing heartily at them. . . .

As a result of a second sally of "the mob," in which they burned the Militia lists—in the frying pan?—the cavalry was called out, and "Quarter Sessions were removed to Derby and never again held at Bakewell."

The world may never know why the mob wanted a frying pan and what they did with it when they got it. However, the report is invaluable for its tip on what to do when being mobbed: take no notice.

*CHATSWORTH HOUSE* ∗ From the steps of the Rutland Arms, the Stately Home of the Dukes of Devonshire is an easy walk of three miles (some uphill work in the early stretch). But since the bus leaves from across the street, it takes a strong mind to resist riding for two-thirds of the way. (You can walk back, as we did.) Get off at The Cuttings. Amble down hill past Edensor (*Enzr*); across the road you find without difficulty the footpath through Chatsworth's superlatively beautiful park. The Cavendish family, Dukes of Devonshire, are among the highest peers in the land, although not among the most ancient. Chatsworth, their seat, is a huge pseudo-classic pile, luxurious and stately. In the eighteenth century it sheltered a passion more sophisticated and unconventional than the fictional Vernon-Manners affair. Then its lady was Georgiana, the great beauty of her day, painted by Gainsborough. Her dearest friend was Elizabeth Foster, her husband's mistress, and the three lived together in perfect amity. Elizabeth bore her lover two children, and on Georgiana's death inherited the widower, as Georgiana had hoped she would. The memory of this odd *ménage à trois* does no harm at Chatsworth's turnstiles. It's a human touch. Another is the matiness of the attendants, which nicely offsets the awesome fact that the treasures of Chatsworth are greater than those of any other private house in the land.

Either coming or going, visit Edensor, the model village built by a duke for the estate's hired hands, with a family-and-tenants church. It's a pretty village in soft brown stone, everywhere gardened. Mrs. Wood, who runs the little store-P.O.-tearoom, will cheerfully prepare something for you; and if you're too tired to walk back or wait for the Bakewell bus, Mr. Wood will taxi you. We walked, taking the country road behind the church. Do likewise if you possibly can.

*HOTELS* * You can make headquarters of either the Peacock at Rowsley or the Rutland Arms at Bakewell. The Peacock is the better hostelry, but Rowsley is only a hamlet. The Rutland Arms is poor in lounges and in food, but Bakewell has more interest than Rowsley. Solution: stay in both, as we did. At the Rutland Arms ask for a room in the main building. The annex down the street is grim. The Peacock also has an annex, across the road from the main building; better than that of the Rutland Arms, but there too you'll prefer to stay at the inn itself.

*MORE DALES* * Consider Dovedale. Lovely was the walk we did there some years ago, from Ashbourne up to around Hartington. Ashbourne is thirteen miles northwest of Derby, about the same distance southwest of Matlock. Its Green Man is a noted inn. The church has a touching marble monument to a child who died at five years eleven months, earning this epitaph: "The unfortunate parents ventured their all on this frail Bark, and the wreck was total."

If you'd like a couple of *joie-de-vivre* weeks tramping in perfect country, buy the Penguin guide, *Derbyshire and the Peak District*, join the Ramblers' Association, get the Ordnance Survey map of the Buxton–Matlock region, put the necessaries into a rucksack, and—afoot and lighthearted—take to the open road. If you have the strength, time, and inclination, you can walk all the way to the Scottish border, now that the Pennine Way is finished. A shorter but unusual trail is the seven-mile north–south footpath made of the former railway line from Hulme End on the Manifold River, just west of Hartington, to Waterhouses on the Hamps. From there you can catch a bus to some other beauty spot and conquer another segment of landscape. There are youth hostels and, of course, inns.

We hate being dogmatic—but unless you've done some cross-country tramping, how can you say you have known England?

*TRAVEL FACTS* * Bakewell is 153 miles and almost four hours by rail from St. Pancras station, London. Buses leave opposite the Rutland Arms for all the nearby beauty spots (chiefly south, west, and north), but also for Derby, Nottingham, Sheffield, and other cities. British Railways and London Transport offer a combined railway–motor-coach tour on certain Sundays in summer, leaving at 9:15 A.M. and returning in the evening, which takes in Dovedale, the Izaak Walton country, and the Peak, the fare a mere $3.40.

§ *LINCOLN*

County town that seventy thousand call home, Lincoln has two merits, neither transcendent. It has a famous cathedral. It is on the York–Durham–Edinburgh road.

What's wrong with Lincoln? It gives us the impression of

frowziness, of bad civic housekeeping. It's made a mess of its river frontage. Downtown is commonplace. The much-photographed sixteenth-century House on the Bridge (the not-too-good best tearoom in town) is remarkable only as a picture snapped from the tourist-inaccessible river below.

Strait Street is alleylike, and Steep Hill, which ought to be picturesque, looks sadly neglected. High Street peters out ignominiously. We seemed to meet mostly curt, unfriendly people.

Lincoln has a pleasant section—up on the height where the castle and its gardens keep company with the wide-shouldered cathedral. Here are also the two hotels, a bank in half-timber, and some nice lanes to wander in.

The cathedral is famed for its Angel choir, stained glass, carvings, gargoyles, misericords, the vast west front, and the central tower with its 5½-ton deep-toned bell, "Tom o' Lincoln." (Its bongs rank in mellowness with those of Big Ben and the bell in St. Peter's, Zürich.)

It's the only cathedral we know where admission-money is bullied from you. The choir is iron-fenced off and guarded by a verger who holds out to each entrant a medieval reticule. You could, of course, ignore it, but it would be an independent spirit indeed who would venture that. One always leaves a donation, but likes it to be voluntary; and that is the universal practice to which Lincoln is an exception. There is also something against the grain about the cassocked official's carefulness not to touch the proffered coin. Lawrence tried to put a shilling into his hand, but he drew it back quickly. Money is repulsive, but how necessary! Near the west door is a tablet:

This stone is erected by the Dean and Chapter in grateful recognition of many generous gifts from citizens of the United States of America and a grant of £20,000 from the Pilgrim Trust for the preservation of this cathedral church (1922–1932).

We wish the Pilgrim Trust would make its next gift to Norwich Cathedral, which needs it desperately.

Lincoln's great church is magnificently sited, and when the surly workers digging and hacking in the close are finished and go away, you will be able to enjoy the far-reaching view. The interior is disappointing. It feels empty, like a house that hasn't been lived in

for a long time but has been kept in repair, and dusted, and polished. Others may not feel this way. We were affected thus by
Salisbury's cathedral. It happens that both are in the Early English
style. Is it possible that E.E. is an adolescent Gothic compared to
Norman on the one side and Perpendicular on the other?

For us the interesting experience was dinner at the White Hart.
Our fellow diners were Provincial Society, with bells on. It was too
bad, we assured each other, that Anthony Trollope wasn't there to
watch and make notes. (By all means read the man's Barchester
novels before visiting an English cathedral town!) Such hats,
clothes, gestures, such business with gloves, such U-tone English!
At the table next to ours a fierce old dowager in black velvet and
precious stones banged the floor with her stick. How the headwaiter came running, how he cringed and massaged his palms! The
next act was set in the lounge, and as it filled with coffee-and-
liqueur sippers, it suddenly was something out of a very dated
Somerset Maugham comedy starring John Drew and Mrs. Patrick
Campbell. Lawrence, carried away, ordered port and watched for
gout to develop.

HOTELS  *  The White Hart, furnished with caressable antiques, has style and good service. It is evidently the haunt of the
Quality; the rates confirm it. The Eastgate, nearby, is the businessmen's choice. It's being extended.


# § YORK

"For my pleasure in the past," wrote William Dean Howells, "I
could not choose any place but York." To him it outranked Florence, Venice, Genoa, even Paris, as a city "where history is hos-
pitably at home and is not merely an unwilling guest."

This is to damn by overpraising. York is not all that wonderful.
But it's wonderful enough—one of the three most interesting pro-
vincial capitals of England, the others being Norwich and Chester.
It's the best of the three.

While ancient, York impresses as a young, dynamic city, very
much alive and in business. Vigor characterizes the walk, talk, gestures, and faces of the good burghers. We like the Yorkshire accent

in all its varieties. We like the directness of the Yorkshiremen who, if it is English to be reticent and reserved, aren't English. A friendly lot, rather American, we told each other; had second thoughts, and amended: "Like the best kind of Americans."

So the first good thing about York is that it is full of Yorkshiremen.

It has much else besides.

York is a walled city of 106,000 on the banks of the river Ouse, more medieval than modern in appearance, and with a cathedral as magnificent as Canterbury's but very different.

YORK MINSTER  *  The cathedral is the seat of England's No. 2 archbishop. Are you fed up with churches, great and small? Since we ourselves have been attacked by that feeling, we don't call it cultural defeatism and a sin. Soon we get our second wind. The ship rights itself.

In France as a young man in his twenties traveling the hard way, Robert Louis Stevenson wrote: "I find I never [he probably meant "seldom"] weary of great churches. It is my favorite kind of mountain scenery. Mankind was never so happily inspired as when it made a cathedral; a thing as single and specious as a statue at first glance, and yet, on examination, as lively and interesting as a forest in detail."

York Minster is no place for an attack of boredom. It is great "mountain scenery." If you are statistically inclined, be impressed by the fact that this is the largest of all English churches in area, covering sixty-one thousand square feet. Be impressed, further, by the wealth of medieval stained glass. Those windows, taken down for safety at the beginning of the first and second world wars, came to more than two hundred thousand pieces and took ten years to put together again. The jigsaw puzzle colossal!

And colossal is the word for the cathedral. It is a tremendous, powerful structure. It has the highest and widest nave in England, and the largest central tower. In one window alone—that at the east end—it displays, says an expert, "the greatest single area of fifteenth-century glass in Europe." It has a glorious fifteenth-century carved stone screen with wrought-iron gates, a beautifully light and graceful chapter house, a Norman crypt with weird hellish sculpture, and— Well, it's quite a cathedral.

If you're there on any but a warm day, take a sweater. The church can be chill enough to strike to the bone.

CATHEDRAL VICINITY * York Minster was a secular—nonmonastic—cathedral, which means it has no cloisters or remains of monastic buildings; no close or precincts to speak of. But its south side and west front stand right on the Middle Ages. The old houses of Petergate, Duncombe Place, and Stonegate crowd up against it, and on the fourth side, off Dean's Park, are the Treasurer's House and College Street.

The Treasurer's House used to be the residence of the Minster's treasurer. It's been through many hands and while keeping some of its original features shows "parlor and bedroom" architecture and furnishings of many periods—a remarkable house for its small size. The National Trust recently acquired it, and keeps it open daily 10 to 1, 2 to 6 (shorter hours in winter).

College Street is a short curved lane with Williams College on it (1461; open to the public, just ring for the caretaker), Tudor buildings, an old house bridging it at one end, and a small garden to set all off. It's a lovely little street.

Stonegate, a long, narrow, and busy shopping street, is one of the most pleasing in York for its variety of shops and buildings. You'll probably find yourself walking up and down it many times. In the eighteenth century it was the street of coffee houses. Look for the house with the gargoyle, the Stonegate Devil.

THE WALL * It almost, but not quite, encloses the city. Stronghold of the Sixth Legion, York was walled from Roman times, and before that was probably earth-walled by the tribes the Romans pushed out. The eastern tower near Monk Bar and the Multangular Tower in the Museum Gardens, dating from 200–400 A.D., were part of the Roman fort.

The present fortifications are of the thirteenth and fourteenth centuries. If you enjoyed Chester's wall you will like this one even better. It's more open, more green and flowery in outlook, and altogether more jolly. If you have to ration time or energy, confine your mural promenade to the stretch between Bootham Bar and Monk Bar, which can be strolled in half an hour. It includes the Lord Mayor's Walk, which gives the best over-all view of the

cathedral—a view enhanced by the lawns and gardens of the deanery and various old houses.

The wall and its moat are so attractive it isn't easy to realize
how serious and bloody a thing we have here. York was a Roman,
then a Saxon, then a Danish, then a Norman garrison town. Under
the Normans it was in the midst of a people who would gladly
have slit the usurpers' throats—and in fact did, and so ably that
the Normans finally gathered in force, sallied out, and slaughtered,
burned, ravaged for years before what was left of the North Folk
settled down.

Micklegate in the south wall was the favored bastion for expos-
ing the heads of traitors and rebels. It is also the spot where the
city fathers met Royalty and escorted It in colorful procession
into the city. All four Bars (gates) used to have drawbridges and
barbicans. Walmgate alone still has its barbican.

The wall is popular not only with tourists but also with the
Yorkshiremen. On it you meet lovers, promenaders, family picnic
parties, schoolchildren, and hikers bent under rucksacks. On a summer Sunday it's crowded (watch your footing) while the broad
river promenade below goes begging.

For a humorous touch, note the tower at Lendal Bridge—which
is frankly and unashamedly "Ye Olde Novelty Shoppe." And
there's an unexpected treat between this and the Royal Station
Hotel. It's that hideous Victorian red-brick building, part cock-
eyed Gothic, part pseudo-Arabic. Look above its upper windows
and you'll see stone-carved letters telling of days great-grandfather
knew: "Botterill's Horse and Carriage Repository." A large cloth
sign below announcing "Used Cars and Car Hire" is twentieth-
century non-Gothic.

OLD HOUSES, OLDER STREETS  *  In York
the old houses come not singly but in battalions. Most famous is
the little street called The Shambles. In medieval times it was the
street of the butchers, and right merrily must it have smelled with
the slaughter yards behind. Two meat markets still do business
here but they may not last much longer. The Shambles is so heavily
touristed that it has become a street of artsy crafts and curio shops.
At least nine hundred years old, it may well be the oldest intact
row of houses in England. In some places the upper projecting

gables of facing houses are only a yard apart. "Dear, we're invited to the Robinsons. 'Don't dress,' they say, 'and just come by the window.'"

Off The Shambles is Little Shambles, a side alley opening onto a square which on Saturday is jammed with a market and crowds cheerfully making a shambles of it. In olden times when York was cramped inside its walls, nearly all of it consisted of narrow streets like The Shambles, Stonegate, and Goodramgate, shutting out the sky and keeping in foul odors. The Middle Ages weren't sanitary. But have no fear of York today; it's kempt and couth.

The Pavement is a broad short street between The Shambles and All Saints Church, and at the Shambles end of it is Whip-ma-whop-ma Gate, of note principally for its name. A gallows used to stand on The Pavement.

On St. Helen's Square is the guild hall. It was a beautiful little stone building of 1440, its hall ornamented by supporting pillars each made of a single oak tree. It was almost entirely destroyed by bombs during the war. Rebuilt, its hall is a fine replica of the old, plus heat and light. You'll want to see it. We were arrested by a sign outside: MR. LONGBOTTOM INTERVIEWS. It turned out that the local M.P. was making himself available to constituents.

The Assembly Rooms, eighteenth-century, built for functions aristocratic and genteel, were a discovery of ours when we were tracking Madame Tussaud (the waxworks woman) around England 130 years late for a novel Sylvia subsequently wrote. In the grand Egyptian Room of this building Mme T. exhibited her waxworks on a barnstorming tour before settling down in London.

MUSEUMS * Wait! Don't skip this. *Museum* is not a depressing word in York. We know of no other city that offers such first-rate entertainment in the museum line.

1. The Castle Museum is the world's most friendly, intimate, and ingenious. Its high point is the part called The Street, which is not just one street but a complex that gives the impression of a whole town, life-size and in a state of suspended animation. There are cobblestones under foot, and on that main street, under oriel windows, bow-fronted shops, and half-timbered houses, a hansom cab with horse and top-hatted coachman waits for a passenger to come out of the hairdresser's. (Hansom, who invented the cab,

was born in York.) A sparrow realer than real sits on a lamppost. Here's an inn, a post office, a fire-station, an apothecary, Terry's the confectioner with a huge christening cake in his window. The cobbler sits in his shop bent over his work, and James Brown the Saddler is waiting for custom. The displays in the shops' windows are so tempting you want to go in and buy.

In this perfect reproduction, this "street where time stands still," children go starry-eyed and grownups become as children. Such is its enchantment that whenever we visit it Sylvia is afraid she'll forget her age and will have to be dragged out kicking and bawling.

Lawrence it affects in another way. Why, he asks in hot indignation, don't we have such museums in the States? The English, says he, have these houses and shops and streets all around them; we don't. For the price of one superbomber—he cries—or one nuclear submarine, or even one nagging but useless congressional investigation, any number of American cities could have The Street of their own past, providing education and delight in one stroke.

But The Street is only a part of the Castle Museum. Even its more run-of-the-mill sections show treasures so well arranged as to make you blissful well before the climax. Take the reproduction of period rooms upstairs—that marvelous Victorian parlor, for one. And that Yorkshire moorland cottage which gives you quite a turn because of the dog lying on the hearthrug and looking straight into your eyes with friendly inquiry. Then there are the fans, and the valentines, and the pincushions, and the Victorian jewelry, and many other joys, whole galleries of them.

SPECIAL NOTE. In the Agricultural Gallery, look for the box with the sign YORKSHIRE DIALECTS. PRESS HERE AND WAIT A FEW SECONDS. Follow the directions.

The museum owes its being to Dr. John Kirk, a physician with a hobby of collecting folk items and with definite ideas about how they should be displayed. Before he died in 1940, he realized his dearest ambition. You see his "office" in The Street.

2. The Debtors' Prison. The building which houses the Castle Museum used to be the Female Prison. The Debtors' Prison is at right angles to it, facing Clifford's Tower, which is all that remains of the castle itself. It might be better to see the Debtors' Prison first, because after the Castle Museum it's bound to be a let-down. Yet it has its fascination—the original prison and craft workshops

on exhibition on the ground floor; upstairs, period costumes, uniforms, toys, arms and armor.

3. The Railway Museum. It's off Queen's Street a quarter of a mile south of the railroad station, and displays steam locomotives from Stephenson's first on to the great express engines of the recent past. Here's another place that children love. It's great fun to watch them, the younger ones clambering up into the cabs and pretending to be engineers, the older ones listening soberly to the attendant's lecture. There's another railway museum of smaller, more technical objects near that Horse and Carriage Repository.

4. The Museum Gardens. Near Lendal Bridge, this charming retreat contains, in an expanse of lawn and flowers, the remains of St. Mary's Abbey, once a wealthy and powerful Benedictine foundation going back to 1080. Here you also find the Multangular Tower (Roman) and the Yorkshire Museum. Mainly archeological, this museum's main feature is Roman relics dug up hereabouts. The digging still goes on. A piece of Roman wall has recently been uncovered.

The Gardens are haunted by peafowl. When we were there, the peacock gave us a display of shocking temper. He shrieked, he displayed his remarkable spread of feathers, he quivered, he strutted ragefully, he hopped up on a sill of the museum building and pecked at the window. Through all this commotion the peahen, his mate, paid not the slightest heed. Under his very beak she kept pecking away at the ground like a housewife getting on with the chores. Lawrence, whose father was an upholsterer, informed the irascible peacock that he looked like a bird badly stuffed in a dark cellar by an amateur taxidermist who was slightly drunk and had broken his eyeglasses. We left the stupid creature screaming curses.

SHOPPING HINT.   Hunter & Smallpage, producer of heraldic emblems, flags, shields, etc., get out a tablecloth designed with a heraldic map of England. A sample hangs in the corridor.

SIGHTSEEING NOTES.   The Tourist Information Bureau, which has folders, booklets, a good staff, is in the Museum Gardens near the entrance. They supply honorary city guides (no fee, no tipping), but you have to apply well in advance; guides are usually taken up by large parties. . . . In summer there are excursions by river launch. Buses go to villages roundabout.

*HOTEL* * The Royal Station Hotel is beside the railroad station, within ten minutes' walking distance of St. Helen's Square. It's something of a monstrosity (enormous), and overpriced too. But it's *the* hotel. Ask for a room facing the gardens. It will give you a view of a piece of city wall and the cathedral. Rooms on the other side overlook (and overhear) the railroad station.

*RESTAURANTS, TEAROOMS* * Terry's and Betty's face each other across St. Helen's Square. Most English towns don't have even one good restaurant—York has two. Terry's is an institution. It grew out of the little confectionery shop you see reproduced in the Castle Museum. To cater a royal wedding reception with two thousand guests, as it did in 1961 when a member of the royal family married a Yorkshire girl, is nothing at all to Terry's. It can also take care of you and your humbler wants. It serves lunches and teas, but doesn't restrict you to either by the clock. It also has a bakery, and is still a candy-maker; Terry's chocolates are famous. But alas, Terry's won't give you dinner; it closes at about five-thirty.

That's where Betty's comes in. Saturday-night dinner at Betty's is an experience. You book in advance, and even so have to wait in the bar-lounge for a table to be vacated. In the jam-packed dining room excellent food is served with acrobatic agility by a team of Italian waiters captained by an Italian maestro who supervises the cooking of specialties at table and who cares nought for his life so long as your dinner is a success. The place resounds with talk and laughter. We tried the *tournedos* made at the table. There was hardly space for both our waiter and the *maître* who was on hand to coach with his eyebrows, and the *maître* almost went up in flames, but nonchalantly wiped the fire from his sleeves and carried on.

*TRAVEL FACTS* * York is midway between London and Edinburgh, or about two hundred miles from either, and is on the main line. The crack express train makes it in three and a half hours.

*ENVIRONS* * Castle Howard, twelve miles north, is an eighteenth-century Stately Home, seat of the Earl of Carlisle; open in summer on Wednesday, Thursday, and Sunday, afternoons only. . . . Beverley, twenty-nine miles east and a little south, is a market town with one big tourist attraction—the Beverley Minster, "largest parish church in England." It is in fact larger and grander than some cathedrals, with the greatest number of misericords of any church. Misericords are our passion, but having saved a Sunday for Beverley we found there was no train to it that day; nor could railway Enquiries explain why. And by then it was too late to take the bus. If driving, take road A1079. . . . Harrogate, twenty-two miles west, is a spa, the Bath and Cheltenham of the North, but not so distinctive. . . . To the north: Helmsley, various ruined abbeys, unspoiled dales. Daily bus tours in summer, but here's a region that shouldn't be done in a hurry. (See next section.)

NOTE.    The greatest thing hereabouts is Fountains Abbey, about twenty-five miles northwest of York. It's four miles from the town of Ripon, but you won't want to stay in Ripon. If you want to do Fountains Abbey from York, take an excursion bus. There's no problem if you have your own car; there is if you hire one with driver because of the time you'll want to spend at the abbey. We did it in a lazy, roundabout way—next section tells all.

## § RURAL YORKSHIRE

The Helmsley bus shot out of York into the wide flat plain of York Vale populated with red-brick villages. Helmsley is twenty-five miles from York. We expected to make it in an hour—maybe less, at that smart pace. An hour later we were wiser.

Abruptly, the country changed from flatland to hilly, the villages from red brick to stone, the roads from straight bands to narrow curving ribbons. The change is from the plain to the dale. A dale is something definite—a system of green and wooded hills watered by streams flowing down from higher hills, and usually named for its principal river. This one was Rye Dale.

But no driving difficulties delayed our bus. It had errands to run. It turned off its route to visit the village of Huby, deposited a mother, pram, and child, and bumped back again. It made a longer side trip through Oswaldkirk and Ampleforth to deliver shoppers with parcels.

We learned that Yorkshiremen of vale and dale have a special fondness for the Reliance bus line. Its motto is, "We never leave a passenger behind," and it enjoys rush-hour hassles with the York police for packing in yet one more over the legal limit. It is obliging. If Miss Oliver of Easingwold has news for Aunt Jane in Stillington, she informs the conductor, and there's a pause while Miss Oliver and Aunt Jane get together. If Mr. Smith in Helmsley wants to make a certain train in York some minutes before the usual bus-arrival time and gets his request in before Mrs. Green, who has an errand in Crayke, Mrs. Green makes other plans and a somewhat shaken busload arrives early in York.

The conductors are women. They know family affairs as the captain of a coastal vessel knows the underwater hazards. They grow old in the service; they don't quit. Every night but Sunday the last bus out of York (the 10:15) for Helmsley stops at Easingwold for fish and chips. The Reliance is like an Emmett railway, except that it's a busway—the ideal way to enter rural Yorkshire.

We were glad to be out in the country again, away from pavements and crowds. Fickle? Disloyal to York? No—merely making the best of both worlds. We were looking forward to Helmsley. It was *off the beaten track*—magic phrase.

Meanwhile, we observed that Ampleforth has a large, modern Benedictine priory and school on which extensive new work was being done. A monastic comeback? Has the wheel come full circle? Ampleforth looks interesting.

We were deposited in Helmsley in a little over two hours out of York.

*HELMSLEY* ＊ The big square has a small market cross in it. This is trumped by a monument to an Earl of Feversham (rhymes with *ever*), said to be a mortification to the region's present earl and boss-landlord. On one side we spotted "Ye Olde Police Station Snack Bar." But the square's ornament was the Black Swan.

Let us say at once that the Black Swan is the best-run and most hospitable inn that ever slept and fed us. Its folder says its great attraction is friendliness. This is true. It also gave us the most charming room (with bath). The Black Swan has architectural interest. It is three buildings thrown into one—the original inn, some four hundred years old; a Georgian house; and a half-timbered cottage next to that. Finally, the meals are good and excellently served. Packed lunches are available for trippers.

So we were not surprised when we came out, after having had our tea, to find no less than eight excursion buses disgorging their loads. Off the beaten track? We had a good laugh. No village with such an inn (and two more getting the spill-over business) could be off the beaten track.

Helmsley is an attractive, rambling river village in the heart of the dale. The high hills around, blue in the distance, are the Clevelands and the Hambletons. It's a friendly place. Poking about, we were greeted by a housewife at her door. She kept up a local-lore conversation although carrying a heavy load of firewood. We must have stood there ten minutes in talk, with Lawrence offering to carry the wood and she tossing the suggestion aside. Suddenly she dashed into the house, and the next minute popped out sans firewood but with a bunch of lilies-of-the-valley for Sylvia.

We had a chat with the railway stationmaster digging in his garden, which resulted in a pleasant at-home evening with his family. The railway here has abandoned passenger service except for special excursions. Nunnington station along the line has been turned into a guest house.

Helmsley has some sights—the old parish church with colorful wall paintings, the ruins of a castle, and Duncombe Park. Deep in the park, which is always open, stands the Feversham manor house, now a girls' school. Then there's Gate Street. Walk from the bottom to the top—slowly. The river, narrowly channeled, runs along the side with houses by it, and by the small bridge the houses form a highly picturesque cluster, making a study in steeply slanted, red-tiled roofs and mellow gray stone. Cézanne would have set his easel down there.

*RIEVAULX ABBEY* ✷ Three miles from Helmsley, and in the loveliest country of this dale, are the ruins of a twelfth-century Cistercian abbey. You can walk to them, or drive. Mount first to the terrace—a high promenade laid out by the earl with a pseudo-Grecian temple at each end. It provides ecstatic views. Then you amble down to the ruins. They are idyllic.

*WHITBY* ✳ Having heard much of the "quaint" fishing town on the North Sea, we set out from Helmsley on a day's self-made excursion. We took a bus to Pickering, changed there to another for Whitby. Pickering is a stone town chiefly notable for the fact that it did *not* give Dr. Kirk, who lived there, a home for his museum—the one that is now the great Castle Museum in York. It has a good church and some remains of a castle.

From Pickering the bus rolled across the Yorkshire moor—a wild, scrubby, lonesome expanse cut by minor canyons and the mysterious Hole of Horcum. The heather, dull in spring, covers all the moor with purple in fall. We had bright yellow gorse along the way, and leaping lambs. In its somber way the moor is magnificent. The bus wound and unwound, dived down a grade of 1 in 4.5 and up another equally steep with a hairpin turn in it on the edge of nothing. The high point is Goathland, a village with a hotel which is holiday headquarters for people who like moors.

We returned to Pickering (taking bus from there to Helmsley) by one of those new diesel trains which provide optimum views. Our seats were right up front with nothing but glass—a picture window—between us and nature. Where the bus follows the high-road the railway takes the low, snaking through Esk Dale along its river. This was as enjoyable a train trip as we have ever made. In the soft, green, low hills, one would never guess the wild moor was right above.

Oh—and Whitby?

It's a *lumpen* seaside resort slightly quainter than Coney Island.

ASIDE ON SCARBOROUGH. Scarborough (Charles Laughton came from there) is the most popular seaside resort of the North. The English seaside resort is no American tourist lure—but we were tempted by this one.

Toward the end of January in Scarborough a bus queue heard the cuckoo.

Now, in England when the new year brings mild weather everyone listens for the cuckoo. There's a kind of competition to be first to hear him and to write a thrilled, triumphant letter to the *Times* or the local paper—for though his note is inane he is harbinger of spring. But a cuckoo in January in northeast England? Either that bird was out of his mind or the listeners were out of

theirs. Reporters flocked to Scarborough. No question about it—
front-page news. Everyone in the queue had heard the bird. Someone had been saying, "Well, the time is drawing near when we
shall hear the welcome note of the cuckoo." Two minutes later,
from the park behind the bus stop, the voice of the cuckoo was
heard in the land. The queue had swiftly deputized two reliable
bird men of their number to scout. They saw no cuckoo, only an
elderly road-cleaner tidying up the gutter.

The next morning, and the next, it happened again. Even skep-
tical reporters heard the cuckoo. Who was this bird, earliest of
historical record, who dared bare his throat to January's North
Sea air?

The police came into the case. In England such matters are taken
seriously. They laid a trap, and into it fell the road-cleaner. At the
station he made a clean breast of it. "I heard 'em wishin' for the
cuckoo, and thought there'd be no harm in pleasing 'em. So I hid
in the bushes and did the cuckoo."

He compounded his crime by adding: "I used to do the nightingale when I had me teeth in."

Now, who wouldn't go out of his way to see a town where a
human, friendly thing like that happens? It's worth a castle, an
abbey, and sixteen assorted magpies.

But we were unable to crowd Scarborough into our itinerary.

*HELMSLEY TO RIPON*  *  If you want to see as much
as possible of this part of Yorkshire, hire a car with driver. If you
have your own car, note these places for routing: Rievaulx–Scotton–
Sutton Bank–Byland–Newburgh Priory–Coxwold–Kilburn–Thirsk–
Ripon.

In Helmsley we approached Mr. Butler, who has a car-hire business, and he himself was our chauffeur. He knows and loves the
country, and understands what a tourist wants to see. A chauffered
trip of seventy miles costs just under ten dollars—a lot to pay for
mere transportation, but not for a zigzag tour that can't handily
be done any other way, and not when the driver is also an intelligent guide. Have an advance understanding about stopover time
at the various sights. In the mileage you have to count the car's
return, with or without you, to home base.

Now, the trip itself. By way of Scotton you go up to 1000–1200 feet, among firs and low stone walls, and feel on top of the world. On the right is Hambleton Heath, an expanse of springy turf where race horses are trained—Hambleton stables are among the oldest in England. The great place is the Sutton Bank, a little farther along. It's a gap in the Hambleton Hills with great views over York Vale, and the cliff which serves the Yorkshire Gliding Club. The gliders push off over the cliff, being held aloft by undercurrents of air. The Bank is a favorite spot for picnickers.

Mr. Butler, having brought us to see the Bank, backtracked, and then branched off on the road to Wath and Byland. Wath Bank provides another grand view. Byland has another ruined abbey like that of Rievaulx, but not as lovely.

Newburgh Priory is a little piece out of the way. A handsome place, unruined, it is sometimes open to the public. It wasn't for us, but even from the outside it is worth a look and a few extra miles.

Coxwold is reputed to be the prettiest village hereabouts. (We prefer Helmsley.) It's a one-street village rising to its church; view from churchyard, and the church itself is interesting. Across the road is Shandy Hall (plaque), where Laurence Sterne, that unclerical cleric, wrote *Tristram Shandy* while holding down a living in the church.

It is out of Byland that you begin to see the White Horse of Kilburn on its hill. You see it more clearly from Coxwold to Kilburn. Said Mr. Butler: "Twelve people can stand on its eye."

You may be amazed to see huge stacks of wood in Kilburn village. A lumberyard? In a way. Kilburn is the village of the Mouse Man. Robert Thompson, a self-made artist in carpentry, adopted the title in the days when they called him poor as a church mouse. He began to carve a wee mouse into the tables, chairs, and even the choir stalls he turned out to order. With that gimmick and his skill he never looked back. Since he was called by the Eternal Carpenter, his grandsons Robert and John have been carrying on as Robert Thompson Craftsmen, Ltd., with thirty-three workmen drawn from a radius of six miles. The work is first-rate and is known to Americans, some of whom have ordered whole suites of furniture. We contented ourselves with a cheese board, very appropriate with that mouse on it.

Kilburn is part stone, part red brick. The ride is now in the vast bowl of the plain and through Thirsk—mildly interesting, its name remarked upon by the witty as "a penchant for Russian vodka"—to Ripon.

*Ripon* is the key stop on this trip. It goes back to the seventh century, has a small, squat cathedral with a Saxon crypt, and a little museum in the thirteenth-century Wakeman's House. The blowing of the wakeman's horn is one of those survivals dear to England. Wearing a three-cornered hat, the wakeman (watchman) blows that horn at the mayor's house and the market cross every evening at nine.

This town on the river Skell is gateway to Nidderdale and the moorlands, to Ilkley and Wharfedale and Wensleydale. These dales, more lonesome than Rye Dale or the Derbyshire dales, are made for walkers.

The importance of Ripon, however, is its proximity to

*FOUNTAINS ABBEY* ∗ This awesome Cistercian ruin, four miles from Ripon, is one of the most glorious in one of the most beautiful situations in England. It is probably more imposing in its ruined state than it ever was whole. The floors of the abbey church, cloisters, and extensive monastic buildings are of the greenest turf. The pillars and arches frame wooded hills. The river Skell flows by and under. It is a vast garden of rest and dream.

Give yourself plenty of time for Fountains Abbey. One could dream away an afternoon here—but not in the tourist season. The admission price also includes Fountains Hall, a Jacobean manor house.

You can stay overnight in Ripon. *Hotels.* The Unicorn, the Old Deanery. They are so-so.

We preferred to go on to

*RICHMOND* ∗ High above the river Swale, and with a ruined castle giving views up and down the river, Richmond, by all we had heard and read, should have been at the least "charming," at the best, "the most medieval-looking town in England." It is neither.

There's a big bare-looking market place; our hotel was on it, and also derelict Trinity Church from which the curfew is rung. Much of the town looks like a stone-built slum. We hunted and found the Theater Royal—a tiny thing, built 1788 and the second oldest in England. Half a dozen workmen were sitting on a stage littered with tools and lumber, having their lunch. They all stared —here a hand with sandwich was frozen halfway in transit, there a mouth fell open in midbite. They looked like Pirandello characters struck to stone. Lawrence bravely said, "Good afternoon." No one moved so much as an eyelash. We fled.

Most of Richmond is something like that. Its air is bleak. It has the feel of having been forgotten and of having decided, in revenge, to ignore you.

When the time came for us to catch our train to Durham, the entire hotel staff—manager, receptionist, porter, had disappeared. The policeman in the square was new to the place and didn't know where a taxi might be found. There was a hearse in the garage around the corner. We'd have taken that, but the driver was elsewhere. We had to give up that train, and by inquiring of the bus drivers in the square found a bus that would take us and luggage to the station.

For goodbye we wished we could have read the manager, when he appeared, a passage from our R. L. Stevenson book: "They [the innkeepers] had taken so little notice of me that I hardly thought they would have condescended on a bill. But they did, with some smart particulars, too."

*Hotel*. The King's Head. May they do better by you than they did by us.


§ *DURHAM*

Durham was gray and grim under a grim-gray sky that seemed permanently fixed over it. Somehow dark weather fits the ancient fortress town. As we checked in at the Three Tuns we asked the receptionist, "Does the sun ever shine here?"

"Oh yes," she said brightly. "We saw it one day only nine weeks ago."

You go to Durham (rhymes with *purr-em*) primarily for the magisterial cathedral. Its architecture speaks eloquently of harsh old times, of terror in the land, of tyranny and bloodshed. The view from the train windows as you come from the south is impressive. The great stone pile crouches on its craggy height above the loop of the river Wear, the castle behind it just as formidable. They were both fortresses, built here in the far north by the Conqueror's baronial and episcopal lieutenants to keep back the Picts and Scots—those northern clans who caused so much trouble that the ancient Britons imported Hengist and Horsa from across the North Sea as allies, to their later regret.

The castle burned, was rebuilt, crumbled, rose again. The church stands intact. Its cut is heavy no-nonsense Norman. It is the Church Militant; its bishops were counts Palatine, barons temporal as well as spiritual. Here and there later centuries have tampered with the original massiveness and softened it, but it remains Norman. Its Chapel of the Nine Altars is distinctive, and the nave, "Galilee," and choir are asterisked Sights. Look for the rich golden clock in one transept—frivolous time in a monument to timelessness—the tomb of the Venerable Bede, St. Cuthbert's shrine; and find in the cloisters the tablet which bears these words

Remember in these cloisters which were finished in his day
JOHN WASHINGTON
of Washington in this county, Prior of this Cathedral
Church 1416–1446, and whose family has won an everlasting
name in lands to him unknown.

Between cathedral and castle spreads the Palace Green, bordered by old stone buildings. Here where knights and clerics used to brawl, students are tearing about. We were surprised to learn that the old buildings are part of the University of Durham. The only Durham University we had known was the one Bull Durham built, out of tobacco profits, down in Dixie.

After doing the cathedral we went to the castle. When we had paid our fee, the gatekeeper pushed a bell-button and, pointing out a doorway across the courtyard, told us to go there to wait for a guide. While we waited, students flowed and surged by and around us. We couldn't figure out what they were doing in the castle itself.

A pert blonde girl of about eighteen, in a trim red smock, materialized and introduced herself briskly as our guide. Off we went, with guide rattling off the mechanical kind of information that goes in one ear and out the other. "And this is the castle kitchen, 1499," she was saying, when suddenly her voice altered and she confided in her natural tone—"Isn't it lucky it's 1499? I *do* think that's a much better date than 1500, don't you?" We agreed. The next moment she had resumed her formal guide's manner and we proceeded to the Great Hall. Our faces must have betrayed that it wasn't up to Oxford-Cambridge standards. Miss Smock said hastily:

"It's been lengthened and shortened many times, you see, and now it's shorter than before, when it was longer, but they are going to make it longer than it was before the last time when— Oh dear!"

We said it was very clear, and she rewarded us with an enchanting smile.

We came to a useless but beautifully stoneworked archway. "This is the greatest Norman doorway in England," she said, and her tone again slipped—"and the Victorians or somebody plastered it over and hid it because it was barbaric for them, and it was the original entrance to the castle. Isn't it lovely?"

It was. But by now we were thoroughly confused, not so much by our delightful chameleon of a guide as by what we were seeing. Nothing looked castlelike; nor did the halls, corridors, galleries, stairways, seem to make up any known kind of building.

"Where," we asked the dear girl, "*is* the castle? Where *are* we?"

She laughed. "Oh, this is the castle, sort of—it's in bits and pieces all around us, and through, and under. It's come down many times and gone up again, and once it was up people would shear a part off, or tack a part on, or plaster something over, or dig something out."

Unless you have as good a guide as ours turned out to be, you'll be bewildered by Durham Castle. The university and the castle are all mixed up together. This is a castle in a university, a university in a castle.

As if that isn't puzzling enough, the castle also serves as a bishop's palace, and as the Assizes headquarters. That is, parts of it are bishop's quarters, and other quarters are set aside for the judges and staff of the traveling Assizes. Our Miss Smock confided that everyone was in a dither because the court was to sit in two days, and it had been discovered that they were bringing one judge too many for the old quarters. He was going to have to sleep in the dining room.

But most of the castle serves as dormitory for students who, as against those lodged elsewhere, are distinguished by the title of Castlemen. Every year they perform an original show on the castle steps. Said our guide: "They always have good weather for the performance. That's what it is to be a Castleman!"

The students have a TV lounge in the undercroft. They have a Victorian chapel, and the bellows of its organ are in a bathroom of the Norman gallery, which before it was a bathroom was used to store coal. One Old Boy who returned to visit his alma mater was shocked at the bathroom. "In my day we didn't need such refinements. Don't know what's coming over the young people. They're soft."

The castle that used to keep the terrible Scots at bay now welcomes them. "Every year at the Caledonian Ball," said our guide, "the Scots parade in the courtyard blowing bagpipes like anything, in a castle built to keep them out."

In the Norman gallery, she pointed out the room with the trapdoor. A student occupant of this dormitory room discovered the trapdoor under the carpet, and in the dead of night explored the secret passages it covered. He passed the word along. For years class after class of Durham's venturesome students crept back to their quarters by a devious and dangerous route after a night on the town—all popping up through the trapdoor in this one room whose occupant was thus privileged beyond any other. The student-delinquent had to climb a wall, pass over a chasm on a shaky plank (no mean feat if he'd taken a load aboard), slide down a stone chute imperfectly cleared after centuries of use for dumping rubbish, and mount a black, steep, spiral stone stair to come out through that trapdoor. Those heroic days stopped when a chump, assigned the room, let the secret out to the enemy. Now trapdoor and the rest are blocked up.

Some years ago the press published the news that a Norman chapel had been discovered in the bowels of the castle. Durham's excitement about the find subsided when it was revealed that it was only the old discard room, familiar to all as the place where unwanted odds and ends had been dumped for a hundred years or so. It tickles one to realize that after all those years someone, taking a good look at that dark chamber, woke up to the fact that Durham had a treasure there.

Restored, the Norman chapel is beautiful. It is built of a strange tinted stone, like none we ever saw before, and is excellently illuminated. The great columns have carved capitals. The famed Norman chapel in the Tower of London is inferior to this one.

The too-easy way to cathedral and castle is up Saddler Street. If you don't mind a twenty-minute walk, there's a better approach. Cross Elvet Bridge, turn right into New Elvet, and after entering Church Street take the footpath which cuts through the yard of St. Oswald's church (visit this church if you have time—it's very old), and keep following this along the river as it makes its hairpin turn under the cathedral cliff. From various points you have stunning views up to Durham's "acropolis," and the banks along which you walk are very pleasant. You cross the river again by the Prebends' Bridge, pausing for another view—and, perhaps, for reading some lines by Walter Scott on the bridge—and then climb steeply up to the cloisters and the rest.

And that should wrap up Durham for you.

*HOTELS* * We stayed at the Three Tuns, and managed to bear it. It leaks noise and kitchen smells. We canvassed, or cased, the Royal County, which gets an extra star in the automobile guide, but were unimpressed. The receptionist at the Three Tuns was a gem, and the porter helpful.

*TRAVEL FACTS* * Durham is 259 miles by railway from London; 63 miles north of York. Newcastle-on-Tyne and the eastern end of the Roman Wall, which runs across this northern neck of England to the Bowness Firth, are only 15 miles north.

# § *HADRIAN'S WALL*

A problem of traveling in England is that there's always something else a little farther on, around the bend, up the valley, that entices. When you've got as far as Durham, to which you have been lured by having got as far as York, you say to your spouse: "Spouse, we may never be this way again, so how about taking a look at that Roman Wall?"

The Chinese Wall is barred, being Communist, but this one is safely within NATO. Its eastern end is only fifteen miles from Durham, and what's fifteen miles, especially if you have a car?

Built by the Roman legions between A.D. 122 and 126 on order of the Emperor Hadrian, the seventy-three miles of wall was the northernmost defense line of the Roman Empire. It was originally fifteen feet high, seven and a half wide, and was constantly patroled from sixteen forts stationed on it and from turrets built at regular intervals between the forts. It was the Maginot Line against the savage Highlanders whom the Romans tried to tame and couldn't. But it was a Maginot Line effective for 250 years, or as long as the legions were there.

The Wall, nowhere more than a mile from an east–west road, rises and falls with the land's contours. The country is lonesome, the effect awesome even where only jagged bits of Wall remain. The main points to visit are Corstopitum, Chesters, and Housesteads, excavated remains of the Roman forts with good museums in connection.

NOTE FOR THE CARLESS.  Hexham, picturesque old town near Chesters, is center for Wall hikers and has a bus tour of the Wall (Thursdays, late June–August). Hexham has an ancient church with Roman stones, a Moot Hall, and a long main street one part of which is called Priestpopple. Hotel: the Royal.

Above Durham, Corstopitum lies seventeen miles west of Newcastle, just outside Corbridge. Chesters is five miles west, Housesteads another nine miles. Your road out of Newcastle is A69 to Heddon on the Wall, and from there on, B6318. If you keep going as far as Brampton, you may be tempted to take a side road to Gretna Green, the famous elopement haven, and once there plunge into Scotland.

And why not?

So here at Hadrian's Wall we leave you.

# INDEX

§ ABOUT THE AUTHORS

Lawrence and Sylvia Martin write while traveling and biding in various parts of the world—Rabat, Ninfield, Ancla dos Reyes, Cuernavaca, Lavenham, Taormina, Llao Llao, Merano, Vaduz, Port of Spain. . . . (Challenge: How many of these can you locate on the map?) It all began when Lawrence, in his seventeenth year of university teaching, was hit on the head by a pile of travel magazines while rummaging in a closet. When next heard of, he and his bride, who had been looking forward to a serene life of faculty teas, were at the corner of Hoyne and the Equator, so to speak. The mobile Martins dream of settling down someday in a garden—she with a cat and six kittens, he with the finest hi-fi set in the world and all the Mozart there is on disks. Meanwhile they are prowling the boulevards and boutiques of *la ville lumière* for their next book in this series, *Paris!*

125 — gag rule